Michael Haugh

m/Politeness Implicatures

Mouton Series in Pragmatics

Volume 11

Michael Haugh

Im/Politeness
Implicatures

—

DE GRUYTER
MOUTON

ISBN 978-3-11-048329-1
e-ISBN (PDF) 978-3-11-024007-8
e-ISBN (EPUB) 978-3-11-039466-5
ISSN 1864-6409

Library of Congress Cataloging-in-Publication Data
A CIP catalog record for this book has been applied for at the Library of Congress.

Bibliographic information published by the Deutsche Nationalbibliothek
The Deutsche Nationalbibliothek lists this publication in the Deutsche Nationalbibliografie;
detailed bibliographic data are available on the internet at http://dnb.dnb.de.

© 2015 Walter de Gruyter GmbH, Berlin/Munich/Boston
Typesetting: PTP-Berlin Protago-T$_E$X-Production GmbH, Berlin
Printing and binding: CPI books GmbH, Leck
♾ Printed on acid-free paper
Printed in Germany

www.degruyter.com

Contents

List of tables and figures

Transcription conventions

]	overlapping speech
(0.5)	numbers in brackets indicate pause length
(.)	micropause
:	elongation of vowel or consonant sound
-	word cut-off
.	falling or final intonation
?	rising intonation
,	'continuing' intonation
=	latched utterances
underlining	contrastive stress or emphasis
CAPS	markedly loud
° °	markedly soft
.hh	in-breath
hh	out-breath/aspiration
↓ ↑	sharp falling/rising intonation
> <	talk is compressed or rushed
< >	talk is markedly slowed or drawn out
( )	blank space or talk in parentheses indicates uncertainty about the transcription
(( ))	double brackets indicates extra contextual or non-verbal information

Morphological gloss conventions

Acc	accusative
ASP	aspect
C	counter
Cont	contrastive marker
Cop	copula
CP	complement
Dim	diminuative
Imp	imperative
M	mood marker
Gen	genitive
Hon	honorification
Imp	imperative
Neg	negation
Nom	nominative
Nomi	nominaliser
Past	past tense
PL	plural
Pol	"polite" form
Pot	potential
Prog	progressive
PRT	particle
Q	question marker
Quot	quotation
Tag	tag question marker
Te	"te"-form
Top	topic marker
Vol	volitional
%	code-switch

Preface

This book has its genesis in my doctoral dissertation, "Politeness implicature in Japanese: a metalinguistic approach". However, given I completed my dissertation in 2003, many of my original ideas have subsequently changed considerably. Reflecting on the differences between the two, I begin to wonder what kind of book I might write about im/politeness implicatures another ten years down the track! I suspect it would be somewhat different in its approach. Yet despite such differences the heart of this work has remained the same. Throughout the years I have remained committed, as it turns out, to developing an account of im/politeness and implicature that is firmly grounded in pragmatics. And while I have consistently emphasised the understandings of participants as they arise in interaction as the proper focus of an account of im/politeness implicature, I have also remain committed to developing an account of im/politeness implicatures that takes seriously the emic viewpoint of members themselves. The work presented here is an attempt to bring together these multiple perspectives in a systematic and coherent way.

The approach I have developed here has, naturally, been influenced by the work of many, many scholars – too many for me to list here. The long list of references at the conclusion of this book offers some idea of the various influences on my work. However, some people deserve special mention. The first is my PhD supervisor, Yasuko Obana, who shaped the early form of this work and set me firmly on the path towards developing a pragmatic account of im/politeness implicatures. The second is my long-time mentor, Robert Arundale, whose work has not only inspired much of what I have developed here, but with whom I have long had discussions since near the beginning of my PhD studies that inform nearly every aspect of this book. They both deserve full credit for the best parts of this book. Any errors are, of course, mine alone.

I would also like to thank others who have had an influence in shaping particular aspects of this book, including a special thanks to my co-authors of other works, Dániel Kádár, Jonathan Culpeper, and Wei-Lin Melody Chang, as well as other collaborators with whom I have had many discussions over the years and who have had a positive influence on the ideas presented in this book, including Francesca Bargiela-Chiappini, Kasia Jasczcolt, Şukriye Ruhi, Helen Spencer-Oatey, Marina Terkourafi, and many others besides. In addition, I would like to thank Istvan Kecskes, not only for his immense patience and support as editor of this book series, but also for our ongoing discussions about his work on sociocognitive aspects of pragmatics.

Finally I would like to acknowledge the support of a grant from the Chian Ching-Kuo Foundation ("Politeness in Taiwan", RG025-P-10) which has assisted me immensely in the final stages of completing this book.

Michael Haugh
September 2014

Introduction

1 Im/politeness implicatures

It is widely known that implying something, or leaving something unsaid rather than saying it, can be regarded as "polite". Consider, for instance, the following short excerpt from the film "Trains, Planes and Automobiles". While waiting for their plane to depart, Del has been making conversation with Neal despite the latter's best efforts to avoid any extended interaction with Del.

(1)   Neal: Eh, look, I don't want to be rude, but I'm not much of a conversationalist, and I really want to finish this article, a friend of mine wrote it, so...

          Del: Don't let me stand in your way, please don't let me stand in your way. The last thing I want to be remembered as is an annoying blabbermouth. You know, nothing grinds my gears worse than some chowderhead that doesn't know when to keep his big trap shut. If you catch me running off with my mouth, just give me a poke on the chubbs.
                (*Planes, Trains and Automobiles*, 1987, director and writer: John Hughes)

Neal is attempting here, rather unsuccessfully as it turns out, to break off the conversation with Del and get back to reading an article. This proposal to close the conversation is accomplished through formulating two possible accounts or reasons for closing the conversation (i.e. "I'm not much of a conversationalist" and "I really want to finish this article [that] a friend of mine wrote"), followed by a turn-final "so", which not only explicitly marks the prior assertions as reasons, but projects that some upshot has been left unsaid. In pragmatics this kind of "unstated upshot" has generally been termed an "implicature", following Grice's (1967, 1975, 1989) seminal work. However, as Raymond (2004) points out, in projecting an "unstated upshot" the speaker is also anticipating some kind of (non) verbal response from the recipient, namely, that he will display understanding of this upshot. The upshot here, of course, is that Neal wants the conversation with Del to end, and so the anticipated response is that Del will let the conversation naturally trail off. What is most interesting to note here is that Neal, in attempting to break off the conversation with Del, makes explicit reference to the possibility of this unstated upshot (i.e. that Neal wants the conversation to end) being perceived as "rude". His turn is formulated, however, to occasion exactly the opposite perception, namely, that he is attempting to be "polite" in spite of the poten‍tially offensive nature of drawing the conversation to a close (prematurely from Del's perspective). In drawing from recognisable practices for doing just that, that is, by *implying* (rather than *asking* or *demanding*) that he would like the conver‍sation to end, a recognisably polite stance on Neal's part is thereby occasioned. Certainly there is nothing in Del's response that indicates he has taken offence at Neal's prior turn. Indeed, Del reassures Neal that he does not want to inter‍rupt Neal any further, although ironically does so in continuing to talk about how annoying it is when some people don't get the "hint" about finishing a conversa‍tion (which is what makes the scene amusing for the overhearing audience). By reciprocating Neal's polite stance in the prior turn through these reassurances, then, it appears that an understanding of not only what has been implied, but also an evaluation of the prior turn, and thus Neal himself, as polite, has been interactionally achieved by Neal and Del.

This kind of interactional practice, where we imply something and thereby occasion politeness, has been termed a "politeness implicature" (Haugh 2007a, 2008a. To characterise a politeness implicature as an interactional practice is distinct from the claim that politeness itself constitutes an implicature (e.g. Brown and Levinson 1978, 1987; Christie 2007; Kallia 2004; Leech 1983; Terkourafi 2001, 2003, 2005). Instead, it refers to instances where a polite stance or attitude appears to be indicated through implying something.

However, implicatures do not always give rise to politeness. As we can see from the following example, one can imply something that may be regarded as offensive or rude. Leading up to the following excerpt from the movie, *The Social Network*, Mark and Erica have been talking about Mark's focus on getting into a "final club" – an undergraduate social club – at Harvard University where Mark studies. However, Mark appears to be frustrated with Erica's apparent lack of interest in his plans at the point this excerpt begins.

(2)   Mark: I want to try to be straightforward with you and tell you that I think you might want to be a little more supportive. If I get in I'll be taking you to the events, and the gatherings and you'll be meeting a lot of people you wouldn't normally get to meet.

Erica: You would do that for me?

Mark: We're dating.

Erica: Okay, well I want to try and be straightforward with you and let you know that we're not anymore.

Mark: What do you mean?

Erica: We're not dating anymore, I'm sorry.

Mark: Is this a joke?

Erica: No, it's not.

Mark: You're breaking up with me?

Erica: You're going to introduce me to people I wouldn't normally have the chance to meet? What the fff-
What is that supposed to mean?

Mark: Wait, settle down.

Erica: What is it supposed to mean?
(*The Social Network*, 2010, director: David Fincher, writer: Aaron Sorkin)

It is apparent here that Erica gets offended. This offence arises from what Mark has implied by saying that she'll get to meet a lot of people she wouldn't normally get to meet if he gets into a final club, namely, that she is not as 'good' as the kinds of people who are members of a final club at Harvard University. Erica initially responds sarcastically, a form of what Leech (1983) terms "mock politeness" (see also Culpeper 1996, 2011a), before going on to say she does not want to continue dating him. She then explicitly holds him accountable for what he has implied by asking him "what is that supposed to mean?", thereby displaying her apparent anger at his remarks, in part through the prosodic contour of her responses, as well as through an incompletely uttered "what the fuck?" We can see here, then, that Mark has implied something about Erica, casting her person as occupying a lower social status than members of those final clubs. Given that Mark initially seems oblivious to the potentially offensive implications of his remarks, it is apparent that Mark and Erica have not evaluated his initial remarks in the same way. On the one hand, Erica is upset and offended and moves to break up with Mark. On the other hand, Mark is initially oblivious to the offensive implications of his remarks, and even later maintains they are only potentially offensive because Erica misunderstood him.

This kind of interactional practice, where someone implies something and thereby occasions impoliteness, can be termed an "impoliteness implicature" (Haugh 2011a). Once again, the question of whether this impolite stance or attitude itself constitutes an implicature is treated as a distinct issue here. An impoliteness implicature may be ostensibly "unintended", as claimed by Mark in relation to his implied evaluation of Erica's social status, although Erica herself treats it as an instance of "genuine" impoliteness (cf. Culpeper 2011a), and the over hearing audience may, of course, form their own views of it as well.

We can also see from the above excerpt that "genuine" impoliteness may be implied through an ostensibly "polite" formulation. This is evident in Erica's initially sarcastic response to Mark's chiding of her lack of enthusiasm, where an ostensibly "polite" formulation (i.e. "You would do that for me?" to express appreciation) serves to mask an impolite stance on her part (i.e. that she thinks Mark's offer, and underlying attitude towards her, is contemptible). This latter implicature can be termed a "mock politeness implicature". A mock politeness implicature is similar in many ways to an impoliteness implicature. However, mock politeness arises through the occurrence of an ostensibly "polite" (non-) linguistic form or practice (i.e. that would in other circumstances be associated with a polite attitude), in a situated context with which it is somehow incongruous, thereby implying a negative assessment of, or impolite attitude towards, the addressee.

One feature of mock politeness implicatures that appears to mark them as somewhat distinct from (genuine) impoliteness implicatures, however, is that the target of the mock polite attitude is often positioned in such a way that it is difficult to respond without appearing churlish, or inadvertently putting "on record" that which has been left "off record" (Brown and Levinson 1987), thereby scoring an interpersonal "own goal" as it were.

In the following excerpt from the film *Four Weddings and a Funeral*, for instance, a server in a shop implies a highly condescending stance towards Charles, yet he remains relatively helpless to respond directly to this impolite stance, given the way in which it is framed within an ostensibly "polite" service encounter.

(3)   Charles: Do you have the wedding list for Banks?

       Server: Certainly, sir. Lots of beautiful things for around about the £1,000 mark.

       Charles: What about things around the sort of £50 mark? Is there much?

       Server: Well, you could get that Pygmy warrior over there.

       Charles: This? Excellent!

       Server: If you could find someone to chip in the other 950 pounds. Or our carrier bags are £1.50 each. Why don't you just get 33 of them?

Charles: Well, I think I'll probably leave it. Thanks very much.
You've been very...
(*Four Weddings and a Funeral*, 1994, director: Mike Newell, writer: Richard Curtis)

The server appears to maintain a "polite" demeanour throughout the interaction by making what appear to be helpful suggestions. However, these suggestions actually mask a negative assessment of Charles, in that his request that she suggest a cheaper wedding gift is implied to be absurd through the patently ridiculous suggestions she makes in response. To imply that a customer's request is absurd is, of course, open to evaluation as "impolite". The superficially helpful and seemingly "polite" manner of the server are incongruous with the implied negative assessments of Charles's request for assistance, and thus mask an impolite attitude towards Charles. It is this clash between the ostensibly polite attitude of the server, the implied negative assessments of Charles's request, which are clearly "not polite", and the mocking or even hostile stance towards Charles that is implied through these sarcastic suggestions, that gives rise to "mock politeness" (and it is this that provides amusement for the overhearing audience for whom the interaction is constructed).

Finally, in some instances what is implied can give rise to what appears to be an ostensibly impolite attitude, but is framed by the speaker as "not impolite". Such instances can be termed "mock impoliteness implicatures". In the following excerpt from the television series, *Seinfeld*, George is being introduced to the husband of a friend of Elaine's.

(4) Beth: Oh, uh, George, this is my husband, David.

George: Oh, hi, David.
((they shake hands))

David: Hello. So, George, uh, you're the one who works for the Yankees, right?

George: Yeah. Why, what do you do?

David: Well, I sell insurance, but Beth used to be Don Mattingly's doctor.

George: Really?

Beth: Mm-hm.

David: Yeah.

> George: Ha! A physician married to a salesman. Heh heh. Well, I gotta tell
> you, Beth, you coulda, done a lot better than him.
> ((George and Elaine both laugh out loud))
> ("The wait out", *Seinfeld*, Episode 23, Season 7, May 9 1996, director:
> Andy Ackerman, writer: Peter Mehlman)

However, as we can see in the interaction that follows, this kind of ostensibly
light-hearted teasing, which in the above case was achieved in part through
implicatures, can be treated seriously by others.

(5) Jerry: Hey, remember Beth and David from yesterday?
             They got separated.

     George: Really? ((pause)) Well, you don't think it had anything to do
             with what I said, do you?

     Jerry: What'd you say?

     George: You know, that, that thing about her being too good for him.
             I mean, I was just bein' folksy. They could tell I was just being
             folksy?

     Elaine: Yeah, I thought you were being folksy.

     George: Totally folksy.
     ("The wait out", *Seinfeld*, Episode 23, Season 7, May 9 1996, director:
     Andy Ackerman, writer: Peter Mehlman)

Here we can see evidence that George's mocking tease may have led to Beth
separating from her husband, and thus what was mockingly suggested has been
taken seriously. George himself tries to head off this conjecture by claiming he
was being "folksy" (which normally means to be "informal" or "unpretentious",
but in this case appears to be used to indicate a non-serious or joking attitude).
Elaine affiliates with George's claim that his teasing was meant non-seriously.
Such examples, albeit ones constructed for an overhearing audience, indicate
that in some instances what is implied is not necessarily evaluated in the same
way by all the participants involved.

The claim that implicatures can give rise to politeness is not a new one.
Indeed, politeness has long been associated with implicatures, and indirectness
more generally, in pragmatics. However, the puzzle to be explored in this volume
is why it is that implicatures only *sometimes* give rise to politeness, while in other
instances they can give rise to other kinds of evaluations, such as impoliteness,

mock politeness, mock impoliteness and shades between. And, indeed, in many cases implicatures do not give rise to any kind of im/politeness-related evaluation at all. The relationship between implicatures and im/politeness is, as we shall see, a complex one. The aim of this book is to start to unravel this relationship: to explain how and why implicatures give rise to politeness, impoliteness, mock impoliteness and related evaluations in some cases, but not in others.

2 Overview of the volume

Chapter One focuses on the broader notion of indirectness, arguing that because it is conceptualised in so many different ways, it is better treated not as an analytic notion per se, but rather as a discursively attributed quality or characteristic of interaction. In other words, participants, and thus we as analysts, can evaluate utterances or sequences of utterances (i.e. discourse) as *indirect* to varying degrees. The assumed relationship between indirectness and politeness, which predominated in earlier work on politeness and speech acts in pragmatics, is also questioned in light of the multitude of different interpersonal functions that can be ascribed to being perceived as *indirect*. It is concluded that the notion of implicature is more well defined in scope as an analytic category, hence the focus of this book is on im/politeness implicatures rather than indirectness more generally. However, various useful analytical insights can nevertheless be garnered from the broader literature on indirectness, and many of these are explicitly drawn upon in the analysis and theorisation of im/politeness implicatures in the subsequent chapters of this book.

Chapter Two offers an overview of various approaches to the analysis of implicatures. It is argued that insights into the analysis of implicatures can be obtained from both (neo)-Gricean and post-Gricean approaches. In the case of (neo)-Gricean theories of implicature, it is suggested that such approaches highlight the systematic (i.e. normative) ways in which implicatures can be made available by speakers, the various different types of implicatures that can be observed, and the need to distinguish between the inferences that give rise to implicatures and implicatures themselves. The fundamental distinction between implicatures that arise through reasoning about the speaker's "intentions" in particular, localised contexts (nonce implicatures), and those that arise through reasoning based on more general expectations about how language is used (default implicatures), is also highlighted by neo-Griceans, as well as by post-Griceans working on default or conventional accounts of language use. Relevance theory, on the other hand, offers useful insights into the ways in which implicatures vary in their degree of (in)determinacy (from strong through to weak implicatures), how they can arise through implicated premises (cf. *supposing, assuming*) as well as through impli- cated conclusions (cf. *implying, indicating*), and thus how the processing of impli- catures is not necessarily constrained by what is said. It is concluded, however, that neither (neo-)Gricean nor Relevance theoretic accounts of implicature are particularly well placed to account for how users attend to the interpersonal implications of what speakers are taken to be implicating, as well as the fact they are implicating something (as opposed to *saying* it) in the first place, and how they are implicating it (e.g. *implying, hinting, alluding, suggesting* and so on).

In Chapter Three, building on these observations, the focus is on the relation- ship between implicatures and social action. It is proposed that not only are par- ticipant understandings of implicatures mediated through understandings of the social actions together with which they arise, but in some cases, implicatures can be observed to be constitutive of particular social actions. This leads into a dis- cussion of the way in which implicatures can arise through different "meaning- actions", such as *implying, hinting, supposing*, and so on, and the extent to which they can be treated as indeterminate. It is argued that these two characteristics both afford and constrain the degree to which participants can be held committed to, or accountable for those implicatures. Overall, in this chapter an interactional approach to implicatures is postulated, where they are conceptualised as reflex- ively intentional state-processes on the part of individual participants that vary in their degree of (in)determinacy, as they are realised both in the course of interac- tionally achieving a particular trajectory of social actions, and also through par- ticular forms of social action (i.e what are termed meaning-actions). It is for this reason that participants can be held accountable to varying degrees for implica- tures. The variable degree of accountability for (pragmatic) meaning afforded by implicatures also underpins the ways in which through implicating participants can implicitly orient to moral or interpersonal concerns.

In Chapter Four, the focus moves to the relationship between implicatures and im/politeness, and the broader interpersonal milieu in which implicatures and im/politeness arise. However, rather than treating im/politeness as a specific form of implicature, as neo-Griceans have generally done thus far, it is argued that im/politeness needs to be theorised as an evaluative social practice because such evaluations demonstrably do more in interaction than simply marking someone or some behaviour as im/polite. This move towards an account of im/ politeness as evaluative social practice opens up the space necessary in order to consider two key analytical questions in relation to the analysis of im/politeness vis-à-vis implicature: (1) *how* do we recognise that something (potentially) counts as im/polite, and (2) *for whom* does something count as im/polite. It is proposed that in order to address the former question, we need to analyse more carefully the moral underpinnings of evaluations of im/politeness. More specifically, it is argued that any such analysis needs to situated with respect to the moral order that is invoked by participants in interaction in making such evaluations, but which is also itself co-constituted through ongoing interactions across relational or social networks. In order to address the latter question, it is suggested we need to situate our analysis of im/politeness vis-à-vis the complex array of participation footings that constitutes the participation order, which are not only invoked in making such evaluations, but are themselves co-constituted through the interaction in question.

This move away from a treatment of im/politeness-as-implicature to an account of im/politeness as evaluative social practice grounds the subsequent characterisation in Chapter Five of im/politeness implicatures proper. In this chapter, it is argued that treating im/politeness implicatures as a form of social practice allows us to observe not only how evaluations of im/politeness can be occasioned through implicating (i.e. im/politeness as occasioned by implicatures), but also the way in which scalar implicatures generate, at least in part, the broader evaluative field in which im/politeness arises (i.e. implicatures as constitutive of im/politeness), as well as the way in which evaluations of im/politeness can themselves occasion implicatures (i.e. implicatures as occasioned by im/politeness). In doing so, the importance of situating the analysis of im/politeness implicatures in interaction becomes evident. It is thus proposed that the two interpretative orders discussed in the previous chapter, namely, the moral and participation orders, need to be complemented by close examination of the temporal-sequential order and the socioinferential order. The temporal-sequential order encompasses the way in which interpretations and evaluations by participants of current talk are systematically related to both prior and forthcoming talk, as well as the sequential positioning of the im/politeness implicature itself as either first-positioned (i.e. initiating an action trajectory) or next-positioned (i.e. responsive to an ongoing action trajectory). It is in this way that we can account for why im/politeness implicatures are both calculable by participants (i.e. they can be understood more or less by participants at the point they arise in interaction), yet also recalculable (i.e. their understandings of what has been implicated can change). The socioinferential order, on the other hand, is argued to encompass the complex array of intentional state-processes that both afford and constrain the interpretations and evaluations underpinning participant understandings of im/politeness implicatures. A distinction between "default" and "nonce" im/politeness implicatures is also argued to be motivated by the socioinferential order. It is then subsequently proposed that modulating the (speaker's) accountability for what has been implicated is implemented in systematically different ways in the case of default and nonce im/politeness implicatures. Finally, the analytical threads in the chapters thus far are drawn together in a framework that highlights the key dimensions for understanding the (meta)pragmatics of im politeness implicatures. This analytical framework underpins the more detailed examination of practices by which politeness implicatures and impoliteness implicatures arise in the subsequent two chapters.

The focus in Chapter Six is on the way in which politeness implicatures do no merely indicate a "polite" stance on the part of a participant, but are taken to be accomplishing particular interactional and relational work as "unofficial" business. In examining politeness implicatures vis-à-vis social action, then, emphasis is placed on what participants are *doing* through politeness implicatures in interaction. It is proposed that this interactional work is accomplished as "unofficial" business through avoiding, masking or even disguising social actions in various ways. Six inter-related practices by which politeness implicatures arise and accomplish such "unofficial" business are discussed in turn, including attenuating, withholding, pre-empting, soliciting, disattending, and doing delicacy. In doing so, it is suggested that while considering the metalanguage of meaning-actions such as *implying*, *hinting*, and *suggesting* is a useful starting point for analysis, in order to gain firm analytical traction we also need to examine the interactional practices by which politeness implicatures arise. In this way we can avoid being unnecessarily constrained by the emic conceptualisations that such metalanguage represents in our analysis of the interactional and relational work accomplished through politeness implicatures.

Chapter Seven then moves on to consider impoliteness implicatures, and the related notions of mock politeness implicatures and mock impoliteness implicatures. These are argued to be closely inter-related in that they involve, in some form or another, an orientation to potential or perceived offence. The chapter builds on the observation that implicating negative assessments can occasion evaluations of impoliteness, mock politeness and mock impoliteness. It is argued that the degree of perceived offence can be exacerbated by implicating negative assessments, as the inferable formulation of these negative assessments can be delivered unmitigated through implicatures, that is, without hedging, hesitations, and the like, and in this way can also position agreement with that implicated negative assessment as the preferred response by other participants. It is subsequently observed that not only can offence be occasioned through implicatures, but participants can also register and sanction (perceived) offence through implicatures. A more considered examination of mock impoliteness implicatures follows, with a focus on the complex and nuanced relational work that can be accomplished through them, in addition to the already well-attested functions of building "solidarity", disguising "coercion", and providing "entertainment". The final section then moves on to an analysis of the ways in which implicated offence can be disputed by participants, and the insights into the moral substrate underpinning interpersonal interaction that these kinds of analyses can offer. It is suggested that such analyses thus complement other ongoing work to better understand the metapragmatics of im/politeness.

A brief conclusion, in Chapter Eight, which summarises the key themes and claims in this treatment of im/politeness implicatures then follows, alongside an outline of the main implications for theorising implicature and im/politeness more broadly. The theorisation and analysis of im/politeness implicatures is then situated within a broader framework of the interpersonal work achieved through talk in interaction, on the basis of which it is proposed that this study lays the groundwork for subsequent studies of relational implicatures more broadly.

Chapter One:
Indirectness and im/politeness

In this chapter we start by exploring a number of key analytical themes associated with the broader notion of indirectness, themes which seed the exploration of im/politeness implicatures in the subsequent chapters of this book. In the first section of this chapter, the presumed relationship between politeness and indirectness is critically examined, before moving on in section two to consider the various interpersonal functions of indirectness. The different ways in which indirectness itself has been conceptualised not only in pragmatics, but also in conversation analysis and linguistic anthropology, are then teased out in section three. In the course of deconstructing the notion of indirectness a number of key analytical themes are identified. This chapter thus concludes in section four by explicating these key themes, and the ways in which the subsequent chapters will build on them.

1 Politeness and indirectness

It has traditionally been assumed in pragmatics that one of the main reasons for being indirect is a concern for politeness. Searle (1975, 1979) was one of the first to explicitly link indirectness to politeness.[1] He claimed that in the case of directives (e.g. requests, commands and so on), "politeness is the chief motivation for indirectness" (p.36). This claim was built on the observation that some requests are realised not through imperatives (e.g. *pass me the salt*), which in Speech Act theory is treated as the so-called basic sentence type for directives and thus a "direct" speech act (Searle 1969, 1979), but rather "indirectly" through interrogatives (e.g. *can you pass me the salt?*) or declaratives (e.g. *this could do with a little more salt*). Searle's intuition was that the latter two "indirect" speech acts tend to be regarded as more "polite" than requests realised through imperative formulations. Searle recognised, of course, that there might be other motivations for these kinds of indirect forms, but nevertheless claimed that "politeness is the *most prominent* motivation for indirectness in requests" (Searle 1979: 49, empha-

---

1 Grice ([1975]1989) noted in passing that "nonconventional implicatures" may also be generated by other maxims such as "Be polite" (p.28). Given that, in Grice's view, violating or flouting maxims gives rise to implicatures, this amounts to the claim that certain kinds of implicatures are motivated by politeness concerns. We will return to consider in Chapter Three how the (neo-) Gricean view of the relationship between implicatures and politeness differs from the relationship between indirect speech acts and politeness that is posited in Speech Act theory.

sis added), particularly those indirect forms that are conventionalised for use as requests. The "can you" form, for instance, is commonly treated in pragmatics a conventionalised for making "polite" requests in English. Searle went on to argue that conventionally indirect forms of requesting are polite for two reasons:

> Firstly, *X* does not presume to know about *Y*'s abilities, as he would if he issued an impera-tive sentence; and, secondly, the form gives – or at least appears to give – *Y* the option of refusing, since a yes-no question allows *no* as a possible answer. Hence, compliance can be made to appear a free act rather than obeying a command. (Searle 1979: 48)

This sort of approach was subsequently extended by Searle (1979) to encompass indirect commissives (i.e. indirect promises, apologies and so on) (pp.54–55).

Searle's line of argumentation in relation to politeness as the motivation for indirect speech acts, and for indirect requests in particular, arguably reflects two of the so-called "rules of politeness" that were proposed by Lakoff (1973), "Don't impose" and "Give options" (p.298), respectively. In formulating these rules for politeness, Lakoff also noted that indirectly requesting via a conversa-tional implicature (Grice 1967, 1975) can be regarded as "polite".[2] However, she went on to point out that such conversational implicatures "may or *may not* be a polite way of saying [something], depending on the situation" (Lakoff 1973: 302, emphasis added). For instance, saying "It's cold in here" in order to implicate that one would like the addressee to "shut the window" may be construed as polite when it is assumed the speaker is giving the addressee options (p.302). However, if the speaker is actually in an institutionally superior or more pow-erful position than that of the addressee, Lakoff argues that a different set of implications can arise. She claims that given such an indirect request is actually masking an order in the latter situation, it could be interpreted as further impli-cating something like, "You must interpret my every wish as your command, you are so beneath me" (p.303), and so could be regarded as quite impolite in that case.

In both Searle's and Lakoff's early work, then, a somewhat qualified claim about the presumed relationship between politeness and indirectness was devel-oped. Searle argued that such a relationship held for indirect requests and other select speech acts, in particular, those forms conventionalised for use as indirect speech acts, while Lakoff noted that conversational implicatures can be inter-

---

2 A conversational implicature refers to a type of speaker meaning that encompasses meaning beyond what is literally said Grice (1967, 1975, 1978, 1989). We will return to the question of how conversational implicatures differ from indirect speech acts, as well as with other approaches to implicature, in Chapter Three.

preted as either polite or not depending on the context. However, in spite of these provisos, the assumed relationship between politeness and indirectness began to treated as much more widely applicable in subsequent theorisations of politeness.

Leech (1983), for instance, is often read as claiming that politeness correlates with indirectness, that is to say, the more indirect an illocution, the more polite it will be. This was initially based on his claim that by being more indirect in making a request the "degree of optionality" for the hearer to comply is increased, while the "force" of the act becomes "more diminished and tentative" (p.108). However, Leech extended his claims about the correlation between indirectness and politeness beyond requests to other speech acts, such as offers, and noted a general "connection between politeness and obliquity (indirectness)" (p.169). Yet he also noted, although this is generally not well recognised in the literature as Culpeper and Haugh (2014) point out, that increasing the degree of indirectness can actually work in the opposite way in the case of impoliteness. That is to say, increasing indirectness can also result in an increase in the degree of impoliteness in the case of so-called "impolite beliefs" (Leech 1983: 171).

The strongest claims about the correlation between politeness and indirectness are thus in fact made by Brown and Levinson (1978, 1987). They propose in their overall ranking of politeness super-strategies that off-record strategies are generally more polite than conventionally indirect strategies, which are, in turn, generally more polite than bald on record strategies. Off record strategies refer to instances where there are a number of "defensible interpretations" of an act, such as in the case of hints, allusions, understatements and so on, where the speaker can avoid "responsibility" for such acts by "leav[ing] it up to the addressee to decide how to interpret it" (Brown and Levinson 1987: 211). Conventionally indirect strategies, on the other hand, encompass the "the use of phrases and sentences that have contextually unambiguous meanings (by virtue of conventionalisation) which are different from their literal meanings. In this way the utterance goes on record, and the speaker indicates his desire to have gone off record (to have conveyed the same thing indirectly)" (p.132). Finally, bald on record strategies include instances where there is no mitigation or modification of the basic speech act, as in the case of direct imperatives (p.95). Thus, according to Brown and Levinson, albeit depending on the particulars of the social distance and power relations between the speaker and hearer (thereby perhaps dealing with Lakoff's earlier concern to some extent), a hint such as "This soup's a bit bland" (p.215) is considered more polite than a conventionalised indirect form such as "Can you pass the salt?" (p.133), which is regarded as more polite, in turn, than a direct imperative such as "Pass the salt."[3] This claim builds on a general "folk understanding" of indirectness a "speaking in a roundabout, circuitous, or even devious way, serving ulterio motives, such as tentativeness, politeness, deniability and so on" (Terkouraf 2013: 214).

Brown and Levinson (1987) went on to argue that "in the absence of defini tive evidence that we got the ranking wrong, there are good arguments for insist ing that off-record strategies are generally more polite than on-record" (p.20). However, subsequent research has since called this broad claim into question. There is now a growing body of evidence that off-record indirectness (e.g. hints) are not universally or uncontroversially perceived as polite (e.g. Blum-Kulka 1987; Dillard, Wilson, Tusing and Kinney 1997; Félix-Brasdefer 2005; Holtgraves and Yang 1990; Lwanga-Lumu 1999; Marti 2006; Marquez Reiter 2000; Pinker, Nowak and Lee 2008; Terkourafi 2002, 2011b; Weizman 1993; Yu 2011).[4] There is also strong evidence that while conventional indirectness might be perceived as more polite in some languages (such as English or Hebrew – see Blum-Kulka 1987), this generalisation does not hold for all languages, even in the apparently straightforward case of directives (Field 1998; Wierzbicka 1985; Yu 2011).

The relationship between politeness and indirectness has thus turned out to be much more complex than originally assumed in early work in pragmatics. While being "indirect" can certainly give rise to politeness in some instances, it is not necessarily always interpreted as polite. As we shall see in the following section, one of the reasons that indirectness is not always perceived as polite is that it can in fact give rise to a whole range of interpersonal effects, of which politeness is just one.

---

3 Brown and Levinson's choice of examples was perhaps somewhat unfortunate, however, given that while "This soup's a bit bland" might count as a hint in regards to requesting the addressee pass the salt and so is interpretable as polite, it is also hearable as a negative assessment, that is, a criticism of the soup and thus the cook, and in that sense, is also interpretable as impolite. Thus, while the existence of "a number of defensible interpretations" can offer an "out" for the speaker (Brown and Levinson 1987: 211), it can also work in the opposite way, that is, (inadvertently) trapping the speaker into being held responsible for interpretations of their talk that they may not necessarily wish to be held to.

4 Brown and Levinson (1987) have argued that the results of Blum-Kulka's (1987) study may have been "due to the experimental design" because "the requests chosen for this experiment all assumed a relatively low R", and also because "the use of off-record hints to do requests of a certain R level is limited to certain kinds of alters" (p.19). However, given the results have been replicated in numerous other studies in various languages it would appear the jury is now in on Brown and Levinson's claim, namely, that off-record strategies are *not* inherently more polite than on-record ones (see also note 3).

2 Interpersonal functions of indirectness

One of the main interpersonal functions of indirectness was initially assumed to involve politeness. However, subsequent work has identified a whole range of interpersonal functions that can arise as a consequence of indirect speech. The various functions of indirectness that have been identified in the literature revolve largely around four key interpersonal loci: persons, relationships, interactional goals and language play.

A person, following Mead (1934), refers to a (biologically autonomous) individual as construed by a cultural group with whom he or she is linked in social interaction. Indirectness in relation to persons involves positioning the self vis-à-vis the other. This encompasses enacting, attributing, ratifying, and challenging identities and relational roles, including power relationships, an interpersonal function that has been well attested to in the literature (Chang 1999; Kiesling and Johnson 2010; Macauley, 2001; Morgan 2010; Rundquist 1992; Tannen 2010; Terkourafi 2011a, 2013). It also involves defending the self through avoiding responsibility or sanctions on the speaker (Bell 1997; Morgan 2010; Nemesi 2013), avoiding loss of face (Tannen 1981; Roberts and Kreuz 1994; Weiser 1974), and maintaining self-interests, such as 'privacy' (Bazzanella 2011).

A relationship, on the other hand, can be understood as "establishing and maintaining of connection between two otherwise separate individuals" (Arundale 2010b: 138), in non-summative system of two or more persons. Such relational systems can range from dyads to relatively closed social groupings through to large, diffuse social networks. Indirectness vis-à-vis relationships can involve, on the one hand, indexing "solidarity" or closeness/intimacy (Bazzanella 2011; Boxer 1993; Holtgraves 1997; Kiesling and Johnson 2010; Sifianou 1993, 1997; Soltys, Terkourafi and Katsos 2014; Terkourafi 2011a, 2013). For instance, Tannen (1981) makes reference to "the satisfaction of being understood without explaining oneself, of getting what one wants without asking for it" (p.223). On the other hand, indirectness can also enable or facilitate relationship negotiation itself (Chang 1999; Lee and Pinker 2010; Pinker, Nowak and Lee 2008; Silverstein 2010; Terkourafi 2011b). Pinker, Nowak and Lee (2008) argue that this is because

> [t]he literal form of a sentence is consistent with the *safest* relationship between speaker and hearer. At the same time, by implicating a meaning between the lines, the speaker counts on the listener to infer its real intent, which may initiate a different relationship. (Pinker, Nowak and Lee 2008: 835, original emphasis)

In other words, relationships can be maintained or re-negotiated through various forms of indirectness. Chang (1999) also refers to the way in which being indirect can generate an "indeterminate linguistic space", which "allows interactants to negotiate their relational status *without* directly challenging the well-defined cul tural rules of relationship, while at the same time protecting and serving thei own ends" (p.542, original emphasis). In this way, the interconnections betweer these two key functions of indirectness, that is, between addressing person-ori ented and relationship-oriented concerns, can also be seen.

The way in which being indirect helps maintain relationships with others is also discussed in the context of politeness research, as we briefly noted in the pre vious section. Through indirectness participants can occasion perceptions they are being polite, or at least avoid offending others (Bazzanella 2011; Lakoff 1973; Leech 1983; Roberts and Kreuz 1994; Searle 1975; Weiser 1974), as well as main-tain relational harmony or minimise social tension more generally (Brown and Levinson 1978, 1987; Obeng 1994; Tsuda 1993). However, indirectness can also be drawn upon in interpersonal attacks or conflict, or what is broadly termed impo-liteness (Culpeper 1996, 2011a; Kiesling and Johnson 2010; Lakoff 1973; Lee and Pinker 2010; Leech 1983; Obeng 1994), a point which will be explored in greater depth in the subsequent chapters. Thus, as we noted in the prior section, while indirectness is involved in various forms of person/identity and relational work, it is not restricted to being "polite" by any means.

A third key loci of indirectness involves what might be termed "interactional goals" (Spencer-Oatey 2005, 2009). Interactional goals refer to those (higher order) intentions that participants are held to be committed to, or accountable for, by other participants in interaction. These can range from mundane tasks such as "obtaining written approval for something, clinching a business deal, or finishing a meeting on time" or more relationally-oriented concerns, such as "peace-making, promoting friendship, currying favour or exerting control" (Spen-cer-Oatey 2005: 107). Indirectness in relation to the achievement of interactional goals has been found to be associated with negotiating or consensus building (Bazzanella 2011; Chang 1999; Georgakopoulou, 2001), on the one hand, and per-suading or even (covertly) manipulating others (Obeng 1994; Parrett 1994; Roberts and Kreuz 1994; Tsuda 1993), on the other. As Spencer-Oatey (2005) argues, the way in which persons are evaluated as in/appropriate, im/polite and so on, for instance, depends on the way in which the interactional goals at play are per-ceived by participants. Indirectness can also enable the "efficient" achievement of interactional goals through decreasing verbal redundancy, given indirectness can serve as a "convenient shorthand" amongst participants (Bazzanella 2011; Terkourafi 2011b, 2013).

A final key interpersonal loci of indirectness encompasses what can be broadly termed "language play". This includes the way in which indirectness can occasion humour or joking sequences (Bazzanella 2011; Holtgraves, 1998b; Kiesling and Johnson 2010; Rundquist 1992; Tsuda 1993), a function of indirectιess that is often linked with indexing relational solidarity or intimacy and positioning the self vis-à-vis others. It also includes aesthetic or stylistic phenomena realised through indirectness (Hickey 1992; Nemesi 2013).

These various functions of indirectness are summarised in Figure 1 below.

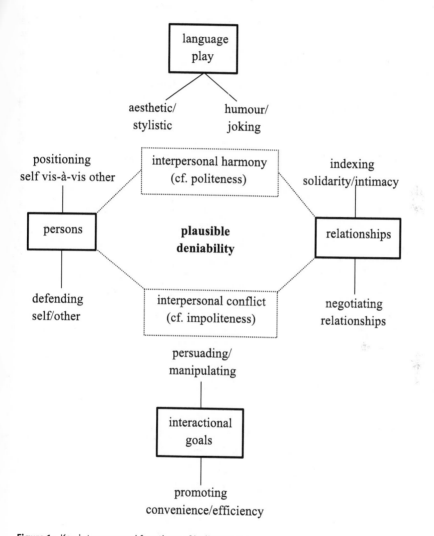

Figure 1: Key interpersonal functions of indirectness

It is suggested in this figure that the various interpersonal functions of indirectness, ranging from indexing solidarity or intimacy through to persuading or manipulating others, all play off the way in which there is inevitably some degre of "plausible deniability" in what is being communicated (Pinker, Nowak and Le 2008; Terkourafi 2011b). In other words, indirectness arises, in part, as a functior of the degree to which participants can either deny being committed to, or be helc responsible for a particular meaning, social action, stance, interpersonal atti tude/evaluation, and so on. This is because indirect speech inevitably involve: some perceived degree of indeterminacy, or at least a lack of complete certainty. Indirect speech thus contrasts with what is (literally) said, which is held to be certain and determinate, and thus something for which participants can be helc accountable, at least amongst speakers of English (Culpeper and Haugh 2014). It is also suggested that so-called interpersonal harmony (cf. "politeness") and interpersonal conflict (cf. "impoliteness") arise through a combination of positioning and defending self/other, and indexing and negotiating relationships, alongside the pursuit of interactional goals and, in some cases, the instantiation of language play.

It is thus clear from research to date that indirectness has a variety of interpersonal functions in communication, of which giving rise to politeness is just one. In other words, one of the main reasons why indirectness does not always give rise to politeness is because it is in fact associated with a whole range of different interpersonal phenomena. The challenge for any investigation of the relationship between im/politeness and indirectness is thus to determine when and why indirectness gives rise to im/politeness in some contexts, but not in others. Another key question to consider is how indirectness arises in the first place, a point to which we now turn.

3 Analysing indirectness

Indirectness has generally been conceptualised as a "not direct", "inexplicit" or "nonliteral" form of meaning that involves some kind "mismatch" between what is expressed by linguistic form and what is intended by the speaker, or, alternatively, as a way of "mitigating" what is communicated by the speaker.

Directness, according to Kiesling and Johnson (2010), involves a path "that goes straight from a point of origin to the destination with no other stops" (p.293), and so, when applied metaphorically to language use, it encompasses instances where "there are no intervening steps that need to be taken to arrive at a meaning. In other words, the meaning is completely conventional and arbitrary" (ibid: 293). In this view, "indirection is an alternate path, one that must go through some extra steps and often take a circuitous route. It is another way of arriving at the same destination" (p.293). (In)explicitness, in contrast, rests on the distinction between what is derived from the "logical form" of an utterance (termed "explicit") and what is derived solely through inference (termed 'implicit") (Carston 2002a; Sperber and Wilson 1995). Finally, "nonliteralness" is grounded in a distinction between "literal" and "nonliteral" illocutionary acts (Bach and Harnish 1979: 66–72), where the latter refers to an illocution derived primarily through inference that is meant *instead of* what is said (as opposed to *in addition* to what is literally or non-literally said as in the case of so-called indirect illocutionary acts). Despite some differences in formulation, however, all of these conceptualisations of indirectness involve some kind of inference on the part of the hearer that either results in some kind of "mismatch" between linguistic form/structure used by the speaker and its (inferred) communicative function, or "mitigation" of the force of the communicated meaning (or sometimes both). The rather fuzzy conceptualisation of indirectness that is referenced in the field is arguably one of the main reasons why so many different ways of theorising and analysing it have emerged in the literature.

In this section, we first examine how indirectness has been conceptualised and analysed in pragmatics, before moving on to consider alternative accounts of indirectness that have been developed in conversation analysis and linguistic anthropology.

3.1 Indirectness as pragmatic mismatch

The conceptualisation of indirectness as involving some kind of "mismatch" underpins a number of binary distinctions in the analysis of speaker meaning in pragmatics, including Grice's distinction between "what is said" and "what is implicated" (Grice 1975, 1989), Searle's distinction between "direct" and "indirect speech acts" (Searle 1975, 1979), Bach and Harnish's (1979) distinction between "literal" and "nonliteral illocutionary acts", and the Relevance theoretic distinction between "explicature" and "implicature" (Sperber and Wilson 1995).[5] Building on these distinctions, there are arguably six key types or forms of indirectness that have been identified in pragmatics (cf. Cheng and Warren 2003):

---

5 The notions of "indirect speech act" in Speech Act theory (Searle 1975, 1979) and "conversational implicature" in (neo-)Gricean theory (Grice 1975, 1978, 1989; Horn 2004; Levinson 2000) both draw implicitly from the underlying distinction between "direct" versus "not direct" meaning, while in Relevance theory the notion of "implicature" rests on the distinction between "explicit" versus "implicit" meanings (Carston 2002a; Sperber and Wilson 1995). This has generated somewhat different, albeit overlapping, conceptualisations of implicature, as we shall see in Chapter Two.

(1) conversational implicatures (Grice 1975)
(2) indirect speech acts (Searle 1975, 1979)
(3) indeterminate illocutionary acts (Austin 1962; Sew 1997)
(4) nonliteral illocutionary acts (Austin 1962; Bach and Harnish 1979)
(5) collateral acts (Bach and Harnish 1979)
(6) pre-sequences (Levinson 1983)

We now move to discuss each of these different forms of indirectness in turn.

A conversational implicature refers to a type of speaker intended meaning that goes beyond what is literally said (Grice 1975, 1989). More specifically, a conversational implicature encompasses a "speaker-intended meaning that arises in a principled way from the cooperative principle and conversational maxims through defeasible inference" (Haugh 2013e: 2659). They involve instances where a speaker means something else *in addition* to what is said (Bach 1994, 2012; Haugh 2002). For example, if I am in a café with a friend who is eating some cake with her coffee, and I comment that the cake looks really nice, my friend might respond by offering me some of her cake. By making this offer, my friend has shown that she thinks I was implying that I would like to try some of her cake. Since I did not actually say I wanted to try her cake, I could deny that I meant to imply this, either directly by saying something like "Oh, I didn't mean I want to try it", or indirectly by saying something like "Oh, I'm not hungry at the moment". However, unless I make some sort of denial, what has been implied, in part due to my friend's response, is that I would like to try (some of) her cake (Haugh 2013f).

Yet while much of the work to date on conversational implicature has proceeded on the tacit assumption that speakers imply something relatively determinate, Grice (1975, 1989) himself acknowledged that they may involve a "disjunction of specific explanations" (Grice 1989: 40), and so may be relatively indeterminate. Indeed, Relevance theorists specifically claim that "an utterance may communicate multiple, stronger or weaker, explicatures and implicatures *at the same time*" (Terkourafi 2013: 202, original emphasis, citing Sperber and Wilson 2008). Terkourafi (2013) refers to this as a "conjunction of inferences" that can be indirectly communicated by utterances, particularly amongst intimates (p.203). For instance, if a wife calls her husband and says, "I have to work late tonight", a whole range of inferences can be taken by the husband to have been implied by the wife through that informing. For example: "don't wait for me", "don't make dinner for me", "go ahead and have dinner without me", "you can have your favourite food which I can't stand", "don't worry that something bad happened to me", "don't call looking for me", "I will miss our favourite TV program", "I'm sorry I won't be able to watch it with you", "please record it for me", and so on (Terkourafi 2013: 201–202). In other words, through informing her husband she has to work late, the wife can simultaneously accomplish multiple indirect meanings. The degree of (in)determinacy of this "conjunction of inferences" depends, of course, on numerous factors, including the beliefs that are assumed to be shared between the participants, the individual mindsets of those participants, and the frequency with which the utterance in question arises in that relationship.

An indirect speech act, somewhat similar to the Gricean notion of "conversational implicature", refers to instances "where the speaker means what he says but he also means something more" (Searle 1979: ix), and so concerns "the relations between literal sentence meaning and speaker's utterance meaning" (p.viii). However, due to it being defined in terms of speech acts rather than propositional meaning, an indirect speech act refers, more specifically, to instances where the basic sentence type of the speech act does not match its illocutionary point in that particular context, as noted earlier in section one of this chapter. Thus, a request is indirect, for example, when it is realised through an interrogative or declarative rather than imperative sentence type. An indirect speech act more generally is where the primary illocutionary point of an utterance, which represents the speaker's intended meaning, is achieved through a secondary illocutionary point that arises through a literal or sentence meaning. Notably, Bach and Harnish (1979) go even further in their Speech Act Schema in claming that the former is "subordinate" to the latter in the sense that "securing uptake requires H to identify the indirect act by way of identifying the first [direct] act" (p.70). For example, if Y responds to X's invitation to go to see a movie by saying "I have to study for an exam", he has indirectly refused X's proposal by asserting something about his current circumstances (Searle 1979: 33). In Speech Act theoretic terms, he has committed himself to some future course of action (i.e. not going to the movie), which counts as a "commissive", more specifically a refusal, through committing himself to the truth of some state of affairs (i.e. he is studying tonight), which counts as an "assertive". The refusal thus counts as indirect because this commissive is achieved through an assertive by Y.

An indeterminate illocutionary act, in contrast, refers to utterances or turns at talk where two or more "illocutionary points" (i.e. the basic purpose of a speech act) are intended by the speaker to be plausible. An indeterminate illocutionary act is thus similar in some respects to Brown and Levinson's (1987) notion of "off-record indirectness", that is, where indirect utterances are designed in such a way that "it is not possible to attribute only one clear communicative intention to the act" (p.211), although it is not limited to illocutionary points that are realised through implicatures. In other words, indirectness in this case involves some degree of indeterminacy in regards to what is meant by the speaker, which may be interpreted as deliberate in some cases, while remaining unnoticed by hearers in others (Weiser 1974, 1975). For instance, if the host of a party find a plant which was given as a gift the next day after the party, but is not sure who it is from, although she suspects it might be from a particular guest, she might say to that guest something like, "I found the most gorgeous plant in my front room this morning" (Weiser 1975: 655). Weiser argues this utterance is inde terminate between two illocutionary points. On the one hand, it can be inter-preted as informing the guest about the plant (if the guest responds to this as new information). On the other hand, it can be interpreted as a pre-thanking, which will subsequently lead into thanking for the gift (if the guest responds to this as already known information, and so presumably was the one who gave the plant to the host). In other words, "the addressee's next utterance would tell [the host] whether they are feeling informed or thanked, and she can respond accordingly" (p.655). Indeterminate illocutionary acts, or what Weiser (1974, 1975) terms "deliberate ambiguity", can be resolved through the responses of hearers in some cases. However, in other cases they may be left unresolved or indetermi-nate for particular relational ends (Chang 1999; Sew 1997). According to this view, then, indirectness can, in some instances at least, involve a considerable degree of indeterminacy.

The finding that some implicatures or indirect speech acts are relatively determinate, while others are relatively indeterminate has been formalised in the oft-quoted distinction between "conventional indirectness" and "off-record indi-rectness" (Brown and Levinson 1978, 1987), which was briefly noted in section one of this chapter. Blum-Kulka and Olshtain (1984) took this basic distinction further, however, in arguing that these two types of indirectness, which they term "conventional indirectness" and "nonconventional indirectness" respectively, form a scale of different types of indirectness (p.201). In their view, conventional indirectness involves speech acts that are locution derivable (i.e. the illocution-ary point is derivable directly from what is said, e.g. "Madam, you'll have to move your car"), scope stating (i.e. the utterance expresses the speaker's intentions, desire or feelings, e.g. "I really wish you'd stop bothering me"), involve a lan-guage-specific suggestory formula (e.g. "How about cleaning up?", "Why don't you get lost?"), or make reference to preparatory conditions for that speech act (i.e. ability, willingness, possibility of the act being performed, e.g. "Could you clear up the kitchen?" or "Would you mind moving your car?"). Nonconventional indirectness, on the other hand, involves speech acts that arise through either strong hints (i.e. utterances that contain partial reference to the objects or ele-ments required for the implementation of the act, e.g. "You've left this kitchen in a right mess"), or mild hints (i.e. utterances that contain no reference to the request proper or any of its elements, e.g. "Have you been busy lately?" to a flat-mate who has left the kitchen in a mess) (p.202).

As we noted in section one in this chapter, conventional indirectness has been found to have a more robust relationship with politeness than nonconventional indirectness across languages, although clearly given the range of pragmatic effects that indirectness may occasion, which we discussed in section two, this is not a straightforward relationship. Moreover, the classification of references to preparatory conditions, such as "can you pass the salt?", as indirect has been challenged by some scholars. Haverkate (1988), for instance, argues that since particular contextual information is not required for their interpretation, conventionally indirect speech acts do not necessarily rely on "logical" inferences for their illocutionary point to be derived by the hearer. A series of empirical studies has also undermined the processing model presumed by Searle, Bach and Harnish, and others to underpin conventionally indirect speech acts (e.g. Gibbs 1979, 1981, 1983, 1986; Holtgraves 1998a, 1998b, 1999, 2002), although it is worth noting that other studies seem to support the idea that the "direct" or "literal" meaning is accessed as well as the "indirect' meaning, at least in some instances (Clark 1979; Clark and Schunk 1980, 1981). The most recent consensus seems to be that conventionally indirect speech acts appear to arise through some kind of "associative" (Mazzone 2011) or "metonymic" form of inference (Gibbs 1999c; Gibbs and Colston 2012; Panther and Thornburg 1998; Perez Hernandez and Ruiz de Mendoza 2002). Nevertheless, putting such debates aside, the claim that conventionally indirect forms are regularly associated with evaluations of politeness remains one that is now fairly well established in pragmatics, albeit one which remains to be explained with regards to the forms of inference through which they arise.[6]

Two other forms of indirectness that have been identified in the literature are what Bach and Harnish (1979) refer to as "nonliteral illocutionary acts" and "collateral acts", respectively. The former refers to instances where "we mean not what our words mean but something else instead" (Bach 2004: 468), or what are sometimes referred to as figurative meanings. These include instances of understatements/overstatements, irony/sarcasm, metaphors, and other figures of speech. While Grice (1975, 1978) treated these as instances of conversational implicature, Bach and Harnish (1979) argue that these constitute quite distinct pragmatic phenomena. Indeed, as Terkourafi (2013) points out, nonliteral illocutionary acts do not necessarily rely on recognition of a speaker's "illocutionary intention" (roughly, the reflexive intention that one's intention to mean something be recognised as intended). In the case of metaphorical utterances, for instance, "not only is experience, rather than rational inference, what is needed for the metaphor to mean for

---

6 We will return to discuss this point again in more detail in Chapter Five (see section 3).

the hearer roughly what is also means for the speaker, the potential interpretation of metaphorical utterances may also be open-ended, and they may go beyond whatever intention the speaker may originally have had in formulating her utterance" (Terkourafi 2013: 214). It is for this reason, then, that there have been on-going calls for figurative meanings to be treated as a distinct set of pragmatic phenomena in their own right (Bach 2004, 2012; Bach and Harnish 1979; Gibbs and Colston 2012; although cf. Arsenault 2014), rather than being subsumed under the notion of conversational implicature as originally proposed by Grice.

Collateral acts, on the other hand, refer to "conversational acts which can be be performed in conjunction with or in lieu of illocutionary acts" (Terkourafi 2013: 198; see also Bach and Harnish 1979: 96–103). Overt collateral acts involve various forms of "non-serious" acts where the speaker "intends to say something without meaning it" (Bach and Harnish 1979: 97), that is, without being held committed to what has been said, including "kidding", "joking", "punning", "mimicking" and so on. Covert collateral acts, in contrast, involve cases where speakers "perform with intentions that are intended not to be recognised" (Bach and Harnish 1979: 101). Innuendo, deliberate ambiguity and "sneaky presupposition", where "the idea is to get someone to think you think something and thereby to get him to think it without recognising that's what you want him to do" (Bach and Harnish 1979: 101), are proposed to constitute overt instances of collateral acts. It remains debatable whether overt collateral acts are actually instances of indirectness. However, it is clear in the case of covert collateral acts that we are indeed dealing with yet another form of indirectness, albeit one that overlaps in part with instances of indeterminate illocutionary acts.

Finally, pre-sequences refer to instances where a speaker tests the waters as it were, and, depending on the response of the addressee, goes on to perform the intended speech act (Levinson 1983). A request can thus be preceded by a pre-request, an invitation by a pre-invitation, an announcement by a pre-announcement, and so on (Schegloff 2007). Levinson (1983), for instance, argues that the following interaction involves a pre-request in line 1.

(6) 1 A: Hullo I was wondering whether you were intending

2   to go to Popper's talk this afternoon

3 B: Not today I'm afraid I can't make it to this one

4 A: Ah okay

5 B: You wanted me to record it didn't you heh!

6 A: Yeah heheh

7   B: Heheh no I'm sorry about that ...

(Levinson 1983: 358)

A's question about whether B is going to attend (Karl) Popper's talk is one of the preparatory conditions for making a request that B record this talk for A, and so counts as a pre-request according to Levinson. As Haugh (2009) points out, however, it is not entirely clear that B was in fact treating A's utterance in lines 1–2 as a pre-request, or simply as a request for information at the point of his response in line 3. It is evident through B's mention of this incipient request in line 5 though, that he has understood at that point A's initial question as a pre-request (see also Haugh and Jaszczolt 2012). In this view, indirectness is a function of sequences of utterances, that is, of discourse.

This kind of "roundabout talk" where indirectness arises through discourse rather than one particular utterance has also been noted more generally in relation to indirectness in a number of languages, including English (Bertuccelli Papi 2000: 149–153), Chinese (Chang 1999; Zhang 1995) and Japanese (Maynard 1997; Yamada 1997). In the following example, for instance, what is most striking is that the primary speech act in question, which is driving the interaction (i.e. a request), is ultimately delivered through a fairly explicit formulation (highlighted in bold), yet it is accompanied by numerous supportive moves that render the request somewhat indirect overall.[7] Here, due to limitations of space, we start by examining only the English translation of the original Chinese example.

(7)   (A and B are two students talking about forthcoming exams)

2   B: Speaking of the exam, I feel really bored and extremely (   ). Look, I don't even have a clue as to how to review. Sometimes, you know, it isn't easy to ask for help from the teacher or the students. Hey, do you think they'd like it if I went and asked some questions? Or is it ...

3   A: If you really must ask, you'd better not ask those exam-related questions. Even if they decide to answer your questions, you know, they'll feel more intimidated to answer exam-related ones. They don't even dare to show any unusual facial expressions for fear that you would say 'yes, I got it'. The other day when I was talking to this person, his facial expression was very strange and I knew immediately that this item would be on the exam.

---

7 This example is translated from Mandarin Chinese. A copy of the original text can be found in Zhang (1995: 103–111).

4   B: Usually, you know, the teacher will give some review topics and things like that. Unfortunately, I didn't come to class last week. Of course, you know, I can study by myself, but I really hope, you know, to receive some help, you know, from the teacher or fellow students. What do you think? As you said just now, there's always a crowd bothering you before every exam, <u>so now I feel like, you know, asking, but I'm afraid that people will resent me</u>. I feel very uncomfortable you know.

5   A: That depends. I don't mind if they are good friends. Otherwise, I hate to help, especially those who come to you only when they need you, you know. Also you must be very careful when you give help. If you give the wrong information by accident, you know, for example, tell people something you are not sure of, people will say, look, you told me such-and-such. Of course they are not blaming you but what they say will make you uncomfortable. Therefore, I usually take it easy with those who are not my friends. But I must appear to be serious. I must pretend it is real. That is a very hard job.

6   B: Really. Because I am now very anxious. The exam is only two weeks away. I don't know where to start and what to review. **Do you think you can help me if you know? Just tell me what the teacher said the other day and give me a rough idea, like some direction.**

7   A: That's no problem. I'll make a photocopy of the review sheet for you and that will take care of everything, right?

8   B: That's wonderful.

9   A: This won't take too much time. Perhaps the two of us can study together. I can learn something from you too. All you missed was one day. Then ...

10 B: That's wonderful.
(Zhang 1995: 105–110)

The overall trajectory of this interaction involves B seeking help from A in order to study for the upcoming exam. The request for help is realised in two steps, underlined in turn 4 and highlighted in bold in turn 6. A responds to the latter explicitly formulated request with an offer to copy the review sheet (turn 7), and an offer that they study together (turn 9).

If we examine this example more carefully, we can see that the initial formulation of the request in turn 4 is somewhat indirect in that the target, that is, the person who is expected to offer help, is not made clear. Consider the following utterance taken from turn 4, which is reproduced in the original Chinese below:

(7a) 4 *Ni kan wo xianzai jiushi shuo you   xiang wen ba,*
      you look I   now   PRT   say have want ask PRT
      keshi you   pa   tongxue   shuo
      but   have fear classmates say
      (lit. 'You see I now say want ask but afraid students talk')

This request is subsequently upgraded into a patently direct request in turn 6, when an imperative directive is issued, albeit mitigated by the prior conditional clause, as illustrated below:

(7b) 6 *Ni   kan ni   neng bu   neng bang wo   neige, ni   yaoshi*
      you look you can Neg can help me   one   you if
      zhidao de   hua, ni   jiu gen wo shuoshuo laoshi   nei   tian
      know   PRT talk you just give me say   teacher that day
      shuo shenme laizhe. Jiu   gei wo daigaiqi de   jiu   rang wo
      say what   PRT   just give me rough   PRT just let   me
      xinli qima   you dian shu-er. Dianbo   dianbo
      heart at least have little idea-DIM give advice give advice
      what-PRT
      shenme-de.
      (lit. 'You see you can help me [or not] if you know, you
      just to me talk talk teacher that day said what. Just let me in general let
      me heart at least have some idea, some direction)

Ultimately, then, B's makes an on record request, as we can see from the detailed gloss of turn 6 in example (7b) above. However, while the request itself is in the end achieved through an imperative directive, it is embedded in discourse that features numerous "supportive moves", including "seeking advice", "stating problems", "expressing worries and wishes" (Zhang 1995: 92). The request is thus framed within indirect talk, although the request itself is ultimately not indirect but formulated through an imperative directive.

Notably, despite the length of time it takes for B to make the request itself, Zhang reports, based on subsequent interviews with the two participants, that throughout the interaction, "A and B know perfectly well what the other wants ...

Yet each tries to get the other to accept what she does not want, i.e., A does nc want to be asked for help and B does not want to be refused" (p.92). Given the par ticipants are aware of what is being negotiated here throughout the interaction through this "roundabout talk" the participant are clearly orienting to relationa concerns, as well as defending the interests of the self (here glossed as avoiding "loss of face" or *diu mianzi* by participants). This kind of discourse-level indirect ness is thus clearly recognisable and so oriented to by the two participants in the course of this interaction.

Bertuccelli Papi (2000) has termed this kind of phenomena "implicitude", which she defines as instances where there is "an implicit agreement on what can remain unsaid and on recognition and acceptance of the intention to leave it unsaid as a mutually shared premise for the construction of what is meant" (p.153). This raises an interesting problem for standard accounts of indirectness in pragmatics. The supportive moves that give rise to this discourse-level indirectness cannot be treated as simply indirect requests or pre-requests in and of themselves, although they clearly do ground and frame an incipient request. This is because these so-called support moves are also recognisable social actions in their own right, with their own interpersonal consequences, and so are not simply just a means to an end (i.e. to make a request). They cannot be considered indeterminate illocutionary acts either, given the participants are well aware throughout the interaction what is really being negotiated here. Instead, these supportive moves are oriented to by participants as implying or hinting about, or alluding to, the negotiation of an interactional goal, which itself remains unspoken until near the end of the interaction. In other words, the phenomenon of implicitude arguably arises through an intertwining series of implicatures. This indicates that implicatures can have discourse-level effects, and so in many cases are better analysed as they arise in interaction. This move to examining indirectness in interaction contrasts, however, with the traditional utterance-level treatment of implicatures, and indeed the other forms of indirectness identified in pragmatics, a point which will be further elaborated upon throughout the course of this book.

3.2 Indirectness as mitigation

As we noted at the beginning of this section, the notion of indirectness has also been conceptualised in pragmatics as involving some kind of "mitigation", that is, as the "weakening, attenuation, downgrading, downtoning" of a particular speech act (Caffi 1999: 882). Sbisà (2001) has argued that mitigation is not simply a "stylistic phenomena" that is "superficially adjoined to the speech act", but rather is constitutive of the illocutionary effect or force itself (p.1791). This argument is extended by Thaler (2012), who proposes that "mitigation processes can be described as operations on components of illocutionary force, namely on the preparatory conditions, the sincerity conditions and the degree of strength of one of the act's sincerity conditions" (p.907). For example, by asking "would you mind passing the salt?" the speaker "indicates a reduction of the hearer's obligation to carry out the requested act of passing the salt" (p.909) through an additional preparatory condition (i.e. that the request may intrude on the other's territory) (p.912), and sincerity condition (i.e. that the speaker is dissatisfied with this intrusion on the hearer's territory) (p.913).[8] In that sense, then, mitigation can be treated as another key form of indirectness – alongside conversational implicatures, indirect speech acts, indeterminate illocutionary acts, nonliteral illocutionary acts, collateral acts, and pre-sequences – which has particular interpersonal or relational implications in its own right.

Various forms of mitigation have been identified by researchers, building and extending upon the notion of "hedge", which was initially coined by Lakoff (1972) to refer to expressions associated with "fuzzy propositional content". In Caffi's (1999, 2007) framework, for instance, a distinction is made between (1) "bushes" on propositional content that either decrease precision or increase indeterminacy or vagueness, (2) "hedges" on illocutionary force that decrease speaker commitment, and (3) "shields" on the target and/or source of talk. Schneider (2010) argues that, overall, mitigation inevitably involves reducing the speaker's or hearer's degree of commitment to the speech act in question in some way. In doing so, mitigation "facilitates the management of interpersonal relations during verbal interaction insofar as it makes an utterance as acceptable as possible to the interlocutor without the speaker having to give up his or her standpoint" (p.255).

Consider, for instance, the following excerpt from the film, *Four Weddings and a Funeral*. Here, Charles is finally declaring his hand and asking Carrie if she will go out with him. This declaration and proposal, however, is accomplished through a rather long and heavily mitigated monologue:

---

8 Thaler (2012) formulates this "intrusion on the other's territory" specifically in terms of Brown and Levinson's notion of "negative face".

(8)   Charles: Ehm, look. Sorry, sorry. I just, ehm, well, this is a very stupid question and, particularly in view of our recent shopping excursion, but I just wondered, by any chance, ehm, er, I mean obviously not because I guess I've only slept with nine people but- but I- I just wondered, er. I really feel, er, in short, to recap it slightly in a clearer version, uh, the words of David Cassidy in fact, uh, while he was still with the Partridge family, uh, "I think I love you," and er, I- I just wondered by any chance you wouldn't like to, er, er (pause) No, no, no of course not. I'm an idiot, he's not. Excellent, excellent, fantastic, er, I was gonna say lovely to see you, sorry to disturb. Better get on. ((to himself)) Fuck!

Carrie: That was very romantic.

Charles: Well, I thought it over a lot, you know, I wanted to get it just right.
(*Four Weddings and a Funeral*, 1994, director: Mike Newell, writer: Richard Curtis)

Apart from the fact that Charles never actually completes the utterance where a proposal is evidently forthcoming (that is, "I just wondered by any chance you wouldn't like to"), the unfinished proposal itself is accompanied by a large number of hedges, bushes and shields, thereby mitigating its force. Notably, while the declaration of love itself ("I think I love you") is direct in its formulation, and the unfinished proposal itself ("I just wondered by any chance you wouldn't like to") is also arguably fairly straightforward in its intent, the overall effect is that Charles is being highly indirect here. Once again, then, we can see that indirectness is not simply a property of individual utterances, but rather can be attributed more holistically to a sequence of utterances.

As Caffi (1999, 2007) points out, then, mitigation can be understood as either a strategy or a result, or both. In other words, mitigation, and so indirectness more broadly, can be understood either as an *analytic category* used to label or group together particular phenomena, or as a *discursive attribute*, that is, an evaluation of some utterance or discourse as mitigated and thus indirect. This begs the question, however, as to what are the grounds on which an individual utterance, or a sequence of utterances in discourse, can be evaluated as indirect? In pragmatics, as we have seen, this has generally been based on a set of criteria formulated by analysts or theorists. In work by conversation analysts and linguistic anthropologists on indirectness, in contrast, evaluations of indirectness have generally been grounded in the understandings of participants themselves.

3.3 Indirectness as social action

In conversation analysis (CA), the focus has been on the actions that are interactionally achieved by participants through indirect speech acts or indirect responses (Drew 1984; Schegloff 1995, 1996a; Stivers 2011; Walker, Drew and Local 2011). Indirectness is thus treated as a property of the relationship between the actions that are being accomplished through current and preceding turns. Walker, Drew and Local (2011), for example, treat responses to polar questions as indirect when they meet the following three conditions: (1) they are non-type-conforming (that is, they are not yes/no prefaced), (2) they do not use ellipsis, repetition or pronominalization to tie the response back to the preceding inquiry, and (3) they require inferences, which draw from prior talk that is non-contiguous (i.e. not in the immediately preceding turn) or from shared knowledge, in order to be understood as responses to the prior turn (p.2339–2340). They go on to claim that indirect responses to polar questions can be used to "reveal" the perceived purpose or agenda displayed in the prior turn, or to treat the prior inquiry as "inapposite", that is, lacking or deficient in some way.

In the following example, for instance, the two speakers are talking about an ESL (English Second Language) program in an American university. What is notable here is that they are former colleagues who have similar jobs setting up and administering such programs, and so are licensed to make a range of assumptions about what the other knows. Up to this point, A has been talking about how they have been spending quite a bit of money upgrading the facilities at the ESL centre at his university.[9]

(9)   IND77 CHAm4247

8   B: do they have any scholarships for foreign students

9   A: .hhhhhh I- I'm- I've never heard of a scholarship

10   for an English language program personally

11   b[ut I think

12   B: [>we never did< either but I keep thinking

13   I'm going to fin::d one one of these days uh huh

14   ((laughter))
(adapted from Walker, Drew and Local 2011: 2446)

---

9 The transcription conventions followed here, and subsequently for other detailed transcripts, are those standardly used in CA (Jefferson 2004a).

The formulation of A's response (in lines 9–11) to B's polar question (in line 8) about scholarships for foreign students is indirect from a CA perspective, as it is non type-conforming, it does not involve any structural tying back to the prior turn and it requires some kind of inference on the part of B to make sense of it. More importantly, this indirect response enables A to display an understanding of B's question as inapposite, because B should already know that no scholarships of that type exist, given their shared background experience in the field. B herself admits the inappropriateness of her question in her subsequent turn (lines 12–13), when she claims that she was pretty sure that such scholarships don't exist. In this way, then, an indirect response is used to display an understanding of a prior question as inapposite in some way. The key assumptions underlying a CA approach to indirectness is thus that particular actions can be achieved through indirect responses or turns, and in that sense, indirectness itself constitutes a social action.

3.4 Indirectness as culturally imbued practice

Linguistic anthropologists have not only called for an expansion of the scope of phenomena that fall under the umbrella of indirectness, but have also called for attention to be paid to the culturally-specific ways in which indirectness is manifested. In a seminal study drawing from various anthropological studies of meaning practices, Brenneis (1986: 341) argues that if indirectness involves cases where "speakers 'mean' more, or other, than what they have said", then it is predicated on "active involvement" by hearers, and it is this active involvement which allows the speaker to imply something about his stance vis-à-vis what has been indirectly conveyed, as well as to avoid or disavow full responsibility for what he or she is taken to mean. Brenneis goes on to suggest there are at least four different types of indirectness: text-centred, voice-centred, audience-centred and event-based indirection (see also Kiesling and Johnson 2010).

Text-centred indirectness refers to instances where "features of the message itself … suggest the intended meaning and … let listeners know that they should attend to such meanings" (Brenneis 1986: 341). Conversational implicatures, indirect speech acts and the like fall under this category of indirectness, although Brenneis also notes that it is the hearers "who must determine *for themselves* why and how a puzzling or apparently out of place comment actually makes sense, and to whom it might apply" (pp.341–342, emphasis added), thereby implicitly challenging the assumption that indirect meanings are determined by the speaker's intentions, or even simply the hearer's perception of those intentions.

Voice-centred indirectness encompasses instances where there is "ambiguity concerning who is really responsible for a message" (Brenneis 1986: 342), such as when speakers co-narrate with others, or when they echo the words of others (Goodwin, M. H. 1980, 1990). Tannen (2010), for instance, analyses examples of "ventriloquising" where one family member speaks in the voice of another, thereby directing the hearers away from the speaker to the person whose voice is being ventriloquised. In the following example, for instance, a father issues a directive to his daughter through the "voice" of her mother.

(10) Father: Oo! And olives, oh.
        Now your mom would say,
        "Oh, you need more lettuce!"

   Daughter: Yeah, I was just gonna put more lettuce into it.
   (Tannen 2010: 311)

Tannen suggests that by ventroliquising the voice of her mother, the father is able to deflect the impression that he is the one giving orders (p.312). In other words, indirectness is used here to decrease the speaker's responsibility for the speech act in question.

Audience-centred indirectness in contrast, refers to cases where comments ostensibly addressed to one party are also meant for another party, as in the case of cultural practices such as "dropping remarks" (Fisher 1976), "indirect teasing" (Haviland 1986), and "signifying" (Morgan 1991, 1996), where the recognition of unsaid meaning is obscured by the ostensible content or function of what is said.

Consider, for instance, the following instance of "pointed indirectness", where "a speaker ostensibly says something to someone (mock receiver) that is intended for – and to be heard by – someone else and is so recognised" (Morgan 1996: 406). This excerpt is from an ongoing interaction between African American family members, including the researcher (Marcyliena) and three others (Judy, Ruby and Baby Ruby). Marcyliena is Judy's daughter, Ruby is Judy's sister, and Baby Ruby is Judy and Ruby's niece.

(11) 1 M: what- what- what- I MEAN- what was teena-

    2   being a teenager like I mean what was::

    3 J: O:h I was: gor[geous

    4 BR: [OH well by that time

    5   HO:NEY? her hea:d was SO: [big

    6 R: [O:H my GO:D

7		O:H my GO:D
8		(.)
9	M:	this is the Coca Cola pha:se?
10	BR:	O:H BABY The whole works
11		(.)
12		she was the only one
13		(.)
14		she ran in the Miss black WHAT↑EV?:ER
15		thing they was RUNNING in those da:ys=
16	R:	=sure di:d

(Morgan 1996: 418)

This signifying episode is triggered by Judy's response in line 3 to the researcher's question about what it was like being a teenager at that time. Baby Ruby employs pointed indirectness by addressing the researcher, who is also Judy's daughter, rather than Judy herself, when she formulates a negative assessment of Judy in lines 4–5, that is, casting her as already being conceited at that time (despite the fact Judy probably had good reason to think she was beautiful according to the researcher). What makes this a matter of *signifying* on Judy, rather than just simply teasing or mocking her, is the way in which it is indexed as such through a number of features of Baby Ruby's and Ruby's talk. These include AAVE (African American Vernacular English) lexical items and prosody that signal a negative assessment amongst African American women, such as "honey" (line 5), which is "often used among women to introduce a gossip episode or an unflattering assessment", and "baby" (line 10), which "can imply a negative assessment as well as address those present" (p.420). The concessive noun phrase "whatever" also functions as a negative quantifier of "thing" (line 14), which in this case refers to an "attitude, belief or life"; in other words, meaning something like "whatever fit her ego" (p.420). Finally, Judy's silence also confirms that signifying has occurred here, since any response would only confirm Baby Ruby's negative assessment, thereby admitting the pointed indirectness to be true.

The culturally-nuanced character of various forms of audience-centred indirectness is well also illustrated through Silverstein's (2010) discussion of the *rambarr* register in Worora (which is an Aboriginal language of the North Kimberley, in Western Australia). This register is used specifically in communiation between a "classificatory mother-in-law (and mother-in-law's classifica-tory brother) and classificatory son-in-law (or classificatory son-in-law's sister)" (p.347), in order to overcome the taboo on direct talk between such relatives. For example, in order "for one *rambarr* relative to ask the other 'Do you(sg.) want to drink some tea/water/sugar bag [honeyed drink]/grog [alcoholic beverage]?' he or she would say, addressing the mediating third party, 'Are we (du. incl.) consuming fluid?'" (p.348). Silverstein points out that here the *rambarr* relative is treated as a "figurative 'third person' present in the interactional triad but excluded from the 'participant' dyad that includes both speaker and shill [ostensible] 'addressee.'" (p.348), thereby maintaining the taboo on (direct) communication between them.

Finally, event-based indirectness refers to instances where "the event's occurrence is itself a significant message, in fact the most important message being conveyed." (Brenneis 1986: 344). This involves reading particular meanings from the fact a particular performance is taking place. Brenneis (1986) gives the example of Fijian Indians participating in shared emotional experience through the staging of particular communicative events.

The notion of indirectness is stretched even further by Kiesling and Johnson (2010), who argue that there are other forms of indirectness, such as "topic indi-rection" where there is "a 'shadow' topic for which the current topic is a conduit" (p.296). They also examine instances of what they call "stance indirection", where "forms conventionally associated with one kind of social relationship are used to create a different, sometimes opposite one" (p.296). In the following interaction, Saul and Alex are talking about their fraternity's basketball team. At the begin-ning of this excerpt Alex holds a cordless lapel microphone, which Saul has been previously holding, up to his mouth like a traditional microphone.

(12) 1   Alex: We're live here at Lee University,

2   with the sec- world's second best to Al King,

3   the fraternity's second best athlete to Al King,

4   and to the state's second best athlete Al King,

5   Saul what does it feel like to be overshadowed by

6   Al King? Talk to me.

7   Saul: I don't know man you- it's a little intimidating

8   when he wears flowers on his tie, and he thinks

9   he's better than me y'know.
(adapted from Kiesling and Johnson 2010: 301)

Here Alex insults Saul by suggesting he is not as good as "Al King". The insult i. indirect in a number of senses according to Kiesling and Johnson (2010). Firstly the insult is disguised in the form of an "innocent interview question" in being formulated in the (culturally familiar) "how do you feel" frame, and so consti tutes an instance of an indirect speech act. Secondly, the insult is not only com petitive (i.e. Alex is trying to get "one up" on Saul), but also at the same time cooperative as through it Alex "engages with Saul and builds connections with him" (p.301), and thus constitutes an instance of what Kiesling and Johnson term "stance indirection". Thirdly, Alex echoes a "generic 'sports announcer voice'" thereby using "another character to do the animating for his insult" (p.301), and so constitutes an instance of voice-centred indirection (or what they term "pro- duction indirection").

We have seen thus far that various different forms of indirectness have been identified not only in linguistic pragmatics, but also in conversation analysis and linguistic anthropology. In these later studies, however, a more critical stance has generally been taken towards the notion of indirectness, and the complex ways in which indirectness arises in interaction has consequently been highlighted. In this way, such studies have gone beyond the traditional treatment of indirectness in pragmatics as involving some kind of mismatch between a particular "linguis- tic form" and its "communicative function". Indeed, it has become evident from such studies that indirectness cannot always be analysed in terms of denotations (i.e. mismatches with "what is said" or "sentence meaning") (Kiesling 2010: 279), as the basic metaphor of indirectness has been stretched, on the one hand, by conversation analysts to encompass the relationship between actions accom- plished through adjacent turns at talk, and by linguistic anthropologists, on the other hand, to instances where indirectness arises through "indexical and meta- phorical meaning[s]" at a more basic level than denotational meaning (Kiesling 2010: 279). It also becomes apparent that there are different ways of being indi- rect that vary across languages, cultures, social or relational networks, and so on (Kiesling 2010: 279; Silverstein 2010; Terkourafi 2011a: 2864). Indirectness thus evidently encompasses a very wide range of phenomena indeed.

4 From indirectness to implicature

The sheer breadth of phenomena that can fall under the label of indirectness has led some to conclude that virtually all language use is in some sense "indi- rect". Caffi (1999), for instance argues that her "view of speech acts as clusters of multi-level and multidimensional features which range along a continuum of gradual variations both within a given type of illocutionary force and between

.wo different types ... leaves no space for a notion such as that of 'indirect speech act'" (p.892). Silverstein (2010) goes further in arguing that "there is no unity of membership in what would have to be considered to be 'indirect' usage—making the concept otiose as an analytic tool" (p.338). The usefulness of indirectness as an analytical category thus remains open to question, because it encompasses a broad range of quite disparate phenomena that are arguably not well explained within any single theoretical paradigm. And even if one were to take an eclectic view of indirectness, the theoretical paradigms in question cannot necessarily be reconciled with each other, which means the same pragmatic phenomena could end up being explained in multiple, potentially contradictory ways. It is for this reason that implicature rather than indirectness more broadly has been chosen as the focal construct underpinning this study.

However, this does not mean to say that the notion of indirectness need necessarily be abandoned in pragmatics. As was previously alluded to, indirectness can be theorised not only as an analytic category used by theorists, but may also be theorised as an evaluation by participants themselves of an utterance, or a sequence of utterances in discourse, as "indirect" (and consequently talk can be evaluated as such by analysts on that basis as well). In the latter sense, indirectness constitutes an attribute of discourse that is ascribed to it by participants. Conceptualising indirectness as a discursive attribute means treating it as yet another way for participants to evaluate talk, and thus as something that is always open to dispute by those participants, given the interpersonally consequential implications of such evaluations in many instances.

A focus on implicature also does not preclude gleaning a number of important lessons from studies of indirectness. A number of key themes have emerged in the course of this survey of the literature on indirectness. The first is that indirectness phenomena are inevitably situated in discourse or interaction. Indeed, the complex ways in which chains of implicatures can become intertwined is only observable at the level of ongoing discourse or talk-in-interaction. For that reason, the analysis of implicatures must be situated at the level of discourse, rather than at the level of isolated utterances or pairs of utterances, as so often has been done in studies of implicature to date.

Second, indirect meanings have been observed to have a close, intimate relationship with social action. To analyse implicatures thus means to examine not only the social actions that are accomplished through implicatures, but also to examine the social actions through which implicatures themselves are accomplished.

Third, indirection inevitably involves some degree of indeterminacy. The raison d'être of implicatures is that what is implied, hinted at, alluded to and so on remains unsaid and so must be inferred by participants. In being critically dependent on inference there inevitably remains space – albeit for all practical intents and purposes rather small in some instances – in which the precise nature of what has been implied, hinted at, alluded to and so on, or the speaker's commitment to that, can be negotiated or disputed.

Fourth, indirectness more often than not allows the speaker to avoid or disavow taking full responsibility for that which has been indirectly communicated. An examination of implicatures thus inevitably involves a consideration of issues of accountability, that is, the real-world social or interpersonal consequences of what a person is taken to be committed to meaning.

Fifth, understandings of indirectness can be situated relative to different speaker voices and audience positions.[10] An analysis of implicatures thus needs to go beyond a basic speaker-hearer model to consider the various participation footings relative to which implicatures can arise.

Sixth, indirectness has been shown to be linked to multiple interpersonal functions ranging from indexing solidarity and negotiating relationships through to positioning or defending oneself, and persuading or manipulating others. Politeness, impoliteness and related evaluations are thus arguably a useful lens through which to examine the nature of implicatures, given the way in which im/politeness cuts through multiple interpersonal functions. It is for reason that im/politeness implicatures constitute the primary analytical focus of this book. It is important to remain cognisant, however, of the fact the implicatures do not necessarily always give rise to such evaluations.

In the following chapter, we begin to review work on implicatures to date in light of these six analytical themes. This review of approaches to implicature then underpins the account of implicature as social action that is developed in the subsequent chapter.

---

10 A similar point is made by Bertucelli Papi (1999, 2000), as we shall see in Chapter Three.

Chapter Two:
Approaches to implicature

The notion of implicature was first introduced by the philosopher Paul Grice in the William James Lectures in order to discuss instances in which what a speaker means goes beyond the meaning literally expressed by a particular utterance in communication (Grice 1967, 1989). In ordinary talk such meanings are often treated as instances of *implying*. However, the word *imply* has two key senses in English:

> a. To involve or comprise as a necessary logical consequence.
> b. To express indirectly; to insinuate, hint at.
> (Oxford English Dictionary Online 2013)

The terms "implicate" (cf. *imply, mean*), "implicature" (cf. *implying*) and "implicatum" (cf. *what is implied*) were coined by Grice ([1975]1989: 24) in order to exclude the first sense of *imply*, which is traditionally used in logic and semantics to refer to logical inferences and entailments of utterances. The term implicature (and related terms implicate and implicatum) is thus limited to the second sense of *implying* as "expressing indirectly", "insinuating" and "hinting at", and so is generally contrasted with *saying* (in Grice's "favoured sense") and "what is said".[11] Notably, the term implicature was coined as a cover term to encompass speaker meanings that arise not only through *implying*, but also through *suggesting, indicating, hinting*, and so on (Grice [1975]1989: 24; [1969]1989: 86; [1987]1989: 360, 368).

In this chapter, the focus is on presenting Grice's original claims about implicature, and subsequent developments of it by the so-called (neo-)Griceans, as well as attempts to replace his framework by the so-called post-Griceans. In the

---

11 The Gricean notion of "what is said" refers to meaning that is "closely related to the conventional meaning of the words (the sentence) [the speaker] has uttered" (Grice [1975]1989: 25), that is, "the particular meanings of the elements of S [sentence], their order, and their syntactical character" (Grice [1969]1989: 87). It arises through a combinatorial understanding of word meaning, syntax, and processes of reference assignment, indexical resolution and disambiguation (the latter referring to both different senses of words and different possible syntactic structures). What is said for Griceans and neo-Griceans is thus akin to what ordinary users understand by the folk notion of literal meaning (i.e. what is literally said). As Börjesson (2014) argues, what is said is nevertheless a *pragmatic* notion given it is demonstrably context-dependent, hence Levinson's (2000) arguments about "pragmatic intrusion" into what is said, and ongoing debates about the boundary between semantic and pragmatic contributions to meaning (see Börjesson [2014] for a useful overview of these debates).

course of this discussion it will become apparent, as Carston (2005) has pointed out, that "we have three rather distinct projects, the Gricean, the neo-Gricean and the Relevance theoretic, each with its own goals and orientation, but all intersecting with each other at certain points" (p.5), which have all developed out of Grice's original work. The Gricean project has been largely philosophical, focusing on "accounting for the nature and conditions of the possibility of communication", while the neo-Gricean project has been largely linguistic, "focusing on the stable aspects of meaning which are related to lexical and structural features of sentences" (Bianchi 2013a: 122). Post-Gricean accounts, on the other hand, have been largely cognitive in focus, and so primarily "concerned with the mental processes underlying [the] comprehension" of implicatures (Bianchi 2013a: 122). While these different approaches are unlikely to be "complementary in all respects" (Carston 2005: 5), there are nevertheless useful lessons to be learned from all three approaches, lessons which inform the development of an interactional account of implicature in the following chapter.

1 Gricean and neo-Gricean approaches to implicature

The notion of implicature was intended by Grice to encompass a range of different species of implicature. However, Grice's primary concern was to explain what he termed "conversational implicatures", that is, implicatures that are implicated by speakers vis-à-vis "certain general features of discourse" (Grice [1975]1989: 26). In introducing his theory of conversational implicature, Grice made three key claims (Haugh 2013b, 2013f). First, Grice claimed that the inferences underlying conversational implicatures are made in a principled way. In other words, conversational implicatures are made available to recipients by speakers with reference to normative assumptions about the nature of cooperative interaction. Grice formalised this claim in postulating the Cooperative Principle and four related conversational maxims. Second, conversational implicatures can be contrasted with other kinds of implicatures, including conventional implicatures and non-conventional, non-conversational implicatures. Grice also proposed a distinction between conversational implicatures that arise through once-off reasoning in a particular context (particularised conversational implicatures), and those that arise through regularised or conventionalised reasoning across contexts (generalised conversational implicatures). Third, since conversational implicatures are claimed to be generated through ordinary, as opposed to strictly logical reasoning, these inferences are inherently defeasible, from which it follows that a conversational implicature, which is necessarily putative by definition in Grice's account, can always be cancelled.

Each of these claims has subsequently become the subject of considerable debate in pragmatics On the one hand, Grice's initial proposals have been further developed and expanded upon by researchers often identified as neo-Griceans. On the other hand, scholars who fall into the post-Gricean camp have called into question all three of Grice's claims about implicature in positing alternative frameworks to replace those proposed by Grice and the neo-Griceans. In this first section, then, Grice's original three key proposals about implicature alongside neo-Gricean developments of them will be discussed. Post-Gricean alternative accounts of implicature will then be discussed in the section two of this chapter.

1.1 Conversational implicatures and normativity

The first key claim made by Grice was that conversational implicatures arise in principled ways. The "general features of discourse" by which conversational implicatures are made available by speakers to hearers was formalised by Grice in the postulation of the Cooperative Principle: "Make your conversational contribution such as is required, at the stage at which it occurs, by the accepted purpose or direction of the talk exchange in which you are engaged" (Grice [1975]1989: 26). The notion of cooperation referred to in the Cooperative Principle is a technical one in that it encompasses the expectations we normally have about the kinds of things people will say, how they will say things, how specific we need to be, the order in which things are said, and so on, when engaging in talk, rather than referring to the folk sense of *cooperative* as joint engagement in an activity with a common purpose (Davies 2007). These expectations will, therefore, change depending on the kind of talk involved, or the "activity type" of the talk exchange in question, as Mooney (2004) points out.

However, rather than leaving it to empirical research to ascertain just what those expectations might be, Grice went on to postulate four key types of expectations in the form of the conversational maxims: Quality, Quantity, Relevance and Manner (Grice [1975]1989: 26–27).[12] According to Grice, a speaker makes avail-

---

12 The Quality maxim was formulated in the form of a supermaxim, "try to make your contribution one that is true", and two specific maxims, namely, "do not say what you believe to be false" (Quality1) and "do not say that for which you lack adequate evidence" (Quality 2) (Grice [1975]1989: 27). The Quantity maxim relates to the amount of information that is provided by the speaker, and was formulated in the form of two maxims, namely, "make your contribution as informative as is required for the current purposes of the exchange" (Quantity1) and "do not make your contribution more informative than is required" (Quantity2) (*ibid.*: 26). The Relevance maxim was formulated simply as "Be relevant", although Grice pointed out that there are both different kinds and different foci of relevance that can "shift in the course of a talk exchange"

able a conversational implicature through the normative expectation that he or she is observing the Cooperative Principle overall, and either observing or not observing specific conversational maxims in order to maintain that assumption. An example of the former given by Grice is when A, who is standing by a car that is not moving, says to B "I am out of petrol", to which B responds "There is a garage round the corner" (Grice [1975]1989: 32). Here B arguably implicates that the garage is, or may be, open. This (particularised) conversational implicature arises through A assuming that B is observing the maxim of Relevance in interpreting B's response. An example of a speaker flouting a maxim given by Grice is when A says at a "genteel tea party" that "Mrs X is an old bag", to which B responds, after a significant pause, that "The weather has been quite delightful this summer" (Grice [1975]1989: 35). Here B implicates that what A has said should not be discussed, or is an inappropriate thing to say. This (particularised) conversational implicature arises through B flouting the maxim of Relevance in his response to A's comment. In other words, it is generated by A assuming B is still adhering to the Cooperative Principle, and thus means something by making this comment about the weather, despite it appearing on the surface to not be related to what A has just said (i.e. flouting the maxim of Relevance).

One critique of the Cooperative Principle and conversational maxims framework, however, has been that it is not actually rigorous enough to account for the conversational implicatures it supposedly generates. Davis (1998: 62–113), Kiefer (1979: 70–71), Sadock (1978: 287), and Thomason (1990: 351–355), among others, claim that the conversational maxims are too general in their formulation to adequately explain individual cases of implicature. Davis (1998: 33–60) also argues that the maxims generate erroneous predictions as readily as they generate correct ones: that is, the maxims can be used to generate implicatures which do not actually occur in conversation. Indeed, while the conversational maxims can be used to explain – at least post facto – various instances of implicatures, their broad formulation means they end up being able to explain virtually any implicit forms of meaning. Sadock (1978: 287), for instance, has shown how the meaning of idioms, such as "spill the beans", can be worked out using the maxims and Cooperative Principle. Yet it does not seem reasonable to suggest that speakers actually use these maxims in making available the meaning of such idioms to hearers. Instead, it is more likely that some kind of conventionalised

---

(*ibid.*: 27). Finally, the Manner maxim was formulated in the form of a supermaxim, "be perspicuous", which was elaborated in a set of specific maxims, namely, "avoid obscurity" (Maxim1), "avoid ambiguity" (Maxim2), "be brief" (Manner3), and "be orderly" (Manner4) (*ibid.*:27), although Grice also left open the possibility that other Manner maxims might be required to account for all cases of conversational implicatures.

route is involved (Davis 1998; Wierzbicka 1985). The main point made in such critiques is that (neo-)Griceans have not demonstrated how it is that in the interpretation of utterances the Cooperative Principle and conversational maxims give rise to implicatures in some cases, but in other cases they do not. In other words, it is argued that Grice did not demonstrate a means by which the power of the Cooperative Principle and conversational maxims to generate implicatures is restricted. The notion of specific activity types remains one possibility given the original formulation of the Cooperative Principle, but one that has only been explored in passing (e.g. Davies 2007; Mooney 2004)

A second argument against the Gricean framework for calculating conversational implicatures has been that it is not only inadequate, it is also unnecessary (Davis 1998: 114–131; Gauker 2001: 173–180; Sterelny 1982: 192–193). Marmaridou (2000: 271) and Gauker (2001: 164), for instance, both argue that (particularised) conversational implicatures are drawn from inferences about what the speaker has said in particular situations without recourse to the Cooperative Principle and conversational maxims. A number of models of the generation of implicatures that do not exclusively rely on the Gricean conversational maxims have thus been proposed, including plan-based approaches (Green 1999; Green and Carberry 1993, 1999; Hinkelman and Allen 1989; McCafferty 1990; Thomason 1990), schematic models (Cooren and Sanders 2002; Sanders 1987), game-theoretic models (Parikh 2001), and preference-based approaches (Bilmes 1993), a point to which we will return to consider in later sections.

Grice ([1987]1989) himself acknowledged in his retrospective epilogue that the formulation and configuration of the conversational maxims had turned out to be less than ideal, in conceding that the maxims were not of the same order, nor completely independent of one another. He argued that flouting or violating the Quality maxim, for instance, was not actually a means by which a speaker could make a conversational implicature available, but rather "spell[s] out the difference between something's being and (strictly speaking) failing to be any kind of contribution at all" (p.371). He also acknowledged that in order to judge whether one has undersupplied or oversupplied information one needs to determine the relevance of an utterance, and so the maxims of Quantity and Relevance are not necessarily independent (pp.371–372). Grice also questioned the utility of the Manner maxim in generating conversational implicatures (p.372). However, as Bach (2012) points out, the role of the conversational maxims was never intended to "determine implicatures", but rather to "help explain how they get conveyed" (p.60). In other words, the conversational maxims were intended to only form part of the normative background against which conversational implicatures are made available by speakers to hearers.

Indeed, it is often not well recognised in critiques of the Gricean framework that in focusing on these "general features of discourse", Grice was proposing a normative apparatus by which speakers make what is implicated available to hearers, rather than attempting to explain how what is implicated is actually communicated or understood by hearers (Saul 2002a, 2002b; cf. Bianchi 2013b). Or as Jary (2013) puts it, Grice's aim was to "to show *why* a hearer is justified in drawing a certain conclusion about a speaker's communicative intent, rather than *how* he does this" (p.639, original emphasis). A conversational implicature (as opposed to a conversational implicatum) refers only to what the speaker intends to implicate (Bach 2006, 2012; Feng 2013; Horn 2004), and it is in that sense that conversationally implicating something only involves *making available* a particular meaning representation beyond what is said to the hearer in question. What the hearer understands to have been implicated is thus a distinct issue (as indicated through the separate term for conversational implicatum). Bach (2012) goes on to argue that "the hearer does not have to infer the thing the speaker implicates. He merely has to infer that the speaker implicates (means) it" (p.60). The process by which a hearer might understand what is implicated (or the speaker infers what a hearer might have understood to have been implicated), thereby yielding a conversational implicatum (that is, either a speaker-implicatum or a hearer-implicatum), is thus of a different order to that of conversationally implicating something. The distinction between implicature and implicatum has been largely lost in subsequent developments of implicature theory (Haugh and Jaszczolt 2012), a loss that arguably lies at many of the ongoing debates about the proper scope of implicature, and how they should be analysed and theorised.

In sum, then, the first key lesson to be gained from the Gricean framework for conversational implicatures is arguably the emphasis Grice himself placed on the *normative* ways in which implicatures are made available by speakers. As Grice ([1957]1989) noted in relation to speaker meaning more generally, "an utterer is held to convey what is normally conveyed (or normally intended to be conveyed)" (p.222). To implicate something, on Grice's account, is to make a speaker-intended inference or set of inferences available to others. But to be speaker intended does not necessarily encompass what the speaker idiosyncratically has in mind in implicating something, but rather refers to a *normative* notion, that is, what a speaker is normally held to intend to implicate through a particular utterance (see also Sanders 2012, 2013, forthcoming; Sanders, Wu and Bonito 2013; cf. Feng 2013) (see also section 1.2 in Chapter 3). While it is, of course, possible for speakers to imply things in highly idiosyncratic ways, as Davis (1998) demonstrates in his critique of the Gricean framework, if we are to make sense of what speakers are implicating in the normal course of interacting with each other, then ve, as users, need to draw from underlying normative, or recurrent practices by which implicatures are made recognisable to us. And it is arguably in large part these normative procedures that Grice was attempting to tap into in proposing the Cooperative Principle and conversational maxims, although the specific formulation of these has since come into question, including from Grice himself. Indeed, it is somewhat doubtful whether the conversational maxims can be legitimately extended from the analysis of implicatures in English to other languages. However, the more basic claim that implicatures are made available by speakers in recurrent ways is an important theme that will be revisited in later chapters.

1.2 Types of Gricean implicature

The second key claim made by Grice was that what is implicated should be further divided into those implicatures that are conventionally implicated and those that are non-conventionally implicated, with conversational implicatures constituting a subset of the latter (Grice [1975]1989: 25–26). This resulted in the postulation of three main types of implicature: (1) conventional implicature, (2) conversational implicature, and (3) non-conventional implicatures which are not conversational (i.e. non-conventional, non-conversational implicatures). Conversational implicatures were further subdivided into those that are meant unless something in the context, including the utterance itself, blocks them (generalised conversational implicatures), and those are meant in specific contexts (particularised conversational implicatures), based on the distinction Grice made between once-off reasoning in a particular context (i.e. nonce inferencing), and regularised or conventionalised reasoning across contexts (i.e. default inferencing) (Grice [1975]1989: 37; see also Grice 2001). These different types of implicature are summarised in Figure 2 below.

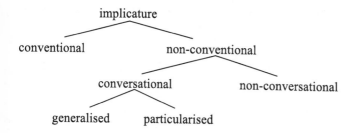

Figure 2: Types of Gricean implicature (Levinson 1983: 131; cf. Birner 2013: 99)

In the remainder of this section the various different types of implicature theorise̶ in (neo-)Gricean accounts are discussed in further detail.

1.2.1 Conventional implicature

Conventional implicatures were briefly characterised by Grice as instances where "the conventional meaning of the words used will determine what is implicated, besides helping to determine what is said" (Grice [1975]1989: 25). Drawing upon definitions of conventional implicature from Horn (1999: 392) and Levinson (1983: 127), they can be defined as implicatures that arise through non-truth-conditional non-logical inferences, which are not constitutive of "what is said" nor calculable in any general way from "what is said", but rather are attached by convention to particular lexical items or expressions.[13] Commonly cited examples of conventional implicature include the implication of "contrast" associated with the use of *but*, the implication of something being "contrary to expectations" associated with *even*, and the implication that "the present situation is expected to be different, or perhaps the opposite at a later time" associated with *yet* (Yule 1996: 45).

Some researchers have argued that conventional implicatures are theoretically otiose, and so an unnecessary as an analytical category in pragmatics (Bach 1999; Blakemore 2000, 2002; Iten 2005; Wilson and Sperber 1993). However, such critiques have arguably targeted an impoverished understanding of conventional implicatures that is limited to what is expressed by the words in question. As Potts (2005) points out, conventional implicatures involve not so much what is expressed by those words, but rather "commitments made by *the speaker of the utterance* 'by virtue of the meaning of' the words he chooses" that are "logically and compositionally independent of 'what is said'" (p.11, original emphasis). According to this view, while not all of the candidate examples proposed by Grice have turned out to qualify as good examples instances of conventional implicature (Potts 2005), there are nevertheless other cases where the speaker does appear to implicate a (metapragmatic) comment or stance on what is said through his or her choice of particular expressions. In such cases we are arguably dealing with instances of conventional implicature.

Consider the following excerpt from the novel *High Infidelity*, where Rob is trying to find out whether or not his ex-girlfriend, Laura, has slept with Ian (Culpeper and Haugh 2014).

---

13 It is worth noting that on some accounts, conventional implicatures are treated as part of what is "conventionally meant" along with what is said (Neale 1992; see Birner 2013: 100), reflecting the somewhat uneasy position of conventional implicatures vis-à-vis the distinction between what is said and what is implicated.

(13) Rob: Is it better?

      Laura: Is what better?

      Rob: Well. Sex, I guess. Is sex with him better?

      Laura: Jesus Christ, Rob. Is that really what's bothering you?

      Rob: Of course it is.

      Laura: You really think it would make a difference either way?

      Rob: I don't know.

      Laura: Well, the answer is that I don't know either.
                We haven't done it yet.
(adapted from Nick Hornby, *High Infidelity*, 1995, p.95)

As we can see, Laura ultimately responds that they "haven't done it yet". In the following excerpt we can see that Rob takes the addition of *yet* to "mean" that Laura is planning to sleep with Ian.

(14) this business about not sleeping with Ian...she only said she hasn't slept with him *yet*, and that was on Saturday, five days ago. Five days! She could have slept five times since then! (She could have slept with him twenty times since then, but you know what I mean). And even if she hasn't, she was definitely threatening to. What does 'yet' mean, after all? 'I haven't seen *Reservoir Dogs* yet.' What does that mean? It means you're going to go, doesn't it?
(Nick Hornby, *High Infidelity*, 1995, p.95)

Rob evidently interprets *yet* as meaning that some action which has not occurred is nevertheless likely occur at some point in the future. However, in this case, he takes it further in interpreting this as a threat on the part of Laura that she expects she will sleep with Ian (sooner or later). On Rob's view, then, it involves a comment on the current status of Laura's relationship with Ian: while they "haven't done it", Laura indicates that she is not committed to maintaining this state of affairs. In Grice's terms, Laura conventionally implicates a particular stance on that state of affairs (i.e. that it hasn't happened so far but it may well happen). Given Rob debates what Laura means by *yet* in this particular context, it is evidently not straightforwardly interpretable, suggesting that some kind of inference about Laura's stance is indeed involved.

From this example we can observe two important characteristics of conventional implicatures which distinguish them from conversational implicatures.
The first is detachability, namely, that an alternative expression with the same
truth-conditional meaning does not carry the same implicature, as can be seen
when we compare example (16) with example (15). The second is non-cancellability, as illustrated by example (17).

(15)   He is rich yet honest.

(16)   He is rich and honest.

(17)   *He is rich yet honest, but I'm not meaning to imply by saying that that we
        might expect rich people to be less than honest.

In example (16) the utterance has the same truth-conditional content as example
(15), but it does not carry the same implicature. In example (17), the attempt to
cancel the implicature is unsuccessful because it simply does not make sense
given the implicature carried by saying *yet* in this particular utterance. Thomas
(1995: 57) takes the non-cancellability of conventional implicatures to mean that
they are always conveyed regardless of context. However, they nevertheless do
evidently trigger some kind of inference on the part of the hearer, as we can see
from Rob's debate about what Laura means by *yet* in this instance (see also Bach
1999: 343–344). This suggests that such inferences are modulated vis-à-vis the
context, and so while they can't be easily cancelled, the stance they are taken to
be implicating is nevertheless sensitive to the locally situated context in which
the expression occurs.

The category of conventional implicatures has been further developed (and
much debated) in work by neo-Griceans. On the one hand, Potts (2005, 2007)
argues that conventional implicatures are not instances of implicatures per se,
but nevertheless encompass a layer of meaning distinct from what is said and presupposition, citing instances where distinct meanings arise from the use of sup-
plements and expressives (including honorifics). On the other hand, Feng (2010),
Levinson (1979, 1983) and Salmon (2009, 2011) have developed and defended the
more traditional Gricean account of conventional implicature, which is generally
associated with particular expressions or linguistic forms. Levinson (1979, 1983),
for instance, has proposed that that socially deictic expressions, such as honorifics, can analysed as giving rise to conventional implicatures (although cf. Potts
2005), as they share similar characteristics with other examples of conventional
implicatures given by Grice (that is, they are neither detachable nor cancellable).

In the following example, for instance, a student asks his teacher whether he is going to a seminar.[14]

(18) *Sensei*   *wa*   *irasshai-masu ka.*
      Teacher(Pol) Top go(Hon)-Pol   Q
      ('will you go?')

On a neo-Gricean analysis, two conventional implicatures arise from the use of the honorific form *irasshaimasu* when used in place of the so-called plain form *iku* of the verb "to go" in Japanese.

(19) a.   With respect to the speaker, the addressee is socially higher

      b.   With respect to the speaker, the addressee is socially distant

According to Levinson (1979, 1983), (19a) is conventionally implicated by the *irassha(ru)* form, while (19b) is conventionally implicated by the *masu* form. Even when used ironically, the conventional implicatures of higher social status or greater social distance remains (Haugh 2007a; Okamoto 2002, 2007), so these implications are not easily removed. However, they can clearly give rise to a range of different interpersonal implications depending on the situated context (not just "politeness" as was originally argued by Levinson), and so evidently occasion some degree of inference about the speaker's stance vis-à-vis what is said.

Bach (1999) has countered Levinson's (1979, 1983) claims in arguing that these so-called conventional implicatures should actually be regarded as contributing to what is said. Yet an analysis of instances where utterance containing honorifics are indirectly quoted seems to undermine his claim. For instance, example (18) can be reported in an indirect quote, as illustrated below:

(20) *Tanaka san wa   sensei*   *ga*   *iku to*   *kii-ta.*
      Tanaka Hon Top teacher(Pol) Nom go Quot ask-Past
      ('Tanaka asked if the teacher will go')

Here the plain form of the verb "to go" in Japanese is used in the indirect quote, and thus the implicatures described in (19a) and (19b) do not arise. The conven-

---

14 The conventions used in the morphological glosses of examples from Chinese and Japanese are listed in the front matter of this book following the list of transcription conventions.

tional implicatures that arise through the use of honorifics by speakers do not appear to pass Bach's "indirect quotation" test for inclusion in what is said.[15]

There thus remains a *prima facie* case for retaining something like the notion of conventional implicature as means of accounting for instances where speakers implicate a stance or comment on what is said via particular contextually-sensitive expressions or linguistic forms. However, while inferences can be triggered by the occurrence of such forms or expressions given this context-sensitivity, the fact that the basic stance indicated by such forms cannot be removed, means that they should be treated as peripheral to implicature theory proper. As Culpeper and Haugh (2014) argue, they are better examined within the context of a metapragmatic analysis, that is, as indicators of reflexive awareness on the part of participants about what the speaker thinks the hearer knows, expects, and so on. For this reason, conventional implicatures are not analysed in any further detail in this book.

1.2.2 Conversational implicature

The second category of implicature, conversational implicature, was the primary focus of Grice's account, as we noted at the beginning of this section. Grice drew a distinction between particularised and generalised conversational implicatures, one that has subsequently generated a considerable amount of debate. Particularised conversational implicatures, according to Grice, refer to "cases in which an implicature is carried by saying that *p* on a particular occasion in virtue of special features of the context" (Grice [1975]1989: 37), while generalised conversational implicatures refer to cases where "the use of a certain form of words in an utterance would normally (in the absence of special circumstances) carry such-and-such an implicature or type of implicature" (Grice [1975]1989: 37). In other words, conversational implicatures can be made available by speakers through once-off, situated reasoning relative to a particular context (i.e. nonce reasoning), thereby giving rise to particularised conversational implicatures, or they can be made available through regularised or conventionalised reasoning that cuts across contexts (i.e. default reasoning), thereby giving rise to generalised conversational implicatures. The basic difference between a particularised and generalised conversational implicature is that the former requires specific contextual information in order to be implicated, while the latter is implicated unless something in

---

15 The indirect quote test for inclusion as part of what is said (Bach 1999) rests on the assumption that if an indirect quote must include an element that is considered to give rise to a conventional implicature, then this supposed conventional implicature must, in fact, constitute a part of what is said.

the context, including the utterance itself, blocks it from being implicated in the first place.

Generalised conversational implicature

Most neo-Gricean developments of Grice's work on conversational implicatures have focused on generalised conversational implicatures, in particular, so-called "scalar implicature", which are a particular type of generalised conversational implicatures that arises through the use of a weaker term in an implicational scale (Gazdar 1979; Horn 1984, 1989, 2009; Hirschberg 1991; Levinson 2000; Matsumoto 1995; Schwenter 1999). It is claimed by neo-Griceans that the first submaxim of Quantity[16] motivates the establishment of quantity scales, such as <and, or>, <all, most, many, some>, and <the, a>, the existence of which underpins the generation of scalar implicatures (Horn 2009: 5).[17] Horn (2009) goes on to argue that "based on such scales, the speaker's assertion of a relatively weak value Q(uantity)-implicates that she was not in the epistemic position to have asserted any stronger value (to its left) within the same scale ... On this approach, scalar values are lower-bounded by their literal meaning ('what is said') and upper-bounded by quantity-based implicature" (p.6). For example, if I say that "John ate some of the cookies" I implicate that he did not eat them all. The defeasible nature of the inferences underlying such scalar implicatures can be illustrated through commonly cited examples, such as "John ate some of the cookies. In fact he ate them all" (Levinson 2000: 42).

One key debate in relation to scalar implicatures noted by Horn (2009) is that arising between those scholars who claim that the speaker implicates a "strong" epistemic claim through scalars, and those scholars that insist the speaker only implicates a "weak" epistemic claim. On the strong epistemic account (e.g. Gazdar 1979; Levinson 2000), it is assumed that "a speaker who asserts $p(i)$" (e.g. John ate some of the cookies) "implicates that he knows $\neg p(j)$" (i.e. the speaker knows it is not the case that John ate all of the cookies), "where j>i on the relevant scale" (i.e. <all, some>) (Horn 2009: 9). On the weak epistemic account (e.g. Geurts 2009, 2010; Hirschberg 1991; Horn 1989), however, a two-stage process is assumed. That

---

16 That is, "make your contribution as informative as is required for the current purposes of the exchange" (Grice [1975]1989: 26).
17 While Horn (1972) originally listed cardinals as an example of generalised conversational implicature (e.g. by saying "John has three children" the speaker normally implicates John has no more than three children), he has subsequently acknowledged there is now considerable evidence that the scalar view of such expressions is not tenable (Horn 2009: 7) (see, e.g., Bultinck 2005; Carston 1988, 1998; Geurts 2010).

is, a speaker who asserts *p(i)* (e.g. John ate some of the cookies) only implicate: that she doesn't know/believe *p(j)* (i.e. the speaker doesn't think or believe tha John ate all of the cookies), where j>i on the relevant scale (i.e. <all, some>). It': only if the hearer assumes the speaker has full knowledge of the situation tha the speaker implicates, and so the hearer is licensed to infer, that ¬p(j) (i.e. the speaker knows it is not the case that John ate all of the cookies) (Horn 2009: 9). Horn (2009) goes on to argue that the weak epistemic account of scalar implicatures is more consistent with our intuitions:

> In saying it's warm, I implicate that I don't know for a fact that it's hot. If you believe I know the actual temperature, you will strengthen my statement to infer that I'm communicating that (I know) it isn't hot, but since there's no guarantee of my epistemic security, this can't be a first-order implicature. (Horn 2009: 10)

In other words, through relevant scales, speakers can implicate for all they know that a stronger value does not hold, that is, they think or believe that *j* is not the case where j > i. This difference is important as it underpins the basic claim that implicatures are inevitably indeterminate to some degree, a point which is developed in further detail in the following chapter. In the case of scalar implicatures, indeterminacy arises as to the degree of speaker *commitment* to what is (taken to be) implicated.

This kind of indeterminacy vis-à-vis the speaker's commitment to what is putatively scalar implicated can be observed in the following excerpt from the British television series, *Merlin*, where a group of knights from Camelot have stopped for a rest after patrolling in the woods

(21)   Elyan: Alright. Who drank all my water?

      Gwaine: ((burps))

      Arthur: I believe you have your answer.

      Gwaine: You said I could have some.

      Elyan: I said you could have some. I didn't say you drink every last drop!

      Gwaine: I was thirsty.
("A Herald of the New Age", *The Adventures of Merlin*, Season 4, Episode 10, Dec 3 2011, director: Jeremy Webb, writer: Howard Overman)

The focus of this exchange is the interpretation of "some", and whether it can be taken to standardly mean "not all". Gwaine feigns innocence of this when he jusifies finishing off Elyan's water by claiming "you said I could have some". Elyan, on the other hand, invokes the standard understanding of "some" implicating "not all", by explicitly arguing that was what was meant by his offer for Gwaine to have "some" water. That Gwaine is taken to be teasing Elyan for the fact he didn't actually say "not all" of the water becomes obvious as the other knights subsequently join in to tease Elyan as well. This example shows us that ordinary users are indeed aware that a standardised meaning representation (i.e. "not all") can be implicated by uttering "some", but whether a speaker is held committed to that generalised scalar implicature can be debated, and it is the latter that is the source of Elyan's frustration.

Neo-Griceans have also refined or reformulated Grice's original conversational maxim, in arguing that they apply not only to scalar implicatures, but to generalised conversational implicatures more broadly as well. Horn (1984), for instance, proposes two principles to replace the Quantity, Relation and Manner maxims, while retaining Grice's original Quality maxim. The first is the Q Principle, which is formulated as "Make your contribution sufficient. Say as much as you can (given R)" (p.13). For example, by saying "It's possible she'll win", the speaker Q-implicates "it's possible *but not certain* that she'll win" (p.13). The second principle is the R Principle, which is formulated as "Make your contribution necessary. Say no more than you must (given Q)" (p.13). For example, in asking "Do you know the time", the speaker thereby R-implicates "What is the time?" According to Horn, a key difference between Q-based and R-based implicatures is the way in which they behave under (metalinguistic) negation. The former can be "cancelled" by explicit negation (e.g. "It isn't possible she'll win" can implicate "It's certain she'll win"), whereas the latter is not straightforwardly removed (e.g. "Do you not know the time?" does not eliminate the speaker implicating, or at least presupposing, that he is asking "What is the time?").[18]

An extension of Horn's account of Q-implicatures can be found in Geurts' (2010) recent work, where he rails against what he regards as the overly narrow neo-Gricean focus on scalar implicatures to date. He suggests that quantity implicatures are of two basic types: Q_c-implicatures which are "derived on the basis of closed sets of alternatives", and Q_o-implicatures, which "do not involve closed sets of alternatives" (p.125). Examples of the former include scalar implicatures, ignorance inferences licensed by 'or', and free-choice inferences (p.125), while examples of the latter include question-answer implicatures and conditional perfection implicatures (p.130). In contrast to Horn and other neo-Griceans, however, Geurts (2010) argues that "hearers do not primarily reason in terms of alternatives

---

[18] In the latter case, the neg-raised form is likely to result in an additional implicature, however, namely, seeking an account as to why the addressee presumably does not know the time.

but rather in terms of intentional states the speaker might be in" (p.129). In other words, he challenges the general neo-Gricean claim that generalised conversational implicatures arise by default independently of the speaker's intentions (e.g. Levinson 2000), and in that sense, his work is, to a large extent, more post Gricean than neo-Gricean in character.

Levinson (2000) also proposes a refined set of maxims that account for generalised conversational implicatures, based on the principles of Quantity ("what isn't said, isn't"), Informativeness ("what is expressed simply is stereotypically exemplified") and Manner ("what's said in an abnormal way isn't normal") (p.34). These three principles underpin the three kinds of generalised conversational implicatures postulated by Levinson: Q-implicatures, I-implicatures and M-implicatures. Q-implicatures arise through the Q-maxim: "do not provide a statement that is informationally weaker than your knowledge of the world allows, unless providing an informationally stronger statement would contravene the I-principle" (p.76). I-implicatures arise through the I-maxim: "'Say as little as necessary'; that is, produce the minimal linguistic information sufficient to achieve your communicational ends (bearing Q in mind)" (p.114). And M-implicatures arise through the M-maxim: "Indicate an abnormal, nonstereotypical situation by using marked expressions that contrast with those you would use to describe the corresponding normal, stereotypical situation" (p.136). Examples of Q-, I- and M-implicatures respectively are given in examples (22) to (24) below (+> is used here to indicate implicates).

(22)   A: So is she married?

      B: She's engaged.
          +> She's not yet married.
          (Levinson 2000: 107)

(23)   Harry and Sue bought a piano.
      +> They bought it together, not one each.
      (Levinson 2000: 117)

(24)   Larry caused the car to stop (cf. Larry stopped the car)
      +> Larry caused the car to stop in an abnormal way, e.g., by using the emergency brake
      (Levinson 2000: 141)

In each case, Levinson (2000) argues that these implicatures arise *ceteris paribus*, unless something in the context (including subsequent talk) blocks them.

However, as Carston (1998) points out, it is not made clear what blocks generalised conversational implicatures in cases where they do not arise despite being predicted on a standard neo-Gricean account. For example, if in response to A saying "Which of your colleagues support the strike?", B says "Some of them do", one would predict, following Levinson's (2000) account, that B saying this will generate a generalised conversational implicature by default, namely "Not all of them do". Yet in reality, something like "I don't want to [or can't] say who supports the strike" is more likely to be implied. Carston (1998) argues that not only the Gricean maxims, but also the refined neo-Gricean principles result in implicatures being predicted that do not actually arise in interactions.

However, one key difference between Levinson's (2000) account of generalised conversational implicatures, and that of most of the other neo-Griceans, which is often missed in such critiques, is the question of whether they involve local defaults attached to particular lexical items, as Levinson (2000) argues, or they are more properly associated with default contexts (Garret and Harnish 2009; Geurts 2010; Horn 2005, 2009; Terkourafi 2003, 2005; cf. Sauerland 2012). The latter position is perhaps closer to what was originally intended by Grice ([1975]1989: 37, [1978]1989: 46–49), who invoked "normal circumstances" in characterising generalised conversational implicatures.

Evidence from experimental studies is clearly mounting against the view that generalised conversational implicatures involve local defaults attached to particular expressions. There is a growing amount of experimental work, for instance, which appears to largely counter Levinson's position that "some" implicates "not all" by default (Bezuidenhout and Cooper 2002; Bezuidenhout and Morris 2004; Breheny, Katsos and Williams 2006; Bott and Noveck 2004; Geurts and Pouscoulous 2009; Katsos 2008, 2012; Noveck 2001; Sauerland 2010), as well as evidence against his view that "or" implicates the speaker is not in a position to make a stronger statement (Breheny, Katsos and Williams 2006; Chevallier et al. 2008; Paris 1973; Pijnacker et al. 2009). However, as Horn (2009) points out, "an implicature may arise in a default context without thereby constituting a default or automatic inference" (p.23). In this sense, then, such experimental results do not falsify the existence of generalised conversational implicatures per se, but rather undermine the local default view postulated by Levinson (2000). Moreover, the current consensus amongst most neo-Griceans is that "a major benefit of a default inference is not that it is *automatic*, but that the system knows *what* to infer, given that it is to make an inference" (Garret and Harnish 2009: 98, original emphasis). This latter position is consistent with the experimental findings of Storto and Tanenhaus (2005), who examined scalar implicatures arising from "or" relative to default contexts (see also Jaszczolt 2005: 211). It is also arguably consistent with Börjesson's (2012) proposal that particular expressions in an utterance can evoke conceptual frames in light of surrounding co-text. For instance, "John broke a finger" is claimed to implicate that "John broke *his own finger*" through the expression "finger" (which is an "Observable_Bodypart" evoking the frame elements of "Body-part" and "Possessor". The latter is, by default, the most readily accessible referent, namely, John.

In the default contexts account, then, generalised conversational implicatures remain a viable species of implicature for analysis, although considerable work remains to be done to further our understanding of the default contexts that trigger such implicatures. An important characteristic of such implicatures, in particular scalar implicatures, is that while there is often very little indeterminacy in regard to what is implicated that has been noted in this course of this discussion, there can be some level of indeterminacy with respect to the speaker's degree of commitment to that which has been (scalar) implicated

Particularised conversational implicature

Particularised conversational implicatures have, for the most part, been addressed only in passing in neo-Gricean work. Indeed, many subsequent accounts of particularised conversational implicatures have abandoned Grice's original conversational maxims framework in favour of alternative accounts of how such implicatures arise (see section 1.1, this chapter). However, one notable exception to the relative neglect of particularised conversational implicatures by neo-Griceans is the work of Bertuccelli Papi (1996, 1999, 2000, 2014) on "insinuation" and other forms of "subplicit" meaning.

Bertuccelli Papi (2000) argues that the "unsaid" can be further subdivided into that which is "implicated", and that which is "subplicit" (p.145). Implicatures, following the standard Gricean account, "derive from the reflexive intention that they be recognised by the hearer as intentionally meant by the speaker" (ibid: 147), although Bertuccelli Papi (2000) claims they arise primarily with respect to the Gricean Maxim of Relation (pp.162–163). Subplicit meanings, on the other hand, are those that "glide into the mind of the hearer as side effects of what is said or not said, and become the most relevant information that is retained of a whole message or be used as premises for the derivation of other implicated meanings" (ibid: 147). Examples of subplicitness include *alluding, insinuating, hinting,* and "implicitude" (i.e. talk "based on the assumption that a common background of shared knowledge is reciprocally accessible for referent identification" (ibid: 149).

One example of this kind of subplicit meaning is presented in Bertuccelli-Papi's (1996, 2014) analysis of *insinuations* by Iago in the Shakespearean play *Othello*. She argues that the act of insinuating "occurs when *A* want *B* to know *p* out does not want *B* to judge that *A* wanted to tell him *p*" (where *A* is the speaker, *B* is the addressee, and *p* is what is insinuated) (1996: 197). For instance, in the following excerpt from Act III, Iago works on planting doubt in Othello's mind about his relationship with Desdemona, in particular, the idea that she may be having an affair with Cassius.

(25) Iago: My Noble Lord.

Othello: What dost thou say, Iago?

Iago: Did Michael Cassio
When he woo'd my Lady, know of your loue?

Othello: He did, from first to last:
Why dost thou aske?

Iago: But for a satisfaction of my Thought,
No further harme.

Othello: Why of thy thought, Iago?

Iago: I did not thinke he had bin acquainted with hir.

Othello: O yes, and went betweene vs very oft.

Iago: Indeed?

Othello: Indeed? I indeed. Discern'st thou ought in that?
Is he not honest?

Iago: Honest, my Lord?

Othello.: Honest? I, Honest.

Iago: My Lord, for ought I know.
(Othello, Act III, scene iii; First Folio, 1623)

In this exchange, Iago brings up both the issue of Cassio's relationship with Desdemona, and then subtly steers the conversation to the question of Cassio's "honesty". Yet while Iago subsequently declares "Why then I thinke Cassio's an honest man" (data not shown), his initial expressions of uncertainty (e.g. "Honest, my lord?", "My lord, for ought [all] I know"), is enough to plant a seed of doubt in Othello's mind about Cassio. It is this insinuation that ultimately leads Othello to doubt Desdemona's faithfulness to him, which results in disastrous consequences for all (cf. Culpeper and Haugh 2014: 150).

Bertuccelli Papi (1999, 2000) also points out that one question that is often neglected in accounts of implicature is for whom is something left unsaid? In the above case of insinuation, Iago is voicing a doubt from which he himself ostensibly dissociates (and thus cannot be held committed to by Othello), yet behind this is the "genuine" voice of Iago that remains hidden to Othello, but is apparent to the overhearing audience. Bertuccelli Papi (1999, 2000) goes on to suggest that implicated and subplicit meanings are thus sensitive to the different types of audience for whom the utterance may be relevant. She introduces Goffman's (1979, 1981) participation framework, where distinctions are made between addressees, side participants, and overhearers, and so on, to account for different kinds of unsaid meanings, arguing that "the tailoring of an utterance in terms of explicit/inexplicit information crucially depends on whom the utterance is addressed to" (Bertuccelli Papi 2000: 172). This move to analyse implicatures vis-à-vis the participation framework is arguably a very important one, and so will be further developed in subsequent chapters.

However, while on the whole, Bertuccelli Papi's (1999, 2000) is certainly appealing, at least *prima facie*, a hard and fast distinction between "implicated" and "subplicit" meanings is, in practice, difficult to maintain. This is because it essentially rests on the degree to which, or ways in which, a speaker can be held committed to or accountable for a particular meaning beyond what is said (a point to which we will return later in this chapter). In being a matter of degree, this consequently motivates a continuum rather than a categorical distinction. It is thus proposed here that what is implied, insinuated, hinted at, alluded to and the like can all be treated as lying within the scope of a technical notion of implicature, a position that is arguably consistent with Grice's original intent as was alluded to at the beginning of this chapter. It can be thus argued that while Bertuccelli Papi's framework represents a genuine, and indeed important, extension of the neo-Gricean account of implicature, as it forces us to consider more carefully the different ways in which particularised implicatures arise, and also the participation framework in which they are situated, so-called subplicit meanings do not warrant a separate treatment distinct from that of implicatures.

1.2.3 Non-conventional, non-conversational implicature

Grice himself had little to say about the final category of implicatures that he proposed, namely, non-conventional non-conversational implicatures, although he suggested in passing that these might encompass other dimensions of pragmatic meaning such as politeness (Grice [1975]1989: 28) or irony (Grice [1978]1989: 53). Non-conventional, non-conversational implicatures were subsequently further investigated by neo-Griceans who proposed other kinds of implicatures, including "politeness implicatures" (Brown and Levinson 1978, 1987; Leech 1983), "irony implicatures" (Leech 1983), and what are variously termed "short-circuited implicatures" (Horn and Bayer 1984; Morgan 1978) "standardised implicatures" (Bach 1995, 1998; cf. Bach and Harnish 1979), or "*generalised conversational implicatures (*GCI)" (Terkourafi 2003, 2005).

Politeness implicatures, in a neo-Gricean account, refer to the attribution of polite beliefs or intentions to the speaker in the form of an implicature. This is referred to in this volume as the "politeness-as-implicature" view (Brown and Levinson 1987: 6, 95; Kallia 2004; Leech 1983: 170–171; cf. Terkourafi 2001, 2003, 2005). In some accounts, politeness is said to arise only through particularised conversational implicatures (Brown 1995, 2001; Brown and Levinson 1987; Kallia 2004; Leech 1983), while in others it is said to arise through both particularised and generalised implicatures (Terkourafi 2003, 2005). However, one key problem with the notion of politeness-as-implicature is that for the most part, with the notable exception of work by Terkourafi (2001, 2003, 2005), where politeness is defined as a perlocutionary effect (i.e. "the addressee holding the belief that the speaker is polite", Terkourafi 2003: 149) that arises from an implicature of politeness (i.e. "the speaker is being polite", Terkourafi 2003: 150), it neglects the complex relationship that obtains between politeness and implicature, as we shall see in Chapter Four.

Irony implicatures refer to instances whereby being overly polite the speaker can implicate impoliteness (Leech 1983: 82–82). This is summarised in Leech's (1983) Irony Principle: "If you must cause offence, at least do so in a way which doesn't overtly conflict with the PP [Politeness Principle], but allows the speaker to arrive at the offensive point of your remark indirectly, by way of implicature" (p.82). In the following example, for instance, B implicates that they won't miss Agatha.

(26)　A:　We'll all miss Bill and Agatha, won't we?

　　　B:　Well, we'll all miss *Bill*.
　　　(Leech 1983: 80)

In doing so, B also implicates a (potentially) impolite stance, according to Leech.

Finally, short-circuited implicatures (which are also termed standardised implicatures or *GCIs) refer to instances "where the implicature is in principle *calculable*, but in practice it is not actually *calculated* by speakers operating with the relevant usage conventions" (Horn and Bayer 1984: 404, original emphasis). In other words, the inference that underlies the implicature is compressed by precedent, but could still be worked out via nonce inference if there were no such precedent (Haugh 2008c: 58). For example, by asking the whereabouts of a particular person when making a phone call (e.g. "Is John there?"), a speaker can thereby standardly implicate that he or she would like to speak to that person. As Terkourafi (2003, 2005) points out, a "minimal context" is required in order for short-circuited implicatures (or what she terms *GCIs) to arise – in this case, that the speaker is making a phone call – and it is this which differentiates them from generalised conversational implicatures, which arise in all contexts, *ceteris paribus*.[19] Short-circuited implicatures are distinct from conventional implicatures and idioms because of their potential defeasibility, and because what is implicated is communicated *in addition* to what is literally said, rather than *instead of* what is literally said, as is the case for idioms (Bach 2006, 2012). For instance, when asking whether a person is there when making a phone call, the implicature that the speaker would like to speak to that person can be blocked by additional contextual information, such as the caller and the call receiver both knowing that the caller doesn't like John, in which case he might be checking if they can talk without being overheard by John (Haugh 2008c: 58). On the other hand, short-circuited implicatures are also distinct from conversational implicatures, because they are detachable, that is, the implicature disappears when an utterance with the same denotation but a different linguistic form is used. For example, asking "Is John there?" standardly implicates that the caller would like to speak to John, while asking "Is John present?" does not as straightforwardly generate the same implicature.[20]

1.2.4 Types of neo-Gricean implicature

In sum, then, Grice's original "typology" of implicatures has been somewhat expanded by neo-Griceans. This expanded set of different types of implicature is summarised in Figure 3 below.

---

19 A minimal context refers to contextual information which is perceivable to speakers (and hearers) prior to making any particular utterance, including the interlocutor's gender or relative age, the setting of the exchange and the timing of the utterance, and the expectations that information gives rise to (see Terkourafi 2001, 2005).

20 The notion of "sentence implicature", defined as "what speakers using the sentence with its regular meaning would commonly use it to implicate" (Davis 1998: 6), while superficially similar to these types of implicature, in fact cuts across the neo-Gricean categories of short-circuited implicatures and generalised conversational implicatures, a point to which we will return in the following section.

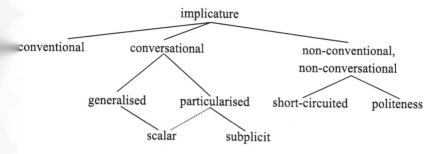

Figure 3: Key types of neo-Gricean implicature

While most types of implicature are relatively straightforward to classify in the neo-Gricean account, the dotted line between "particularised" and "scalar" is meant to reference ongoing debates about whether or not scalar implicatures are exclusively generalised, or may on occasion constitute instances of particularised implicatures.

From the preceding discussion, then, the second key lesson that can argu-ably be taken from the (neo-)Gricean framework is that implicatures are hetero-geneous. While the postulation of various different species of implicature has been much debated, the distinctions that are drawn between these different species of implicature allows us to start to explore a variety of analytical issues, including the different ways in which implicatures can arise, and the interper-sonal consequences of the ways in which speakers are taken to be committed to or accountable for those implicatures to varying degrees. Neo-Gricean work on implicatures also alerts us to a basic distinction between implicatures that arise through situated reasoning about the speaker's meaning in particular, localised contexts (i.e. nonce implicatures), and those that arise through inferences based "on general expectations about how language is normally used" (Levinson 2000: 22) (i.e. standardised or default implicatures). In that sense, these distinctions prove useful in exploring the relationship between im/politeness and implicature in more nuanced ways, a point to which we will return to consider further in the chapters that follow.

1.3 Implicatures and cancellability

The third key claim made by Grice was that conversational implicatures, and indeed non-conventional implicatures more generally, are cancellable. This is because implicatures arise through ordinary as opposed to strictly logical reasoning, from which it follows that the inferences underpinning implicatures are defeasible. Grice argued that a conversational implicature can be cancelled in two different ways. Explicit cancellation involves adding a subsequent cancel lation clause that either retracts the putative implicature (e.g., "not that I mean [to imply x]"), or blocks it from arising in the first place (e.g., "in fact [not x]". Contextual cancellation involves identifying situations in which the putative implicature would not arise in the first place (Grice [1978]1989: 44). The standard position in pragmatics to date has thus been that Grice's "cancellability test" is useful way of differentiating implicatures from logical implications, semantic entailments and the like (see, e.g., Blome-Tillmann 2008: 156). Cancellability, in other words, has often been assumed to be one of the necessary, albeit not sufficient, tests for identifying implicatures; although it is worth bearing in mind that the two types of cancellation tests clearly apply at different orders of analysis (Jaszczolt 2009b).

In recent years, however, there has been considerable debate as to whether implicatures are always in fact cancellable. There have been three key arguments made against the (neo-)Gricean claim that implicatures are, by definition, cancellable (Haugh 2013b). First, implicatures may, in some instances at least, be entailed, and given that such cases involve logical inferences that are not defeasible, entailed implicatures cannot, strictly speaking, be cancelled (Bach 2006: 24, Carston 2002a: 138–140, Higashimori and Wilson 1996: 122, Vicenti 1998; cf. Wilson and Sperber 1986: 61). Second, something which is speaker intended, such as a particularised conversational implicature cannot be "un-intended", and so such implicatures cannot, by definition, be cancelled (Burton-Roberts 2010, 2013; Capone 2009; Feng 2013). Third, there are instances of implicatures where explicit cancellation phrases are either non sequitur or end up reinforcing the implicature, that is, so-called "cancellation-resistant implicatures" (Huitink and Spenader 2004; Mayol and Castroviejo 2013; Weiner 2006).

One reason for such ongoing debate s, however, is that in making the case that implicatures are not cancellable, they have often been treated by analysts as more determinate than is actually warranted. For instance, the following examples have been proposed as instances where what is implicated is also entailed by the utterance in question (NB. +> represents implicated, while ‖ represents entailed)

(27)   Peter: Would you like to listen to my Rolling Stones record?

        Mary: No. I'd rather hear some music.
               +> Peter's Rolling Stones record is not music.
               ‖ Peter's Rolling Stones record is not music.
        (Higashimori and Wilson 1996: 122)

(28) Adam: Does John drink slivovitz?

Bob: He doesn't drink any alcohol.
+> John does not drink slivovitz.
‖ John does not drink slivovitz.
(Carston 2002a: 139; cf. Wilson and Sperber 1986: 61)

In the examples above, what is implicated by the speaker also follows logically from what is said by analytic rule. Carston (2002a) argues that such examples demonstrate that "non-contradictory cancellability is not a necessary property of implicatures" (p.140). However, she subsequently concedes that

> the concept of entailment and the concept of implicature belong to different explanatory levels, in fact different sorts of theory – the one a static semantic theory which captures knowledge of linguistic meaning, the other an account of the cognitive processes and representations involved in understanding utterances (Carston 2004: 644).

As Carston (2004), argues, then, there are fundamental differences between analysing something as an entailment, as opposed to analysing it as an implicature.

One key difference between analysing implicatures and entailments is that the former are not required to be formally determinate in the same way as the latter (Haugh 2013b). Higashimori and Wilson's (1996) gloss of example (27), for instance, brushes over all sorts of possible indeterminacy in the interpretation of Mary's response. For a start, while they claim that Mary implies the Rolling Stones is "not music", clearly we're dealing with something more than that. Mary's response could be interpreted as her implying it is "not real music", "not good music", "not pleasant to listen to music" and so on and so forth. It also remains indeterminate as to who this evaluation is attributed to. Is it just Mary who thinks this, or is she implying that others (e.g. people of good taste) might also share the same belief? Such issues of indeterminacy in interpretation lie outside the scope of formal analyses of entailments, which are attached to utterances, but they are critical for the interpretation of implicatures, given the latter are treated as part of what a person is taken to mean. Importantly, it is these indeterminacies in what is being implicated by Mary that allow her to subsequently deny particular interpretations that are made by Peter on the basis that she didn't *say* that which has been specifically attributed to her.

A second key difference is that while any understanding of an implicature is inevitably contingent on context, including what comes before and after the utterance in question, as well as the presuppositions of speakers (and recipients), entailments involve a strictly defined and fixed set of assumptions. In example (28), for instance, Bob could subsequently add something like "except for the odd tot of slivovitz" without contradiction of what is said, thereby removing the entailment relation between his utterance and what would have been implicated without this proviso (i.e. "John does not drink slivovitz"). In that case, what is implicated is something along the lines that John's habit of drinking slivovitz (albeit not often) is quite striking in light of his general abstinence from drinking alcohol.

Finally, proponents of this ongoing debate have often not acknowledged the way in which "cancellability" obtains depends on whether we are analysing inferences that can lead to implicatures (i.e. sociocognitive processes) or the implicatures themselves (i.e. products of those sociocognitive processes). While a number of scholars treat implicatures as essentially synonymous with (pragmatic) inference (Carston 2002a, 2002b, Levinson 1983, 2000, Sperber and Wilson 1995), others scholars insist that assimilating implicature to inference constitutes a conceptual and analytical error (Bach, 2006; Feng 2013; Horn 2004, 2012).

One good reason to maintain a distinction between implicatures and inferences is that while speakers can be held committed to or accountable for implicatures to varying degrees, neither speakers nor recipients are held accountable for all the inferences they make when participating in interaction (except when they make available such inferences to others through saying or implicating). A second reason for doing so is that close examination of implicatures and (pragmatic) inferences vis-à-vis "cancellability" indicates that this occurs in quite different ways. While pragmatic inferences can be either "blocked" or "suspended", implicatures can be either "repaired" or "disputed" (cf. Mayol and Castroviejo 2013).[21]

Blocking inferences encompasses instances where a potential inference, which could conceivably follow from something that has been said, is not allowed through by the speaker. It is thus prospective or anticipatory in nature. Suspension, in contrast, involves removing the speaker's commitment to an inference that has already likely been drawn, and is thus retroactive in orientation. A speaker can block (unwanted) inferences that the recipient might be expected to otherwise draw through various connectives that implicitly orient to what could have been inferred, including "but (not) x", "if not x", "in fact/actually x" and so on (Haugh 2013b). In example (29), for instance, the second phrase blocks the (unwanted) inference that (A knows that) Smith has a girlfriend in New York. Notably, it does not block the inference that Smith *might* have a girlfriend there, but rather reinforces it (albeit depending on the intonation with which B utters this response).

---

21 Cancellation phrases may also "reinforce" an implicature, that is, reiterate what is implicated without redundancy. In such cases, the implicature remains open to clarification, although it cannot be readily retracted or denied (Haugh 2013b).

(29)   A: Smith doesn't seem to have a girlfriend these days.

B: He has been paying a lot of visits to New York lately, but I don't think he has a girlfriend there.
(Huitink and Spenader 2004: 10; cf. Grice [1975] 1989: 32)

In such cases the connective itself (i.e. *but*) orients to a possible inference that is subsequently blocked, by indexing a contrast with what could have been inferred (i.e. that the speaker knows Smith has a girlfriend in New York).

A speaker can also suspend an inference, which he or she assumes the recipient may have made, through subsequent talk. In the following excerpt from a conversation between two friends, a potential default inference is suspended by a subsequent nonce inference.

(30)   (Cameron has called up Steve on the phone)

18   C: Whadaya doing tonight?

19   S: I dunno, what are you gonna do?

20   C: Oh I've been invited to a party that I don't wanna really want to go to.

21   Hope to find an excuse.

22   S: Oh right. I see.

23   Um, hav'eya seen Lethal Weapon?
(adapted from Haugh 2009a: 105)

In this short interchange, Cameron's initial question in line 18 is in the form of a standard pre-invitation (Schegloff 2007: 129), whereby a speaker standardly implicates (through this utterance-type in a minimal context) that he is going to subsequently invite the recipient to do something together, if the preparatory condition that has been invoked is met (i.e. that the other person is available). Steve orients to this possible invitation (and thus a *putative* short-circuited implicature) by inquiring about what the invitation might involve (line 19). This default inference, however, is subsequently suspended in Cameron's next turn, when he outlines the preparatory conditions for another kind of invitation, namely, an invitation from Steve (lines 20–21), thereby implicating that he would like Steve to invite him somewhere (and so provide the means by which he can be excused from going to a party he doesn't want to attend). This latter implicature, through which Cameron solicits an invitation from Steve, arises from a nonce inference that requires specific contextual information. Steve indicates he has reached a new understanding through his use of "oh" and "right" (Heritage 1984b; Scheglof 2007: 118), and through the way he subsequently launches an invitation sequence starting with a standard pre-invitation (line 23) (cf. Haugh 2009a: 104–107). From this example, then, we can see how the response of the recipient (Steve) helps constrain what is inferred amongst the potential interpretations initially afforded by that same speaker's (Cameron) initial utterance, an understanding which is subsequently qualified by the first speaker (Cameron). It is the contingency of this inferential work that allows for the suspension of the default inference that was drawn at first by the initial recipient (Steve) (Haugh 2013b).

An explicit "cancellation" of an implicature, in contrast, activates a kind of "not-frame" which necessarily presupposes there is something there to cancel in the first place. This means we cannot talk of an implicature being removed or no longer existing per se, and for this reason a distinction between "cancellation" and "correction" of implicatures is difficult to maintain in practice (cf. Bultinck 2005: 35; Feng 2013: 126; Jaszczolt 2009b: 266–267). Instead, we can talk of implicatures being "denied" (e.g. claims that the implicature was not speaker-intended), "retracted" (e.g. claims that the implicature is no longer relevant or applicable to the current discourse), or "clarified" (e.g. claims that what was meant is different to how it was understood or might have been understand by the recipient). All of these actions involve modulation, in some form or another, of the degree of the speaker's commitment to, or accountability for the implicature in question. The plausibility or legitimacy of the actions of denial, retraction or clarification is a function of the degree of indeterminacy of the implicature in question, as well as the degree to which the implicature is taken to be made normatively available through what has been said. In cases where it is clear that something has indeed been implicated, the speaker can usually only clarify what was implicated. In cases where it is open to interpretation whether or not something has been implicated in the first place, then the implicature(s) in question may be more readily denied or retracted, as well as clarified. In all cases, however, repair actions are always open to dispute by participants as to what exactly was implicated, or the degree of speaker commitment to what was taken to be implicated, given the existence of both speaker and recipient implicatum.

When considering the issue of the "cancellability" of implicature, then, it is arguably critical to distinguish between the defeasibility of inferences, which is a consequence of contingent reasoning on the part of individual users, and the way in which implicatures can be repaired or disputed through social actions that are jointly achieved by participants through interaction. The fundamental indeterminacy of implicatures is an issue which we will revisit in more detail in the following chapter. However, before doing so, we will first consider a number of post-Gricean developments in theorising implicature.

2 Post-Gricean approaches to implicature

The focus of Gricean and neo-Gricean approaches to implicature has primarily been linguistic. Grice's original project was to account for the ways in which speakers can mean things that are not strictly speaking said, which he termed implicatures. Neo-Griceans, as we saw in the previous section, have extended Grice's original program to include a consideration of the nature and conditions for obtaining such meanings, with a particular focus on theorising "stable aspects of meaning which are related to lexical and structural features of sentences" (Bianchi 2013a: 122). The focus of the variety of approaches that are loosely termed "post-Gricean" is, however, markedly different. In post-Gricean approaches the primary focus has been on the mental or cognitive processes that underlie the comprehension of implicatures.

In this section, we will discuss the two main streams into which post-Gricean approaches to implicature fall. The first stream encompasses a range of broadly linguistic-philosophical approaches that emphasis default or convention-based processes in relation to implicatures. The second is the Relevance theoretic approach to implicature, where the focus is primarily on "particularised" implicatures, since Relevance theorists argue that the generalised-particularised distinction is theoretically otiose. What unites these two streams as post-Gricean, and differentiates them from most neo-Gricean approaches, is their emphasis on the cognitive processes by which implicatures are understood by hearers.

2.1 Implicature and defaults

One of the most contested aspects of the theorisation of implicature to date has been the question of whether default interpretations or conventions play a significant role in their derivation. While most Relevance theorists have explicitly rejected a role for default inferencing (e.g. Carston 2002b: 142), other post-Gricean approaches to implicature have essentially argued the opposite, that Grice did not go far enough in accounting for the role of defaults or conventions in accounting for implicatures. There are arguably two key post-Gricean accounts of defaults vis-à-vis implicature: (1) Meaning Expression theory (Davis 1998, 2003), where the role of conventions vis-à-vis the generation of implicatures is emphasised, and (2) the Default Semantics approach (Jaszczolt 2005, 2009a), where a model that theorises different kinds and sources of defaults is proposed.

In an extensive critique of the Gricean approach to implicature, Davis (1998) makes a distinction between speaker implicature and sentence implicature. The former is tied to what a particular speaker is meaning *by* meaning something else. In other words, speaker implicature is a kind of indirect speaker meaning which is defined more formally by Davis (1998) as follows: "S implicates that p if S means or implies that p by saying something other than p" (p.13). The notion of speaker implicature thus overlaps to a considerable extent with the (neo-)Gricean notion of particularised conversational implicature, although it is not completely synonymous with it. The notion of sentence implicature, on the other hand, moves away from an account of generalised conversational implicatures framed in terms of neo-Gricean principles. Instead, it is defined as "what speakers using the sentence with its regular meaning would commonly use it to implicate" (p.6). In moving to a convention-based account, Davis (1998) allows for the fact that although implicatures may arise in regular or recurrent ways these conventions can vary across languages.

A convention is defined by Davis (1998) as "an arbitrary social custom or practice: a regularity in the voluntary action of a group that is socially useful, self-perpetuating, and arbitrary" (p.133). A "regularity in action" is meant to refer to a common way of doing something (p.137), although this does not amount to the claim that it must apply at all times (that is, it is not necessarily universal), nor that the action itself must be common. Rather, Davis (1998) claims that while an action itself may be uncommon, a common way of doing it may still exist, suggesting that "how common a way W of doing A is, is determined by the *relative* frequency of W *given* A, not the absolute frequency of W" (p.137, original emphasis). In addition, while the regularity in action must hold across two or more individuals to qualify as a convention, he argues that there is no reason to assume that conventions need always be universally known (that is, be common or mutual knowledge) (p.139). Finally, Davis claims that a social custom or practice is "socially useful" when it serves a mutual interest. In other words, it is something people want not only for themselves, but for others or for society as a whole. It is argued to become "self-perpetuating" based on a variety of factors including: mental association between an expression and an idea and frequency of the pairing; precedent of past conformity to conventions and tradition; and social or normative pressure to conform to the conventions of the group.

Davis (1998) goes on to differentiate between "first-order conventions" and "second-order conventions". This allows him to explain why idioms – which prima facie do not involve expressing something by expressing something else – do not qualify as implicatures in his framework (although see Arsenault [2014] for a recent counter-argument). First-order conventions are defined as conventions for using sentences to "directly" express certain thoughts (that is, meaning *p* by the expression *e*), or what Davis (1992a, 1992b) terms a regularity in "cogitative speaker meaning". The meanings of words, phrases and sentences are assigned using first-order conventions. Idioms are also considered to arise from first-order conventions, since they involve a regularity in direct meaning. Davis goes on to argue that "we can of course still hear the literal meaning of the sentence as we use it, and this gives the idiom its colour. But we are not using the sentence with its literal meaning at all" (Davis 1998: 159).

Second-order conventions are conventions which apply to implicatures, in particular, sentence implicatures. Second-order conventions involve regularities in "indirect" meaning (that is, meaning that p by uttering e), or what Davis (1992a, 1992b) terms a regularity in "cognitive speaker meaning".[22] Thus, in his account, "Some S are P" is regularly used to mean "Not all S are P" in English. Sentence implicatures are essentially synonymous with the (neo-)Gricean category of generalised conversational implicature, but they are rooted in conventional practices for a particular language, not in universal principles. However, while such an approach opens up the door to a more empirical approach to implicatures where defaults are examined more carefully across languages rather than simply being searched for and found, it does leave somewhat unexplained the existence of phenomena that are commonly found across many languages, such as some instances of scalar implicatures.

A more nuanced account of defaults is proposed in Default Semantics (Jaszczolt 1999, 2005, 2009a, 2009b), which although not directly focused on implicatures, nevertheless offers a number of potentially useful insights. Default Semantics represents a radically contextualist approach to meaning in that it replaces the traditional said/implicated distinction with a distinction between primary and secondary meaning. The latter is distinguished on the basis of the sources of information from which meanings are derived, and by the types of processes involved in their derivation. A primary meaning is defined as a "merger representation" of word meaning and sentence structure (WS), world knowledge, situation of discourse, society and culture, and properties of the human inferential system, while a secondary meaning arises from situation of discourse, stereotypes and presumptions about society and culture, and world knowledge (Jaszczolt 2009a: 132). More specifically, primary meanings arise through decoding word meaning and sentence structure (WS), social, cultural and world-knowledge defaults ($SCWD_{pm}$), cognitive defaults (CD), and conscious pragmatic

---

22 There is also a third type of convention Davis (1998) makes note of, namely, conventions of use associated with speaker implicature. For example, we commonly make a request in English by using a declarative sentence to describe a problem that can be solved by doing something, such as in saying "It is cold" in here to implicate "Close the window (please)" (Davies 1998: 171). This kind of convention is not associated with any particular linguistic form, but rather involves particular interactional practices. Such interactional practices, or third-order conventions in Davis's approach, are discussed in further detail in Chapters 6 and 7.

inference (CPI_{pm}), while secondary meanings arise through social, cultural and world-knowledge defaults ($SCWD_{sm}$) and conscious pragmatic inference (CPI_{sm}). However, these primary meanings are not constrained by the syntax of the utterance in question, as there is no priority assigned to WS in the processes leading to a merger representation.

The distinction between primary and secondary meanings is important, as it enables us to account for cases where the implicature in question seems to be what is really being communicated by the speaker. In the following example, for instance, it is what is implicated rather than said that is likely to be of greater relevance to the child:

(31) Child: Can I go punting?

   Mother: You're too small.
   Jaszczolt (2009b: 274)

What is said is something like the child is too small to go punting, while what is implicated is that the child is not able to or allowed to go punting. In Default Semantics, it is the implicature which would be considered the primary meaning in this situation despite it not being a straightforward pragmatic development of WS. This is important as it accounts for our intuition that it is the latter which is really *meant* by the mother in this instance.

The distinction between "cognitive defaults" (which can only contribute to primary meanings) and "social, cultural and world-knowledge defaults" (which can contribute to both primary and secondary meanings) is also potentially useful. The former accounts for defaults that appear to obtain across languages (such as some instances of scalar implicatures), while the latter accounts for defaults that are much more language specific (such as honorific forms). It also moves the discussion of default implicatures beyond a narrow focus on local defaults for particular expressions (as in Levinson's account of generalised conversational implicature) towards an account of defaults for contexts.

While the issue of convention or defaults vis-à-vis implicature will be revisited in Chapter Five (section 3.1), it is important to first acknowledge that the other major post-Gricean approach to implicature has taken a radically different stance on the status of defaults vis-à-vis implicatures, as we shall see in the following section.

2.2 Implicature in Relevance theory

Relevance theory is primarily a theory of utterance comprehension. While it takes Grice's conversational maxims as its springboard (Wilson and Sperber 1981), it does not attempt to explain how speakers make meanings available to hearers as did Grice, but rather focuses on the cognitive processes by which hearers understand what speakers are meaning (Sperber and Wilson 1995). The Cooperative Principle and conversational maxims are reformulated in the guise of the Principle of Relevance, namely, that "every act of ostensive communication conveys a presumption of its own optimal relevance" (Sperber and Wilson 1995: 260). In Relevance theory, "ostensive communication" refers to utterances and other non-linguistic behaviours that are intended by the speaker to be recognised by the hearer as intended to mean something (p.63), while "optimal relevance" refers to the assumption that the utterance is "relevant enough for it to be worth the audience's effort to process it" and is "the most relevant one compatible with communicator's abilities and preferences" (p.270).

Relevance itself is defined in Relevance theory primarily in terms of information. Based on the assumption that information has greater value for users when it is new as opposed to given, and that users will prefer, other things considered equal, information that is more easily processed, Relevance theory formalises these as two concerns as "contextual effects" and "processing effort" respectively (Sperber and Wilson 1995: 260–270). Contextual effects are divided into three types in Relevance theory: (i) those that produce new information, (ii) those that confirm or strengthen an existing assumption, and (iii) those that contradict or weaken an existing assumption (pp.108–117). When discussing contextual effects that arise in an individual user's mind, that is, "changes in the individual's beliefs" (p.265), they are termed "positive cognitive effects" in cases where they contribute "positively to the fulfilment of cognitive functions or goals" (p.265). Positive cognitive effects are contrasted with cognitive effects that do not provide any new information or do not strengthen/weaken existing assumptions for that user. The interplay of cognitive effects and processing effort is argued to be what determines the degree of relevance of information for an individual:

a. Other things being equal, the greater the positive cognitive effects achieved by processing an input, the greater the relevance of the input to the individual at that time.
b. Other things being equal, the greater the processing effort expended, the lower the relevance of the input to the individual at that time. (Wilson and Sperber 2004: 609; cf. Sperber and Wilson 1995: 265–266)

The general idea is that the greater the cognitive effects, and the smaller the degree of processing effort, the greater relevance information has for an individual. The degree of relevance that arises in the course of processing an utterance is thus argued to be the basis on which hearers understand speaker meaning including implicatures, given the assumed primacy of the Principle of Relevance

One challenge facing this definition of relevance for an individual, however, is that positive cognitive effects have not been the object of sustained empirical investigation. In other words, there is no clear definition of what counts as positive cognitive effects in a particular situated context, apart from what the analyst him or herself claims to be the positive cognitive effects in their own analysis of that particular case. A second challenge is that processing effort has generally been reduced to processing time, which is only a rough measure of processing effort at best. One upshot of this is that Relevance theory has had, on the whole, little to say about how implicatures are made available to hearers in the first place, apart from the general platitude that implicatures arise when their content is of some relevance to the individual(s) concerned. In the following sections, it will thus be argued that while Relevance theoristsy have made important contributions that have broadened our understanding of the nature of implicatures more generally (section 2.2.1), there are problems with the way in which implicatures have been specifically conceptualised vis-à-vis explicatures in their approach (section 2.2.2).

2.2.1 Implicatures as implicitly communicated assumptions

Implicatures are defined in Relevance theory as implicitly communicated assumptions (Sperber and Wilson 1995: 182). More specifically, an implicature constitutes "a distinct implicitly communicated proposition" (Carston and Hall 2012: 64), which is intended by the speaker, and recognised as intended by the speaker (Sperber and Wilson 2002; although cf. Jary 2013), and so arises solely through pragmatic inference without any contribution from the logical form of the utterance involved (Carston 2002a: 134).[23] They are contrasted with explicatures, which are defined as "a development of (a) a linguistically encoded logical form of the utterance, or of (b) a sentential subpart of a logical form" (Carston 2002a: 124; cf. Sperber and Wilson 1995: 182). The latter definition means that in Relevance theory, "explicit utterance content [i.e. explicatures] can include constituents

---

23 A logical form refers to "a structured set of constituents, which undergoes formal logical operations determined by its structure" (Sperber and Wilson 1995: 72). In other words, it is pared-down representation of what is encoded by "words" and the syntactic structure of an utterance. Logical forms are thus arguably a precursor to the Gricean notion of what is literally said, that is, they encompass a combinatorial representation of word meaning and syntax prior to the processes of reference assignment, indexical resolution and disambiguation.

which are not articulated in the linguistic form of the utterance" (Carston and Hall 2012: 47). The relevance theoretic notion of implicature is thus grounded in a distinction between implicitly and explicitly communicated propositions.

There are three important claims made about implicatures in Relevance theory that arguably advance our understanding of implicature. The first is the observation that not only "conclusions" but also "premises" can be implicated (Carston 2002a; Sperber and Wilson 1995). In the following example, for instance, B indicates that he cannot (or does not want to) assist A with a problem with one of the computers in the department's lab, but that Graeme can help.

(32) A: Can you help me?

B: Graeme's office hour is in five minutes.
(Culpeper and Haugh 2014: 136)

A's understanding of what B means through his response arises in the form an implicated premise and two implicated conclusions. The implicated premise is an assumption something spite "Graeme helps with computing problems". The two related implicated conclusions involve something like "B thinks Graeme can help A with her computing problem" (i.e. a suggestion), and "B should ask Graeme for help rather than him" (i.e. a refusal). Carston (2002a) argues that "the distinction between implicated premises and implicated conclusions is, transparently, a distinction between two different inferential roles that implicatures may play in the derivation process" (p.142). However, it is arguably more than this. Sperber and Wilson (1995) claim that implicated premises "must be supplied by the hearer, who must either retrieve them from memory or construct them by developing assumption schemas retrieved from memory", while Clark (2013) further elaborates that implicated premises are "inferred from the presumption of relevance and the fact that utterance has been made" (p.228). Implicated conclusions, on the other hand, are "inferred from the explicatures of the utterance and contextual assumptions" (Clark 2013: 228). This points towards the distinction between implicated premises and implicated conclusions being between two qualitatively different ways in which implicatures arise, namely, between speakers *implying*, *indicating*, *suggesting* and the like (what Grice termed "implicating"), on the one hand, and hearers *supposing* or *assuming*, on the other, a point to which we will return to consider further in the following chapter.

The second key claim is that implicatures can vary in their degree of "strength" from strong through to weak. In other words, something may be "strong implicated" through to "weakly implicated". At a certain point, then, "the hearer receives no encouragement at all to supply any particular premise and conclusion, and he takes the entire responsibility for supplying them himself" (Sperber and Wilson 1995: 199). For example, in the following response to Peter's question it remains an open question just what exactly Mary is implicating.

(33)   Peter: What do you intend to do today?

       Mary: I have a terrible headache.
       (Sperber and Wilson 1995: 56)

Sperber and Wilson (1995) point out that what Mary can be taken to be implicating here ranges from not doing anything, doing as little possible, or even doing as much as she can in light of her headache. While more detailed contextual information might go some way towards narrowing down this set of possibilities, Sperber and Wilson subsequently argue that in this case "there is no precise assumption, apart from the one explicitly expressed, which she can be said to intend Peter to share" (pp.56–57). The continuum of strong through to weak implicatures thus explicitly acknowledges the indeterminacy of instance of implicature such as this. As Sperber and Wilson (1995) go on to point out, most discussion of implicatures in the literature have neglected the existence of such cases, despite Grice ([1975]1989: 40) noting in his original discussion that many implicata are in fact indeterminate. Moeschler (2012) argues that the distinction (or more accurately continuum) between strong and weak implicatures represents one of the most important post-Gricean developments in theorising implicature, as it is through it that a distinction can be made between implicatures for which the speaker are held primarily responsible, and those for which the hearer is left responsible for deriving (Moeschler 2012: 423–424). The relative indeterminacy of many implicatures, and how this intersects with issues of speaker commitment or accountability, is another theme which we will return to consider further in the following chapter.

The third key claim made by Relevance theorists is in that in the process of understanding implicatures, the hearer does not necessarily have to derive explicatures before being able to draw implicatures:

> interpretive hypotheses are made rapidly, on-line, and in parallel. The mechanism that mediates the inferences from logical form to communicated propositions is one of 'mutual parallel adjustment' of explicatures and implicatures, constrained by the comprehension strategy. (Carston 2002b: 139; see also Wilson and Sperber 2004: 615)

In other words, hearers do not necessarily have to fully work out what the speaker is saying (in the Gricean sense) in order to infer what he or she is implicating. This contrasts with the assumed position of Grice in regards to the process whereby implicatures are understood (cf. Grice [1987]1989: 370). This third key claim also encapsulates the Relevance theoretic focus on how implicatures are comprehended or processed at the utterance level by hearers, rather than on what speakers are doing with such implicatures.

The Relevance theoretic conceptualisation of implicature thus contrasts with that of the (neo-)Griceans in a number of ways. One key difference is that implicatures in Relevance theory are grounded in the distinction between "explicit" versus "implicit" meaning, as opposed to that between "direct" and "indirect" (or "not direct") meaning, which underpins the (neo-)Gricean conceptualisation of implicature. This has generated somewhat different, albeit overlapping, conceptualisations of implicature.

A second key difference, which follows from the first, is that the Relevance theoretic notion of implicature is a vastly pared down concept, which only encompasses a portion of what are treated as "particularised conversational implicatures" in the (neo-)Gricean account (Carston and Hall 2012: 71).[24] Relevance theorists have argued that phenomena which are termed conventional implicatures (Blakemore 1987, 2002; Iten 2005; Wilson and Sperber 1993), short-circuited implicatures (Groefsema 1992; although cf. Ruytenbeek 2012), and most instances of generalised conversational implicatures (Carston 1988, 1995, 1998, 2002a, 2004; Sperber and Wilson 2002; Wilson and Sperber 1998) actually contribute to the explicatures of utterances, and so do not constitute valid instances of implicature.

However, there are a number of problems with the reduction of all these different neo-Gricean species of implicature to either implicatures or explicatures. One problem is that it fails to account for our folk or pre-theoretic intuitions

---

24 In fact, the Relevance theoretic conceptualisation of implicature also does not include figurative meanings such as metaphor, litotes, hyperbole, tautologies and so on. Instead, they are generally treated as part of explicatures (Carston 2002a, 2004, 2010, 2012; Ruiz de Mendoza 1998; Sperber and Wilson 1995; Wilson and Carston 2007), and thus part of what is explicitly as opposed to implicitly communicated. While figurative meanings were were originally treated as particularised conversational implicatures on the Gricean account (Grice [1975]1989: 33–35), they have subsequently been reanalysed as nonliteral meanings, that is, as instances where the speaker means something *instead* of what is said (Bach 2012). Such meanings can in some cases, although not always, be treated as utterance-token meanings. However, it would be fair to say that a comprehensive neo-Gricean account of figurative meaning remains to be developed. In any case, most neo-Griceans do not treat idioms and the like as implicatures following the basic distinction between a speaker meaning something *instead* of what is said (i.e. nonliteral meaning) versus *in addition* to what is said (i.e. implicature) (Bach 1994, 2006, 2012; Davis 1998). Arsenault's (2014) recent treatment of idioms as arising through conversational implicatures thus represents a significant divergence from the position of most neo-Griceans, and post-Griceans for that matter, on the status of figurative meanings vis-à-vis implicature.

about such phenomena. Groefsema (1992) and Yus (1999), for instance, claim that a request arising from "Can you pass the salt?" constitutes an explicature of that utterance rather than involving a short-circuited implicature. However one problem with this argument is that a Relevance theoretic approach appears to neglect to account for the potential politeness effects that are associated in some instances – although not always Ruytenbeek (2012) quite rightly points out – with the choice of "Can you pass the salt?" over a direct imperative ("Pass the salt") in formulating a request (Haugh 2002: 122–123). It is hard to see how one would explain why politeness arises in account where the "ability" and "permission" interpretations of "can you" are treated as simply indicative of two different potential explicatures (depending, of course, on the context) (see also Terkourafi 2001: 148–149). It also does not adequately account for why the "ability" interpretation remains available to be invoked by users, even in request contexts where one can offer "smart-alec" responses such as "I can pass the salt, but I'm not going to", for instance.

Putting such debates aside, however, the key issue facing the Relevance theoretic account of implicature is arguably the question of whether pragmatically derived meanings (i.e. meanings derived through inference) should be counted as instances of implicatures, or as a pragmatic contribution to an explicature. It is to this issue that we now turn.

2.2.2 On differentiating implicatures from explicatures

One challenge facing the Relevance theoretic approach to implicatures is our pre-theoretic intuition that explicitness and implicitness are gradable attributes. That is, something can be more or less explicit, or more or less implicit, from which it follows that the point where less explicit explicit meaning ends and less implicit implicit meaning begins is not in fact clear-cut. Consequently, something which is regarded as less explicit in some cases, can in other instances also be regarded as somewhat implicit, and vice-versa. For this reason, the line between implicitly communicated propositions (i.e. implicatures) and explicitly communicated propositions (i.e. explicatures) can be somewhat fuzzy, in some instances.[25]

One example that has generated conflicting responses from Relevance theorists involves cases of what neo-Griceans term scalar implicatures. Example (34), for instance, is held by neo-Griceans to scalar implicate (35) as a generalised conversational implicature (Horn 1984; Levinson 2000).

---

25 This gradability is acknowledge by Chaves (2010: 122), for instance, who proposes a distinction between "explicit import" and "implicit import", which vary in their degree of explicitness and implicitness, respectively.

(34)   Some of the children were sick.

(35)   Some *but not all* of the children were sick. (Carston 2004: 646)

According to Carston (2004: 646), the communicated assumption in (35) is likely to be an explicature on a Relevance theoretic account. Yet according to Sperber and Wilson (2002: 4), it is implicated.

Instances where "trailing-off" utterance-final conjunctives project "unstated upshots" (Raymond 2004; cf. Haugh 2008d) also prove somewhat difficult to account for on the basis of the current definition of implicature in Relevance theory (see also Haugh 2002: 123–125). In the following excerpt from a conversation between three friends, for instance, the turn-final "so" in line 19 projects an "unstated upshot", namely, that Laura will want to get drunk (because the fact her ex-boyfriend is getting married will most likely make her feel depressed).

(36)   SN-4

6   Mark: en then I got s'mthing planned on Sunday

7   with Lau:ra

8   (0.5)

9   Mark: She- she wen- she 'n I are gonna go out

10   'n get drunk et four o'clock in the

11   afternoon

12   Sher: huh-huh hhh [h

13   Mark: [It's a religious: (0.3) thing

14   we're gonna have.

15   (0.3)

16   Mark: I d'know <u>why</u>:, °b't

17   (0.5)

18   Mark: Uh::m () No- her ex boyfriend's getting married

19   en she:'s: gunnuh be depressed so:,

20   (0.8)

(adapted from Schegloff 2007: 125; cf. Raymond 2004: 189–190)

Given explicatures are defined as "a development of (a) a linguistically encoded logical form of the utterance, or of (b) a sentential subpart of a logical form" (Carston 2002a: 124) this "unstated upshot" (i.e. Laura will want to get drunk) could conceivably count as an instance of an explicature that is developed from the utterance in lines 18–19 ("her ex-boyfriend's getting married and she's gunna be depressed so"). Yet this is obviously highly counter-intuitive, because by trailing off, Mark is treating this upshot as better left unsaid. The basic problem lies with the Relevance theoretic notion of logical form, and what is meant by its development. A logical form is defined as "a structured set of constituents, which undergoes formal logical operations determined by its structure" (Sperber and Wilson 1995: 72). It follows that discourse connectives such as "so" constitute part of the logical form of an utterance. Given that part of the logical form of the utterance in question triggers a kind of bridging inference, namely, that it is because Laura is "gunnuh be depressed" (line 19) that Mark and Laura are "are gonna go out 'n get drunk et four o'clock in the afternoon" (lines 9–11), the utterance in lines 18–19 is interpretable as meaning Lara will be *wanting* to go out and get drunk (i.e. because she is "gunnuh be depressed"). In other words, the likelihood that Laura will be "wanting to go out and get drunk" is what can be inferred from "she's gunna be depressed" (line 19), and what Mark previously said they will be doing, which is to "go out 'n get drunk" (lines 9–11). But this inference, which is triggered by the utterance-final "so" in line 19, clearly develops out of the bridging inference back to the explicature arising from the utterance in lines 9–11. The line between what is explicitly and implicitly communicated thus becomes very fuzzy indeed given the "unstated upshot" (i.e. Laura will want to get drunk) develops in part out of the logical form of what has just been said by Mark a few turns earlier (lines 9–11), as well as in part from the logical form of the utterance in line 19.

Carston (2004) has countered that discourse connectives such as "but", "so" and "after all" are treated as "encoding procedural constraints on the inferential processes involved in deriving conversational implicatures" (fn.1, p.654), and so "do not contribute conceptual constituents to the content of implicatures" (fn.2, p.654). In other words, elements of the logical form that "encode procedural meaning which constrains the derivation of implicated premises and conclusions" (p.654) do not presumably count as developments of the logical form of utterances. However, in the example of utterance-final "so" above, these "procedural constraints" lead the hearer back to an explicitly communicated assumption, that they're "going to go out and get drunk", from which is developed the "unstated upshot", that is, Laura is "going to *want to* go out and get drunk" (based on the assumption that that is what people who are depressed sometimes do). In other words, this qualification from Carston (2004) does not appear to remove the definitional fuzziness arising from the Relevance theoretic distinction between implicitly and explicitly communicated propositions.

Another problem that Carston's (2004) qualification highlights is that implicatures cannot actually be rigorously identified on the basis of the current Relevance theoretic definition of implicitly communicated propositions. This has generated an ongoing debate about what other criteria might be used to distinguish between implicatures and explicatures (Breheny 2002; Carston 1988, 2002a, 2004; Carston and Hall 2012; Recanati 1989). A number of potential criteria have been postulated (see Carston [1988] and Recanati [1989] for more in-depth discussion), but it is the "functional independence principle" (Carston 1988), the "scope principle" (Recanati 1989), and the "availability principle" (Recanati 1989, 2004) that have been most favoured in such discussions.

The "functional independence principle" involves the claim that "implicatures have distinct propositional forms with their own truth conditions and they function independently of the explicature as the premises and conclusions of arguments" (Carston 1988: 157). In other words, the inferences leading to implicatures "must function as autonomous premises in inferential interactions with other assumptions and must be stored in memory as separate assumptions" (pp.157–158). Carston (2002a) consequently qualifies this to mean not "logical independence" – a reading of the functional independence principle which is critiqued by Recanati (1989) and Vicenti (1998) – but rather that an implicature should "function independently as a premise in arguments" (Carston 2002b: 190). However, example (25) above appears to be somewhat problematic even for this qualified formulation of the functional independence principle. The unstated upshot triggered by Mark uttering "she's gunna be depressed so" (line 19) is that Laura is "going to want to go and get drunk", but this does not appear to be functionally independent of the explicitly stated premise that they are "going to go out and get drunk" (lines 9–11), because the unstated upshot here is closely connected to a previously explicated premise. In any case, Carston (2002a) herself regards the functional independence principle as "only a useful heuristic" and not necessarily "worth any kind of vigorous defence" (p.191).

This therefore leaves either the "scope principle" or the "availability principle" to do the work of differentiating between pragmatic contributions to explicatures and implicatures (Carston and Hall 2012). The "availability principle" encompasses Recanati's claim (1989, 2004) that "we should always try to preserve our pre-theoretic intuitions" in relation to what is said. The idea is that if ordinary speakers would treat something as part of what is said then it cannot be an implicature, and so must be part of the explicature (or "enriched what is said" in Recanati's terminology). While no one denies such pre-theoretic intuitions exist, tapping into them in a systematic way through experimental work has proved challenging.

Gibbs and Moise (1997) and Hamblin and Gibbs (2003), for instance, tested a number of different instances of phenomena treated as generalised conversational implicatures by neo-Griceans, and found that they were considered to be part of what is said, rather than implicatures, by ordinary speakers. Gibbs (1999b, 2002) subsequently argued that these results support something akin to the Relevance theoretic distinction between explicature and implicature. However, identifying which intuitions are actually being tapped into in these kinds of experiments proves somewhat difficult. Bach (2001: 26) and Levinson (2000: 197) both argue that what ordinary speakers consider to be "said" depends on how one elicits the response. This is because what is said can be interpreted in at least two distinct ways (Berg 2002: 347; Carson 2002a: 169; Wilson and Sperber 2002): in an indirect-quotational sense (what the utterance itself standardly means) or and in a commitment sense (what the speaker is committing herself to in producing the utterance). Ordinary speakers vacillate between these two senses in describing what a speaker is saying, which creates problems for empirical studies such as those conducted by Gibbs and Moise (1997) and Hamblin and Gibbs (2003). Bach (2002) argues that ultimately what Gibbs and Moise's (1997) results show is:

> how people apply the phrase 'what is said' and perhaps of what they mean by the word 'say'. It tells us little about what is said, much less about the cognitive processes whereby people understand utterances. (Bach 2002: 23)

Moreover, other experiments demonstrate that ordinary speakers may perceive unequivocal examples of implicature to be a part of what the speaker has said in some cases (Ariel 2002; Bezuidenhout and Cutting 2002; Nicolle and Clark 1999). And even when the intuitions of respondents are tapped into through contextualised examples (Noveck 2004; Noveck and Sperber 2007), such intuitions have not been found to be consistent across speakers. Such results indicate that intuitions about what is said may actually overlap with what is implicated unless experiments are designed to enable respondents to differentiate between the two conflicting ways in which *saying* can be interpreted. The fundamental challenge, however, is that in actual language use these two senses are difficult if not impossible to divorce. What a speaker is taken to be committed to saying is a local, situated concern, given speakers are inevitably held accountable for what they say (Haugh 2010c, 2013a), a point to which we will return in the following chapter. It is thus not surprising that trying to ascertain what an utterance "standardly means" divorced from such concerns is only possible in decontextualised situations where such intuitions are consequently unreliable, as the mixed results of the above experiments clearly indicates. As Carston and Hall (2012) argue, then, while we "do want to preserve pre-theoretic intuitions regarding what a speaker says/implicates as much as we can" (p.67), in practice, this proves somewhat difficult.

One way of trying to sharpen such pre-theoretic intuitions further is by embedding such cases under logical operators, that is, the so-called "scope principle", as proposed by Recanati (1989). The scope principle is formulated as follows:

> A pragmatically determined aspect of meaning is part of what is said (and, therefore, not a conversational implicature) if – and, perhaps, only if – it falls within the scope of logical operators such as negation and conditionals. (Recanati 1989: 114)

It follows from this that if a pragmatically derived meaning falls under the scope of a logical operator such as negation, disjunction, conditionals, or comparatives, then it cannot be an implicature, and so must be taken as contributing to the explicature of an utterance (Carston and Hall 2012: 67). Carston and Hall (2012) go on to argue that the scope test shows that the "scalar implicature" arising from "some" (i.e. "not all") contributes to the truth-conditional content of that utterance because it falls under the scope of the subsequent conditional clause. They offer the following example to illustrate their claim:

(26)   Sam doesn't care if some of his students fail, but if they all do, he'll be worried.
(Carston and Hall 2012: 68)

Carston and Hall (2012) take the first clause in example (26) to mean that "Sam won't be upset if *just* some *(not all)* of his students fail" (p.68, emphasis added), and so assume that "not all" contributes to the explicature of that utterance. However, they neglect to explain why the second clause is not redundant if "not all" is explicated by the first clause. One problem with examining "not all" as part of the explicature is that its formulation, "Sam doesn't care if not all of his students fail", is actually rather difficult to follow given the double negative. Indeed, this double negative would likely give rise to some kind of marked interpretation (i.e. that Sam believes that a number of students will fail). The point is that the contrastive conjunction "but" is contrasted with something, namely, that which is arguably only implicated at the point the speaker is uttering "some of his students" (i.e. "not all"). This something subsequently becomes fixed as part of what the speaker is meaning here in light of the second clause. If Relevance theory is really to be a theory of online utterance comprehension, as it is often claimed to be, then it needs to take into account this kind of shift in the determinacy of what is meant by the speaker as utterances are incrementally processed by hearers.

There are also other potential problems with the scope principle. The main sticking point is that it tests "utterance types", and so "it cannot predict or decide in advance whether some such element *does* contribute to explicature or not on any particular occasion of utterance" (Carston and Hall 2012: 68, original emphasis). A related problem is that it cannot be applied to test actual instances of implicature (i.e. utterance tokens) without creating relatively decontextualised and thus unnatural utterances in many cases. It is thus impractical to consistently apply as a test differentiating implicatures from pragmatically-derived contributions to explicatures (Haugh 2002: 126).

It appears, then, that the Relevance theoretic definition of implicature, even when supplemented with various pragmatic tests is not able to consistently identify whether something counts as an implicature or not.[26] Given Relevance theory is a theory of utterance comprehension, it is perhaps not surprising that they ultimately retreat to differentiating between implicatures and explicatures on the basis of how they are processed. Carston and Hall (2012), for instance, conclude that "the line between explicature and implicature can vary from occasion to occasion of utterance of the same sentence type, and will be determined by how the utterance is processed" (p.68), more specifically, "based on the distinction between two ways of deriving communicated assumptions: by developing a linguistically given logical form and by pragmatic inference" (Carston 2002a: 142). Carston (2002a) goes even further in suggesting that "the distinction between explicatures and implicatures, the two kinds of communicated assumptions, is primarily a derivational distinction and *may have no greater import than that*" (p. 366, emphasis added). Breheny (2002) argues, however, that this does not actually solve the problem, since as he points out "there really is no principled way of saying how a given derivation is made" (p.180). In other words, claiming that implicatures can be distinguished from explicatures on the basis of how they are processed makes the distinction even more difficult to maintain empirically. As Breheny points out, "it would not be surprising to find that such obvious 'implicatures' are not always derived in the manner Carston suggests" (Breheny 2002: 180), which undermines the attempt to distinguish implicatures from explicatures on the basis of how they are derived.

In some respects, this problem might be regarded by some as largely definitional rather than being a substantive issue. In other words, it might appear that (neo-)Griceans and Relevance theorists are simply disagreeing about whether

---

26 Wilson (2012) also notes in a recent paper on the explicit-implicit distinction that there are questions remaining as to whether a sharp distinction between the two is necessary, or whether there is in fact a gradient or continuum between the two, although she does not yet appear to take a clear position on this issue.

certain pragmatic phenomena should be labelled as implicatures, or alternatively as contributions to explicatures. However, here it is argued to be much more than that. The problem is that an account of the distinction between implicatures and other forms of pragmatic meaning which is grounded in how they are derived or cognitively processed does not seem amenable to accounting for the existence of the phenomena that are the key focus of this book, that is, im/politeness implicatures. As I have argued in earlier work,

> the fact that by implying something one can give rise to politeness indicates that implicature is not simply a category to be distinguished on the basis of its derivational process, but rather that implying something sometimes has crucial implications for interpersonal aspects of communication. (Haugh 2007a: 107)

As is now well known in pragmatics, implicatures do not arise in isolation through relatively decontextualised utterances in the way that debates about implicature between Relevance theorists and (neo-)Griceans have often framed them. Instead, implicatures arise through sequences of utterances in discourse, where the interpersonal implications of what speakers are taken to be implicating, the fact they are implicating something, and how they are implicating it, are all issues (among many others) that users may attend to in the course of such interactions.

In the following chapter, it will be argued that an analysis of implicatures as they arise in interaction allows us to explore many of the well-worn arguments around implicature that have been outlined in this chapter from a somewhat fresh perspective. It will be suggested that not only does an interactional perspective on implicature allow us to emphasise characteristics of implicature that have hitherto been noted only in passing, but it also allows us to move towards a more systematic account of how implicatures can give rise to various interpersonal phenomena, including im/politeness, in the first place.

Chapter Three:
Implicature, social action and indeterminacy

1 Implicature and interaction

There have been numerous debates about how to best analyse and theorise implicatures, in particular, whether to explicitly build on Grice's (1967, 1989) original claims, or to posit an alternative framework, as we saw in the previous chapter. However, the basic notion of implicature itself has essentially stood the test of time. While there are various approaches to theorising implicatures, most approaches converge on the claim that an implicature is a type of speaker meaning that goes beyond what is literally said. More specifically, implicatures pertain to separate individual, additional intentional state-processes (i.e. thoughts, beliefs, intentions, desires, attitudes and so on) with their own pragmatic force (Haugh 2002: 128–130, Haugh and Jaszczolt 2012: 96). For the most part it is also assumed by both (neo-)Griceans and post-Griceans, based on, or at least building on, Grice's (1957, 1989) seminal work on "non natural meaning", that implicatures are limited to those additional intentional state-processes that are speaker intended. In other words, implicatures pertain only to those additional thoughts, beliefs, intentions and so on that are intended by the speaker to be recognised (by the hearer) as intended by the speaker. In that sense implicatures have been theorised primarily as a form of cognitive representation that is displayed through, or is occasioned by natural language constructions.

One problem, however, which was noted in passing in the previous chapter, is that implicatures have generally been defined only negatively as what is communicated less "what is said" (e.g. Horn 2004; Levinson 1983, 2000) or less "what is explicated" (e.g. Carston 2002a; Sperber and Wilson 1995). An implicature on that view is thus essentially a kind of speaker intended meaning representation that arises through inference rather than being (literally) said. Yet Grice himself had a somewhat more nuanced take on implicatures, as we can see from is made evident in his initial characterisation of implicature:

> Suppose that A and B are talking about a mutual friend, C, who is now working in a bank. A asks B how C is getting on in his job, and B replies, *Oh quite well, I think; he likes his colleagues, and he hasn't been to prison yet.* At this point, A might well inquire what B was implying, what he was suggesting, or even what he meant by saying that C had not yet been to prison. The answer might be any one of such things as that C is the sort of person likely to yield to the temptation provided by his occupation, that C's colleagues are really very unpleasant and treacherous people, and so forth ... [but] it is clear that whatever B implied, suggested, meant in this example, is distinct from what B said, which was simply that C had not been to prison yet. (Grice [1975]1989: 24)

According to Grice, B implicates something about C himself, or C's colleagues, by saying "he hasn't been to prison yet". From the speaker's perspective what is implicated is termed an implicature. From the perspective of what is actually communicated, what is implicated by the speaker is termed an implicatum. In outlining this example, then, Grice was careful to note how what was implicated by B here is not entirely determinate. There are a number of plausible interpretations as to what B could be implicating on this occasion, some of which Grice points to in his explanation. It is important to note, however, that he did not indicate which of them would actually have been implicated. In other words, what is actually implicated in communication (i.e. the implicatum or set of implicata) is not entirely determinate, and indeed may even be relatively indeterminate. Varying degrees of indeterminacy is thus arguably a key characteristic of implicature according to Grice's original account of them.

In introducing the notion of implicature Grice also explicitly associated implicatures with a particular set of what might be termed *meaning-actions* (given they don't count as speech acts on Searle's account of Speech Act theory), the differences amongst which he regarded as "worth analysing" (Grice [1969]1989: 86). In fact, Grice even attempted a preliminary analysis of differences between two of them, namely, *suggesting* and *hinting* in his retrospective epilogue (Grice [1987]1989: 368), a point that has generally escaped notice in most accounts of implicature to date. The way in which implicatures arise through different kinds of meaning-actions is thus arguably a second key characteristic of implicature in Grice's original account.

In this chapter, it is argued that these two characteristics of implicature become much more salient when implicatures are analysed *in situ*, that is, in the localised, situated interactions in which they arise. Consider, for instance, the following excerpt from an episode of *Seinfeld*. At the point the excerpt begins, George has been arrested, along with his soon to be ex-girlfriend Anna (who works for Elaine), for making pirate copies of movies. Elaine and George's father, Frank, have arrived at the police station to help George and Anna with the charges.

(37)   1   Frank: I'm sitting at home, reading a periodical,
                    and this is the call I get? My son is a bootlegger?
                    ((He hits George on the head))

       2   George: Ow! Dad...

       3   Frank: Who put you up to this, was it her?

       4   Elaine: All right. Wait a minute. I think you've got it backwards.

       5   Frank: My George isn't clever enough to hatch a scheme like this.

6   Elaine: You got that right.

7   Frank: What the hell does that mean?

8   Elaine: It means whatever the hell you want it to mean.

9   Frank: You sayin' you want a piece of me?

10 Elaine: I could drop you like a bag of dirt.

11 Frank: You wanna piece of me? You got it!
            ((They begin to fight))

("The Little Kicks", *Seinfeld*, Episode 4, Season 8, Oct 10 1996, director: Andy Ackerman, writer: Spike Feresten)

Frank starts berating George (turn 1) before moving to accuse Anna of instigating the whole affair (turn 3). Elaine steps in to defend Anna, implying that it was George who was the main instigator (turn 4). The implicature of particular interest here arises when Frank counters that it couldn't be George because he "isn't clever enough to hatch a scheme like this" (turn 5), to which Elaine responds "You got that right" (turn 6). The question is what does Elaine imply by saying "You got that right"? On the one hand, she appears to be affiliating with Frank's stance here, namely, that it couldn't have been George who was the main instigator. On the other hand, she formulates an emphatic form of agreement that goes beyond the specific claim that George isn't clever enough to instigate such a scheme, to implying the more general claim that George is not smart, or is even idiotic or stupid. It is the insulting stance occasioned through the latter implicature that Frank then challenges in turn 7. Notably, rather than explicating what was implied by her prior turn, Elaine responds with a counter-challenge by implying that she does not care how Frank interprets her prior utterance (turn 8). The argument then escalates from threats and counter-threats (turns 9–11) into outright physical conflict.

From this example we can see that implicatures are closely associated with particular social actions, in this case, occasioning insults (turn 6) and subsequent challenges (turn 8). However, the actual content or object of the initial insult is not entirely determinate, although it clearly involves a negative assessment of George, namely, his intelligence or capabilities. Thus, while Elaine remains explicitly committed to occasioning an insult through this implicature in the turns that follow, the object of the insult is left partly indeterminate, and indeed, deliberately so ("it means whatever the hell you want it to mean"). Indeterminacy and social action are thus arguably fundamental to our understanding of implicatures as they arise in interaction.

Indeed, building on the interactional account of implicatures developed in this chapter, an implicature is conceptualised here as more than simply an intentional meaning representation, as the generally received view might have it. Instead, it is argued that an implicature constitutes an indeterminate reflexively intentional state-process (cf. Grice's "implicatum"), which not only arises coordinate with understandings of social action in interaction, but ultimately is itself a form of social action (cf. Grice's "implicate"), and so is something for which participants can be held accountable to varying degrees.

In this chapter, we begin by discussing these two key characteristics of implicature/implicatum in further detail. The intertwining relationship between implicatures and social action is first considered. It is proposed that not only do implicatures arise coordinate with understandings of social action in interaction (section 2), but that implicatures arise through specific kinds of social actions, namely *meaning-actions*, and so in some cases may even be constitutive of social actions (section 3). Following this, the relative indeterminacy of implicature is discussed in more detail (section 4). Three key types of indeterminacy vis-à-vis implicature are outlined, alongside illustrating the ways in which implicatures arise through possible understandings on the part of the participants that are situationally contingent. It is subsequently argued that the relative indeterminacy of implicatures is what allows speakers to be held committed to or accountable for the real-world consequences of what they are taken to be implicating to varying degrees, an analytical theme which underpins the theorisation of im/politeness implicatures that is developed in the subsequent chapters.

2 Implicature and social action

The relationship between implicatures and social action has received a number of competing treatments since Grice introduced the notion of implicature. In this section, three of the main accounts will be discussed, namely, the indirect speech act approach advocated in Speech Act theory (section 2.1), the speaker plan-based approach to implicature proposed primarily by neo-Griceans (section 2.2), and the "indirectness" as social action approach proposed by conversation analysts (section 2.3). This will be followed by a brief consideration of how these different approaches offer various insights into debates around the question of what relationship holds between implicatures and social action (section 2.4).

2.1 Implicature and indirect speech acts

The relationship between implicatures and what people *do* through talk was noted very early in Searle's ([1975]1979) work on "indirect speech acts". Echoing definitions of implicature as instances where the speaker means something in addition to what is said, Searle argued that indirect speech acts involve cases where "the speaker utters a sentence, means what he says, but also means something more" (Searle [1975]1979: 30). In the following exchange, for instance, Searle proposes that there are two speech acts involved:

(38)   X: Let's go to the movies tonight.

        Y: I have to study for an exam.
        (Searle [1975]1979: 33)

It is claimed by Searle that the primary illocutionary act performed by Y's response here is a rejection of X's proposal (i.e. a commissive), while the secondary illocutionary act is making a statement (i.e. an assertive). In order to understand the primary illocutionary act here, Searle argues that X must infer what the speaker has meant, along similar lines to what Grice proposed for conversational implicatures. What a speaker means is, in turn, determined by what he or she *intends* to mean. On Searle's account, then, indirect speech acts involve the speaker doing something through indirectly meaning something. Building on Austin's (1962) seminal account of speech acts, Searle (1969, 1979) proposed that indirect speech acts are both a form of speaker meaning and a form of speaker action, given his definition of an illocutionary act, F(p), as being constituted through an illocutionary force (F) (cf. action) and its propositional content (p) (cf. meaning) (Searle 1969: 31).[27]

One of the key claims in Speech Act theory (SAT) is that speech acts should be classified on the basis of their illocutionary point, rather than trying to use the illocutionary verbs of a particular language, because classification based on the former enables us to see that "there are a rather limited number of basic things we do with language" (Searle 1969: 29); that is:

---

27 The illocutionary force of a speech act refers to its illocutionary point, that is, the "point or purpose of a type of illocution" (Searle 1979: 3), alongside a set of presuppositions and attitudes that accompany that illocutionary point (Searle 1969: 66–67). Propositional content was originally theorised by Searle in terms of modified Gricean communicative intentions (Searle 1969: 42–50) (cf. footnote 32), but was subsequently theorised with reference to intentionality, including conditions of satisfaction (Searle 1983, 2007).

we tell people how things are, we try to get them to do things, we commit ourselves to do things, we express our feelings and attitudes and we bring about changes through our utterances. Often, we do more than one of these at once in the same utterance. (Searle 1969: 29)

These five types of basic illocutionary points are termed assertives, directives, commissives, expressives and declaratives, respectively. Searle argues that the illocutionary force of an utterance is assigned on the basis of the preparatory conditions, propositional content conditions, sincerity conditions and essential conditions of that illocutionary act, alongside the strength of the illocutionary point.

In the case of indirect speech acts, at least two illocutionary points arise through the speaker meaning not only what he says, but also meaning something more in addition to what he says (Searle 1979: ix, 30).[28] It is thus through participants recognising the illocutionary point and force of an illocutionary act, as well attributing particular intentions to the speaker, that indirect speech acts arise in communication.

Notably, in Searle's view, some illocutionary verbs, such as "hinting" and "insinuating", for instance, "do not name types of illocutionary acts, but rather the *style* or *manner* in which a rather large range of types can be performed" (Searle 1979: ix, emphasis added). For this reason they have been regarded as lying outside the direct purview of SAT. This somewhat contentious claim has not gone unnoticed, however. Holdcroft (1976) and Tsohatzidis (1989), for instance, argue that acts such as "hinting" and "insinuating" pose problems for one of the key claims in SAT, namely, the "principle of expressibility", where it is claimed that "whatever can be meant can be said" (Searle 1969: 19). The problem is that "hints" and "insinuations" evidently cannot be said or made explicit without surrendering part of their intrinsic nature.[29] Indeed, as Searle and Vanderveken (1985) themselves note,

---

28 To mean something, on Searle's (2007) view, is the "intentional imposition of conditions of satisfaction onto utterances, the imposition of the same conditions of satisfaction as the intentional state expressed in the utterance" by the speaker (p.29), where "conditions of satisfaction" refer to intentional states being "such and such is the case" (p.13). Searle argues that a speaker means "it is raining" by intentionally uttering that "it is raining" to the condition of satisfaction of uttering that utterance-token, and by imposing a further condition of satisfaction on that utterance, namely, the belief that "it is raining". Thus, if one is just practising English by saying "it is raining", one does not *mean* "it is raining", because one is not uttering to the condition of satisfaction of believing (whether rightly or wrongly) it is raining (Searle 2007: 23).

29 Silverstein (2010) goes even further in arguing that the existence of "hints" exposes a fundamental flaw in Speech Act theory, namely, that "if *all* utterance, not just the recognisably explicit primary performative formulae, consists in 'doing something with words,' the existence of hints, *universally*, means that any arbitrary utterance can be interpreted as any arbitrary illocutionary formula type" (p.344, original emphasis).

boasting, like hinting and insinuating, is one of those illocutionary acts that are intrinsi
cally concealed. To the extent that the speaker makes his intentions explicit, as the perfor
mative verb would serve to do, to that extent his speech act would be less a case of hinting,
insinuating, or boasting.

(Searle and Vanderveken 1985: 180)

Ultimately, then, SAT only attempts to deal with instances where indirect speech
acts are predicated on recognisable – that is, recognisable to other participants –
intentions on the part of the speaker to mean something by meaning something
else. In that sense, it remains at best only a partial account of implicatures
vis-à-vis social action, given implicatures include instances that arise through
"hinting" and "suggesting", and not just "implying", on Grice's original account
(see Grice [1975]1989: 24, [1987]1989: 368).[30]

Another drawback of SAT in accounting for implicatures is that subsequent
work examining indirect speech acts in interaction has found that it is not simply
the speaker's intentions that determine what a speaker is taken to be indirectly
meaning.[31] In the following interaction, for instance, the so-called indirect speech
acts here arise as much through how the other interactant responds to what the
speaker says, as through whatever the speaker himself may or may not be (taken
to be) intending.

(39) (Carl is standing in the hallway of a university speech department, while
      holding the hand of his 15-month-old son, Curtis)

Carl: Hey Debbie. Are you going to be free from 1:30 to 2:30?

Debbie: Yeah, I think so. You want me to watch him?

---

30 Although cf. Bach and Harnish (1979) for an alternative formulation of SAT which also considers "collateral acts" that lie outside of their "speech act schema", including "covert collateral
acts" such as innuendo, and what Weiser (1974, 1975) terms "deliberate ambiguity" (see Chapter 1, section 3.1).

31 Searle (1979, 2007) himself makes a distinction between speaker meaning and communication (see also Davis 2003 for a similar point). On Searle's account, speaker meaning is determined by the speaker's intentions. Speech Act theory is thus claimed to be a theory of speaker
meaning rather than communication per se. The question, then, is whether it is plausible to treat
implicatures as being simply a matter of speaker meaning abstracted from interaction, when
they evidently are recognisable to users as arising in communication. If one takes the latter view,
then while a definition of implicatures solely in terms of speaker intentions is understandable
from a Speech Act theory-internal perspective, such a definition arguably does not adequately
account for the phenomena in question, namely, implicatures as they arise in actual interactions.

Carl: Yeah.

Debbie: I'd love to. It'd be a pleasure.

Carl: Okay. Thanks. I'll bring him around then.
(Geis 1995: 27–28)

Geis (1995) argues that by uttering "You want me to watch him?" Debbie is not only formulating "an inquiry about the prior speaker's goal", but is also implicating "a willingness to watch the child" (p.28). In doing so, Debbie is treating Carl's prior utterance as indirectly requesting that she look after his son for an hour or so through her response, as well as making an indirect offer. Curl (2006) argues that the formulation of this offer constitutes a recognisable practice (in English at least), given "offers of remedy for problems educed from previous talk are always produced with the syntactic format [*do*] *you want me to X*" (p.1257). In this case, Debbie infers from Carl's prior question, the fact that his son is with him, and perhaps based on situations in the past when Debbie has helped out Carl, that his question is hearable as something which is "done not as an action/move in its own right and analysable in its own terms alone, but for its relevance to and bearing on some action/utterance projected to occur" (Schegloff 2007: 28, fn.1). In other words, "Are you going to be free from 1:30 to 2:30?" is interpretable as a pre-request which projects the contingent possibility that a request will be forthcoming, depending, in part, on the response from Debbie in the subsequent turn (Levinson 1983; Schegloff 2007: 62, 72). The object of this request is, of course, educed by Debbie when she makes a pre-emptive offer, which Schegloff (2007) argues to be the preferred response in such situations in that it "pre-empt[s] the need for a request altogether by offering that which is to be requested" (p.90). This pre-emptive offer is, in turn, predicated on Debbie's assumption that Carl's prior question is indicative of a potential or latent problem, namely, that he needs someone to look after his son for a while.

Importantly, while Debbie evidently attributes an agenda to Carl in asking this, namely, wanting to get Debbie to look after his son, Carl's prior question is recognisable as pre-request implicative, not as a request per se. The most plausible communicative (i.e. utterance-level) intention with respect to this utterance itself that could be attributed to Carl at this point, then, is an intention to communicate an utterance hearable as a pre-request. But a pre-request is not a request as such. Thus, it is as much through Debbie's pre-emptive offer – through which she enacts her own agency – as it is through Carl's formulation of his utterance, and Debbie's recognition of a putative intention on Carl's part to communicate a pre-request, that the request itself is indirectly achieved in this instance. Notably, this means the object of that request (and Debbie's offer) constitutes an implicature, but this implicature is not solely determined through recognition of Carl's putative intentions with respect to his initial utterance, but also through Debbie herself exercising agency in making an offer that pre-empts the need for Carl to formulate a request.

As Geis (1995) argues, we have here an instance of

> requesting and offering without requests and offers. If we wish to say that Carl was doing requesting and Debbie was doing offering in this interaction, as is perfectly reasonable, we must say that these actions are in some sense trans-sentential emergent properties of the interaction. (Geis 1995: 29)

This amounts to the claim that speech acts do not arise as properties of utterances but rather as "relations between utterances" (Asher and Lascarides 2001: 223). Such an analysis also undermines ongoing claims that implicatures are determined solely by speaker intentions (Feng 2013) or recognition of those intentions (Wedgwood 2011), given such approaches do not allow for recipients to exercise their own agency in contributing to what is taken to be meant by the speaker in actual communicative interaction.

Whether Speech Act theory, or at least Searle's approach to it, can account for examples like the above instance, where indirect speech acts are interactionally achieved by two (or more) participants, has been much debated (as we shall see in section 2.4). However, no matter what stance one ultimately takes on such debates, Searle's focus on indirect speech acts has nevertheless drawn attention to a critical question facing any account of implicatures: should they be theorised primarily as a form of pragmatic meaning or as a kind of social action?

In the remainder of this section, although it is maintained that implicatures are primarily a form of pragmatic meaning, as was assumed in the previous chapter, it is argued that they are also fundamentally interdependent with understandings of social actions. That is to say, implicatures arise coordinate with the interactional achievement of social actions. This means an analysis of implicatures in interaction cannot be undertaken without a consideration of the social actions together with which they arise. On this view, not only do participants need to form understandings of social actions which are occasioned through talk, but the "object" of social actions themselves may be implicated rather than said in some instances. In cases where the object of social actions remains unsaid, we are more often than not dealing with implicatures.

2.2 Implicature and intentions

The second main approach that explicitly addresses the relationship between implicature and social action encompasses a range of proposals which involve participants making inferences either about the discourse plans of speakers themselves or generalised discourse schema (Cooren and Sanders 2002; Green 1999; Green and Carberry 1993, 1999; Hinkelman and Allen 1989; Levinson 2011, 2013; McCafferty 1990; Perrault and Allen 1980; Sanders 1987, 2012, 2013; Thomason 1990). The key claim underlying such approaches is that what a speaker can be taken to be implicating is a function, at least in some instances, of the participant's perceptions of, or inferences about, the speaker's overall aim or agenda – or what can also be termed a "higher-order intention" (Bratman 1987; Ruhi 2007) – in engaging in the talk in question.

In the following interaction, for instance, Levinson (1983) argues the initial question is an example of a "transparent pre-request", which is thus implicative of a forthcoming request.

(40) 1 A: Hullo, I was wondering whether you were intending to go to Popper's talk this afternoon

  2 B: Not today I'm afraid I can't make it to this one

  3 A: Ah okay

  4 B: You wanted me to record it didn't you heh!

  5 A: Yeah heheh

  6 B: Heheh no I'm sorry about that...
(Levinson 1983: 358)

Similar to example (39) above, it is clear that the two participants here reach an understanding that A wanted to ask B to record (Karl) Popper's talk for him, without a request actually being made, through their (mutual) recognition of A's utterance in turn 1 as a pre-request implicative (Haugh 2009a, 2012b; Haugh and Jaszczolt 2012: 101).

According to the plan-based view, it could be argued that B attributed a communicative intention on A's part to check whether it would be possible for B record Popper's talk for him on the basis of his utterance in turn 1.[32] However, it is

---

32 A communicative intention refers to an intention on the part of the speaker to mean something by intending that the hearer recognise the speaker's intention to mean something. In other

not actually entirely clear from B's response in turn 2 whether he was treating A's utterance in turn 1 as pre-request implicative, or simply as a request for information, although it is evident by his topicalisation of A's *intentions* – in the ordinary, folk sense of *intention* as what A is wanting to achieve by asking these questions – that he did at some point in the interaction understand A's initial question as a pre-request. However, putting aside the issue of exactly when this pre-request implicative communicative intention was inferred by B (Haugh 2008c, 2009a), it can be argued that in order for B to infer this communicative intention in the first place, he would necessarily also have to have made an inference about a possible higher-order intention on A's part, namely, his intention to make a request, as it is only in the context of the latter that the former inference is plausible.

As Haugh and Jaszczolt (2012) note, this means that any *putative* "communicative intention of A is embedded within his higher-order intention" (p.101).[33] In other words, to figure out the implicature that evidently arises here, the participants are necessarily making inferences about some kind of overall aim or higher-order intention on A's part, or at least that is what is (implicitly) claimed in plan-based or schema-based approaches to implicature. According to this view, then, inferences about the intended implicature(s) (i.e. the speaker's communicative intentions) arise concomitant with inferences about the overall aim of the speaker (i.e. the speaker's higher-order intention), the latter of which more often than not constitutes some kind of speech act.

One of the key challenges facing an intention-based approach to the relationship between implicatures and speech acts is therefore the question of how to properly differentiate between different types of intentions, as well as their different usages by researchers in the field (Haugh 2008a, 2012b; Haugh and Jaszczolt 2012; cf. Jary 2013). The notion of higher-order intention, for instance, is generally conceptualised as rooted in some kind of cognitive reality, and so is treated as causative of the talk and conduct of speakers. Yet given higher-order intentions focus on what a speaker is aiming to achieve through talk (or conduct more broadly), they are to a large extent similar in scope to the folk notion of *intention/intending* (Gibbs 1999a: 22–23; cf. Bara 2010: 76–77). The latter encompasses

---

words, a communicative intention involves a first-order intention (i.e., to intend to inform or represent something), which is embedded in a second-order intention (i.e., to intend that this first-order intention be recognized by the addressee) (Haugh 2012b: 164; cf. Haugh and Jaszczolt 2012).

33 As Haugh and Jasczcolt (2012: 101) note, any inference about A's higher-order intention or "plan" to make a request presupposes, in turn, that A and B are "we-intending" the possibility of getting something done (that is, arranging a recording of the talk) as opposed to simply exchanging information about each other's activities, as that higher-order intention would only be consistent with the former interpretive frame.

the ordinary or lay conceptualisation of *intention* as referring to "what oneself or others want to achieve by doing or saying something (i.e., as goal-oriented/directed), or classifying actions as being done with the speaker's awareness of the implications of them (i.e., as deliberate)" (Haugh 2012b: 168).

However, while the scope of higher-order intentions and the folk notion of *intention/intending* are ostensibly very similar, a very different set of assumptions, and thus epistemological commitments, underpins each of these. In particular, the folk notion of *intention* is a discursive construct, which participants themselves invoke when holding themselves or others accountable for talk and conduct. For example, through topicalising *intentions* participants may seek to lay blame, or seek to avoid it (Edwards 2008; Haugh 2008b, 2008c). The folk notion of *intention* is thus a deontological construct rooted in the participants' understandings of what is being meant at a particular point in an interaction. In that sense it contrasts markedly with the concept of higher-order intention, which is generally theorised as a cognitive construct, and thus without much consideration being paid to the moral implications of intentions (from a participant's perspective) (Haugh 2012b; cf. Wedgwood 2011).

Sanders (2013, forthcoming) has recently proposed this apparent contradiction might be resolved through reformulating speaker intentions, which he argues encompass both "utterance-level intentions" (cf. communicative intentions) and "activity-level intentions" (cf. higher-order or folk intentions), as "a property of the utterance in context, not the speaker" (Sanders forthcoming; see also Sanders, Wu and Bonito 2013). According to Sanders (forthcoming),

> the speaker's intention about the pragmatic meaning of an utterance is the intention *any* acculturated, role- and rule-following, member of a given community would have – a generic speaker – drawing on communally shared knowledge of discursive means to ends, who produced that utterance, with that content and those compositional details, in that context, to that hearer in that role/identity, just then, in response to just that. (Sanders forthcoming: 6, original emphasis)

He proposes that, in this way, we can sidestep the various epistemological and ontological problems that treatments of speaker intentions as private intentional states on the part of individuals pose for the analysis of implicatures in situated interactions (Arundale 2008; Haugh 2008c, 2009a, 2012b, 2013b). Such a position is also arguably more consistent with Grice's (1957: 387) original claim that "an utterer is held to intend to convey what is *normally* conveyed (or *normally* intended to be conveyed)".

This contrasts with the common position recently reiterated by Feng (2013), who argues that "in conversation any information independent of the speaker's intention is outside of what is meant [by that speaker]" (p.119), and so "the implicature of the utterance ... is the one intended by the speaker and the one that she expects the hearer to be able to recover" (p.124). Yet Feng's appeal to a notion o. intention grounded in the subjective intentional states of speakers, runs contra to Grice's (1957) emphasis on what is "normally intended to be conveyed" (p.387). The danger, then, in many traditional intention-based accounts of implicature is that it can result in theorising implicatures as arising simply with respect to the relationship between a speaker's subjective thoughts and his or her use of language, without due consideration of the demands on intersubjectivity vis-à-vis any such putative speaker intentions that a communicative context necessarily entails.

However, putting aside such debates for the moment, what is clear is that while intention-based approaches to implicatures have all invoked the notion of discourse plan, that is, the overall aim or purpose of the speaker, in almost all cases what has been invoked – from a theoretical perspective – is a cognitively-grounded notion of higher-order intention. The focus has been primarily on the reasoning processes by which hearers figure out what the speaker has implicated. This leaves open the question, with the notable exception of recent work by Sanders (2012, 2013, forthcoming), of whether such approaches can properly address the ways in which participants hold each other accountable for what is taken to be implicated, along the lines of what participants do through the folk, deontological construct of *intention*. We will return to consider this issue further in the final section of this chapter.

2.3 Implicature as social action

The third main approach that addresses the relationship between implicature and action, albeit somewhat less explicitly, is that proposed in Conversation Analysis (CA). One key claim in CA is that communicative interaction is fundamentally organised as a vehicle of human action (Schegloff 2007): "talk is constructed and is attended to by its recipients for the action or actions which it may be doing" (Schegloff 1995: 187). It follows from this that any analysis of implicatures must necessarily be contextualised with respect to trajectories of social actions accomplished through talk-in-interaction. It is important to note that this should not be taken to mean that only actions are of importance in the analysis of talk-in-interaction (although the analysis of social action is the primary focus of conversation analysts), but rather that meaning cannot be analysed without analytic attention being directed to social actions as well. However, while Schegloff (1995) argues that "it is critical that the analysis of discourse incorporate attention not only to the propositional content and information distribution of discourse units, but also to the actions they are doing" (p.187), the reverse also arguably holds true. Indeed, any analysis of social action necessarily presumes an analysis of the "object" of those social actions, that is, what they are about or directed at (e.g. a request to *x*, an invitation to *y*, a complaint about *z* and so on) (Haugh 2012b: 179). In addition, as Levinson (2013) argues, "stating or asking about the preconditions of an action might end up performing the action itself" (Levinson 2013: 111), as in the case of the recognisable "pre-requests" we observed in the analysis of examples (39) and (40) above. It follows from such cases that one of the means by which participants recognise an utterance or turn as implementing a particular action (or set of actions) is through an understanding of its implicated object.

A second key claim in CA is that intersubjectivity vis-à-vis social actions is locally managed by the participants themselves in conversational interaction (Schegloff 1992a: 1338). Understandings of social actions, and consequently implicatures vis-à-vis those social actions, are thus subject to constraints licensed by the sequential position and composition of the utterances or turns that occasion those social actions. Levinson (2013) succinctly summarises the former claim about the importance of sequentiality in regards to action ascription in arguing that "the location of a turn maps sequential expectations of action content onto it" (p.110). For instance, a possible refusal can be implicated through silence subsequent to a request because the latter makes complying with – or refusing – the request is an expectable next action. It follows, then, that "*withholding* a response, and *implying that one disagrees* without doing so explicitly, are both actions" (Drew 2013: 140, original emphasis). The latter claim is addressed in work on turn design (Drew 2013; Schegloff 2007), where it is argued that the formulation of talk by participants is finely tuned to "the construction of a specific *kind* of that action" (Drew 2013: 145) in a recognizable or accountable way (*ibid*: 132) that avoids unwanted implications (*ibid*: 142). A critical way in which participants sustain intersubjectivity, then, is through the turn-by-turn organisation of actions and the way in which next turns can be taken to reflect, in some respects at least, that person's understanding of the just-prior turn, or what is termed the "next-turn proof procedure" in CA (Sacks, Schegloff and Jefferson (1974: 728). Heritage (1984a) argues that through the interlocking of current turns with prior turns (and next turns), "a context of publicly displayed and continuously up-dated intersubjective understandings is systematically sustained" (p.259). However, it is important to note that such understandings only constitute evidence of such understandings, and are not understandings per se. Heritage (1984a), for instance, cautions that

> the 'official' treatments of talk occurring at the conversational surface are the *starting point* for interpretative and analytic work and cannot be treated simply as unproblematic representations of what the speakers' understandings or *intentions* in the talk consisted of. (Heritage 1984a: 260, emphasis added)

In the case of actions that arise "without every actually being broached", or which are "disguised as other actions" (Levinson 2013: 115), including those that arise through implicatures, the problem is even more acute. As Levinson (2013) concedes, "researching the unsaid is not an easy task: one needs to show that both participants are oriented to something not occurring and deliberately kept off-stage as it were" (pp.115–116). In analysing implicatures, or implicated actions, it is thus of particular importance to draw on other sources of analytical evidence beyond localised interactional data, although only when such evidence is demonstrably relevant to the interactional data in question (Haugh 2012b: 180).

A third key claim in CA that is of particular relevance to the relationship between implicatures and social action is the notion of "possible understandings". That is, the observation that participants may be "pursuing 'possible understandings' of turns at talk – including their own at talk – along *multiple* lines, and are thereby prepared to recognize even ones arrived at by others that might have been thought elusive" (Schegloff 2006: 147, emphasis added). One upshot of this is that interpretations of social actions implemented through utterances or turns, and thus consequently implicatures as well, are very often provisional, in the sense of being both contingent on what follows as well as what has preceded that utterance or turn.

Yet while CA offers useful insights into the analysis of implicature, and their relationship to the interactional achievement of social actions, there are a number of challenges remaining for such an account. The question of how actions are recognised or ascribed as such by participants in interaction is, for instance, far from settled (Haugh 2012a: 266–268). In most CA work to date, the identification (and thus labeling) of actions by the analyst itself has been treated as largely unproblematic. For example, recognizing a "possible complaint" as an action is argued to be "a matter of position and composition – how the talk is constructed and where it is", and so "it is not a matter of divining intentions" (Schegloff 2006: 88). However, while highly fine-grained and nuanced, and consequently very useful, analyses of such social actions have emerged from such work, it is generally never made clear how the analyst (or participants) know this constitutes a (possible) complaint in the first place (Haugh 2012a: 266). Levinson (2013) in a very useful overview of how action ascription is achieved by participants, concludes that it involves,

> a range of factors: format (linguistic shape), content (e.g. mentioning of conditions on another action), position in a sequence, the nature of the prior sequence, by detecting the underlying project from the current and preceding turns, and by tracking epistemic authority and others aspects of context. (Levinson 2013: 127)

While the importance of turn composition and sequential position is well attested to in studies of social action by conversational analysts, one important factor to note in this list that is often neglected is that recognising social actions involves interpretations of the "content" of talk. In other words, understandings of social actions necessarily involve understandings of meanings occasioned by talk (Bilmes 2011). The role "content" plays in action ascription means that the object of social actions may in fact be implicated rather than said, and it is in this sense, then, that social actions can be said to be interdependent with implicatures, at least in some cases. The objects of the requests in examples (39) and (40), for instance, are implicatures. In other words, what these requests are directed at is constituted in part through implicatures. Implicatures can thus play a reflexive role in ascribing particular social actions to turns of talk in situated interaction (i.e. requests in the case of the above two examples).

Another point to note in CA accounts of social action is the reference made by Levinson (2013) to "projects" (cf. Schegloff 2007: 244–250). A project refers to "a 'plan of action' – that is, a course of action that at least one participant is pursuing, which may at first be opaque to others then retrospectively discernible ... and then prospectively projectable" (Levinson 2013: 122). In this sense, a project is arguably analogous with the notion of "higher-order intention" (Bratman 1987), or what is generally understood by ordinary users as *intend/intending* in the folk sense (Gibbs 1999a; Haugh 2012b: 168; Haugh and Jaszczolt 2012: 102).[34] Levinson (2013) himself argues that social actions are made recognisable in part relative to such broader projects, and so social actions are often tiered such that there is a "a hierarchy of actions within a project" (p.126). He suggests that pre-sequences constitute a straightforward example of these kinds of hierarchically-organised sets of actions.

In the following interaction, for instance, Ida makes an "announcement" about the arrival of her long awaited furniture (lines 7–9), which is interpretable as a "pre-invitation" according to Levinson (2011, 2013). This is because, as Drew (1984) notes, "the upshot or consequence of reporting is a proposal to get together ... to come round to see I[da]'s furniture" (p.142).

(41)   Rahman:B:1:1:12:1

1   Jen: *Hello?,*

2   (0.5)

---

34 Indeed, Levinson's (2011, 2013) recent work suggests he is attempting to reconcile plan-based (i.e. intention-focused) and CA-based (i.e. participant understanding-focused) approaches to speech acts/social action.

3   Ida: Jenny?

4   (0.3)

5   Ida: It's me:,

6   Jen: Oh hel<u>lo</u> I:da.

7   Ida: Ye:h. .h <u>uh</u>:m (0.2) I'v jis rung tih teh- <u>eh</u> tell

8   you (0.3) uh the things ev arrived from Barker'n

9   Stone'ou[:se,

10 Jen: [O<u>h</u>:::::.

11   (.)

12 Jen: O[h c'n ah <u>c'm</u> rou:nd,h[h

13 Ida: [An'   [Ye[s please[that's w]'t=

14 Jen: [ha <u>ha</u> [a:h   ]

15 Ida: =I wantche tih come rou:nd.
     (Drew 1984: 142, 2011: 2)

It is clear in this instance that Ida's friend, Jen, has shared in Ida's anticipation of the imminent arrival of Ida's new furniture, given the "announcement's initial position in, and reason for, the call; and J's needing no explanation about what "the thing" refers to" (Drew 1984: 143). Levinson (2011, 2013) claims that the announcement in Ida's turn is recognisable as both an "informing" and as "pre-invitation" implicative. It is recognisable as an informing because it is a declarative that is framed as lying within the speaker's epistemic domain (Heritage 2012a, 2012b), while it is recognisable as a pre-invitation because it "projects a conditional next action, which is how recipients can make informed choices about encouraging (with a 'go ahead') or discouraging the next action" (Levinson 2013: 125). This "duality of function", according to Levinson (2013), "follows from its place in a hierarchy of actions" (p.125), and so it can be dealt with as both an informing and pre-invitation implicative by Jen. Jen's subsequent self-invitation (line 12), which follows her receipting the news about the arrival of the furniture as "new information" through the change of state token "oh" in line 10 (Heritage 1984b), is consequently labelled "pre-emptive" by Levinson (2011). In other words, in Levinson's account, Jenny is construing Ida's prior turn as implicating she would like to invite Jenny to come around to see the furniture.

However, as Drew (2011) points out, this self-invitation is not necessarily pre-emptive, *because Jen does not in fact know what Ida is going to do next*. In other words, this does not constitute a straightforward case of Jen making an inference to Ida's overall project, namely, inviting Jen over to view the new furniture, because that may not in fact be Ida's project. Drew (1984) earlier argues that

> since the initial reportings only provide the opportunity for the recipients to address their possible involvement/participation, without constraining them to do so, any such withholding (i.e., just treating the reportings as news) would be as unofficial as the sociability/invitational relevance of the reportings themselves. And because any proposal that a recipient makes is left as an option for them to do, they – and not the prior speakers – are responsible for the proposals (i.e., the self-invitations) ... [reportings] can be a cautious way of finding out whether recipients are available and would like to ... come round. (Drew 1984: 143)

It follows that Ida's project here could actually have been to solicit an offer from Jenny to come around to look at her furniture without having to go on record as having invited her. In this way, she can avoid the potentially negative relational implications that would arise if Jenny were to go on record and refuse to go and see the furniture. In other words, Ida is *hinting* that she would like Jenny to come around.

As Walker (2007) argues, Ida's "aborted start-up" in line 13 constitutes evidence that Ida's so-called "plan" (whatever it may have been) has been "derailed" by Jenny's enquiry (p.2227, fn.11), and so the direction in which Ida's talk was heading was subsequently adjusted (as in lines 13 and 15). The point is whether Ida's agenda (or higher-order intention) was to proceed to invite Jenny, or to solicit a self-invitation from Jenny, remains opaque to the analyst (and in all likelihood to the participants as well). The difference between these two action trajectories is clearly significant for the ongoing relationship between Ida and Jen, yet it is achieved as "unofficial business" by these two participants in this case (Drew 1995).

Therefore, while speakers may well indeed have projects, and recipients may well make inferences to these perceived projects, what is ultimately implicated is not solely determined by inferences to putative higher-order intentions (or motives), but rather is determined through negotiated understandings of what a speaker is doing – sometimes on multiple levels – in a particular, locally situated interaction. Indeed, Levinson (2013) concludes as much when he claims that "projects are interactionally negotiated, jointly launched, diverted or aborted" (p.126). The way in which projects are inevitably contingent, and so interactionally negotiable, is a consequence of the fact that when "when a recipient treats the prior speaker as having done something, they are doing something", that is to say, "'ascribing an action' is itself an action" (Drew 2011). In this particular case, Jenny construes Ida's prior announcing as *hinting* she would like Jenny to come around, irrespective of whether or not that was what Ida was actually intending.

Whether one labels them projects or higher-order intentions, then, it is evident that these are discursive constructs through and through given they arise with respect to interpretations by others of the speaker's awareness of the implications of what he is saying or doing, and/or interpretations of what the speaker is aiming to do through the utterance in question (cf. Haugh 2012b: 168). A critical feature of a discursive account of intentions, motives, projects and the like is that they involve a moral dimension (Knobe 2010), in the sense that participants are holding each other accountable for particular understandings that arise from their talk or conduct (Garfinkel 1967; Sacks [1964]1992, Vol. I: 4–5). In the case of example (41), Jenny is holding Ida partially accountable for *hinting* that she would like Jenny to come around through the formulation of her response (i.e. an offer achieved through a request to come around to look at the furniture). We will return to the consider issue of accountability in relation to implicatures in more detail in the final section of this chapter.

A final point that is important to reiterate is that "other aspects of context" (Levinson 2013: 127) can also prove critical to recognising social actions. Mey (2010) argues that what makes social actions (or what he terms "pragmatic acts") possible are particular conditions, or what he terms "affordances":

> for any activity to be successful, it has to be 'expected', not just in the sense that somebody is waiting for the act to be performed, but rather in a general sense: this particular kind of act is apposite in this particular discursive interaction. (Mey 2010: 445)

In other words, social actions are dependent on the "situation being able to 'carry' them" (Mey 2010: 445). Attempts to formalise such conditions in philosophical and cognitive pragmatics (e.g. Austin 1962; Kissine 2013; Searle 1969, 1979) evidently have a more important role to play than generally acknowledged by those preferring empirical analyses of naturally occurring data. Indeed, without "precise reflections on what constitutes the nature" of the action in question (Jucker 2009: 1620), analysts may inadvertently reify their own intuitions about social actions to the level of theory (Haugh 2012a: 267).

The central role social action plays in the organisation of interaction, and thus plays in giving rise to implicatures in interaction, is now arguably indisputable. This claim is well illustrated by Schegloff (1995) in his analysis of an interaction where one of the participants (Debbie) repeatedly questions the other (Nick) about whether he has bought a waterbed (lines 37, 40 and 43), which subsequently occasions a complaint from Nick that he has already said so (line 46). Of particular note in this interaction is the role attributed to what Schegloff (1995) terms "intimations" by Debbie in his analysis.

(42) Debbie and Nick, 34–59

34 Debbie: .hhh Urn:: u- guess what I've-(u-)wuz lookin' in

35   the paper:.-have you got your waterbed yet?

36 Nick: Uh huh, it's really nice °too, I set it up

37 Debbie: Oh rea:lly? ↑Already?

38 Nick: Mm hmm

39   (0.5)

40 Debbie: Are you kidding?

41 Nick: No, well I ordered it last (week)/(spring)

42   (0.5)

43 Debbie: Oh- no but you h- you've got it already?

44 Nick: Yeah h! hh=   ((laughing))

45 Debbie: =hhh[hh hh]   ((laughing))

46 Nick: [I just] said that

47 Debbie: O::hh: hu [h, I couldn't be [lieve you c-

48 Nick: [Oh (°it's just)   [It'll sink in 'n two

49   day [s fr'm now (then) ((laugh))]

50 Debbie: [((laugh))   ] Oh no cuz I just

51   got- I saw an ad in the paper for a real discount

52   waterbed s' I w'z gonna tell you 'bout it =
     (Schegloff 1995: 188)

Schegloff (1995) suggests that an important question to ask is "*why* should this information [about buying a waterbed] come in for such scrutiny or doubting?" by Debbie (p.189). He goes on to argue that

> we can get some analytic leverage on what is going on here if we attend to these utterances not only as a matter of information transfer involving issues of truth and confidence and stances toward that information, but as actions in a course of action, constituting an inter-actional sequence of a recurrent form. (Schegloff 1995: 189)

In the analysis that follows, Schegloff (1995) points out that the sequence begins with a recognisable "pre-announcement" (Terasaki [1976]2004; Schegloff 2007: 37–41) by Debbie, namely, "guess what" in line 34. This then develops, he suggests, into a recognizable "pre-offer" when Debbie "*intimates* that what she has to tell is something that one can find (and that she has found) in the newspaper" through saying "I was looking in the paper" (lines 34–35), and then "indicates" in line 35 that "the thing to be told (about) has something to do with waterbeds, and with Nick's possibly being in the market for a waterbed in particular" (p.190, emphasis added). Thus, when asking "Have you got your waterbed yet?" Debbie is not simply asking for information, but seeking a "go-ahead" from Nick for her implicit offer of information. Schegloff (1995) goes on to argue, however, that "as it happens, it appears that Nick has not caught this, and so he responds only at the level of information transmission" (p.191), or at least he acts as if he hasn't got it.[35] In other words, Nick does not appear to orient to what Debbie has "intimated". This intimation is subsequently made explicit in lines 50–52 by Debbie, when she refers to her "baulked intention" (Edwards 2008), that is, what she was going to tell him about (line 52). This baulked intention serves as an implicit account, or explanation, for her repeated questioning (in lines 37, 40 and 43), which appears to be occasioned, in turn, by Nick's complaint (line 46).

Schegloff (1995) argues that such an analysis demonstrates that

> a focus on information will not suffice. It is the action import of utterances and not just what they are about or what they impart – the action import or nonaction import – that regularly drives the interactional construction of extended spates of talk, or discourses. (Schegloff 1995: 202)

However, clearly Debbie's "intimation" does nevertheless play a critical role here. It is not just what Debbie is taken to be saying and doing by Nick that proves important here (cf. Schegloff 1995: 191), but also what Debbie can be seen to be – unsuccessfully as it turns out – implicating as well. In other words, an implicature that is (ostensibly) missed by one of the participants proves to be constitutive of subsequent talk, in that it occasions an explicit account from Debbie of what she had earlier only "intimated" or "indicated".

However, while Schegloff (1995) focuses on analysing what the participants are doing with their utterances with admirable analytical precision, the critical role played by the implicature here (Debbie's "intimation" in Schegloff's terms) is left somewhat neglected. Indeed, the treatment of "intimation", "implying",

---

35 It is, of course, possible that Nick *did* understand what Debbie was intimating, but chose not to attend to it, although his "complaint" in line 46 seems inconsistent with such an analysis.

"insinuating", "alluding", "hinting" and the like, arguably remains ad hoc and largely intuitive in most CA studies up to the present day. Such terms are often used interchangeably, and so are used without any particular analytical precision, with just a few exceptions where more care has been taken in defining the scope of the "unstated" or "unsaid" phenomena in question (see, e.g., Drew 1984; Lerner 2013; Pomerantz 1980; Raymond 2004; Schegloff 1996a, 2003). However, given the various approaches to implicature we discussed in the previous chapter have not paid much attention to such differences either, this is hardly a weakness limited to work in CA. We will thus be returning to further consider this point in section 3.

2.4 Implicature and action ascription

While the three main approaches to analysing the relationship between implicatures and social action that have been outlined in this section all arguably contribute something to our understanding of that relationship, the claim that they are simply complementary to each other is not a tenable one. It has been argued that SAT, for instance, is not well equipped to account for the fact that social actions are not straightforwardly realised through individual utterances by speakers, but rather arise in discourse, and so must be analysed relative to their sequential context (Schegloff 1988a, 1992b), and the participation footings of the participants involved (Brenneis 1986; Kiesling and Johnson 2010). Yet while Searle (1992) himself claims the empirical question of how speech acts are realised in interaction lies outside the purview of SAT proper, others have defended the view that either SAT, or at least Austin's (1962) original account of speech acts, can in fact be productively extended to the analysis of how speech acts are accomplished in discourse (Cooren 2005; Geis 1995; Sbisà 1992, 2002; Sbisà and Fabbri 1980; Vanderveken 2013; cf. Kissine 2013). It has also been claimed that by some conversation analysts that plan-based approaches are problematic. Drew (2011), for instance, has argued that inferences to discourse plans or projects cannot straightforwardly account for social actions that are done unofficially in ways that mask or disguise the social action in question in some way. In other words, in cases where the object of the social action in question (i.e. what it is about) is realised through an implicature, inferring discourse plans is a complex endeavour.

One particular piece of data that has received multiple treatments from these different perspectives is one which was initially discussed by Schegloff (1988a) in his critique of SAT, and has subsequently also been considered by a number of other scholars (Cooren 2005; Geis 1995; Levinson 2013; Sanders 2012). The way in which these different accounts of the same piece of data coverge and diverge in various ways proves instructive. In the excerpt in question, a mother is talking over dinner with her two boys about her plans for that evening.

(43) 1 Mother: Daddy 'n I have t- both go in different

2 directions, en I wanna talk ta you about

3 where I'm going (t'night).

4 Russ: mm hmm

5 Gary: Is it about us?

6 Mother: Uh huh

7 Russ: I know where you're goin'.

8 Mother: Where.

9 Russ: To the uh (eighth grade)=

10 Mother: =Yeah. Right.

11 Do you know who's going to that meeting?

12 Russ: Who.

13 Mother: I don't kno:w.

14 Russ: Oh::. Prob'ly Missiz McOwen ('n detsa)

15 en prob'ly Missiz Cadry and some of

16 the teachers (0.4) and the counsellors.

(Scheglof 1988a: 57–58)

According to Schegloff (1988a), the mother's question, "Do you know who's going to that meeting?" in line 11 is treated as a pre-announcement by Russ. This can be seen from his subsequent response, which "forwards the sequence to the announcement position for mother" (p.59). However, the mother's subsequent response (line 13) indicates that Russ's understanding of her prior turn is "incorrect" as she "does not have the required information" (p.59). Russ thus "re-analyses it as a request for the information asked by the embedded question" (p.59), and proceeds to offer that information (in lines 14–16). Schegloff goes on to argue that an interpretation of the mother's utterance as an indirect request for information would be "the one which speech act theory would propose to be the ordinary one", but as we can see that in this example, "it is tried only after another analysis has been tried and proved incorrect" (p.59). He concludes that SAT neglects the way in which talk is situated within a particular sequential context. While the way in which current talk can project further talk, for instance, is something about which participants are reflexively aware (p.61), Schegloff (1988a) argues that this is ignored in a typical Speech Act analysis.

Levinson (2013) subsequently builds on Schegloff's (1988a) analysis in suggesting that Russ's interpretation of his mother's question as a pre-announcement, which turns out to be treated as incorrect by the mother, is likely occasioned by his own prior utterance in line 7, which could be "characterised as a pre-guess, a wager taken up by [mother]" (p.109). In Levinson's (2013) analysis, then, the mother's question is interpretable as a "counterpart challenge", although it turns out to be "not what was intended" (p.109). What Levinson's (2013) analysis adds to Schegloff's (1988a) is that Russ's initial interpretation is likely grounded in the way a prior turn of his own has been treated by his mother as a pre-announcement.

However, Schegloff's analysis has been challenged on a number of counts. Cooren (2005), for instance, argues that the class of "pre-announcement" is in fact a viable one in Speech Act theory.

> Given that the speech act of "announce" is in the class of assertives, then we know from speech act theory that if you want to inform or announce something to somebody, the preparatory condition consists of presupposing that the recipient does not know the information content (Vanderveken, 1990–91), otherwise there would not be any point in reporting or announcing something. Given this preparatory condition of informing, it appears that speech act theory can, in fact, explain why it is possible for Russ to orient to this question about his state of knowledge as anticipating an announcement. (Cooren 2005: 28)

Cooren (2005) goes on to claim that Russ's answer in line 12 (i.e. "Who") "implies, by definition, he believes that there might be an information deficit on his part" (p.29), and this reflects his initial interpretation of her question as a pre-announcement.

Geis (1995), on the other hand, argues that it is not self-evident that the interpretation of the mother's question as a "pre-announcement" is in fact due to its sequential location. He suggests there are in fact three possible readings of the mother's question in line 8 ("Do you know who's going to that meeting?"): (1) an indirect *wh*-question where the mother does not know the information but believes Russ may know it (i.e. an indirect request for information); (2) a direct *yes-no*-question where the mother does not know the information, and thinks Russ should know it, but is not sure whether Russ knows it or not (i.e. an indirect suggestion or directive); and (3) a pre-announcement where the mother knows the information, and thinks Russ should know it, but is not sure whether Russ knows it or not (Geis 1995: 188–189). Geis goes on to argue that to distinguish between these three interpretations "we do not need to refer [to] the sequential location of the utterance at all. We need, instead, to know what the contextual presuppositions of the participants are" (p.190). In other words, the participants' assumptions about their respective epistemic states vis-à-vis that particular information drives their interpretations of what the mother may be implicating through her question.

However, while Cooren (2005) and Geis (1995) both appeal to putative knowledge states, and the participants' assumptions about each other in that respect, Sanders (2012) re-analysis of this interaction indicates that while assumptions about epistemic states may indeed be involved, a gloss of this interaction as Russ "incorrectly" assuming that his mother knew the information in question is an inadequate one. He suggests that even Schegloff's (1988a) analysis cannot account for "why would Russ have understood it in this way" (p.18), at least in the first instance, because it ignores the broader "activity" (cf. project) in which the interaction is assumed to take place, a point which is alluded to but not fully articulated in Levinson's (2013) subsequent presentation of Schegloff's (1988a) original analysis. Sanders (2012) claims that from the mother's perspective it is an "information-seeking activity", which is evident from her response in line 13 ("I don't know"), while from Russ's perspective it is an "information-giving activity", and thus a kind of "guessing game", which is evident from how Russ appears to respond to his mother's question in line 12 ("Who"). On an interpretation of the activity here as a "guessing game", Russ is "challenging" his mother's implied boasting about her knowledge of the meeting, and so indirectly "inviting" her to make true on this boast. Thus, according to Sanders (2012), Russ "almost certainly understood Mother's question as a request to tell her what he knew, not as Schegloff contended, a pre-announcement. What he had wrong was what activity she was engaged in" (p.21). This line of analysis is supported by Russ's subsequent turn where he "expresses his realisation" with an elongated change of state token ("Oh::" in turn 14) (p.21), and the subsequent shift to an information-seeking activity where Russ tells his mother what he knows.

The ongoing debate about how Russ was interpreting his mother's question in line 11 highlights deeper questions about just how do we (i.e. participants) know what action(s) are being implemented through talk, and thus how this question might be approached by analysts. From this debate it has become evident that the participants negotiations about the "project" (or "activity") at stake (including the ways in which they attribute *intentions* to each other in the course of doing so), their assumptions about their respective epistemic states (or background knowledge more generally), and what sequentially precedes and follows the talk at hand, can all play a role in reaching understandings of what speakers are doing through talk-in-interaction. It has also become evident that the assignment of illocutionary points/forces (from a SAT perspective), or action ascription (from a CA perspective), is not a trivial issue. As we saw from the discussion of example (39), understanding what is implicated can turn on the participants' interpretations of the social actions involved. The fact that (neo-) Gricean and post-Gricean accounts of implicature have not addressed the issue of how participants assign illocutionary points or forces to utterances in any detail, as Kissine (2013) points out, thus constitutes a critical gap in our theorisation of implicatures. However, as we saw from the discussion of examples (40) to (43), the question of which social action(s) are ascribed to talk can itself turn on the participants' interpretations of implicatures. This is because the ascription of social action is dependent, at least in part, on what is taken to be the object of that social action. And we saw through those examples how the object of social actions can be constituted through implicatures. It follows that the analysis of implicatures cannot be divorced from the analysis of social actions. This is because implicatures are inevitably understood by participants coordinate with the social actions together with which they are interactionally achieved, and in some cases, of which they are even constitutive.

3 Implicature and meaning-actions

The proper scope of which pragmatic meanings are encompassed by the notion of implicature has been the subject of ongoing debate, as we discussed in Chapter Two. What has often been missed in such debates, however, are the distinctions Grice originally proposed between the technical notions of "implicate" (cf. *imply, mean, suggest, indicate, hint at,* and so on), "implicature" (cf. *implying, suggesting, indicating, hinting,* and so on), and "implicatum" (cf. *implication, suggestion, indication, hint,* and so on) (Grice [1975]1989: 24; [1969]1989: 86; [1987]1989: 360, 368). That is, critical distinctions between the various "meaning-actions" through which implicatures arise have been largely neglected in subsequent work. In many of the approaches that have arguably been subsequently developed, implicatures have been equated with pragmatic inference (e.g. Carston 2002a, 2002b; Levinson 2000; Sperber and Wilson 1995), or with (perceived) speaker's intentions (e.g. Bach 2001, 2006, 2012; Feng 2013; Horn 2004; although cf. Horn 2012, Saul 2002a, 2002b). However, such a move is arguably overly reductive, as it misses a critical feature of implicatures, namely, that implicatures constitute a social action in and of themselves (Bianchi 2013a: 118; Haugh 2002: 127).

One problem with the reduction of implicatures to either inferences on the part of hearers, or to the (perceived) intentions of speakers, is that such approaches do not do justice to the distinction between what Saul (2002a) terms "utterer impli-catures" and "audience implicatures". The former refers to instances where a speaker means the hearer to understand he or she has meant something beyond what is said in a particular interaction, but the hearer does not necessarily rec-ognise this, or at least does not recognise what has been meant (cf. "implicate"). The latter refers to instances where a speaker is taken to mean something beyond what is said that he or she has not necessarily intended, or at least does not want to be held accountable for meaning (cf. "implicatum/implicata"). In hearer-infer-ential or speaker-intention based accounts of implicature such phenomena are generally treated as instances of "miscommunication". However, they are argu-ably much more than that. As Horn (2012: 85–86) has pointed out, in some cases participants will recognise an "implication" or "suggestion" as "unintended", and yet maintain that it was nevertheless *implied*. Jary (2013) has also recently argued that some implicatures arise without recourse being made to inferences about the intentions, beliefs, and so on of the speaker in question, instances of which he terms "material implicatures".

In the following interaction between two university students getting acquainted, for instance, we can observe just such an instance of where some-thing is construed as implicated but not necessarily as intended. The excerpt begins at the point where Peter (an American) and Sally (an Australian) have been discussing foods that are available in Australia but not in the U.S.

(44)   AmAus02: 4:15

   102 P: I like <u>kan</u>garoo though.

   103   you [guys] don't eat it here though for some reason.

   104 S: [yeah?]

   105   (.)

   106 S: ↑n [o::.]

   107 P: [don]'t know why. [it's] <u>wil</u>d there's no <u>hor</u>mones

   108 S: [(I::-]

   109 P: there's no::, there's nothing n it?

   110   it's the healthiest meat you can eat? [bu:t?]

   111 S: [yeah?]

   112   (.)

113 S: I guess [because] (0.2) it's a bit of a <u>cul</u>tural thing?

114 P: [hem hem]

115   like where I'm from people feed kangaroo meat to <u>dogs</u>?

116   so: (0.2) <u>ye</u>:ah.

117 P: >°I guess I'm a dog.°<

118 S: [I- <u>no</u>: I don't mean dogs] <u>eat</u> it

119 P: [I like dogs so that's okay]

120   I just mean because [(I   know   )] that my fath-

121 P: [>that's okay<]

122 S: you know like my stepdad's a farmer? and that's what he

123   does? it's just (0.2) I wouldn't even (0.2) like I would <u>eat</u>

124   it, but I just wouldn't go out of my way to eat it

125   sort of thing?

An implicated premise arises when Sally offers an account as to why kangaroo meat is not widely eaten in Australian, namely, that where she is originally from (i.e. rural Australia), kangaroo meat is fed to dogs, and so it is presumably considered not "good enough" for people to eat (lines 113, 115–116). However, Peter draws an additional implication from what Sally has said, namely, that if he likes eating kangaroo meat then she is implying he must be like a dog (line 117). This elicits two different responses. Sally quickly moves to deny the implication that she thinks people who eat kangaroo meat are like dogs (line 118), by claiming that is just the practice of farmers (including her step father) to feed kangaroo meat to dogs (lines 120, 122–123), and although she wouldn't seek it out, she wouldn't necessarily avoid eating it either (lines 123–125). Peter, on the other hand, reassures her that he "likes dogs" so it is not really such an insult after all to be likened to a dog (line 119), and subsequently reassures her again that he is not insulted (line 121). The conversation then turns to Peter's claim that meat in Australia is better (data not shown). What we can observe here, then, is that Sally is held momentarily accountable by Peter for an implication that she subsequently denies *intending*.

On Clark's (1997) account, this counts as an instance of a "misconstrual", that is, where the speaker is not able to block another understanding on the part of the hearer. Misconstrued implicatures, which are a type of "audience implicature" in Saul's (2002a) terminology, involve instances where the speaker may deny having intended to mean or imply something, but the hearer's understanding nevertheless overshadows the claimed intentions of the speaker. In the above example, for instance, Sally is taken to imply people who eat kangaroo are like dogs by Peter (line 118), which is potentially a rather cutting remark given Peter's prior claim that he likes eating kangaroo (lines 102). However, he lets Sally off the hook as it were in regards to the potentially offensive implications of this (lines 119, 121), and so implicitly recognises that offence was not intended on her part (although it is in fact his construal of the upshot of the account she offers that creates the "offence" in the first place). However, the implication that some people think kangaroo is not good enough for consumption by humans remains. This can be seen from Sally's subsequent attempts to distance herself from that implied stance by attributing it to her stepfather rather than herself (lines 120, 122), and also her claim that she would consider eating kangaroo meat (lines 123–125), albeit perhaps not enthusiastically. The point here, then, is that a misconstrued implicature is not simply a matter of "miscommunication" of the speaker's intentions. What Sally *intended* here is implicitly oriented to by both participants, but she is only able to distance herself from the offensive implications of what she is taken to have implied by Peter (i.e. that Peter is like a dog), not what she has been taken to have implied itself, which is what gives rise to the potentially insulting implication in the first place (i.e. that kangaroo meat is not good for human consumption). This is because by attributing this implication to Sally, albeit in jest, Peter has thereby played an active role in co-constructing what is taken to be implied by Sally at this point in their conversation. This orientation to unintended "implications" or "implying" by ordinary speakers, which is also implicit in phrases such as "didn't mean to imply" or "unintentionally implied", thus suggests that implicatures cannot always be straightforwardly treated as instances of speaker-intended meaning (Horn 2012: 85–86). In other words, implicatures cannot always be readily reduced to the intentions of speakers or the inferences of hearers about those intentions, given the active role participants can play in their interpretation.

A second problem with the reduction of implicatures to either the putative intentions of speakers or inferences on the part of hearers about the speaker's intentions is that such approaches ignore differences in the way in which implicatures arise, and thus the interactional consequences of such differences in regards to what speakers can be held to be committed to, or accountable for meaning. Grice himself recognised this in his original claim that the term "implicate" was intended to subsume various ways in which implicatures can arise (Grice [1975]1989: 24). Indeed, Grice ([1969]1989) explicitly claimed that "'implicature' is a blanket word to avoid having to make choices between words like 'imply', 'suggest', 'indicate', and 'mean'", but that "these words are worth analysing" (p.86). He subsequently argued that *implying, suggesting, hinting* are exploited by speakers in "specifying different ways in which a speaker's *alignment* with an idea or thesis may be displayed or obscured" (Grice[1987]1989: 367, emphasis added) (cf. implicature). What was meant by "alignment" here was the degree to which a speaker can be held to be committed to a particular "implication", "suggestion", "hint" and so on, or the "content" of that "implication", "suggestion", "hint" and so on, itself (cf. implicatum). He outlined in his retrospective epilogue, for instance, how *suggesting* and *hinting* might be characterised and thereby so differentiated. To *suggest* (that so-and-so), according to Grice,

> is perhaps more like, though still by no means exactly like, asserting there to be some evidence that so-and-so...The existence of such a case will require that there should be a truthful fact or set of facts which might be explained by the hypothesis that so-and-so together with certain other facts or assumptions, though the speaker is *not committed* to the claim that such an explanation would in fact be correct. (Grice [1987]1989: 368, emphasis added)

To *hint* (that so-and-so), on the other hand, is where,

> one makes, explicitly, a statement which does, or might, justify the idea that there is a case for supposing that so-and-so; but what there might be a case for supposing, namely that so-and-so, is not explicitly mentioned but is left to the audience to identify. Obviously the more devious the hinting, the greater is the chance that the speaker will fail to make contact with his audience, and so will escape *without having committed* himself to anything. (Grice [1987]1989: 368, emphasis added)

In other words, through *suggesting* (that *x*) one is able to distance oneself from the belief that *x* is necessarily true, while through *hinting* (that *x*), one is able to leave it up to the hearer to figure out, thereby reducing, or even perhaps eliminating, one's responsibility for the implicature in question. Both *suggesting* and *hinting* thus constitute a particular kind of social action, which are here termed "meaning-actions".

Studies of the meaning-actions through which implicatures arise have focused primarily on *hinting* (e.g. Bertuccelli Papi 1999; Brown and Levinson 1987: 215; Haugh 2002: 127; Holdcroft 1976; Weizman 1985), *insinuating* (e.g. Bertuccelli Papi 1996, 2000, 2014; Fraser 2001; Holdcroft 1976; Morgan 2010; Parrett 1994), and *innuendo* (e.g. Bell 1997; Fraser 2001; Obeng 1994), with only passing mention being made about *suggesting* (Bertuccelli Papi 2000; Holdcroft 1976; Goddard and Wierzbicka 2014), *alluding* and *supposing* (Bertuccelli Papi 2000; cf. Brown and Levinson 1987: 215–217). In differentiating between *implying, hinting* and *insinuating*, for instance, Wierzbicka (1987) offers the following glosses:

imply: the speaker wants to cause the addressee to think something ... [but] he refrains from saying the thing that he wants to cause them to think. Instead, he says something else ... the speaker seems to *assume* that the addressee will be able to 'uncover' the hidden meaning as if it were somehow provided in the utterance itself – being hidden, but present. (p.272, original emphasis)

hint: one is thinking something that one would quite like to say aloud, but that one refrains from doing so – presumably because one thinks that one shouldn't say it. (p.271)

insinuate: [the speaker] wants to cause his addressee to think something bad about someone ... [but] the speaker doesn't want his information to be too obvious ... the attitude is 'I don't want people to be sure that I want to cause them to think this'. (p.273)

According to Wierzbicka (1987), what differentiates *implying* from *hinting* is that the speaker expects the hearer will understand what has been *implied*, but only may – and thus may not – understand what is being *hinted at*. It follows that in the case of *implying*, while what has been *implied* might be open to dispute, the fact that the speaker has *implied* something is generally difficult to deny. In the case of *hinting*, however, the degree of plausible deniability is greater, that is, the speaker can more legitimately claim to not be *meaning* anything. What differentiates *implying* and *hinting* from *insinuating*, on the other hand, is that in the latter case not only is the speaker wanting others to think something bad about the target (whereas the content of what is implied or hinted at does not have such a stricture on it), but is also wanting to ensure he or she cannot be held accountable for *meaning* such a thing (cf. Austin 1962: 105; Bertuccelli Papi 1996; Fraser 2001; Holdcroft 1976; Parrett 1994).

However, while offering a useful starting point, such glosses only take us part of the way, as they are invariably grounded in the speaker's perspective. As we have seen from our discussion in the previous section on the relationship between implicatures and social action, implicatures arise as much through the hearer's response to the speaker's prior turn, as through whatever the speaker him or herself is taken to be doing in interaction. To properly understand the meaning-actions through which implicatures arise, then, we must ultimately examine them as they are mediated through interaction.

Consider the following example where a husband "hints" (cf. *honomekasu, sasou mizu*) that he would like his wife to make a special kind of beef dish after commenting about it while seeing it being made on television.

(45)   (Otoboke is watching a cooking programme on television)

1   Otoboke: *Waa, uma-sō.*
            wow delicious-looks
            'Wow, that looks good!'

2   Otoboke: *Shimofuri-no gyūniku nantte shibaraku*
            marbled beef Quot   long   time

3   *tabe-te-nai nā*
            eat-Te-Neg M
            'Gee, we haven't eaten marbled beef for a long time'

4   Wife: *Ja,   konya wa totteoki-no   o*
            well then tonight Top reserve-Nomi Acc

5   *dasu   ka.*
            take out(Pol) Q
            'Well, shall I get the one I especially put aside out tonight?'
(Ueda 1995: 15)

Otoboke first comments (ostensibly to himself) that the marbled beef being made on television looks delicious (line 1), and then says to his wife that they have not eaten it for a long time (lines 2–3). Otoboke thereby indicates that he would like to eat some marbled beef, and also "hints" that he would like his wife make some for him; or at least he is evidently interpreted as doing so by his wife through her subsequent offer (lines 4–5). Importantly, then, it is as much through his wife's response, as it is through what Otoboke himself has said, that Otoboke is taken to be "hinting" he would like to eat some marbled beef (and thus that his wife make some for them). Whether this implicature can be counted as arising through "implying" or "hinting" depends in part on how one defines "implying" and "hinting" (which is itself a concern of participants), an issue which is made more complex by the fact we are dealing here with data from Japanese, and thus other terms with their own particular nuances, such as *honomekasu* and *sasoi mizu*, are available to those participants. But no matter which term the participants (or indeed analyst) might choose to characterise this instance (a choice which counts, of course, as an instance of action ascription with all its attendant implications), there is clearly some degree of "illocution-ary opacity" (Weizman 1985: 160) in regard to this implicature. That is, while it is indicated that Otoboke likes eating marbled beef (line 1), and implied that he would like to eat some (lines 2–3), it is less clear what he wants his wife to do about it at that point in time, and so it is left up to his wife to identify the latter (which she does in making an offer in lines 4–5). The latter upshot thus arguably constitutes a clear instance of an implicature that arises through "hinting", because while Otoboke might assume there is a "good chance the audience [i.e. his wife] possesses the missing premises" (Holdcroft 1976: 153), here, it is by no means certain that she does in fact possess them. There is also the sense here that Otoboke might be "refraining" from asking for something he would like his wife to do, but perhaps thinks he "shouldn't say" (Wierzbicka 1987: 271), presumably because this means he gets what he wants without having to go on-record as having asked for it. In this way, by soliciting an offer from his wife, he avoids giving rise to the attendant interpersonal implications of achieving something through making an outright request.

In the following example, we can also see a similar phenomenon in that a noticing about "good weather" was reported by an informant as being regularly used in by her mother to "hint" that she would like the father to take the children out somewhere.

(46) Mother: *Ashita   tenki   ii   rashii ne.*
            tomorrow weather good seems M
            'It seems like nice weather day huh?'

     Father: *Ja,   kodomo o   kōen ni tsure-te-ik-ō   ka?*
            well, children Acc park   to take-Te-go-Vol Q
            Well then, shall I take the children to a park?'
(Field notes, Tokyo, 10ᵗʰ October 1999)

In this case, the father is left to figure out the upshot of the mother's choice to comment on the weather at this point in time. While it could ostensibly treated as simply chit-chat about the weather, here the father treats the mother's report as "hinting" she would like him to take the children out to a park. This is achieved through the father making a pre-emptive offer that construes the report as "raising the issue of some desired act", namely, taking the children out to a park, thereby framing the mother's prior utterance as "asserting ... the conditions for the act" in question (Brown and Levinson 1987: 215). What is notable about this case, however, is that it was reported as a regular occurrence in that family. In other words, particular instances of "hinting" can be accomplished through practices that are recognisable (to those participants) as "hinting".

Drew (1984) details one such practice, whereby reporting on some kind of troubles, speakers can hint that they would like some form of help from the addressee, yet without having to go on record as requesting help. Such reportings regularly, although not always, elicit an offer from the other participant(s). In the following excerpt, for instance, Emma is talking with Lottie on the phone about Sandra's troubles.

(47) NB:IV:1

    1   E: Wul 'anyway tha's: the deal, so I dunno what to do

    2   about Sandra (.) .hhh

    3   E: Cuz yuh see she's depending on: him takin' 'er in tuh

    4   the el a: deepl s- depot Sundih s[o ('e)

    5   L: [I:ll take er in

    6   Sund[h

    7   E: [.hh Oh:: no: Lottie

    8   E: Oh [my ga:d no Lottie

    9   L: [Yea::(n)h

    10 E: No that's a he:l luv a long trip.
    (Drew 1984: 149, fn.10)

In this case, Emma's reporting of Sandra's troubles about getting somewhere on Sunday (lines 1–4) elicits an offer from Lottie to take Sandra to where she needs to go (lines 5–6). This offer is subsequently rejected by Emma (lines 7–8, 10), although Emma later proposes that they (i.e. Lottie) could "take 'er to thuh .hh Greyhound bus over here on the coa:st highway" (data not shown). In other words, Lottie construes Emma reporting on Sandra's troubles as *hinting* that Emma would like to request some form of help for Sandra from Lottie, although what form this help takes is worked out in subsequent talk. In this case, then, there is "propositional opacity" in regards to the "object" or "content" of the requested help in question (cf. Weizman 1984: 161), although that a request for help is here being implicated is evidently treated as a relatively straightforwardly accessible inference by both the participants.

The use of "hints" or "implications" in order to solicit an offer, as we saw in examples (45) to (47), can also be used to solicit other actions, including to "fish" for information (Pomerantz 1980), to solicit accounts (Robinson and Bolden 2010), and to elicit (self-)invitations (Drew 1984; Haugh 2009a). In the following excerpt from a recording of a telephone conversation between friends, for instance, which we briefly discussed in the previous chapter, we can observe how a reporting transforms what appears initially appears to be an invitation sequence initiated by the call-maker (Cameron) into an instance of soliciting an invitation from the call-taker (Steve) (see also example 41).

(48) WSC: DPF006: 0:18

   18 C: whadaya doing to<u>ni</u>ght?

   19   (0.2)

   20 S: I dun↑no:. >what are< <u>yo</u>u gonna do.

   21   (0.5)

   22 C: o:h I've been invited to a party that I don't wanna-

   23   really want t' go to.

   24   (0.6)

   25 C: hope to find an ex<u>cu</u>se.

   26   (0.6)

   27 S: o:h ↑<u>ri</u>:ght. hh. (0.3) I see.

   28   ↑u::m. hav'ya se<u>en</u> lethal weapon?
(Haugh 2009a: 105)

As Cameron's initial question, "Whadaya doing tonight?" (line 18) is in the form of a standard pre-invitation (Schegloff 2007: 129), Steve orients to the possibility of a forthcoming invitation by inquiring as to what the proposal might involve through a hedged "go-ahead" response (line 20). However, rather than proceeding to issue an invitation in his subsequent turn, Cameron's outlines the preparatory conditions for another kind of invitation, namely, an invitation from Steve (lines 22–23), thereby hinting, or perhaps even implying, that he would like Steve to invite him somewhere (and so provide the means by which he can be excused from going to a party he does not want to attend). Steve's understanding of the upshot of Cameron's prior utterance in line 18, namely, that Cameron wants Steve to invite him somewhere, is evident from his subsequent launching of an invitation sequence, starting with a standard pre-invitation (turn 28). However, this understanding is indicated to be a revised one, which has arisen in light of Cameron's qualification in lines 22–23, through Steve's use of "oh" and "right" (line 27), by means of which he registers that this is new information for him and has generated a new understanding on his part, respectively (Heritage 1984b; Schegloff 2007: 118). We can see here, then, how Cameron is able to solicit an invitation from Steve despite being the one who initiated both the call itself, and the subsequent talk about their plans for that evening. In doing so, Cameron is able to "avoid" a particular social action (i.e. inviting Steve), and leave it to Steve to enact it (Drew 2011). It is in this sense, then, that implicatures can also be regarded, at least in some instances, as constitutive of social actions.

The situation becomes even more complex, as we briefly noted before, when one considers that meaning-actions and related practices can vary in their import across languages and cultures. For instance, the conceptual scope of *anshi, anyu, yiwei, yinshe* in Chinese, and *fukumu, fureru, honomekasu, anjisuru, niowaseru, atetsukeru* in Japanese cannot be straightforwardly mapped onto *implying, hinting, intimating, alluding, suggesting* in English, although this point is not often well-recognised in pragmatics. It is also evident that not all relevant meaning-actions are necessarily named in the vernacular of different languages. For instance, one recognisable practice in Chinese workplaces is to implicate criticism of one individual at a meeting by addressing the criticism at all parties present. In this way, not only does the speaker deny the perceived target of the indirect criticism straightforward rights of reply, it also decreases the extent to which the speaker can be held accountable for criticising that particular person. This practice echoes cases of "pointed" indirectness amongst speakers of African American Vernacular English, "when a speaker ostensibly says something to someone (mock receiver) that is intended for – and to be heard by- someone else and is so recognised" (Morgan 1996: 406). The range of meaning-actions and related practices that can be observed to arise in actual talk-in-interaction is thus much more complex and varied than an account of implicatures in terms of either speaker intentions or inferences by hearers about those intentions can legitimately accommodate.[36]

In summary, then, implicatures arise through a specific set of socially-implicative actions, which have here been termed meaning-actions (e.g. *implying, intimating, hinting, alluding, suggesting, insinuating*, and so on). It is through these different meaning-actions that implicatures may contribute to the interactional achievement of various different social actions. Indeed, implicatures may in some instances be constitutive of social actions, as through *implying, hinting, alluding*, and so on, participants can interactionally "position" social actions vis-à-vis other participants as "avoided", "open to deniability", "deliberately ambiguous", and so on (Drew 2011; Weiser 1974, 1975). Critically it is this range of meaning-actions, and the interactionally positioning that can be accomplished through them,

---

36 It is evident that we have a long way to go in adequately characterising how implicatures arise through meaning-actions, and that we have only been able to just scratch the surface of this issue in the course of this section.

which affords the existence of im/politeness implicatures, a point to which we will return in Chapter Four . However, before doing so, we will first consider the issue of the potential deniability or ambiguity of implicatures in more detail, in moving to discuss another key characteristic of implicatures originally noted by Grice, namely, that they are not necessarily as determinate as might first appear.

4 Implicature and indeterminacy

In characterising implicatures, Grice ([1975]1989) noted that "in order to preserve the supposition that the Cooperative Principle is being observed ... there may be various possible specific explanations, a list of which may be open" (pp.39–40), and so "the conversational implicatum in such cases will be a disjunction of such specific explanations" (p.40). He further argued that "if the list is open, the implicatum will have just the kind of *indeterminacy* that many actual implicata do in fact seem to possess" (p.40, emphasis added). Terkourafi (2013) takes this further in suggesting that in some cases utterances may not involve a "disjunction of such specific explanations", that is, one single albeit indeterminate implicature, but may involve "a conjunction of inferences" (p.203), that is, multiple implicatures arising from a single utterance or turn of talk. She suggests, for instance, that calling one's partner and saying "I have to work late tonight" could be taken to give rise to multiple off-record interpretations, ranging from "Don't wait for me", "Don't make dinner for me", "You can have your favourite food which I can't stand", "I will miss our favourite TV program", "Please record it for me", and so on (pp.201–202). Yet while Grice explicitly recognised right from the beginning that what is taken to be implicated by speakers is very often indeterminate, this point has not, for the most part, been well recognised in subsequent theorising of implicatures. As Sperber and Wilson (1995) argue, "there has been a tendency in modern pragmatics to treat all implicatures ... as *fully determinate* assumptions for which the speaker is just as much responsible as if she had asserted them directly" (p.195, emphasis added).

In Relevance theory, as we briefly discussed in Chapter 2, Grice's original claims about the potential indeterminacy of implicatures has been further developed through a distinction being made between "strong implicatures" (that is, those implicatures for which the speaker is held primarily responsible for their truth), and "weak implicatures" (that is, those implicatures for which the hearer is held primarily responsible for their truth) (Moeschler 2012: 423–424; Sperber and Wilson 1995; Wilson and Sperber 1986). In their view, implicatures can thus vary in their degree of determinacy (Sperber and Wilson 1995). One potential problem with the Relevance theoretic account of weak implicatures, however, is the claim that implicated assumptions or conclusions can be upgraded such that they "conform to the principle of relevance", and in such cases "the speaker is held responsible for the truth (or degree of confirmation) of any assumptions and conclusions upgraded in this way" (Wilson and Sperber 1986: 73). The weakness that making such a claim exposes is that it ultimately leaves the ontological status of weak implicatures open to question (Gil 2011). That is, strictly speaking, weak implicatures cannot be regarded as "communicated" on a Relevance theoretic account, given what is communicated is determined by the hearer's recognition of the speaker's intentions, yet weak implicatures are, by definition, not specifically intended by speakers. However, such a stance seems somewhat counter-intuitive. When we speak figuratively, that is, using metaphors, metonymy, understatement (litotes), idioms, proverbs and the like, it is now well attested in the literature that such meanings are more often than not indeterminate (Gibbs and Colston 2012; Wilson and Sperber 2012). Yet it seems odd to claim that by speaking figuratively one is not communicating, but rather only "conveying" meaning. Indeed, making a distinction between communicating and conveying only makes sense in a paradigm where (inferences about) speaker's intentions are held to determine pragmatic meanings, including implicatures and nonliteral meanings (i.e. figurative meanings).[37]

Yet such issues notwithstanding, the point is well made in Relevance theory that implicatures are not always as determinate as analysts often assume. Even many of the classic examples of implicature originally posited by Grice, which have been discussed ad infinitum in the subsequent literature, have turned out to be more indeterminate than is often recognised in ongoing debates about the so-called cancellability of implicatures (Burton-Roberts 2010, 2013; Capone 2009; Feng 2013; Jaszczolt 2009b). Take, for instance, Grice's oft-quoted example of the implicature arising through the wording of a very brief testimonial written for a candidate applying for a philosophy job.

(49)   Dear Sir, Mr. X's command of English is excellent, and
       his attendance at tutorials has been regular. Yours, etc.
       (Grice [1975]1989: 33)

---

37 It is worth noting that although in Grice's ([1975]1989) original account figurative uses of language (e.g. metaphors, irony etc.) were treated as implicatures on par with other conversational implicatures, these are now generally treated as either "weak implicatures" in Relevance theory (Sperber and Wilson 1995; Wilson and Sperber 2012), or "non-literal meanings" in a neo-Gricean account (Bach 2006, 2012).

Grice ([1975]1989) originally argued that what was implicated here was that A thinks "Mr. X is no good at philosophy" (p.33). However, as Capone (2009) argues, there are in fact at least two possible implicatures that can arise here. One is that the writer does not support the candidate's application for the job. The second is that the writer thinks the candidate is not a very good philosopher. Moreover, on closer examination it turns out that both of these implicatures are, at least to some degree, indeterminate. As Capone (2009) points out, "though A could deny not having supported his student, he certainly could not assert his support" (p.57). In other words, there is indeterminacy in regard to the first implicature as to whether the writer is strongly against the candidate's application, or just indifferent (although in normal circumstances we might assume the former interpretation). As Haugh (2013b) points out, however, the second implicature is also more indeterminate than is commonly assumed. To be labelled as "not a (very) good philosopher" is not the same thing as being labelled "a poor philosopher". There is a difference of degree here in this broadly negative evaluation, and this indeterminacy affords the writer space in which to negotiate exactly what is meant by his testimonial at a later time if what he meant by it is brought into question. The writer could argue, if challenged, for instance, that he is not implying that Mr. X is a poor philosopher, but simply not saying he is a good philosopher. Not saying something good about someone is not the same as implying something bad about them. There are naturally limits to the plausible deniability of implicatures. The writer can hardly deny having implied *something* through writing the testimonial in this way. But what exactly has been implied, as well as the degree to which the writer is committed (or can be held committed) to those implicatures, can nevertheless be debated, because the precise object of those implicatures, and the speaker's stance vis-à-vis those implicatures, is inevitably indeterminate to some degree. In other words, the object(s) of implicatures, and the speaker's degree of commitment to those implicatures, may very often be indeterminate.

In this section, building on these preliminary observations, the different types of indeterminacy vis-à-vis implicatures are first considered (section 4.1). It is argued that indeterminacy is an inherent property of implicatures, because they often arise in the course of participants pursuing multiple possible understandings in interaction. And it is this characteristic that makes them so useful (and hence common) in navigating potentially delicate interpersonal interactions. The implications of this inherent indeterminacy for the degree to which participants can be held accountable for what is (taken to be) implicated is then briefly considered (section 4.2). It is suggested that through implicatures participants can position particular social actions as "avoided", "open to deniability", "deliberately ambiguous" and so on, thereby decreasing the extent to which they can be committed to or accountable for those particular social actions.

4.1 Types of indeterminacy

Implicatures are generally understood in pragmatics, as we observed in the previous chapter, as speaker-intended meaning representations that go beyond what is said by the speaker, a view that originated in Grice's seminal work on speaker meaning (i.e. meaning$_{nn}$). Specifically, implicatures are claimed to arise through inferences by the hearer about a speaker's reflexively intended mental state, namely, recognition of that speaker's belief, thought, desire, attitude, intention and so on, as intended by that speaker to be recognised by the hearer as intended. One important point to note here is that Grice's definition of speaker meaning actually creates a natural source of indeterminacy in that implicatures are determined by the reflexively intentional mental states of speakers.[38] In other words, the fact that implicatures are constituted through reflexive intentional mental states is what makes it so difficult to precisely pin down such meanings in the first place.

One kind of indeterminacy vis-à-vis implicatures, as we noted in our above discussion of example (49), concerns the object of the implicature in question (or what is here termed "type 1 indeterminacy"). Blum-Kulka and Weizman (1988) offer a very detailed discussion of this kind of indeterminacy. In the excerpt below, the analysis turns on what exactly Ruth can be taken to have implicated through her question, which follows some small-talk at the beginning of their conversation.

(50)   (Ruth and Rachel are colleagues; Ruth is a visitor in Rachel's town. Rachel expects Ruth for a visit at her home in the afternoon. Ruth calls Rachel in the morning)

   1   Ruth: I realise now that we won't have the car today.
               Can you tell us how to get to your place by bus?

   2   Rachel: It's Bus no. 7, but it does not run very frequently,
               I think you'd better take a cab.
   (Blum-Kulka and Weizman 1988: 220)

Ruth's question is formulated as a conventionally indirect request for information. However, the fact that Ruth brings up not having a car, and Rachel subsequently suggests that Ruth take a taxi instead of the bus, because "it does

---

38 Grice himself arguably avoided the issue of the indeterminacy of implicatures by positing the additional notion of implicatum which shifts such problems to the hearer, thereby treating understandings of what is meant that arise in communicative interaction and discourse more generally as a separate issue.

not run very frequently", indicates that a further layer of implicated meaning underpins this exchange. The question, then, is what exactly is being implicated here?

As Blum-Kulka and Weizman (1988: 220–229) point out, Ruth's question could be taken as implicating (specifically, *hinting*) a request that Rachel come and pick her up. According to that view, Rachel's response implicates a refusal of this implicated request, albeit attending to the implicit problem that Ruth alludes to in stating that they don't have a car. However, Ruth's question could also be taken as implicating that she would like to cancel the meeting or change the place they are planning to meet (as a consequence of not having a car and the trouble associated with taking a bus). From that view point, Rachel's response implicates a refusal to entertain this proposal, at least at this point in the interaction. Given in both cases the possible refusal is only implicated, Ruth "may conclude that Rachel failed to understand her hint" (Blum-Kulka and Weizman 1988: 229).

However, it is more likely (although not certain), given Ruth and Rachel are acquainted with each other, and so have developed relational expectations as to what they might expect of each other, that we are dealing here with what Bertuccelli Papi (2000) terms "implicitude", that is, talk "based on the assumption that a common background of shared knowledge is reciprocally accessible for referent identification" (p.149). In this case, the referent is the issue of whether expecting Ruth to take the bus to get to Rachel's place is a reasonable or appropriate expectation on Rachel's part. This opens up various possibilities, including Rachel going to pick up Ruth, changing the place or even cancelling the meeting (what Ruth might be hinting in turn 1), or taking a taxi instead (what Rachel proposes in turn 2). However, no matter how they both respectively interpreted Ruth's original question, Ruth's subsequent response is constrained by Rachel's response, given that making the request or counter-proposal more explicit could be evaluated as "impolite", or at least "inappropriate". The fundamental indeterminacy of the implicatures in this case thus allows something to be negotiated off-record (although it is quite possible that the two participants had diverging understandings of the exact nature of what was being negotiated through this off-record exchange). The interactional record thus does not always present unequivocal evidence of what is being implicated or taken to be implicated by participants, as Levinson (2013) points out.

Chang (1999) explores instances of type 1 indeterminacy in the course of an ethnographic study of indirect meanings amongst in-laws in Taiwan. What is notable about this study is that with a broader ethnographic understanding of the situation in which these examples arise, the analyst is able to infer with a greater degree of certainty the unstated understandings of participants. One such instance of this kind of type-1 indeterminacy as to what has been implicated arises in the following short excerpt below, which is taken from a conversation between a mother-in-law and her daughter-in-law (and translated from the original Chinese interaction by Chang):

(51) M: We are going to the department store. We'd better take a bus and take our time getting there.

D: Mom, why do you need to take a bus?
We'll take you there.
(Chang 1999: 544)

Here the mother-in-law's proposal to take a bus and "take their time" getting to the department store is treated as implicating a request that the daughter-in-law give them a lift. There is also an implicated complaint that "the couple is ignoring her" (Chang 1999: 544). However, as Chang (1999) points out, since these requests and complaints are accomplished off-record through "hinting", the daughter-in-law could have responded differently, thereby treating what the mother-in-law has said as implicating something else (p.545). For example, by responding "Mom, there is no need to take a bus – a taxi will do" (p.545), the daughter-in-law would thereby be construing the mother-in-law's prior turn as alluding to hassles associated with taking a bus to the department store, and so treatings the implicated request and complaint as not warranted in the context of their relationship (i.e. the mother-in-law is not entitled to make such requests or complaints). On the other hand, by responding "Oh, Mom. Don't tire yourself with a bus, I know you can afford a taxi!" (p.545), the daughter-in-law could attend to the mother-in-law's implicated complaint through implicating a counter-complaint, that is, her mother-in-law expects her daughter-in-law to give her rides to the department store when she can easily get herself there through by her own means. Notably, Chang (1999) characterises the exchange as a particular practice that is termed "waku" by Taiwanese, where one "puts the other in a hurtful situation by the implication that the listener is not good enough for certain things" (p.544, fn.3). The fact that there is a vernacular label for this kind of phenomenon offers evidence this constitutes a recognised practice in the context of intimate relationships.

The second type of indeterminacy vis-à-vis implicatures concerns the degree of speaker commitment to those implicatures, or what Grice ([1987]1989: 367) characterised as the ways in which "a speaker's alignment with an idea or thesis may be displayed or obscured" (which is here termed "type 2 indeterminacy").[39] Consider, for instance, an exchange in which Burton-Roberts (2010, 2013) claims the (particularised) implicatures that arise cannot be cancelled.

(52) Max: Do you ever speak to Charles?

Ann: I never speak to plagiarists.
(Burton-Roberts 2010: 151; cf. Burton-Roberts 2013: 19)

There are, in fact, at least two implicatures that potentially arise here. The first is an implicated premise (i.e. Charles is a plagiarist), while the latter is an implicated conclusion (i.e. I don't speak to Charles). The latter putative implicature can be straightforwardly cancelled with an "except for" clause (i.e. I never speak to plagiarists, except for Charles). However, the former potential implicature appears more resistant to cancellation, because if Ann attemptings to cancel the implicated conclusion in this way, she the speaker actually reinforces the implicated premise. However, on closer examination, it becomes apparent that there is in fact potential indeterminacy in regards to the speaker's degree of certainty about this suggestion. That is, the speaker is not actually, strictly speaking at least, committed to the belief that Charles is definitely a plagiarist (although Ann would commonly be taken to be so committed). For this reason, the implicature can in fact be removed by Ann simply adding something like "And I think Charles might be one", or "I am not saying that Charles is a plagiarist for sure, mind you, just that I think he probably is one", thereby indicating her uncertainty about such a claim. Max could, of course, dispute such claim by Ann about her degree of commitment to the implicated premise, but that only goes to illustrate the point being made here, namely, that implicatures are not fully determinate, which is why they can be disputed in the first place (Haugh 2013b).

Indeterminacy in regards to the speaker's degree of commitment to an implicated proposal can be observed in the following sequence where the possibility of an invitation to lunch is repeatedly hinted at in the course of implicitly negoti-

---

39 Grice termed this "dictiveness" and argued that it involves consideration of such phenomena as "the presence of absence of an appropriate measure of ardour on behalf of a thesis, a conscientious reluctance to see one's statements falsified or unconfirmed, an excessive preoccupation with what is actually or potentially noncontroversial background material, an overindulgence in caution with respect to the strength to be attributed to an idea which one propounds, and a deviousness or indirectness of expression which helps to obscure even the identity of such an idea" (Grice [1987]1989: 367).

ating this proposal. The sequence begins part-way into the telephone call when Emma asks Nancy what she is doing.[40]

(53) NB:II:2:14

```
 6   E:  Wuddiyuh ↑DOin.

 7       (0.9)

 8   N:  What'm I do[in?

 9   E:             [Cleani:ng?=

10   N:  =hh.hh I'm ironing wouldju belie:ve ↑tha:t.

11   E:  Oh: bless it[s ↓hea:rt.]

12   N:              [In fa :c  ]t I: ire I start'd ironing en I:d- I:

13       (.) Somehow er another ahrning js kind of lea:ve me:

14       co:[ld ]

15   E:      [Ye]ah,

16       (.)

17   N:  [Yihknow,  ]

18   E:  [Wanna c'm] do:wn 'av a bah:ta lu:nch with me?
```
(Drew 2005: 77; cf. Drew 1984: 131–132)

While Emma's initial inquiry about what Nancy is doing is formulated in the manner of a typical pre-invitation (Levinson 1983; Schegloff 2007), thereby implicating the possibility of a forthcoming invitation, as Drew (1984) notes, Emma's invitation in line 18 (i.e. "Wanna come down and have a bite of lunch with me?") is treated by the participants as arising as a consequence of Nancy's report. Specifically, while Nancy initially responds that she is ironing in response to Emma's query (line 10), which is ostensibly a response that blocks the issuing of an invitation by Emma, as evidenced by Emma's subsequent positive assessment of Nancy's current activities (line 11), Nancy subsequently reframes the current activity as something she has only started (line 12), thereby leaving open the possibility

---

40 There are a number of different transcriptions of this conversation that have been published (e.g. Drew 1984: 131–132, 135, 144; Drew 1995: 77–78). The transcript reproduced here draws primarily from that published in Drew (1995), although the analysis draws primarily from that of Drew (1984).

that she is not currently doing it, and moreover, that it is something that she does not like doing (lines 13–14). Given Emma's invitation follows this reformulation of Nancy's reporting of her current activities in line 18, it is interactionally managed as "an upshot of finding in that report that N[ancy] may be ambivalent about continuing with her ironing, or may have already given up on it" (Drew 1984: 132). The initial inquiry in line 6 thus implicates only the possibility of a forthcoming invitation, and so Emma's degree of commitment towards making such an invitation remains ambivalent, and thus contingent on Nancy's response.

In the interaction that follows, Emma's seemingly straightforward invitation is subsequently qualified, as Nancy's response appears to implicate a declination (cf. Haugh 2008c: 52–53):

(54)   NB:II:2:9

18   E: Wanna c'm <u>do:wn</u> 'av [a bah:ta] <u>lu</u>:nch w]ith me?=

19   N: [°It's js] (   )°]

20   E: =Ah gut s'm <u>beer</u>'n stu:ff,

21   (0.3)

22   N: ↑Wul yer ril sw<u>ee</u>t hon: uh:m

23   (.)

24   E: [Or d'y] ou 'av] sup'n [else °(   )°

25   N: [L e t-]   I :] hu. [n:No: I <u>haf</u> to: uh c<u>a</u>ll Roul's

26   m<u>o</u>ther, h I t<u>o</u>ld'er I:'d <u>call</u>'er this morning

27   I [gotta l<u>e</u>tter] from'<u>er</u> en

28   E: [°(<u>U</u>h huh.)°]

29   N: .hhhhh<u>h A</u>:nd uhm

30   (1.0)

31   N: .tch u.-So: she in the l<u>e</u>tter she said if you c<u>a</u>:n why (.)

33   y<u>i</u>h know c<u>a</u>ll me Saturday <u>morning</u> en I jst h<u>a</u>ven't. hh

34   E: °Mm[<u>hm</u>:°

35   N: [.hhhh T's like t<u>a</u>kin' a b<u>ea</u>ting. (.) mhh

36   (0.2)

37   N: kh hh ↑hnhh hnh-hnh-hnh
(Drew 2005: 77; cf. Drew 1984: 135)

As Emma issues the invitation in line 18, it becomes apparent from Nancy's overlapping talk in line 19, the subsequent pause in line 21 after Emma mentions she has some "beer" (a possible attempt at persuasion), and the well-prefaced response in line 22, that Nancy's response is being formulated as dispreferred (Pomerantz 1984a; Schegloff 2007; Pomerantz and Heritage 2013). In other words, Nancy is most likely going to decline the invitation. Indeed, Emma's subsequent response in line 24 orients to this possible implicated refusal when she reframes the invitation as more contingent (i.e. depending on what Nancy wants to do) than her previous one in line 18, and thereby not only decreases her degree of commitment to the said invitation, but also "avoids explicitly recognising and treating what N[ancy]'s reported commitment might implicate for her invitation" (Drew 1984: 136). This indeterminacy in what Emma is taken to be committed to is important, because it allows Nancy to continue on in lines 26–33 to report about the problems she is having (i.e. her ex-husband, Roul's, failure to get in touch with family), without yet resolving the course of that invitation sequence (Drew 1995: 84). As Drew (1984) points out, "E[mma] can be seen to withhold proposing a consequence of N[ancy]'s reported commitment, and thereby to resist what the reporting could be taken to imply (i.e. that N[ancy] might not be able to come for lunch" (p.136). Consequently, "a decision concerning E[mma]'s invitation is left unresolved", although this is "not because one is not stated explicitly by N[ancy] herself, but [is] a result of E[mma]'s withholding proposing an upshot" (p.136). In other words, Emma does not yet commit herself to a particular understanding of what Nancy may have implicated through her dispreferred response to Emma's invitation.

This indeterminacy underpins subsequent talk where Emma once again alludes to the prior invitation and its, as yet, unresolved status.

(55)   NB:II:2

1   E: AW:::rig[ty I don' know what ti:me izit, I- I=

2   N: [°(allri-)°

3   E: =woke up et s::six this mo:rni [g=

4   N: [Oh: [my G↑od

5   E: [God w't izit.

6   Quarter after 'leven?

7   N: Yea(n)h

8   (1.0)

9   N: Yea [(h°yeh ave got°)]

10 E: [The S U : N] S comin out(pt)

11 N: I know it.

12 E: Bee::utiful

13   [(Jus')]

14 N: [(It's)] beautiful.

15   (0.2)

16 N: So: anyway, let me uh hhh call Roul's mother,

17   (.) and uh,

18   (0.5)

19 N: [(Don't)

20 E: [Well give me a bu:zz if you- (.) u↑g'mon down if

21   you- I'd like tih have yih come down fer ...
(Drew 1984: 144)

Drew (1984) suggests that given this sequence occurs in the same call around three minutes after Emma avoided explicitly dealing with the possibility that Nancy was implicating a declination of her invitation (or least was implicating difficulties in accepting it), that Emma's question about the time (line 1), and subsequent indication that it is already late in the morning in lines 5–6 in the excerpt above, may reflect an attempt to "hint at N[ancy]'s coming over for lunch, without directly referring to or suggesting that action" (p.144). This is because by treating the time as "reportable" due to it being late in the morning, Emma can be taken as alluding to "the invitation by implicitly invoking the closeness to lunchtime" (p.145). In addition, the sequence is framed as a pre-closing to the call through the discourse marker "alright" (line 1), which "thereby occasion[s] the relevance of arrangements talk" (p.145), given the closings of calls may be initiated through making arrangements (Schegloff and Sacks 1973: 317–318). Notably, although Nancy appears to "pass over those opportunities" to reconsider Emma's invitation, Emma does not at this point develop her own talk in any other direction, nor does she allow Nancy to do so either, in making reference to the "sun coming out" (lines 10–14). Nancy's subsequent response remains indeterminate as to whether she will come for lunch or not (lines 16–17), which prompts a reissuing of the invitation by Nancy, but this time in a highly conditional form (lines 20–21). Ultimately, then, in the course of this sequence Emma is able to prompt Nancy to "initiate reconsideration of E[mma]'s earlier invitation" (p.146), as evident from Nancy's response in lines 16–17, although Emma does so in a way that leaves her degree of commitment to this implicit line of persuasion indeterminate. Nancy's degree of commitment to her implicated refusal here also remains somewhat indeterminate, in part because Emma avoids treating it as an implicated refusal.

The third type of indeterminacy vis-à-vis implicatures concerns the issue of whether something has been implicated or not in the first place (or what is here termed "type 3 indeterminacy"). In the case of some meaning-actions, such as *hinting, alluding, insinuating* and the like, some degree of plausible deniability is an inherent feature of such implicatures. In other words, being able to legitimately deny one is *hinting at, alluding to,* or *insinuating* something is a necessary (although not sufficient) condition for an implicature to be regarded as arising through *hinting, alluding* or *insinuating.* This type of indeterminacy arises, in part, because talk or conduct can be taken to implicate different things for different participants. Schegloff (1996b) alludes to this point when he claims that

> [s]ome actions, by virtue of the action which they implement vis-à-vis one interlocutor, can be understood as doing another, related action to a different interlocutor ... If I compliment a contributor to this volume as the most elegant writer on discourse, I risk insulting others who feel slighted thereby. Schegloff (1996b: 20)

The insult here arises through the fact that complimenting one contributor can be taken as scalar implicating that the other contributions are not worthy of compliment. The ubiquity of such potential scalar implicatures means that there can be, in some situations, real indeterminacy as to whether or not something has been implicated at all.

In the following example, Michael is initially held accountable for implicating something that the other participant later reported that he did not actually think Michael was implicating.

(56) (Michael and Ned have been discussing with two others who uses the instant coffee that is available in the staff tea room. Michael looks at Ned's coffee)

1 M: So you drink instant coffee.
       ((pause))

2   N: I see. You're looking down on my choice of coffee.
          ((laughter))

3   N: No, I bring my own coffee in.
          (Haugh 2013a: 52)

Through two consecutive responses to Michael's initial utterance in turn 1, Ned orients to two different interpretations of it. The first response by Ned treats it as implicating a negative assessment of Ned's choice of coffee, which is followed by laughter from others in the room who witnessed the exchange. The second response from Ned treats it as a polar interrogative that is seeking information through formulating a candidate answer to the question (Heritage and Raymond 2012; Pomerantz 1988; Raymond 2003; Stivers 2010). The question, then, is whether Michael's initial utterance *should* be treated as a request for information or as implicating a negative assessment of Ned's choice of coffee, or even both (Haugh 2013a: 52).

The laughter from the other participants present, as well as Ned's subsequent report that he thought the negative assessment was only something that *could* be taken as implicated by Michael's prior utterance, but was not actually something he had interpreted as implicated by Michael, is indicative of the fact that this implicature was treated as only a *possible* interpretation, which Michael was caught out in meaning (hence the laughter). In other words, it was the indeterminacy as to whether Michael had in fact implicated a negative assessment or not that afforded Ned's two-pronged response here.

Schegloff (1984, 2006) argues that close analysis of talk-in-interaction reveals there are often various "possible" interpretations/projections utilised in the co-construction of meaning, including "possible invitations" and "possible complaints" (and thus also "possible negative assessments"):

> The ready capacity of the participants in these exchanges to grasp another's understanding even when it is 'incorrect' suggest that they are pursuing 'possible understandings' of turns at talk – including their own turns at talk – along multiple lines, and are thereby prepared to recognize even ones arrived at by others that might have been though elusive. (Schegloff 2006: 147)

Following this train of thought, the notion of "possible understandings" can arguably be extended to social actions that are constituted through implicatures.

Indeed, the demonstrable existence of possible understandings at play in talk-in-interaction can be utilised to illustrate how a single turn at talk can be taken as implicating more than one thing. In the following interaction, for instance, Chris's question, given it follows talk by Emma about how effective acupuncture is, can be taken either as pre-request implicative or as implicating a teasing challenge, or even perhaps both (Haugh 2008a: 62–63, 2009a: 103, 2012b: 178–186).

(57)   ERCH: 8:18

>223 E: and the needles happen to be one of the most effective
>
>224   ways to (0.6) manipulate it
>
>225 C: yea:h?
>
>226 E: mmmm
>
>227 C: can you fix patellar tendonitis? °heh°
>
>228   (1.7)
>
>229 E: ↑maybe ↑ye:ah
>
>230 C: yeah?
>
>231   (0.3)
>
>232 E: yeah you got that?
>(Haugh 2012b: 178)

One possible understanding of Chris's question in line 227 is that through it he is implicating a teasing challenge. This analysis is evidenced by the fact that it is delivered with a "compressed intonation" that is characteristic of mockery (Attardo et al. 2003; Keltner et al. 2001: 324), and is appended by a laughter particle ("heh"), which is often used in orienting hearers to the possibility of joining in to laugh about a possible mocking remark (Glenn 2003; Jefferson 1979; Schenkein 1972). Emma has also been "extolling" the virtues of acupuncture up until this point, which can, as Drew (1987) points out, occasion a teasing response that treats such talk as "overdoing" something (in this case over-extolling). There is also contextual evidence in that in prior talk (around one minute before this sequence), Chris had been taken by Emma as implying he is sceptical or doubtful about the effectiveness of acupuncture (see Haugh 2012b: 183). That Chris has implicated a teasing challenge is thus indeed a possible understanding of Chris's question in line 227 at this point in the sequence.

Another possible understanding, however, is that Chris's question foreshadows a possible request sequence. In other words, Chris's question is taken as implicating a possible forthcoming request for treatment (Schegloff 2007: 62, 90; Stevanovic 2011). It is toward this possible understanding that Emma appears to orient in subsequent talk when she responds that she may be able to treat it (line 229), and then asks whether Chris has that condition (line 232), as it leaves open the possibility of Chris making the request, or Emma pre-empting such a request with an offer, which eventually she makes as it turns out (Haugh 2012b: 181–182). In this case, then, while Emma and Chris subsequently orient to an understanding of Chris's question in line 227 as pre-request implicative, and thus it is this possible understanding that is foregrounded in the interaction, the other possible understanding of it as implicating a teasing challenge remains potentially in play, albeit interactionally backgrounded. The latter thus remains indeterminate as to whether something has (been taken to have) been implicated or not.

4.2 Indeterminacy and accountability

It was briefly noted in the prior section that implicatures are generally claimed to arise from inferences about reflexively intentional mental states (in particular, the speaker's communicative intentions). The traditional cognitive account of implicatures in terms of the recognition and attribution of speaker intentions arguably neglects, however, a deontological understanding of speaker meaning as what a speaker is taken to be committed to or accountable for meaning in interaction (Haugh 2010b, 2012b, 2013a; Haugh and Jaszczolt 2012; Morency, Oswald and de Saussure 2008; Sanders 2013; although cf. Sperber et al 2010; Searle 2010). A deontological approach treats implicatures as meaning representations for which speakers are routinely held reflexively accountable. To be held accountable refers to the ways in which participants treat speakers as socially committed to or responsible for the real-world consequences of what they are taken to be implicating. The term meaning representation refers here to the reflexive intentional (i.e. directed) mental state-processes that are occasioned by talk and/or conduct. A deontological notion of speaker meaning thus goes beyond whatever the speaker may or may not have "intended" to also encompass beliefs/believing, thoughts/thinking, attitudes/evaluating, feelings, and so on (Haugh 2013a: 47).

Through implicatures speakers can reduce their degree of accountability for particular understandings and social actions that arise in interaction (Haugh 2013a; Weiser 1974, 1975). In the following interaction, for instance, Charlie is able to avoid taking full responsibility for delivering "bad news" through leaving it up to Ilene to make explicit the upshot here, namely, that he cannot give her a ride, despite having previously promised to do so.

(58)   Trip to Syracuse: 2

1   C: I spoke to the gi:r- I spoke tih Karen.

2   (0.4)

3   C: And u:m:: (.) it wz rea:lly ba:d because she decided of a:ll

4   weekends for this one tih go awa:y

5   (0.6)

6   I: Wha:t?

7   (0.4)

8   C: She decidih tih go away this weekend.

9   I: Yea:h,

10 C: .hhhh=

11 I: =.kh[h

12 C: [So tha::t yihknow I really don't have a place tuh sta:y.

13 I: .hh Oh::::: .hh

14   .hhh So yih not g'nna go up this weeken'?

15 C: Nu::h I don't think so.

16 I: How about the following weekend.

17   (0.8)

18 C: .hh Dat's the vacation isn't it?

19 I: .hhhhh Oh:. .hh ALright so:- no hassle, (.)

20   s[o

21 C: [Ye:h,

22 I: Yihkno:w::

23 (): .hhh

24 I: So we'll make it fer another ti:me then.
(Drew 1984: 130, 1995: 125)

Charlie outlines potential trouble for their planned trip to Syracuse when he reports that Karen is going away (lines 1–8), and so he doesn't have anywhere to stay (line 12). This is taken by Ilene to be implicating that Charlie won't be going on the trip (line 14). While Ilene then subsequently proposes that they go the following weekend (line 16), Charlie responds by implicating a declination of this proposal through further reporting that it's the vacation (line 18), during which presumably Charlie is not able to go. Finally, it is Ilene who makes explicit the upshot of these reports by Charlie, namely, that they can't go to Syracuse and so they'll have to go "another time" (line 24).

On two occasions in this sequence, then, Charlie avoids a particular social action, here delivering bad news, by putting "Ilene in the position of figuring out and 'announcing' the bad news", thereby leaving Charlie in the position of only having to "confirm the bad news" (Drew 1995: 125). In the first instance, it is Ilene who makes explicit the upshot of the Charlie's reporting of the circumstances surrounding his accommodation in Syracuse, namely, that Charlie will not be going that weekend. In the second, it is also Ilene who makes explicit the upshot of Charlie's reporting about the circumstances of the following weekend, namely, that it is vacation time, and so they'll have to go another time. In this way, Charlie is able to reduce his accountability for delivering the "bad news". We can see from this example, then, the way in which indeterminacy as to what is taken to be implicated can be exploited by participants in reducing their accountability for certain possible understandings on the part of other participants.

Weiser (1974, 1975) notes how such indeterminacy can be exploited through what she terms "deliberate ambiguity" and "selection by reply". The former practice, deliberate ambiguity, refers to talk by a speaker that implicates more than one possible understanding, but through the response from the other party, the speaker is able to work out which states of affairs holds or is allowable (Weiser 1974). She offers the example of a situation where "A wants to know about what happened in a committee hearing, but B strictly speaking is not allowed to talk about it" (p.725). She suggests that an utterance such as "I'm curious about what went on at the hearing" (p.725) is ambiguous as to whether it is meant as an indirect request for information or simply as reporting the speaker's current state of mind, although in not expecting such information to be forthcoming, it thereby implicates some frustration about that state of affairs. In such instances, A has recourse to plausible deniability, as if accused of implicating the former, she can respond "Oh, but I wasn't asking you to *tell* me! I was just saying I'm curious" (p.725).

The latter practice, selection by reply, refers to instances where a speaker focuses on a prior utterance that has given rise to two (or more) possible understandings, and selects the "preferred" understanding (Weiser 1975). For instance, by saying something like "I probably shouldn't ask you in for a drink" at the end of a date, the speaker leaves open two possible understandings, a wistful expression of regret in regards to an aborted proposal or an implicated invitation. The subsequent response from the other party therefore "selects" the preferred understanding for him or her, in a way that allows both parties to avoid the embarrassment of an outright refusal, then, a possible proposal (cf. Weiser 1975: 656). The point Weiser (1974, 1975) makes is that in situations where two (or more) understandings can be implicated, although the speaker may only intend one to be ultimately attended to by the other participant, he or she does not know which one it will be, as it is left up to the recipient to choose how to interpret the speaker's utterance. In this way, the speaker's degree of accountability for implicating something is significantly reduced.

Whether speakers are held accountable for a particular implicature (or set of implicatures) can, of course, be disputed. In the following interaction, two classmates, Jane and Sandra, are talking about Sandra's proposal to skip the next tutorial. Sandra mentions there's a guy in the class that she's "pretty scared of", which appears to be framed as an account as to why she doesn't want to go to class.[41]

(59)   Brown 2013: 0:45

    32 J: but why are you scared of him?

    33 S: hhh because last time I used to like he used to talk to

    34   me a <u>lo</u>:t?

    35 J: yea<u>:</u>h

    36 S: <u>t</u>oo much

    37   and >then I was< like <°ok<u>a::</u>y°>

    38   [heh]

    39 J: [o:]h <u>co</u>me on, not every guy that talks to you

    40   is in love with ya.

    41 S: >NO no no!< NOT in LOVE with me!

    42   but it's li:ke (1.1) >no just because<

---

41 Thanks to Jessica Brown for permission to use this example.

43   Jeff s(h)ai(h)d so(h)me(h)thing,

44   and it was like mm two:, two weeks ago.

45   and I don't wanna be like (0.5) by myself

46   (0.6)

47   J: around him

48   S: yea'

When questioned by Jessica why she's scared of the guy, Sandra responds that he talks to her "a lot" (line 34), which is then subsequently upgraded to "too much" (line 36). This is then followed by an ironic evaluation of this state of affairs" indicated through a stretched "oka::y" (line 37). The upshot here is left attenuated by Sandra, however, although it appears that she is implying she is the object of unwanted attention (hence the proposal to skip class and avoid the guy). Jane, however, responds by attributing an implicated premise to Sandra, namely, her assumption that because the guy is talking to her a lot, that he is in "love with her" (lines 39–40), an assumption about which she takes a somewhat mocking stance. In other words, through her response, Jane holds Sandra accountable for *supposing* that this guy is in "love with her" because he is reported by Sandra as talking to her "a lot" (or even "too much"). However, Sandra subsequently disputes the attribution of this implicated premise (line 41), claiming that she is treating this as "unwanted attention" because of something "Jeff said" (lines 42–44), and it is this which has made her want to avoid the guy (line 45).

From this example, then, we can see how an implicature attributed to one participant can be disputed by that participant because of the negative implications for his/her person in being held accountable for meaning such a thing. This also, once again, underscores the way in which implicatures can be relatively indeterminate, despite arising in locally, situated interactions where participants are able to maintain a coherent action trajectory. Indeed, without such indeterminacy, implicatures could not be legitimately disputed in the first place.

One theme that has been consistently alluded to throughout this chapter, then, is that speakers can be held accountable for implicatures to varying degrees. Or to put it another way, through implicatures speakers can position particular social actions as "avoided", "open to deniability", "deliberately ambiguous" and so on. Furthermore, through implicatures, participants can implicitly orient to moral concerns such as rights, obligations, responsibilities, permissibility and the like, or to as the way in which it casts their persons or "social image" in that particular, situated interaction. As Chang (1999) has argued implicatures provide opportunities for interactants "to protect and serve their own ends", yet also allows them "considerable flexibility in negotiating relational position and role behaviour within the confines of a relational system" (p.535). It is to such concerns that we will now turn in starting to consider the relationship between implicatures and im/politeness in more detail in the following chapter.

Chapter Four:
Implicature, im/politeness and social practice

In previous chapter we discussed the relationship between implicatures, social action and accountability. It was argued that implicatures are inevitably indeterminate to some degree, because they are constituted through reflexively intentional state-processes (cf. implicatum). Yet implicatures are nevertheless meanings for which participants can be held accountable, because of the ways in which they arise as objects of social action, as well as constituting a form of social action in and of themselves (cf. implicature). In outlining how speakers can be held accountable for implicatures, and how speakers may attempt to modulate their degree of accountability through implicatures, we briefly alluded to relational or interpersonal issues, that is, the ways in which participants can implicitly orient to moral concerns, such as rights, obligations, responsibilities, permissibility and the like. It was suggested that grounding the analysis of implicatures in interaction draws analytical attention to the ways in which users consistently attend to the interpersonal implications of what speakers are taken to be implicating, the fact they are implicating something, and how they are implicating it. Such interpersonal concerns arguably need to be incorporated into a comprehensive theory of implicature.

In this chapter, and the one that follows, we thus move to consider the *moral* grounding of implicatures, focusing in particular on the intersection between implicatures and im/politeness. In doing so, we also return to consider in more detail some of the issues raised in our discussion in Chapter Two, including debates about the various types of implicature proposed by (neo-)Griceans and the pared-down Relevance theoretic conceptualisation of implicature, as well as the issue of whether im/politeness itself constitutes a type of implicature. It is argued in the course of these two chapters that while politeness, impoliteness, mock impoliteness, over-politeness and so on do indeed have an intimate relationship with implicature, as originally proposed by Searle, Brown and Levinson, Leech and others, as we discussed in Chapter One, this relationship is much more complex and nuanced than originally anticipated.

However, before starting to consider the relationship between implicature and im/politeness in more detail, this chapter begins, in section one, by considering the broader interpersonal milieu in which implicatures arise drawing from the threads that emerged from the discussion of implicatures vis-à-vis social action in Chapter Three. In section two, we then return to discuss in more detail a claim that was alluded to in passing in Chapter Two, namely, that im/politeness itself constitutes an implicature. It is subsequently argued, in section three, that such an approach is problematic on two counts. First, it confounds two conceptually distinct phenomena, namely, implicatures, which are the object of social actions, and im/politeness, which are attitudinal evaluations occasioned by implicatures (and by social actions more generally). Second, it leaves us unable to explain why implicatures can give rise to im/politeness in the first place. Finally, in section four, a proposal for how im/politeness itself can be theorised vis-à-vis social practice, and consequently how there are inevitably multiple perspectives in which evaluations of im/politeness can be grounded is outlined (Haugh 2012b, 2013c; Kádár and Haugh 2013). This lays the groundwork for the framework introduced in the following chapter, where it is proposed that im/politeness implicatures themselves be analysed as a form of social practice that arises in and through locally situated interactional contexts.

1 Implicature, relationality and (im)propriety

In the previous two chapters we briefly touched upon the various ways in which through implicatures participants can display a concern for interpersonal relationships, issues of propriety, and so on. In this section, it is argued that im/politeness represents just one aspect of this broader interpersonal context, albeit an important one, and so any analysis of (im)politeness needs to be grounded in a broader perspective that takes into account the relational or inter-personal work achieved through participants orienting to or invoking (im)politeness.

In the following interaction, for instance, we can observe the broader relational milieu in which issues of (im)propriety arise. In this excerpt, an understanding by the participants, Donnie and Marica, of what is being requested and subsequently refused arises without Donnie actually explicitly requesting or Marcia explicitly refusing to give Donnie a ride (Schegloff 1995; cf. Geis 1995: 210; Haugh 2008c: 55–56; Levinson 2013: 116; Mandelbaum and Pomerantz 1991: 153–154; Schegloff 2007: 64–65; Sidnell 2010: 10; Wong and Waring 2010: 86–87). Given the object of these two social actions remains unsaid, that is, they arise through "hinting" and "implying", respectively, we are arguably dealing here with instances of implicature. However, not only do these implicatures arise through an interactional trajectory that is actively shaped by both participants, the way in which this trajectory develops is indicative of an orientation by both participants to concerns that go beyond the immediate interactional project (i.e. Donnie's implicit request), to a concern for issues of propriety and implications for their ongoing relationship.

(60) MDE: Stalled

   2 M: Hello?

   3 D: 'lo <u>Ma</u>rcia,

   4 M: Yea [:h   ]

   5 D: [('t's) D]onny.

   6 M: Hi Donny.

   7 D: Guess what .hh

   8 M: What.

   9 D   .hh My c<u>a</u>:r is st<u>a</u>::lled.

  10   (0.2)

  11 D: ('n) I'm up here in the Glen?

  12 M: O<u>h</u>::.

  13   [(0.4)]

  14 D: [.hhh]

  15 D: A:nd .hh

  16   (0.2)

  17   I don' know if it's: po:ssible, but .hhh see

  18   I haveta open up the b<u>a</u>:nk.hh

  19   (0.3)

  20 D: a:t uh: (.) in Brentwood?hh=

  21 M: =Yea<u>h</u>:- en I know you want- (.) en I whoa- (.) en I

  22   <u>wo</u>uld, but- except I've gotta leave in about five

  23   min(h)utes. [(hheh)

  24 D: [Okay then I gotta call somebody

  25   else.right away.

  26   (.)

  27 D: Okay?=

28 M: =Okay [Don   ]

29 D: [Thanks] a lot.=Bye-.

30 M: By<u>e</u>:.
(Schegloff 1995: 193)

The phone call opens with a recognisable pre-announcement in line 7 that foreshadows delivery of urgent news, given its position at the beginning of the call without any preceding "howareyous", and its "rushed, charged, almost breathless quality" (Schegloff 1995: 195). Following the go-ahead response from Marcia (line 8), Donnie announces the news, namely, that his car is stalled (line 9). Notably, this telling is not followed by any indication of "information uptake", either through "registering the information as new through *oh*" or through an assessment of Donnie's telling (*ibid.*: 197). This is then followed by a reporting of his current situation, namely, that he is up in "the Glen" (line 11). Given the way in which this reporting is framed as urgent, it appears that Donnie is making "a remedy or help of the offer of a remedy or help" (*ibid.*: 198) contingently relevant. However, while it is left to Marcia to "extract the upshot and the consequent appropriate response" (*ibid.*: 206, fn.16) to this reporting (cf. Drew 1984), Marcia responds by simply registering this as new information through an elongated "oh" (line 12). In lines 15–20 that follow, Donnie incrementally adds to these prior reportings in "a multiply renewed effort (or series of efforts) to elicit help from Marcia, without ever requesting it (as we say in the vernacular) explicitly" (Schegloff 1995: 199), although the use of "parenthetical inserts" (e.g. line 17) also portends "incipient disagreement or rejection" (*ibid.*: 206, fn.18). Yet despite multiple points at which "an offer of help" from Marcia "might be relevant", no such offer is forthcoming (*ibid.*: 199). Instead, in lines 21–23 Marcia explicitly makes reference to an underlying project or agenda on Donnie's part, and then follows with an account of her current situation, namely, she has to leave very soon herself. Thus, without actually saying what project is involved here, Marcia displays "her understanding that a solicitation of help was being made relevant ('en I know what you want') and that she would ordinarily comply ('en I would'), but for a disabling circumstance" (*ibid.*: 200–201).

Yet while such an analysis illustrates how the request and the subsequent refusal of the request is achieved through implicatures, that is, through Donnie initially hinting, and subsequently implying, that he would like some help, and Marcia implying that she is not able to offer that help, it leaves the core CA question of "why that now" somewhat unanswered. In other words, *why* is it that Ronny "provid[es] for help to be offered without requesting it explicitly", and *why* is it that Sheila "declines to offer help, without ever saying 'no.'" (Schegloff

1995: 200). Schegloff (1988b) himself appears to take a strong line against any explanation vis-à-vis the notions of "impoliteness", "rudeness" or "incivility", or at least so far as they are invoked by Goffman:

> Such notions as impoliteness or rudeness need to be recognised as parts of the *vernacular culture* which is the mark of competent membership in the society. They are parts of the apparatus of social control, used for the treatment of occasional violations, lapses, violators, the prospects of which are used to socialise new members to avoid the behaviour which will earn them, and their families or social groups, such epithets.

> But the vernacular culture's proper business concerns the *running* of the society, not the building of a discipline for its rigorous description. 'Impoliteness' and 'incivility' may work as vernacular accounts of *occasional lapses* in the turn-taking order (and other orders), but do not serve as an account for the existence and character of *the orders themselves*. The fact that violations of some normative structure may be labelled in some fashion does not account for why there was a normative structure there in the first place, or why *that* normative structure. (Schegloff 1988b: 98, original emphasis)

Yet while Schegloff appears to argue strongly against invoking matters of im/politeness or in/civility in analysing interaction in his critique of Goffman's work, closer examination of the CA literature suggests that relational and moral matters are in fact demonstrably oriented to by participants in the guise of references to "preference organisation" (Pomerantz 1984a; Pomerantz and Heritage 2013), "affiliation" (Heritage 1984a; Lindström and Sorjonen 2013), "entitlements" (Curl and Drew 2008), "epistemic rights and authority" (Heritage 2012a; Stivers, Mondada and Steensig 2011), "delicacy" (Drew and Holt 1988; Lerner 2013), "improper talk" (Jefferson, Sacks and Schegloff 1987: 160), "relationship (categories)" (Bolden 2006; Pomerantz and Mandelbaum 2005), and even in explicit references to "face" (Heritage 1984a: 268; Heritage and Raymond 2005: 16; Lerner 1996; Robinson 2006), and "im/impoliteness" itself (Bayraktaroğlu and Sifianou 2012; Cook 2006; Ferenčík 2007; Goodwin and Heritage 1990: 296–300; Hutchby 2008; Merrison 2011; Piirainen-Marsh 2005). In explaining the notion of "preference" vis-à-vis assessments, for example, Pomerantz (1984a) argues that

> across different situations, conversants orient to their agreeing with one another as comfortable, supportive, reinforcing, perhaps as being sociable and as showing that they are like-minded ... across a variety of situations conversants orient to their disagreeing with one another as uncomfortable, unpleasant, difficult, risking threat, insult, or offense. (Pomerantz 1984a: 77)

In principle, then, there is no reason why issues of im/politeness, and thus im/politeness implicatures, cannot be analysed in a manner that is consistent with the epistemological commitments of CA (Arundale 2006, 2010a). What Schegloff

(1988b) can be taken to be arguing against, then, is "the depiction of an organisation of interaction [by Goffman] which is driven by, whose *raison d'etre* is, the individual and his/her interest – namely 'face'" (p.95), and not against a consideration of moral and relational matters per se in interaction.

Mandelbaum and Pomertanz (1991), for instance, suggest in their analysis of the above interaction that while getting help is the primary concern that drives the organisation of this interactional sequence, or what might be labelled the project in CA parlance, there are also contingent concerns that can be inferred from Donnie and Marcia's conduct. And it is these continent concerns that arguably enable Donnie and Marcia to recognise how each is implicating their respective positions on that project. The issue here, then, is the analytical question of *how* we approach matters of im/politeness vis-à-vis the interactional achievement of social actions and meanings, including, of course, implicatures.

On Donnie's part, we can find evidence that he is implicitly orienting to issues of relational entitlements from the way in which he formulates that request.[42] Through only *hinting* at what he would like Marcia to do (lines 9, 11), and subsequently *implying* in such a way that portends "incipient rejection" (lines 15–20), not only is Donnie is treating the implicated request as dispreferred (Robinson and Bolden 2010; Sacks 1992; Schegloff 2007), he is also leaving it up to Marcia to "extract the upshot" and figure out the "appropriate response", namely, offering help. In leaving the upshot of the reporting up to Marcia, Donnie thereby signals a lower degree of entitlement to be making such a request (Curl and Drew 2008), as well decreasing the degree to which he can be held accountable for making a request in the first place (Pomerantz and Heritage 2013: 219–220). This is also evidenced by his immediate uptake of her implicated refusal (lines 24–25), which takes place without him either questioning or challenging it (Mandelbaum and Pomerantz 1991). In addition, in offering "a basis that [Marcia] might have for not helping him that minimized the potential *offensiveness* of her not helping him out" (Mandelbaum and Pomerantz 1991: 156, emphasis added), that is, "I don't know if it's possible" (line 17), Donnie indicates an orientation to the possible relational repercussions of Marcia not offering the help in question, namely, it could be seen as offensive.

On Marcia's part, we can also find evidence that she is orienting to a concern for their ongoing relationship. This can be inferred from the way in which she displays "a sympathetic and friendly attitude toward his asking" (Mandelbaum and

---

42 cf. Mandelbaum and Pomerantz (1991) who characterise this concern on Donnie's part as "trying to minimize the degree to which he was imposing on [Marcia]" (p.155), thereby alluding to Brown and Levinson's notion of negative face.

Pomerantz 1991: 155). This is partly evidenced from the way in which the impli-cated refusal is produced with disfluency (that is, with multiple restarts), which is "interpretable as a show of discomfort at turning him down" (*ibid*.: 158). It is also evidenced by the content of the account itself, namely, the claim to be willing to undertake the favour (lines 21–22), but an inability to do so due to circumstances beyond her control (lines 22–23) (*ibid*.: 157–158). In addition, by formulating the response as dispreferred (Davidson 1984; Pomerantz and Heritage 2013), and also in implying rather than saying she is not able to help, Marcia indicates her reluctance to refuse Donnie's implicated request. In this way, she also displays an orientation to the possible relational repercussions of not offering the help in question, namely, she could be perceived by Donnie as unconcerned about his plight, and so not sufficiently concerned with maintaining their ongoing relation-ship. The latter could, of course, also be interpreted as offensive by Donnie given they are evidently well acquainted enough for Donnie to assume it is legitimate to be making such a last-minute request for help in the first place (albeit impli-cated). Both Donnie and Marcia are thus evidently orienting to inherently moral concerns here, including Donnie's degree of relational entitlement to make such a request, and Marica's degree of relational obligation to grant such a request, alongside an orientation to the interactional contingencies of the moment in question. Notably, these concerns all evidently turn on the potential offence that could arise from a refusal of the project in question, namely, Donnie's request for help.

However, while there are evidently a number of different relational and inter-personal concerns at play in the above example, the focus in the remainder of this book is more specifically on the notion of im/politeness implicature, that is, where im/politeness arises through implicating. While various kinds of rela-tional implicatures can arise in interaction, a point to which we will return in the penultimate chapter of this book, it will be argued that im/politeness impli-catures themselves play a pivotal role in the constitution of relationships over time in many cases. This is because im/politeness involves taking into account "the feelings of others as to how they think they should be treated in working out and maintaining our sense of personhood as well as our interpersonal relation-ships with others" (Kádár and Haugh 2013: 1). Being perceived as polite at the right time, or impolite at the wrong time, for instance, can be highly consequen-tial for the development or maintenance of interpersonal relationships. In the view being forwarded here, then, im/politeness implicatures constitute only one element of the broader tapestry of interpersonal relationships, although arguably an important one. In the remainder of this chapter we thus move to consider more deeply the relationship between implicatures and im/politeness.

2 Politeness as implicature

The claim that politeness itself constitutes an implicature is a view most readily attributed to (neo-)Gricean accounts of implicature, as was briefly noted in Chapter Two (section 1.2.3). Brown and Levinson (1987: 6, 95), for instance, have claimed that politeness arises through the hearer attributing a "polite intention" to the speaker in the form of a particularised implicature (see also Brown 1995: 169, 2001: 11623). As Bertuccelli Papi (2000) points out, however, these inferences do not constitute "face" as such, but rather involve "feelings that are related to the possibility of losing or enhancing one's face" (p.78). Indeed, as Brown (2001) also argues,

> polite utterances are not necessarily communicating 'real' feelings about another's social persona, but [are] expressing contextually-expected concern for face. This concern is an *'implicature'*, an inference of polite intentions, not a feature inextricably attached to particular linguistic forms. Politeness is ascribed to a *speech act*, or to an *interactional move* (if you prefer), not to a strategy or its linguistic realization per se. (Brown 2001: 11623, original emphasis)

In Brown and Levinson's account, then, politeness-as-implicature arises through particularised or nonce inferences about the speaker's "polite" intentions vis-à-vis positive and negative face. The content of this politeness-as-implicature is, as Pfister (2010) points out, something like "I intend to be polite" (Fraser 1990: 228) or, more specifically, "I'm intending to be polite here by showing I'm sensitive to your face needs" (Fraser 2005: 66, cited in Pfister 2010: 1268). This treatment of politeness-as-implicature is extended by Levinson (1979, 1983), who argues that politeness arises through conventional implicatures in the case of honorifics (see Chapter Two, section 1.2.1).

Leech (1983) also retains the politeness-as-implicature assumption in his approach, but proposes that these implicatures arise from utterances, which although sometimes in conflict with Grice's Cooperative Principle, are nevertheless consistent with the Principle of Politeness: "Minimise (other things being equal) the expression of impolite beliefs" and "Maximise (other things being equal) the expression of polite beliefs" (p.81).[43] The Politeness Principle is elaborated by Leech (1983), analogous to the conversational maxims, through six politeness maxims:[44]

---

43 This has subsequently been reformulated as the Grand Strategy of Politeness: "In order to be polite, S expresses or implies meanings which associate a high value with what pertains to O (other person(s), mainly the addressee) or associates a low value with what pertains to S (self, speaker)" (Leech 2007: 181).
44 These were subsequently re-organised in Leech's (2007: 182) revised list of pragmatic constraints that follow from the Grand Strategy of Politeness, namely: Generosity/Tact (place high

tact maxim (minimise cost to other; maximise benefit to other), generosity maxim (minimise benefit to self; maximise cost to self), approbation maxim (minimise dispraise of others; maximise praise of others), modesty maxim (minimise praise of self; maximise dispraise of self), agreement maxim (minimise disagreement between self and other; maximise agreement between self and other), sympathy (minimise antipathy between self and other; maximise sympathy between self and other). (Leech 1983: 132)

It is claimed that the Politeness Principle and attendant polite maxims can explain not only why implicatures arise (and in that sense complements the Cooperative Principle), but also explain instances where implicatures arise despite the conversational maxims being ostensibly fulfilled (Leech 1983: 80).

In the following excerpt, for instance, Leech argues that the response orients to an implicated accusation, but that this reading is only interpretable with reference to the Politeness Principle

(61)   A: Someone's eaten the icing off the cake.

        B: It wasn't *me*.
        (Leech 1983: 80, original emphasis)

It is argued by Leech that an implicature only arises from A's assertion if one assumes that he is adhering to the approbation maxim, in this case, suppressing a potentially offensive accusation towards B.

Leech (1983) also argues that the degree of politeness associated with various forms can be explained with reference to politeness-as-implicature. However, he diverges from Brown and Levinson's focus on attributing polite intentions to the speaker, in focusing instead on the attribution of polite beliefs (a move echoed in Terkourafi's [2001, 2005] subsequent work). He suggests that the following utterances would be perceived as increasingly polite because of the attribution of polite beliefs arising through implicatures.

(62)   a.   Will you have anything to eat?

        b.   Will you have something to eat?

        c.   Won't you have anything to eat?

---

value on O's wants and low value on S's wants), Approbation/Modesty (place high value on O's qualities and low value on S's qualities), Obligation (place high value on S's obligation to O and low value on O's obligation to S), Opinion (place high value on O's opinions and low value on S's opinions) and Feeling (place high value on O's feelings and low value on S's feelings).

d. Won't you have something to eat?
(Leech 1983: 169, 171)

According to Leech (1983), utterance (62b) is interpretable as more "polite" than utterance (62a), because the former implicates a "polite belief", namely, that the "s assumes [or believes h to assume] that h wants something to eat" (p.170), consistent with the generosity maxim (where s refers to speaker, and h refers to hearer). Utterance (62c) is argued to be more "polite" than utterances (62b) and (62a), in turn, because it gives rise to two implicatures, namely, the speaker's belief that it is polite to offer someone something (consistent with the generosity maxim), and the hearer's belief that it is more polite to decline than to accept an offer (consistent with the tact maxim). This is argued to be "doubly polite because it pays the hearer the compliment of assuming he is being polite. It gives the hearer a chance to withdraw of suppress a polite refusal" (Leech 1983: 170). Finally, utterance (62d), in turn, is argued to be even more "polite" than utterances (62c), (62b) and (62a),

> because it countermands the hearer's polite assumption (or the hearer's anticipated refusal) by an equally strong polite assumption on the part of the speaker: the speaker refuses, as it were, to accept the politeness of the hearer, since to do so would involve himself in being impolite at further remove. (Leech 1983: 170)

In other words, the latter utterance (62d) gives rise to three implicatures: the speaker's belief that it is polite to offer someone something (consistent with the generosity maxim), the hearer's belief that it is more polite to decline than to accept an offer (consistent with the tact maxim), and the speaker's belief that it is polite to reject the hearer's anticipated polite refusal of the offer (consistent with the generosity maxim). According to Leech, such politeness-as-implicatures can be generated ad infinitum, at least in theory.

Yet while it is not often very well appreciated in the literature, Leech (1983) further claimed that *im*politeness arises through implicatures in proposing the Irony Principle, whereby speakers can implicate "offence", as briefly noted in Chapter Two (section 1.2.3). He also observed that increasingly indirect accusations are actually more impolite than an "ordinary yes-no question" (*ibid.*: 171). For instance, the following utterances are argued to not only be increasingly indirect but also "progressively more impolite" by Leech.

(63) a. Have you anything to declare?

b. Have you something to declare?

c. Haven't you anything to declare?

d. Haven't you something to declare?
(Leech 1983: 160)

In other words, the attribution of increasing number of impolite beliefs (i.e. impoliteness-as-implicature) leads to a perception that these utterances are increasingly impolite, in a manner analogous to the attribution of polite beliefs (i.e. politeness-as-implicature).

Both Brown and Levinson's (1987) and Leech's (1983) approaches have been challenged, however, in subsequent neo-Gricean developments of the basic claim that im/politeness itself constitutes an implicature (Culpeper 2011a; Kallia 2004; Pfister 2010; Terkourafi 2001, 2003, 2005). One key problem with the view that politeness arises through particularised implicatures, according to a number of subsequent accounts, is that it does not accord with the well-versed claim that politeness is more often than not seen but unnoticed, and thus generally anticipated in interaction, rather than arising through inferences about the speaker's particular intentions at that moment in time (Escandell-Vidal 1998; Fraser 2005; Haugh 2003; Jary 1998; Kasper 1990; Kingwell 1993; Terkourafi 2003). It also does not necessarily accord with the observation that speakers can be perceived as both unintentionally polite and unintentionally impolite (Pfister 2010: 1270; see also Terkourafi 2001).

The emphasis on politeness as largely anticipated, as opposed to being inferred, has been developed in two key ways. In one approach to politeness-as-anticipated, it has been argued that the largely seen but unnoticed quality of politeness can be explained through subsuming politeness maxims under an expanded version of the Cooperative Principle (Kallia 2004; cf. Pfister 2010).[45] The maxim of politeness is reformulated as follows:

> Be appropriately polite (i.e. politic in Watts' sense) in form (choice of how) and content (choice of what).
> – Submaxim 1: Do not be more polite than expected.
> – Submaxim 2: Do not be less polite than expected. (Kallia 2004: 161)

---

45 Pfister (2010) takes Kallia's (2004) approach in a somewhat different direction in suggesting that the maxim of politeness consists of two directives: "do not impose on the hearer (avoid unnecessary imposition) and "show approval of the desires and actions of the hearer" (p.1277). However, given his formulation of the politeness maxims bears more than a passing resemblance to Brown and Levinson's (1987) original formulation of negative and positive face respectively, it appears that Pfister (2010) is taking the maxims approach to politeness back full circle to Brown and Levinson's original claims about face, in spite of his purported critique of Brown and Levinson's approach (p.1270).

Kallia's claim is that standard particularised implicatures arise when speakers observe the maxim of politeness, but since these standard implicatures (cf. Levinson 1983: 104) are "weak background messages" to the effect that the speaker is "being polite", these are generally not noticed (Kallia 2004: 161). Kallia suggests that politeness-as-implicature, on the other hand, can arise through clashes between the politeness maxim and other conversational maxims, as well as through flouting the politeness maxim itself (e.g. being more polite than expected). Being polite, in Kallia's account, involves the hearer recognising implicated polite claims, such as "I share your feelings", "I like you", "I respect you", "we belong to the same group" and so on (*ibid.*: 162). It is further claimed that instances of impoliteness-as-implicature arise through being more polite than expected, as well as through being less polite than expected, although Kallia does not offer any principled way of distinguishing between cases where being more polite than expected gives rise to impoliteness as opposed to politeness.

Kallia's (2004) treatment of politeness as arising relative to what is expected by participants is largely echoed in the Relevance theoretic treatment of politeness (Christie 2007; Jary 1998; Padilla Cruz 2007; Ruhi 2007, 2008). According to Jary (1998), for instance, "behaviour that is compatible with the hearer's assumptions ... is not relevant enough for the hearer to pay attention to it and, hence, will not be marked in terms of politeness" (cited in Padilla Cruz 2007: 352), and so it is only behaviour that is "incompatible with the hearer's assumptions ... [which] will be relevant enough for the hearer to pay attention to it because it evidences that the speaker is being more (im)polite that expected (ibid.: 352). However, in Relevance theory, (im)politeness is argued to be constituted through higher-level explicatures, where the proposition expressed (either through explicature or implicature) is embedded under a propositional-attitude descriptor (Wilson and Sperber 1993), rather than through implicatures. Politeness thus consists of a polite belief or stance that is attributed by the hearer to the proposition expressed or implicated by the speaker (Ruhi 2007, 2008; Padilla Cruz 2007). In that sense, it constitutes a "metarepresentation of speaker's meaning", where an (im)polite attitude towards that meaning is attributed to the speaker by the hearer relative to a set of background expectations and beliefs (Ruhi 2008). Such higher-order explicatures, or metarepresentations, generally remain in the background consciousness of the participants, that is, as registered but not attended to, in cases where these attitudes are consistent with convention. However, they can be brought to primary consciousness when the attributed attitude or metarepresentation of the speaker's attitude is unexpected in some way (Ruhi 2008). In the latter case, "metarepresentations of (communicative) intentions" are integrated with "evaluative metarepresentations of the interactants' social acts (e.g., being kind, considerate, rude, etc.)" (Ruhi 2008: 288).

One potential problem with the Relevance theoretic treatment of politeness-as-higher-order-explicature, however, is that it leads to a highly problematic, and as yet empirically unsupported distinction between "communicating" and "conveying" (cf. Jary's [2013] distinction between "material" and "behavioural" implicatures). Ruhi (2008), for instance, argues along exactly those lines in reference to an example of a politeness implicature analysed by Haugh (2007a: 95), where a mother says to herself that "I thought I had brought a hankie along but ..." (*Mama, hankachi motte-kita to omotta-n-da kedo ...*), to which the daughter responds by passing her a handkerchief (thereby treating the reporting as implicating a request). She claims that "any assumption that the daughter derives would not be 'communicated' but only 'conveyed" given the daughter does "not rely on speaker intention but draw[s] on background knowledge and the situation to interpret the utterance" (Ruhi 2008: 300). However, this distinction is less instructive than might first appear. In fact, the daughter reported that she believed that the mother *was* intending to solicit an offer from her, and, moreover, that this is a common practice on the part of her mother.[46] Such a practice draws, in turn, on the value placed on "attentiveness" (*kikubari*) amongst (middle class) Japanese speakers, that is, by demonstrating one is "attentive" to the needs of others, one thereby indexes a polite stance (Fukushima 2004, 2009; cf. Haugh 2007a: 95–96). To say that the implicated request here was only somehow "conveyed" rather than being "communicated" (or constituted a "material" implicature as opposed to a "behavioural" implicature in Jary's [2013] terms) thus potentially neglects two key features of this example. First, it neglects the way in which the mother was able to reduce her degree of accountability for making such a request through the interpretative indeterminacy in regards to the potential upshot of that reporting and her degree of commitment to it, a feature that lies in common with other instances of *hinting*, *alluding* and the like, which we discussed in the previous chapter. Second, it does not recognise the cultural value placed on "attentiveness" by these participants, and the way this allows for such instances to be seen as very much contributing to the conversational record by participants, albeit unofficially or off-record. Such considerations undermine the claim that the implicature (i.e. a *hint*) arising here was only "conveyed" rather than being "communicated".

In the second key approach to politeness-as-anticipated, it is argued that this largely "seen but unnoticed quality of politeness can be explained by treating politeness as arising primarily through generalised conversational implicatures relative to minimal contexts (Terkourafi 2001, 2003, 2005). According to Ter-

---

46 Although whether her mother was in reality actually intending to do so remains opaque to both the daughter and the analyst, as Haugh (2007a: 95–96) points out.

kourafi, politeness consists of a perlocutionary effect, namely, "the hearer holding the belief that the speaker is polite" (Terkourafi 2001: 127; cf. Leech 1983). Notably, in treating politeness as a perlocutionary effect that arises through implicatures, rather than an implicature per se, Terkourafi allows for the possibility that a speaker may be interpreted by a hearer as intending to be polite (i.e. an implicature of the form, "the speaker is being polite"), but nevertheless not be evaluated as such (i.e. the belief that "the speaker is polite" does not arise).

It is argued by Terkourafi (2005) that politeness arises for the most part through the "regularity of co-occurrence between linguistic expressions and frames" (p.248), and that politeness is generated in such cases through a generalised implicature relative to some kind of minimal context in most cases (cf. Escandell-Vidal 1998). Critically, she argues that given this type of generalised implicature arises because of "the addressee's previous experience of similar contexts" where the "expressions x regularly occurs", the addressee does not need to engage in "full-blown inferencing about the speaker's intention", but rather invokes a belief the addressee already holds, namely, that "in uttering expressions x the speaker is being polite" (i.e. a generalised implicature), which can give rise to a further belief that "the speaker *is* polite" (i.e. a perlocutionary effect) (Terkourafi 2005: 251). Notably, Terkourafi (2005) distinguishes between generalised conversational implicatures that are presumed relative to a minimal context (type I GCI, or *GCI), which are arguably akin to short-circuited implicatures (see Chapter Two, section 1.2.3), and Levinson's (2000) generalised conversational implicatures, which are presumed in all contexts *ceteris paribus* (type II GCI).

Terkourafi (2001, 2003) notes, however, that politeness can also arise through particularised implicatures, that is, where a hearer engages in inferencing about the speaker's intentions in cases where the speaker's utterance gives rise to two distinct implicatures, namely, it neglects the way in which the speaker's intention in making the utterance" and "the speaker's polite intention" (Terkourafi 2001: 135), or where the speaker's utterance is "ambivalent and not conventionalised for some use" (p.129). For instance, in uttering "it's hot in here", the hearer may infer that "the speaker wants me to somehow make it 'not-hot' for her", and that "the speaker is being polite", because "avoiding an explicit request gives me options and avoids imposition on my negative face" (p.135). Theorising politeness as a perlocutionary effect that arises through particularised implicature thus represents a subtle but important tweaking of Brown and Levinson's (1987) category of off record politeness strategies, while treating it as something that can also arise through generalised implicatures (*GCI) arguably constitutes an important extension of Brown and Levinson's original framework.

Culpeper (2011a) has recently argued, however, that Terkourafi's framework for analysing politeness as arising through particularised and generalised implicatures cannot be easily extended to impoliteness, as "impoliteness formulae are much less frequent than politeness formulae" (p.130), and so are not seen but noticed, but rather are very often highly salient and thus noticed by participants. Culpeper thus proposes an alternative account of impoliteness that is implicated (by speakers) or inferred (by hearers). He suggests that "implicational impoliteness" can be triggered in three main ways (Culpeper 2011a: 155–156): (1) it is marked through surface form or semantic content (i.e. form-driven), (2) there are evident mismatches between what is said or done and the context (i.e. convention-driven), or (3) inferences are triggered by "strong expectations flowing from the context" (*ibid.*: 180) (i.e. context-driven).

Form-driven implicational impoliteness arises through flouting or violating the conversational maxims (including through mimicry or echoic mention), and so overlaps with what is commonly termed *insinuation, innuendo, snide remarks* and so on in everyday discourse. The following example, for instance, was reported as arising in a conversation between friends who were meeting up in a café during the holidays after attending different universities during the prior semester:

(64)   It's cool we've got one of each ... a lawyer, a medic, an economist ... and Sue.
       (Culpeper 2011a: 159)

Culpeper argues that the utterance flouts the maxim of manner thereby giving rise to an impoliteness implication, namely, "Sue is the odd one out" (p.159).

Convention-driven implicational impoliteness is said to arise in instances where an inference is triggered by multimodal or verbal mismatch (i.e. where verbal, oral and visual elements of talk and conduct from the same speaker are inconsistent), or where talk or conduct is inconsistent with the external context. Culpeper (2011a) suggests that this kind of implicational impoliteness overlaps with what is often termed *sarcasm* and *harsh/bitter humour* in everyday discourse. For instance, a driver saying to someone who has just clamped his car, "have a good day", is interpretable as implicating the opposite given its incongruence with the context at hand (*ibid.*: 179), namely, that they are arguing about his car getting clamped.

Finally, context-driven implicational impoliteness arises when some element of the context is invoked by the speaker in order to imply something impolite. In the following interaction, for instance, the customer reported thinking that the shop assistant was implying "he [the customer] was trying to con him [the shop assistant]" by pointing to his sleeves (Culpeper 2011a: 181).

(65) Customer: You've not given me the pound.

      Shop assistant: ((abruptly)) I think I did

      Customer: Well it's not there. Look. ((opens wallet to show him))

      Shop assistant: Go like that ((points to his sleeves, gesturing to loosen them))

      Customer: ((raised volume)) See ((opens sleeve to show him))

      Shop assistant: ((hands across a pound))

      Customer: Thank you.
      (Culpeper 2011a: 181)

In this case, the perceived implication that the customer is trying to con the shop assistant, and so is dishonest, is regarded, by the customer at least, as impolite.

As Culpeper (2011a) points out, form-driven implicational impoliteness is not easily deniable (see also Bell 1997), and indeed "off-recordness in contexts where the impoliteness interpretation is clear seems not to mollify the offence: if anything, it might exacerbate it" (Culpeper 2011a: 160). However, one could go further in arguing that impoliteness, and indeed politeness, more generally is not as easily denied, retracted or clarified as are implicatures (Haugh 2007a, 2013b). In the following example, for instance, denying an impolite intention in the second utterance only serves to reinforce the sarcastic, and hence impolite, stance that has been implicated through the first utterance.

(66) (Alice and Sarah are in a crowded train. Alice, who is obviously able-bodied, is sprawled across two seats, and Sarah is standing)

      Sarah: I'm curious as to whether it would be physically possible for you to make room for someone else to sit down. Not that you *should* make room; I'm just curious.
      (Weiner 2006: 128, original emphasis)

As Haugh (2013b) points out, we can see here how the second utterance, which is formulated as a denial that she is implicating she wants Alice to move (as well as her receipting offence at Alice's conduct), does not involve correction or repair, but rather reinforcement of a sarcastic stance on the part of Sarah. In this way, the implication of an impolite attitude on the part of Sarah is reinforced rather than being cancelled.

In the following section, it will be argued that such examples point towards two problems that dog both the current neo-Gricean treatment of im/politeness-as-implicature, and the Relevance theoretic treatment of im/politeness-as-higher-order-explicature. First, treating im/politeness as a form of implicated (speaker) meaning (as opposed to arising through implicatures) arguably conflates two distinct pragmatic phenomena that should be treated as conceptually distinct. It is proposed that keeping these two phenomena conceptually distinct enables a much more nuanced account of the relationship between implicatures and im/politeness to emerge. Second, treating im/politeness as kind of implicature (or a higher-order explicature) does not address the question of *why* implicatures can give rise to politeness, impoliteness and so on in the first place. To claim that politeness arises through hearers (or speakers) attributing polite beliefs via implicatures, or higher-order explicatures, does not actually explain the moral grounds on which such attributions are made. It is thus argued that theorising im/politeness-as-evaluation opens up the key question of what is *done* with such evaluations in interaction.

3 Im/politeness as attitudinal evaluation

One key argument in favour of treating im/politeness as an evaluation is that the politeness-as-implicature approach confounds what are essentially two quite conceptually distinct phenomena. An implicature, as we have discussed in the previous two chapters, is a type of pragmatic meaning, and so pertains to what an utterance is about (cf. information) (Arundale 2010a: 2081). More specifically, an implicature encompasses a (sometimes relatively indeterminate) reflexively intentional mental state-process that is the object of the social actions achieved through talk (cf. implicatum), which not only arises coordinate with under-standings of social action in interaction, but is itself ultimately a form of social action (cf. Grice's implicate), and so is something for which speakers can be held accountable to varying degrees. In this view, implicatures are the intentional objects of social actions, where the latter refer to understandings on the part of participants as to what is getting done by producing talk in locally situated inter-actions.

An evaluation, on the other hand, involves an appraisal or assessment of persons or relationships with respect to their perceived worth or value. In CA terms, evaluations are assessments arising from "utterances that offer an evalu-ation of a referent with a clear valence (e.g. as good, bad, outrageous, tragic or funny)" (Stivers and Rossano 2012: 63). More broadly, the notion of evaluation encompasses the interpersonal or relational implications of the social actions and pragmatic meanings (including implicatures) that are interactionally achieved by participants through talk (and conduct more broadly). Evaluations in interpersonal settings thus involve the casting of persons and relationships into particular valenced (i.e., positive-neutral-negative) categories according to some kind of perceived normative scale or frame (see Kádár and Haugh [2013] for further discussion). Accordingly, evaluations not only constitute reflexively intentional mental state-processes directed at referents, specifically subjective attitudes or stances, which are distinct from interpretations of what talk is held to be about (cf. meaning), but they are also vehicles through which participants accomplish particular interactional work, and in the latter sense can also constitute intersubjective attitudinal stances.

A treatment of im/politeness as a kind of (inter)subjective attitudinal evaluation focuses our analyses on evaluations of im/politeness as they arise within situated, localised interactions, consistent with the broadly discursive turn in politeness research (Culpeper 2011a; Eelen 2001; Haugh 2007a, 2007b; Locher 2004; Locher and Watts 2005; Mills 2003; Spencer-Oatey 2005; Watts 2003; Xie 2008). Drawing from studies of "how evaluations are constructed and put together in everyday life" (Augoustinos, Walker and Donaghue 2006: 140) in both discursive psychology (e.g. Potter 1998) and CA (e.g. Goodwin and Goodwin 1987; Pomerantz 1984a), Haugh (2013c) argues that im/politeness be conceptualised as a form of "evaluative practice". In other words, im/politeness is occasioned through the interactional achievement social actions and pragmatic meanings in situated, local interactions, which have implications for the casting of persons and relationships vis-à-vis their talk or conduct as polite, impolite, mock impolite, over-polite, under-polite, neither polite nor impolite, and so on.

A key focus of analysis in theorising im/politeness as evaluative practice is on the "resources for constructing [such] evaluations", including "categories, commonplaces, interpretative repertoires" (Potter 1998: 259). Careful examination of how evaluative social actions and pragmatic meanings are interactionally achieved by participants is also critical to the analysis of evaluations of im/politeness in interaction. A further key feature of a conceptualisation of im/politeness as an attitudinal evaluation is that is not assumed that such evaluations will necessarily always be consistent across individuals from the same "social group" (as defined by traditional sociolinguistic variables), or even within the same individual over time (Haugh 2013c). As Bertuccelli Papi (2001) points out, attitudes are "not fixed or frozen" but rather are "dynamic entities, subject to modification and dynamically interacting with other components of the text" (p.260). Thus, variability in evaluations of im/politeness is to be expected, and so should be theorised as such:

evaluations are flexibly constructed to mesh with specific ongoing practices. Variation is expected as people perform different actions with their talk; for example, as they respond to assessments, align themselves with friends and differentiate themselves from enemies, and as they construct locally coherent versions of the social and moral world. (Potter 1998: 244)

What is done through evaluations of im/politeness, and the potential variability in such evaluations amongst participants, is thus foregrounded when we focus our analytical attention on how the participants themselves are evaluating implicatures vis-à-vis im/politeness.

Consider, for instance, the following excerpt from an interaction where two Australians working in a university are getting acquainted. The excerpt begins when Gary claims that he doesn't have any questions to ask Natalie, despite her prior admonishment that he needs to ask her questions as well.

(67)　NJGR: 8:00

　　　210 G: U:M I haven't got any questions to ask you actually.

　　　211　　(1.2)

　　　212 N: ↑you must be fun at parties.

　　　213 G: .hhh don't like parties

　　　214 N: no: I can imagine. ahe parties probably don't like you

　　　215　　either(h)

　　　216　　(0.6)

　　　217 G: I guess so. ↑OH NO. (0.8) people always like

　　　218　　someone they can saddle up to (2.1) talk to.

　　　219　　at least someone in the corner they can talk to.
　　　(Haugh 2011a: 178)

Gary's apparent refusal to ask her any questions is followed by pause (line 211), and subsequently an ostensibly positive assessment of how Gary would be perceived at social occasions like parties (line 212). However, given the mutually accessible knowledge that Gary has just said he does not have any questions, and the intonational emphasis on "you", this ostensibly positive assessment is hearable as implicating that Gary would not be fun at other parties (i.e. a negative assessment). Natalie also takes a negative stance towards the ostensibly positive assessment through framing it ironically (Clift 1999), and in so doing, also implicates that Gary is socially inept. It thus appears that Natalie is insulting Gary by "ascribing a negative characteristic" to him (Hay 2002: 20). This implicated negative assessment is clearly open to evaluation as "impolite", or at least "not polite", given it is interpretable as achieving an insult (cf. Culpeper 2011a: 142–143). Perhaps somewhat surprisingly, Gary responds by claiming that he doesn't "like parties" in line 213, thereby affiliating with Natalie's implicated negative assessment. This agreement is preceded though by what is hearable as incipient laughter in Gary's in-breath, which may signal here an orientation to the current situation as "sensitive or tense" (Osvaldsson 2004: 517), and so an attempt to defuse it through treating his social awkwardness as a laughable, that is, something to be laughed at (Glenn 1995, 2003). However, in taking the stance that his social awkwardness constitutes a potential laughable, Gary is distancing himself from Natalie's prior scornful stance, and so it is interpretable as mildly disaffiliative (Vöge 2008). Gary's somewhat mixed response thus occasions, in turn, a further negative assessment from Natalie, which is upgraded from only being implicated to being explicated (lines 214–215), although the scornful stance implemented through the ironic framing of this negative assessment remains given Natalie does not reciprocate Gary's prior incipient laughter, thereby passing on the opportunity to laugh with Gary about his apparent social awkwardness. Once again, while this utterance is open to evaluation as "impolite" given it is interpretable as accomplishing an insult, Gary initially agrees with the assessment in line 217, although this is subsequently retracted, and his response is reformulated as qualified disagreement (lines 217–219).

There is thus no indication on the part of either Natalie or Gary that they have interpreted this as an instance of "mock impoliteness" (Culpeper 1996, 2005; 2011a; Haugh and Bousfield 2012; Leech 1983). An analytical puzzle thus arises here as to why Gary does not appear to orient to the apparent "impolite" intent displayed by Natalie, given it appears to be a straightforward case of a prototypical impoliteness strategy, namely, "condescend, scorn, ridicule" (Bousfield 2008: 114–115; Culpeper 1996: 358; cf. Culpeper 2011a: 256). What then is Natalie doing with this negative assessment? And why does Gary not explicitly respond to Natalie's implicit sarcastic stance here, but instead appears to affiliate with these negative assessments?

These two questions are arguably inter-related in that what Natalie seems to be doing through these negative assessments is sanctioning or censuring Gary for not having any questions to ask. In other words, Natalie is treating his lack of questions as an impropriety, and so is in fact receipting offence at Gary's prior implicated refusal to ask her questions (line 210), through her subsequent implicated negative assessments in lines 212 and 214–215. This means that the insults accomplished through these implicatures are in fact framed as tit-for-tat for the perceived insult arising from Gary refusing to ask her questions. Indeed, there is interactional evidence in talk just prior to and following this excerpt from which we (as analysts) can infer that this is indeed what both the participants are understanding Natalie to be doing through these implicated negative assessments.

In the case of Natalie, she has previously invoked the moral obligation to ask questions in conversations, as can be seen in the brief excerpt below.

(68) NJGR: 7:39

195 N: .hhh right. ahehehe feel ↑free to ask me some

196   questions now. That's [the way conversations work]

197 G: [no you s- you   sho-   ]

198   you should talk to the other interviewers actually

199   °because°

200 N: I'm not an interviewer. This is supposed to be a

201   conver[sation   ]=

202 G: [OH RIGHT]

203 N: =you are as free to ask me any questions

Here it appears by asserting that Gary now has the opportunity to ask questions (lines 195–196), Natalie is implicating that Gary should ask her some questions (notably, this is not the first time she has done so in this interaction). She then frames this as a moral obligation in claiming that asking questions reciprocally is the normal way in which conversations progress (line 196). Gary implicates an incipient refusal of this implicated request (lines 197–199), however, in his subsequent response when he suggests that she needs to "talk to the other interviewers", thereby also giving rise to the implicated premise that the interaction is an "interview", and thus that it is Natalie's role to be asking the questions. Natalie orients to this implicated premise (which underpins, in turn, his implicated conclusion) by denying its applicability to this particular interaction (lines 200–201). Gary subsequently responds in line 202 by displaying an orientation to Natalie's claim (i.e. that it is a conversation not an interview) as new information for him through the markedly louder "oh" particle (Heritage 1984b; Schegloff 2007), followed by "right", which here functions as an acknowledgement of the correctness of Natalie's just prior claim (Gardner 2005: 7). Yet while Gary appears to display acceptance of Natalie's claim here (i.e. that it is a conversation not an interview), he declines to ask questions in spite of Natalie's subsequent exhortations that he should do so (line 203). Notably, then, the turn-final "actually", which is subsequently deployed by Gary (in line 210 in example [67], "I haven't got any questions to ask you actually"), orients to the way in which this implicated refusal is likely inconsistent with Natalie's probable expectations about his next interactional move (Clift 2001).

In Gary's case, we also have interactional evidence that he orients to not asking questions as an impropriety. In the excerpt below, which follows the implicated negative assessments by Natalie, Gary explicitly acknowledges the moral grounding of his obligation to ask questions in conversations.

(69)   NJGR: 8:50

    233 G: u:m yeah (0.2) ↑I honestly don't have anything to talk

    234   about really.

    235   (1.2)

    236 G: 'cept I guess (.) to be polite

Here Gary suggests that it is "polite" to ask questions (line 236), subsequent to his reiterated claim that he has nothing to talk about (lines 233–234), thereby scalar implicating that not attempting to make conversation, including through asking questions, can be evaluated as "not polite" or even "impolite". It is evident, then, that both Natalie and Gary are orienting to Gary's prior implicated refusal of Natalie's implicated request that he ask her some questions as an impropriety, thereby grounding an analysis of Natalie's implicated negative assessments as censuring or sanctioning this impropriety on Gary's part. In other words, we can see evidence here that the evaluations in question are doing particular interactional work for these participants.

Through these implicated insults, then, Natalie treats Gary's prior refusal to ask questions as an impropriety, and censures him for this impropriety. The "impolite" (or "aggressive") stance on Natalie's part is thus framed as tit-for-tat for Gary's impropriety, and so from Natalie's perspective at least, the "impolite" attitude indexed through doing insulting is perhaps warranted. Gary's response is, of course, ambivalent in the sense that while he, at least initially, affiliates with the implicated criticism, he does not orient to Natalie's "impolite" or "aggressive" stance in his responses. While he implicitly acknowledges his own conduct in not asking questions is "not polite" (line 236), it remains open to question whether Gary might subsequently treat Natalie's negative assessments as "impolite". There is no evidence, however, from his responses in that interaction to suggest that he has reached such an evaluation, and so he appears to tacitly accept (for the moment at least) that such a stance on Natalie's part is warranted given his prior improprieties (cf. Kádár and Haugh 2013: 214). In other words, Natalie's ostensibly "impolite" stance here is oriented to by both participants as responsive to the impropriety of prior talk on Gary's part, and is thus evaluated accordingly.

It should now be evident that a treatment of im/politeness as an implicature, or even as a higher-order explicature, would make an analysis of the kind of case discussed above somewhat difficult. Rather than being simply a matter of what the speaker is held accountable for meaning, issues of im/politeness and im/propriety are oriented to by the participants vis-à-vis what such evaluations are taken to be *doing* in localised, situated interactions. A treatment of im/politeness as a kind of speaker or pragmatic meaning thus does not easily account for the interactional and relational work accomplished through evaluations of im/politeness, and the ways in which participants may come to different understandings vis-à-vis those evaluative stances. In particular, it neglects to account for the ways in which evaluations of im/politeness that are occasioned by implicatures can be "agreed upon, contested, disagreed with, left uncommented, and so forth" (Haddington 2013: 4618), as long argued by proponents of the discursive approach to politeness research (e.g. Eelen 2001; Mills 2003; Watts 2003).

A second key challenge facing the politeness-as-implicature approach is that it arguably neglects to account for the ways in which implicatures themselves can occasion evaluations of im/politeness, or what are here termed im/politeness implicatures (Haugh 2007a, 2008d; cf. Huang 2012: 151, 225). In other words, such approaches do not readily explain *why* implicatures can give rise to evaluations of politeness, impoliteness, mock impoliteness, over-politeness, and so on and so forth. Brown and Levinson's (1987) approach to what they term off record politeness strategies is instructive in that respect.

According to Brown and Levinson, off-recordness arises in instances where "it is not possible to attribute only one clear communicative intention to the act. In other words, the actor leaves himself an 'out' by providing himself with a number of defensible interpretations; he cannot be held to have committed himself to just one particular interpretation of his act" (p.211). They propose that particularised conversational implicatures can thus function as off record politeness strategies, including through "hinting", "giving association clues" (cf. alluding), "presupposing", and the like. They also suggest that "off-record" communication can be

achieved through being "vague or ambiguous", such that a communicative intention cannot be straightforwardly ascribed to the speaker (p.225).[47]

A key problem with Brown and Levinson's account of off-record politeness
strategies, however, is that there is little in the way of explanation as to why
such particularised conversational implicatures or deliberate vagueness/ambi-
guity would be considered polite in the first place. They argue that "if a speaker
wants to do an FTA [face threatening act], but wants to avoid the responsibility
for doing it, he can do it off record and leave it up to the addressee to decide
how to interpret it" (Brown and Levinson 1987: 211). However, stating that one
can reduce one's responsibility or accountability for a particular social action
through implicatures does not actually explain why doing so would be considered polite. It is not made clear whether it is through showing concern for the
addressee's positive face or for their negative face that so-called polite intentions can be inferred as an implicature, or indeed whether the notions of positive and negative face more broadly are able to adequately account for perceptions of (im)politeness across different languages (e.g. Haugh 2005, 2013d; Mao
1994; Matsumoto 1988).

The examples cited by Brown and Levinson do little to enlighten the reader
either. Instances of "hinting" reported by Brown and Levinson are cited in examples (70) to (72) below.

(70) This soup's a bit bland.
      +> pass the salt

(71) It's cold in here.
      +> shut the window

(72) That window isn't open.
      +> open the window
      (Brown and Levinson 1987: 215)

According to Brown and Levinson these are examples whereby "raising the issue
of some desired act", either through indicating "motives or reasons for doing the

---

47 Brown and Levinson (1987) also argue that "conventionalised indirectness", or what might
be better termed short-circuited implicatures in neo-Gricean terms, can function as a particular
type of "negative politeness strategy", but only offer that the speaker "indicat[es] his desire to
have gone off record (to have conveyed the same thing indirectly)" (p.132) as an explanation for
why these count as polite. Such an explanation rests, however, on the arguably flawed assumption that indirectness can be equated with politeness.

act" (examples 70 and 71), or "by asserting or questioning the conditions for the act" (example 72), the speaker "invites conversational implicatures" (*ibid.*: 215). While this initial claim is plausible to be sure, it is less self-evident that these would actually count as "polite". In each case, the speaker is reporting on a potentially troubling state of affairs, namely, the taste of the soup, the temperature in the room, and the current status of the window. However, given reporting on a trouble is interpretable as orienting to a complainable (Drew and Walker 2009; Schegloff 2005), and that complaints are very often oriented to improprieties (Drew 1998), each of these examples is also interpretable as a negative assessment; in other words, a complaint, criticism or even an accusation or blaming (Pomerantz 1978b) of the other party for the current potentially troubling state of affairs.

It would, of course, depend on the particularities of the situated interaction in which such utterances appear as to how they might be interpreted. But therein lies the point: the implicatures these kinds of examples of "hinting" give rise to are not unambiguously polite.[48] We are consequently left without any clear explanation as to why such off-record strategies are considered instances of politeness in the first place, given they can just as easily occasion so-called face threats as they can mitigate them. Thus, while such implicatures can clearly have relational or interpersonal implications, whether they occasion evaluations of politeness is a distinct question that arguably remains unanswered in Brown and Levinson's account.

Other accounts of politeness vis-à-vis implicature also arguably suffer from the same problem (albeit to varying degrees). On a number of approaches, politeness is said to encompasses beliefs about the speaker and/or hearer (Leech 1983; Terkourafi 2001, 2005). Such beliefs are formulated very broadly, for instance, as "the speaker is being polite" consistent with positive or negative face needs (Terkourafi 2001: 135; cf. Terkourafi 2007), or more specifically, following the politeness maxims, as in "it is polite to offer someone something" (consistent with the generosity maxim), or "it is more polite to decline than to accept an offer" (consistent with the tact maxim) being attributed to speakers and/or addressees (Leech 1983: 170). In other accounts they are formulated as "polite claims", such as "I share your feelings", "I like you", "I respect you", "we belong to the same group" (Kallia 2004: 162), or simply as metapresentations – specifically higher-order explicatures where the propositional content of an utterance is embedded

---

48 Invoking relational distance (D) or power (P), or even the cultural value placed on "imposition" (R), does not help us much either. Rather it is only the details of locally situated interactions, and the relational histories of the participants involved, that would enable participants to come to understanding(s) of what is implicated by such examples.

under an attitudinal descriptor – of the speaker as "polite", "kind", "considerate" (Ruhi 2008: 288).

The problem with such approaches is that it is not the participants, but rather the analyst, to a large extent, who supplies the grounds on which a particular instance of talk or conduct is evaluated as im/polite. While such analytical slippage may not be considered problematic by those adhering to so-called operational definitions of im/politeness, it nevertheless opens up the question of what exactly is accomplished by analyses that are rooted in moral claims by the analyst or politeness theorist that do not take into account the understandings of participants themselves. As Eelen (2001) has argued:

> A situation in which the scientific account contradicts informants' claims and dismisses them as being 'wrong' does not represent a healthy situation. Such a practice immediately leads to a rupture between scientific and commonsense notions, causing the theory to lose its grasp on the object of analysis. In an investigation of everyday social reality informants can never be 'wrong', for the simple reason that it is their behaviour and notions we set out to examine in the first place. (Eelen 2001: 253)

In other words, if we do not orient to the understandings of participants themselves vis-à-vis im/politeness, then we open the door to analyses of artifacts generated by the theory itself. Such theoretical constructs are only useful to the extent that they illuminate pragmatic phenomenon. However, given evaluations of im/politeness are a real-world concern for participants, towards which they can be observed to be demonstrably oriented, it is evident that an account of why implicatures can give rise to im/politeness needs to be grounded in the understandings of participants themselves.

To tap into participant understanding(s) vis-à-vis im/politeness is not, however, a straightforward task. Such evaluations must be inferred, for the most part, by the analyst through careful analysis of the sequentially-grounded achievement of implicatures and related evaluative stances by participants, alongside other forms of metapragmatic evidence (Haugh 2007c; Kádár and Haugh 2013).

Consider, for instance, the following interaction that is reported by Haugh (2007a) as constituting a candidate example of a politeness implicature. In this interaction, which was overheard by the author while visiting the Edo-Tokyo museum, an attendant walks up to a visitor who had sat down on a seat and begun unwrapping her lunch to eat, and starts by issuing an explicit apology (Robinson 2004) formulated through an honorific form apology illocutionary force indicating device (IFID).

(73)   (In exhibition area at the Edo-Tokyo museum, Tokyo)

    1   A: *mōshiwake-gozai-mas-en ...mōshiwake-gozai-mas-en ...*
          excuse(Pol)-have-Pol-Neg excuse(Pol)-have-Pol-Neg
          ('I am very sorry ... I am very sorry')

    2   V: *a', ike-nai?*
          oh acceptable-Neg
          ('Oh, is this not allowed?')

    3   A: *mōshiwake-gozai-mas-en ...*
          excuse(Pol)-have-Pol-Neg
          ('I am very sorry ...')
    (adapted from Haugh 2007a: 86)

Haugh (2007a: 86) claims that through this honorific form of apology the attendant implicates that one is not allowed to eat in the exhibition area; but in implying this directive rather than saying it, an evaluation of politeness thereby appears to arise. On those grounds it is treated as an instance of a politeness implicature. The attribution of politeness, in this case, is grounded in the claim that the attendant is indicating through implicating rather than directly issuing this directive that she still respects the 'place' (i.e. *tachiba*) (Haugh 2005; cf. Haugh and Obana 2011) of the visitor, and the concommitment rights and entitlements associated with that 'place' (Haugh 2007a: 87). In other words, the attendant "shows [she] does not think badly of [the visitor] in spite of some utterance or behaviour [in this case, a directive] that could be interpreted as implying one thinks badly of them" (Haugh 2007a: 87), thereby expressing hesitancy and so reducing the illocutionary force of that directive.

    Xie (2008) counters, however, that here the analyst is actually unwittingly masquerading as the hearer, arguing that "some politeness analysts may consciously or unconsciously, take the position of the hearer in interaction and make (im)politeness evaluations themselves" (p.159). While the implication here that this is not in fact an instance of a *politeness* implicature is not well grounded by any actual counter analysis made by Xie (2008), the point is nevertheless well made that the way in which "politeness" is occasioned here through this implicature is not sufficiently grounded in the perspective of the participants themselves, and indeed is the object of glossing by the researcher (albeit grounded in emic terms) rather than detailed analysis. The point that Xie's objection implicitly raises is that it is incumbent on the analyst to demonstrate the grounds on which evaluations of im/politeness are inferred, and to also more carefully tease out the different loci of understanding vis-à-vis im/politeness at play here. In this way, a more detailed account of why implicatures can occasion im/politeness can be developed.

In this case, through a repeated explicit apology the attendant implicates a particular upshot here, namely, that the visitor is not allowed to eat in the exhibition area (i.e. an implicated informing or reminding), and so she should stop eating there (i.e. an implicated directive). However, the attendant's apology is, in fact, demonstrably oriented to two possible improprieties here. The impropriety that occasions this interaction in the first place is actually the visitor's decision to start eating her lunch in the exhibition area. It is, of course, common for eating to be prohibited inside museums and the like around the world. However, the impropriety in this case is arguably even more marked, as according to various guides to etiquette in Japan, it is uncommon to eat in public areas in Japan unless it is recognised as a specified area for eating, such as a restaurant or a designated lunch area, and so eating in public outside of such areas can be considered "impolite" or "rude", at least by some.[49] Through this implicature, then, the attendant orients to this impropriety on the part of the visitor. In other words, we can see that an implicature is used here to receipt an offence on the part of the addressee.

The other impropriety towards which the apology is directed is the implicated informing and directive on the part of the attendant. In this case, the attendant appears to be apologising for having to issue the informing and directive in the first place. This is in spite of the fact that it is commonly understood that attendants in museums are entitled to stop improprieties on the part of visitors, as such interactional work lies within their institutional role (cf. *tachiba*). Obana (2012), for instance, argues that when a request or directive lies within the recognised *tachiba*-role of the speaker, then he or she is entitled to use an imperative form such as *yoroshiku onegaishimasu* (cf. Matsumoto 1988; Pizziconi 2003). In this case, however, not only does the attendant avoid this kind of directive, through implicating it rather than using what is ostensibly allowable, namely, a directive formulated through an imperative form, but she treats this implicated informing and directive itself as an impropriety through her explicit apology. The apology is also repeated, which indicates a higher degree of commitment by the

---

49 For example: "some consider it rude to eat in public or on trains, but this is not a universally held aversion (Wikipedia 2013, http://en.wikipedia.org/wiki/Etiquette_in_Japan, accessed 25 May 2013); "In general, Japanese people don't eat or drink in public (contrary to how logical it would be for such a fast-paced society)" (Come Japan, http://www.comejapan.org/lifeinjapan/, accessed 25 May 2013); "Generally speaking, Japanese *eat* or drink in designated areas only. In most public areas (e. g., at public transportation: trains, subways, buses etc.) you are not recommended to eat something noticeable" (Top 10 Mistakes Foreigners Make in Japan, http://learn-japanese.com/foreigners-in-japan/, accessed 25 May 2013).

attendant to an evaluation of the implicated informing/directive as an impropri-ety. On those grounds, then, it is clear that the attendant is in fact orienting to this interaction as a matter of (im)propriety, and this is not simply a judgment on the part the analyst himself.[50]

We can find further evidence that the attendant is projecting a "polite" stance from the response of the visitor in line 2, and the attendant's subsequent response in line 3. In line 2, the visitor explicates part of the upshot that has been impli-cated here, namely, the informing that eating in the exhibition area is prohib-ited, thereby checking her understanding of the upshot. However, in doing so it is notable that she does not explicitly confirm the implicated directive itself, instead treats the latter as a "delicacy" (Lerner 2013), that is, orienting to "what can and *cannot be properly said* in conversation – and to when one is overstepping the limits of propriety" (p.95, emphasis added). This treatment of the implicated directive as a delicacy is reinforced in the subsequent response by the attendant, where she confirms the visitor's understanding of the implicated upshot of the prior turn through yet another implicature, where she once again orients to the "impropriety" of having issued such a directive. This thus constitutes an interest-ing case of "confirming allusions" (Schegloff 1996a), where "a recipient explic-itly formulates an understanding of what the first sayer had conveyed without saying, and the first sayer confirms that the sense that had been 'alluded to' had been conveyed without being said" (p.181), given that the "first sayer" (i.e. the attendant) confirms the upshot explicated here by the "recipient" (i.e. the visitor) through yet another implicature.

In this way, then, we can see how both participants are orienting towards what has been implicated here as occasioning "politeness". As Haugh (2007c) argues, evidence that participants are orienting to a concern for issues of polite-ness can also be inferred from identifying "the reciprocation of concern evident in the adjacent placement of expressions of concern relevant to the norms invoked in that particular interaction" (p.312; cf. Culpeper 2011b: 417). In this case, we can see evidence of this "reciprocation of concern" from the way in which both participants are orienting to the potential impropriety occasioned by implicating a directive: in the case of the attendant, through her repeated explicit apologies, and in the case of the visitor, through her confirming the upshot by only partially explicating it. We can also see the way in which they both reciprocate concern through orienting to the implicated directive as a delicacy, that is, by treating it as something that "cannot be properly said" (Lerner 2013). The potential impro-

---

50 In this case, given I was an unratified over-hearer in this instance, I naturally formed my own understanding of politeness vis-à-vis this implicature, which, for the record, was that the attendant was being "polite".

priety, and thus delicacy, of issuing a directive towards a visitor stems, in turn, from assumptions about the 'place' (*tachiba*) of customers in Japan, namely, the oft-quoted quote that the customer should be treated like a deity (*okyakusama wa kamisama desu*, 'the customer is god'), which is generally taken to mean that the customer is "always right" and so is entitled to be treated with respect (*kei'i*).[51]

In this section, it has been suggested that im/politeness is first and foremost an attitudinal evaluation through which particular interactional and interpersonal work is accomplished. In some cases, evaluations of im/politeness can be occasioned by implicatures, or what are termed here im/politeness implicatures. However, in order to better understand how implicatures give rise to politeness, impoliteness, mock impoliteness and so on, it has become evident that we need to properly ground our analysis of im/politeness itself in the interactional practices of participants themselves. In this way, we can start to account for why implicatures sometimes occasion evaluations of im/politeness, but in other cases evidently do not (cf. Xie 2008: 166, fn.11).

In the following section, we therefore move to outline how im/politeness can be theorised as social practice, focusing, in particular, on its moral grounding. This lays the groundwork for analysing how im/politeness implicatures themselves can thus be analysed as a form of social practice in the subsequent chapter.

4 Im/politeness and social practice

In the previous section it was argued that when examining im/politeness implicatures, im/politeness itself should be analysed as an attitudinal evaluation rather than as a type of implicature. In examining im/politeness vis-à-vis evaluative practices, then, the focus was on what is being done through such evaluations in interaction. However, the issue of *why* implicatures are open to evaluation in this way was only briefly alluded to as being grounded in moral concerns, such as the obligation to reciprocate in asking questions when getting acquainted, or in the entitlement of customers (in Japan at least) to be treated like *kamisama* (lit. 'deities').

In this section, this line is further developed with reference to work in ethnomethodology (Garfinkel 1967; Heritage 1984a; Wilson 2012), which underpins the theorisation of im/politeness as something that does not simply arise in social practice (Eelen 2001; Garcés-Conejos Blitvich 2013; Watts 2003), but is itself a form of social practice (Haugh 2013c; Kádár and Haugh 2013). According to the former

---

51 The popularity of the saying is attributed to the singer Haruo Minami, although it is often mentioned in etiquette guide books in Japan, particularly in the context of customer service.

view, im/politeness should be analysed with respect to social practices. The latter view, however, takes this further in proposing that im/politeness be analysed as reflexively occasioned by social actions and pragmatic meanings, including implicatures, which invoke, in the ways they are formulated and accomplished, an orientation on the part of those participants to particular moral dimensions of interpersonal interaction (Haugh 2007c, 2012c, 2013c; Kádár and Haugh 2013).

Theorising im/politeness as social practice in this manner arguably raises two key questions. The first involves the question of *how* do participants (and thus analysts) know something counts as im/polite, im/proper, in/appropriate, and so on? The underlying question here is what constitutes the basis for evaluating something as polite, impolite, over-polite, mock impolite, and so on? It is suggested here that such evaluations can arise because of the way in which our everyday talk or conduct is open to moral evaluation, and so are constituted through what Garfinkel (1967) has termed the moral order.

The second question involves the issues of just *whose* evaluations of im/politeness are we (as observers of interactions) analysing? In other words, for whom does something count as polite, impolite, over-polite, mock impolite, and so on? It is argued here that in order to systematically address this question, we need to consider the broader participation order relative to which such evaluations arise. Building on Goffman's notions of speaker footing and the participation framework (Goffman 1979[1981]), it is proposed here that a broader participation order, where not only speakers but also recipients are able to occupy complex figurations of participation footings (Haugh 2013c), is critical for grounding our analysis of im/politeness as social practice.

4.1 Im/politeness and the moral order

In ethnomethodology the focus is on the procedures and practices by which members make sense of everyday situated activities, and the ways in which members are held accountable for the emergence of such understandings.[52] A key claim is that such procedures and practices are morally organised (Jayuusi, 1984, 1991), and so "practical activities (e.g. asking questions, providing descrip-

---

52 A member can be defined as a person who is recognised as affiliated with a particular social or relational network by other persons in that network. The term member is thus deliberately used here, following the ethnomethodological tradition, in recognition of fact that membership vis-à-vis a particular social group is a morally-imbued matter, and because one's status as a participant in an interaction can be either vis-à-vis a footing as a recognised member or as a non-member (Haugh 2009b, 2012b; Kádár and Haugh 2013).

tions and making 'sense') are also inexorably moral" (Housley and Fitzgerald, 2009: 347). Garfinkel ([1964]1967) terms this the moral order, that is, the "taken for granted" or "'seen but unnoticed', expected, background features of everyday scenes" (pp.35–36). However, this background to interpretation and evaluation is argued to be not just a matter of common knowledge, but is itself treated as "inexorably moral" (Housley and Fitzgerald 2009: 347). This is because "for members not only are matters so about familiar scenes but *they are so because it is morally right or wrong that they are so*" ([1964]1967: 35, emphasis added).

A key claim, then, in theorising im/politeness as social practice is that the moral order is what grounds our evaluations of social actions and meanings as "good" or "bad", "normal" or "exceptional", "appropriate" or "inappropriate" and so on, and of course, as "polite", "impolite", "over-polite" and so on. Conceptualising im/politeness as social practice thus builds on the claim that social actions and pragmatic meanings are not simply the means and basis for accomplishing the multitude of interactions through which we constitute our daily lives, they are also inherently moral in and of themselves. They can thus at any time be interpreted in localised talk-in-interaction as evaluative of persons and/ or relationships.[53]

However, it is important to note that the "seen but unnoticed" expectations which constitute that moral order are also both "socially standardised and standardising" (Garfinkel ([1964]1967: 36). What this entails is that not only do these expectancies afford or constrain the behaviour of members, but they are also the means by which one makes a claim to be a member of society (or some social or relational network) in the first place. As Haugh (2013c) argues,

> not only do practices depend on these expectations in order to be recognisable to members, and thus accessible as interpretative resources, but also as members continually engage in such practices in their everyday interactions, they both sustain the moral order, and over time act to change it. The "seen but unnoticed" expectations of the moral order are thus not something to be simply assumed by the analyst, but rather constitute an important object of study in their own right. (Haugh 2013c: 57)

---

53 A person here is conceptualised as an individual in a social environment, namely, the individual construed as a social being linked with others in social interaction, rather than as biological or psychological being (Haugh 2013c), echoing early work in symbolic interactionalism (Mead 1934). In contrast, a relationship, following Arundale (2010b), is conceptualised as the "establishing and maintaining of connection between two otherwise separate individuals" (p.138). The terms identity or face are deliberately avoided here as these are used in various different, and arguably theoretically incompatible, ways in the literature (see Haugh [2013d] and Garcés-Conejos Blitvich [2013] for further discussion).

The moral order in which evaluations of im/politeness are grounded is, therefore, something in which the analysis of im/politeness implicatures must necessarily be grounded, but towards which such analyses may also contribute a more comprehensive understanding. As Haugh (2013b) argues, the moral order encompasses a very large and rich tapestry, "the workings of which remain an important domain for ongoing research" (p.48). In other words, through the analysis of im/politeness implicatures across languages and cultures we can also gain further insight into the workings of the moral order itself.

In order to illustrate what is meant by im/politeness as social practice in more specific, interactional terms, one aspect of the moral order is briefly introduced here, namely, what Stevanovic and Peräkylä (2012, 2014) refer to as the deontic order. The deontic order encompasses what participants think is "obligatory, permissible, or forbidden" (p.299). It thus encompasses claims to "deontic authority" concerning the respective "rights and obligations" of participants (p.298), among other things. Curl and Drew (2008), for instance, identify relational "entitlements" as a key element of the deontic order that is oriented to by participants alongside contingencies in formulating requests (see also Heinemann 2006). Building on Curl and Drew's (2008) account, the formulation of a request arguably involves an implicit assessment by the participants of the entitlements of the speaker (and in that sense involves an evaluation of his/her person) to make that request in that particular situated context, including vis-à-vis his or her interactional role (Mead 1934). However, such entitlements are invariably constituted relative to an implicit assessment of his/her relationship with the requestee. Analysing evaluations of im/politeness vis-à-vis requests thus means carefully examining how evaluations of persons and/or relationships are occasioned by social actions and meanings, including implicatures, that are recognisable to participants as doing requests.

However, given requests inevitably occasion evaluations of persons and relationships vis-à-vis (role-based or relational) entitlements, they also constitute potential loci for complaints, among other things. Formulating a complaint about a prior request, for instance, involves interactionally achieving an evaluation of that request as an impropriety on the part of an individual (or group of individuals) (Drew 1998; Pomerantz 1978b). This means that such complaints arise due to (often prior) assessments of some person (or group of persons) as formulating a request that is somehow "inappropriate" or "improper" with respect to their respective entitlements. A complaint also implicitly carries with it morally-imbued expectations about how those listening to the complaint will respond to it, and so has implications for the co-constitution of their ongoing relationship.

In the following interaction, for instance, we can observe how participants draw upon aspects of the deontic order, in particular, those pertaining to relational entitlements vis-à-vis requests, in occasioning evaluations of im/politeness. We can also observe in the course of analysing this interaction how im/politeness evaluations are both occasioned by social actions (in this case a request), as well being constitutive of social actions (in this case a complaint) (cf. Haugh 2013c). The excerpt here begins when Lisa asserts that she doesn't want to give another friend, Edna, a ride to church anymore.

(74)   (Three friends, Bob, Lisa and Tom are talking while playing computer games and studying)

15	Lisa:	so I don't <u>w</u>anna,- (1.2) I don't <u>w</u>anna
16		pick up Edna for <u>c</u>hu:rch. (hh)
17		(1.1)
18	Bob:	pick up who?
19		(0.7)
20	Lisa:	Edna:.
21	Tom:	E[dna:?] (.) where does she live?
22	Bob:	[mmm.]
23		(0.6)
24	Lisa:	on Anzac Avenue. <u>b</u>ut- (.) she just- (1.2)
25		like <u>l</u>ast week she made me take her home
26		<u>str</u>aightaway after the service. (0.4) so
27		I had to leave and then (0.7) c[ome back.]
28	Bob:	[come back.]
29		(0.7)
30	Tom:	ah
31	Lisa:	and just- she's just re:ally, (.)
32		doesn't think of anyone but herself.
33		(2.1)
34	Tom:	is she a <u>y</u>outh student?

35   (0.5)

36 Lisa: no=

37 Bob: =<u>no</u>: she's a °friend from school.°

38   (0.4)

39 Lisa: school friend.

40 Tom: ↑o:h (h)o(hh)kay.

41 Lisa: she's just <u>really</u> oblivious to social etiquette=

42 Tom: =oh yeah.

43 Lisa: °basically°

44   (1.1)

45 Tom: <u>khh</u>
(cf. Haugh 2013c: 58)

After a brief pause, Bob and Lisa clarify the person being referred to (lines 18–20), followed by a line of questioning in line 21 where Tom offers an implicated candidate account (Bolden and Robinson 2011; Robinson and Bolden 2010; Schegloff 1988a) as to why Lisa no longer wants to pick up Edna and take her church, namely, that she lives a long way off, and so picking her up is inconvenient. Lisa implicitly dismisses this candidate account through a contrastive structure where she first orients to what is literally asked by Tom, which implicates that it is not because it is inconvenient to pick up Edna that she no longer wants to give Edna a ride (line 24), and then outlines her account, namely, that Edna asked Lisa to take her home straightaway, thereby forcing Lisa to make an extra trip (lines 24–27). In this way, Lisa orients to Edna's request to take her straight home as a complainable (Drew and Walker 2009; Schegloff 2005), the upshot of which is acknowledged by Tom (line 30), but about which no assessment from either Tom or Bob is forthcoming. This is then upgraded to a recognisable complaint in lines 31–32, when Lisa implicates that Edna does not think of others thereby claiming that Edna does not show (appropriate) consideration for others.

It is important to note that the complaint itself is formulated at a more generalised and abstract level than the locally situated context in which the complainable is occasioned which implies that it is not just on this occasion, but possibly on many others as well, that Edna has shown a lack of consideration for others. Formulating the complaint at a more generalised level through abstraction (Deppermann 2011a), also enables Lisa to invoke aspects of the deontic order by casting Edna as someone who "doesn't think of anyone but herself", namely, that not thinking of anyone but oneself is a bad thing, and that everyone (including the other participants present, as well as Edna) should know this. More specifically, Lisa is evidently orienting to their respective entitlements vis-à-vis making such a request, namely, the way in which Edna is positioning herself as entitled to make such a request in that particular situated context (and by implication others), and not orienting to the contingencies of the situation (i.e. Lisa wanting to stay after the service) (Curl and Drew 2008). In this way, we can observe how an evaluative social action (i.e. a complaint) is itself occasioned by a prior evaluation of impropriety, namely, the Lisa's evaluation of the inconsideration of Edna's prior request (and perhaps a long history of such selfish requests).

Tom then offers yet another candidate account for this ongoing impropriety on the part of Edna in line 34, in proposing through a candidate answer that it may be because she is a "youth student" (Pomerantz 1988), and so presumably young and selfish. However, Lisa rejects this account (line 36). The implicit rejection of Tom's candidate account is then further clarified by Bob (line 37), and confirmed by Lisa (line 39), when they assert that Edna is in fact a friend from school. Tom then responds (line 40) by not only treating this as new information through a change-of-state token "oh" (Heritage 1984a), but also "signalling a 'state of readiness' for moving to next-positioned matters" (Beach 1994: 339) through "okay", namely, the issue of what can plausibly justify Lisa's complaint (i.e. Edna's lack of "consideration"). Notably, Tom's response is interpolated with laughter particles, through which he indicates recognition of the inadequacy of his prior candidate account for Edna's impropriety (Potter and Hepburn 2010). Lisa then proffers an account in line 41 by casting Edna as someone who is "really oblivious to social etiquette". In doing so, not only does Lisa explicitly categorise the "impropriety" of Edna's request as a breach of "social etiquette", she also accomplishes a negative assessment of Edna's person. The complaint and subsequent negative assessment thus constitute what Garfinkel (1956) terms a "public denunciation", where Lisa makes a claim to "moral indignation" in relation to Edna's (apparently numerous) breaches of etiquette.

While complaints and negative assessments offer an opportunity for other participants to affiliate with the stance taken by the speaker (Drew and Walker 2009; Stivers and Rossano 2010), in this case, the other participants do not strongly affiliate with Lisa's negative assessment (i.e. that Edna's behaviour constitutes an impropriety that reflects her lack of a proper understanding of "social etiquette") (cf. line 42), nor do they strongly align with Lisa's complaint here, by offering, for instance, some kind of assessment subsequent to it (cf. lines 33–40). Instead, Tom only weakly affiliates with the negative assessment (line 42). Lisa then subsequently downgrades her denunciation through the addition of a turn increment "basically" (line 43) uttered *sotto voce*, whereby she concedes that Edna may not always be "oblivious to social etiquette." Tom then affiliates with this slightly less categorical negative assessment through a frictative "khh", by which he indicates a dismissive stance (presumably towards Edna's impropriety). In either mildly affiliating with negative assessment (Tom), or at least not challenging it (Bob), the complaint and subsequent negative assessment instantiated by Lisa appears to be tacitly accepted by Tom and Bob as consistent with their understandings of the underlying taken-for-granted moral expectancies vis-à-vis entitlements to make requests (to which Lisa's complaint appeals).

There are three key dimensions of im/politeness as social practice that can be observed here. First, Lisa's negative assessment of Edna's person is not framed as an idiosyncratic evaluation, but rather one that is rooted in the moral order, specifically, aspects of the deontic order (i.e. entitlements vis-à-vis requests). Evaluations of im/politeness are thus evidently occasioned by social actions and meanings, in this case, a request that is characterised as inconsiderate and a breach of social etiquette. Second, this negative assessment of Edna's person also has implications for the relationship between Lisa, Bob and Tom in that the degree to which they affiliate with Lisa's stance here has implications for the ongoing co-constituting of their relational connection/separation. Third, we can observe here an instance of a social action (i.e., a complaint) and an implicature (i.e., the object of that complaint) being occasioned by a prior evaluation of someone else's conduct, namely, the breach of social etiquette perceived by Lisa to have arisen from Edna asking Lisa to drive her home straight after church. It follows, then, that evaluating someone as im/polite can occasion subsequent social actions (e.g. a complaint), and in that sense im/politeness can be constitutive of social actions and meanings, including implicatures. It is in these three inter-related senses, then, that we can analyse im/politeness as a form of social practice.

Another key point that has been alluded to in this analysis of im/politeness vis-à-vis the moral order is that these different participants do not necessarily evaluate im/politeness in the same way. While Lisa explicitly commits herself to an evaluation of Edna's prior conduct as displaying a lack of consideration ("she really doesn't think of anyone but herself"), and thus a breach of "social etiquette", Tom only weakly commits himself to that stance ("oh yeah", "khh"), while Bob at most tacitly accepts it through not challenging it, and so is even more weakly committed to Lisa's stance. We do not have access to Edna's perspective on her request, but she is cast as being oblivious to the "offence" by Lisa, and in that sense an understanding of her request as at least "not impolite" can be plausibly attributed to her.[54] These different participant evaluations of im/politeness thus represent different first order (i.e. user) understandings of im/politeness. In other words, in examining im/politeness evaluations a key analytical question is inevitably the issue of im/polite according to whom? It is also evident that the different participants, in particular Lisa and Edna, may have different understandings of a particular aspect of the moral order, namely, their respective entitlements to be making this kind of request. In other words, while participants necessarily ground their evaluations of im/politeness in aspects of the moral order, this does not mean to say that all members have the same understandings of particular aspects of that moral order. An analysis of im/politeness as social practice must also be grounded relative to these different participation footings, a claim we shall now turn to consider in further detail.

4.2 Im/politeness and the participation order

Most approaches to the theorisation of politeness or impoliteness have focused either on the speaker's (putative) intention to be im/polite (e.g. Brown and Levinson 1987; Bousfield 2008; Culpeper 1996, 2005; Terkourafi 2008), or on the hearer's evaluation of the speaker's behaviour vis-à-vis perceived (social) norms (e.g. Eelen 2001; Mills 2003; Watts 2003). More recently, however, there have been calls to go beyond a basic speaker-hearer model of interaction in order to consider more carefully the footings of all participants vis-à-vis im/politeness (e.g. Bousfield 2008: 174–175; Dobs and Garcés-Conejos Blitvich 2013; Dynel 2012; Haugh, Davies and Merrison 2011). Such arguments are foreshadowed in Goffman's (1979[1981]) seminal claim that the folk categories of speaker and hearer need to be decomposed into "smaller, analytically coherent elements" (p.129); and indeed most of these approaches explicitly draw from Goffman's work in some form or another.

Goffman (1979[1981]) made essentially two key claims in relation to how we might further deconstruct the folk notions of "speaker" and "hearer". The first was that the term "speaker" actually conflates four distinct sets of roles and associated responsibilities, which Goffman termed "footings": animator, author, principal and figure. An animator is the person or group of persons uttering the talk, the author is the person or group of persons who formulated or designed the talk, the principal is the person or group of persons held

---

54 Indeed, we could presume that Edna did not consider it a breach of "social etiquette" given she made the request in the first place, and thereby implicitly made a claim to being entitled to make such a request irrespective of the contingencies at hand.

responsible for that talk, and the figure is the person or group of persons por-
trayed in the talk. The second key claim made by Goffman was that the participation status of hearers also confers distinct sets of roles and responsibilities.
One key distinction in the participation status of hearers is that between those
hearing and those *listening* to the talk. While in both cases the talk is audible to
the hearer, in the latter case the hearer is expected to attend to and participate
in the interaction in some way, and so is regarded as a "ratified hearer" (as
opposed to a "non-ratified" hearer). Ratified hearers are further subdivided into
those treated as the "addressee" by the speaker (i.e. the person or persons to
whom the talk is ostensibly directed), and those who are treated as "side participants". Although both addressees and side participants have legitimate rights
to respond to the talk, their degree of responsibility to do so varies (at least
ostensibly). Unratified hearers, on the other hand, are further subdivided into
"bystanders" and "overhearers", with the difference being that it is expected
by the speaker (and other ratified participants) that bystanders will be able to
hear the talk, although they are not expected to respond to it, while in the case
of overhearers, the speaker and other ratified participants may or may not be
aware that those persons are able to hear the talk.

There have been various reworkings of Goffman's original participation
framework (e.g. Dynel 2011; Kerbrat-Orecchioni 2004; Levinson 1988; Verschueren
1999). For instance, the treatment of "overhearers" as unratified hearers has been
challenged, since viewers of broadcast talk (e.g. television, radio, film etc.) can
hardly be considered "unratified" since the talk is expressly designed with them
in mind (Dynel 2011, 2012; Lorenzo-Dus 2009). Such arguments also extend to
talk mediated through various forms of social media (e.g. Facebook, Twitter etc.)
or other computer-mediated contexts, such as blogs, discussion boards and so
on (Lorenzo Dus, Garcés-Conejos Blitvich and Bou-Franch 2011; Marcoccia 2004).
However, one notable gap in the development of Goffman's initial proposals
about the participation framework that has received only passing comment thus
far is that

> there is a marked asymmetry in the analytic frameworks used to describe different kinds
> of actors. The speaker is endowed with rich cognitive and linguistic capabilities, and the
> ability to take a reflexive stance toward the talk in progress. However, all other participants
> are left cognitively and linguistically simple. (Goodwin and Goodwin 2004: 225)

Haugh (2013c) thus proposes that the notion of speaker (i.e. production) footing
need to be complemented by the notion of recipient (i.e. reception) footing. It is
suggested that the animator (or producer) has a counterpart in the various recipients that can (potentially) attend to the talk (or non-verbal conduct). The author

footing is complemented by the interpreter(s) who construct their own understandings and evaluations of that talk. The footing of principal is matched by the accounter(s), who either explicitly or tacitly hold the principal responsible for the meanings and actions accomplished through the talk. Finally, the production footing of figure is also a potential target when the person or character depicted is co-present (i.e. one of the recipients), or when the talk is attributed to someone else other than the animator/producer. These extensions allow for a much more nuanced range of participation footings, as summarised in Figure 4. It is important to note, however, that these participation footings do not in any way pre-exist talk-in-interaction, but are themselves are dynamically co-constituted through talk itself. The array of participation footings which are instantiated through talk in particular, locally situated interactions, and the attendant rights and responsibilities these footings confer on participants constitutes what Haugh (2013c) terms the "participation order".

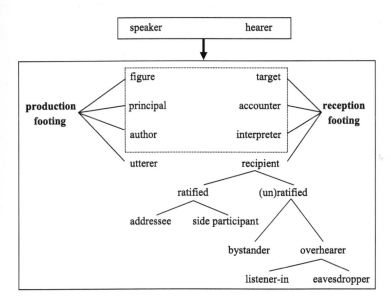

Figure 4: The participation order (adapted from Haugh 2013c: 62)

In sum, the first key element underpinning the locally situated instantiation of the participation order in interaction is the participation framework. This refers to the ways in which recipiency of talk can be configured by participants (Goffman [1979]1981; cf. Levinson 1988; Dynel 2011a; Kerbrat-Orecchioni 2004), that is, how participants are positioned in regards to interpreting and responding to talk. The second key element underpinning the participation order is that of participation footings. These refer to the locally realised configuration of production and reception roles (of users) vis-à-vis particular social action trajectories.

The importance of this complex array of potential participation footings for analysing im/politeness becomes evident when we consider interactions, such as the following, where multiple participants are involved, including a viewing audience. The interaction in question comes from a documentary investigating race relations in Australia. Four Indians have been invited to tour various communities around Australia. In the excerpt in question, there are seven interactants present: Gurmeet, Radhika, an Aboriginal elder from Kamilorau country, another indigenous resident of Kamilorau, along with the host of the documentary Joe, plus two other Indian visitors who remain out of camera throughout. Offence is displayed by the Aboriginal elder in response to what is implicated by a line of questioning from one of the Indians, Gurmeet. Notably, this display of offence by the elder, and the orientation of the others present to this display of offence, are mediated through the locally situated participation order that is co-constituted in the course of that interaction.

(75) 1 Radhika: so do they lack <u>mo</u>tivation? <u>why</u> do they lack

2 [motivation]

3 Elder: [<u>some</u> do] because of, uh, the sss- so I think

4 because they've been so suppressed, you know

5 if you kick a dog so much and call 'em a dog

6 he'll stay there [so that-

7 Gurmeet: [so >there there there< should be

8 uhm, educational institutions, uh specific

9 educational institutions for Aborigines

10 [then,] after that there [will be no (   )]

11 Elder: [there is] [there is a lot of that]

12 here there is a lot of that here.

13 Gurmeet: then what are the complaints.

14 Elder: ((cocks her head)) uh uh, beg your pardon?

15 Gurmeet: why are you complaining then.

16 Elder: ((steps back)) ↑am I com<u>plai</u>ning?=

17 Radhika: =<u>n::</u>o

18 Gurmeet: heh [heh heh

19 Elder: [I'm answering <u>que</u>stions [that they   ] <u>a:s</u>ked

20 Joe: [that's right]

21   yeah that's righ(hh)t

22 Elder: I'm not complain-

23 Radhika: <u>ye:</u>ah

24 Gurmeet: ((shakes head and smiles)) but- but [you are <u>say</u>ing

25 Joe: [(   )

26 Elder: you don't live in <u>my</u> country

27 Radhika: <u>n::</u>o.

28 Elder: ((points her finger at Gurmeet)) you don't live in

29   my- this is <u>my</u> country

30 Joe: <u>y</u>es.

31 Elder: Kamilorau is <u>my</u> country. ((points at self)) I see

32   what happens here, ((points at Gurmeet)) whatever

33   happens in <u>your</u> country.

(*Dumb Drunk and Racist*, Episode 4, July 11 2012, ABC2 and Cordell Jigsaw
Productions)

The excerpt begins when Radhika asks the elder for an account as to why
Aboriginal Australians have struggled to improve their socioeconomic situation
(lines 1–2). The elder responds this is due to the oppression of Aboriginal Australians (lines 3–6), which then leads into suggestion from Gurmeet that there needs
to be "specific educational institutions" for indigenous Australians (lines 7–10).
When the elder responds that such institutions already exist (lines 11–12), Gurmeet
then asks "what are complaints" (line 13), a question that appears to occasion
considerable offence on the part of the elder, especially when it is subsequently
repeated (line 15), as can be seen from what follows.

In order to analyse this display of offence two analytical moves are arguably required. First, we need to examine not only what is said, but what is implicated through Gurmeet's line of questioning here. In other words, we need to acknowledge that we are dealing with an instance of impoliteness implicature in this interaction. Second, we need to examine how this display of offence is formulated and oriented to vis-à-vis the participation order.

What is important to note, first of all, is that the elder appears to treat in subsequent turns what is *supposed* by Gurmeet here in formulating this question (in line 13) as offensive. There are two key implicated premises that the elder treats as arising through Gurmeet's question. The first is his assumption that there are insufficient grounds for her to be claiming that Aboriginal Australians have been oppressed, given that specific educational institutions exist for them. The second is his assumption that the formulation of her prior account (in lines 3–6), which arose in turn in response to Radhika's original question (lines 1–2), constitutes an instance of complaining. These implicated premises then underpin what she appears to take as *implied* (i.e. an implicated conclusion) by Gurmeet, namely, that her complaints are not warranted. Given these implicated premises and conclusions give rise to offence, it appears that an impoliteness implicature has arisen.

This offence, however, is progressively displayed over a number of turns by the elder. And this is where the analytical import of the participation order comes to the fore. The first indication we have that the elder has taken offence at Gurmeet's question in line 13 is apparent from her use of an open class repair initiator (Drew 1997), "beg your pardon?", in response to the question in line 14, alongside the elder cocking her head to display puzzlement. While repair initiation is often associated with troubles in hearing or understanding prior talk, in this case "the repairable trouble is manifestly not a problem of hearing etc., but rather one associated with the *propriety* of the prior turn" (Drew 1997: 95, emphasis added). The preferred response to pre-disagreement achieved through repair initiation is, as Koshik (2005) argues, "a self-correction, or a backdown, which preempts a dispreferred other-correction or disagreement" (p.28; cf. Schegloff, Sacks and Jefferson 1977: 380). In other words, the elder offers Gurmeet an opportunity to reformulate (or even withdraw) what is implicated through his question, thereby holding him accountable for an incipient impropriety. However, Gurmeet does not reformulate or withdraw his line of questioning in a way that alters what is implicated through it (line 15), and so resists her move to hold him accountable for an improper question. Instead, he elects to pursue a response by treating her repair initiation as a problem of understanding (Pomerantz 1984b), by simply reformulating the syntactic structure of his question.

This pursuit of a response, and the lack of recognition of the incipient impropriety by Gurmeet, consequently occasions another display of offence on the part of the elder in line 16. Notably, while the principal, producer and figure are the elder herself (as might normally be expected given she is the speaker talking about herself), the authorship is in fact attributable to Gurmeet, as he is the one construing her prior account as complaining. This interactional detachment from the footing of author allows the elder to display her own stance towards that construal, namely, that it constitutes an offence or impropriety. This stance is indicated, first of all, through a "reversed polarity question" (Koshik 2005), through which the elder attempts to elicit a backdown from Gurmeet,[55] but which at the same time "raises the stakes" by reframing her prior pre-disagreement as a pre-challenge (Reynolds 2011: 423; cf. Edwards and Fasulto 2006: 364), and so alters the potential trajectory here from a simple disagreement between the elder and Gurmeet to an outright argument or conflict. Yet while the stakes are raised through it, a reversed polarity question nevertheless allows this pre-challenge to be suggested "off record" (Koshik 2005: 152), thereby reducing the elder's degree of accountability for this raising of the stakes. The prosodic contour here also contributes to the display of her stance on Gurmeet's prior construal of account. The elder's reversed polarity question is delivered with a markedly raised pitch and emphatic stress on "complaining" (which itself constitutes a modified partial repeat). In this way, the elder displays "astonishment" or "surprise" (Selting 1996; Wilkinson and Kitzinger 2006; cf. Sendra et al. 2013), thereby indicating that Gurmeet's pursuit of a response is unexpected, and indeed inapposite (Couper-Kuhlen 2012).

Yet while the elder nominally positions Gurmeet as the direct addressee, the side participants to this exchange are here positioned as indirect addressees, because the reversed polarity question frames a response that affiliates with her stance that Gurmeet's question is inapposite as the preferred one. Radhika consequently elects to move from her then recipient footing as a side participant to the footing of addressee through a fall-pitch on an elongated negative ("no [you're not complaining]") in line 17, which thereby marks it as a preferred response (Pomerantz and Heritage 2013). In other words, Radhika also indicates an evaluation of Gurmeet's prior questions as inapposite, and so holds him accountable for this impropriety.

The elder then further clarifies her stance by rejecting Gurmeet's construal of her account as "complaining", and reconstruing it as simply "answering questions" (line 19). Once again, while Gurmeet is positioned as the direct addressee,

---

55 A reversed polarity question is similar in form to a rhetorical question, but differ in that the former are designed to elicit a response where the recipient either affiliates or not with the stance suggested through the question (see Koshik 2005: 37), while the latter are designed to make assertions.

one of the side participants, Joe, chimes in to affiliate with her claim (lines 20–21), thereby sharing a co-principal footing for this stance, as well as indicating an evaluation of Gurmeet's construal as inapposite, and so also holds Gurmeet accountable for this offence.

Gurmeet, on the other hand, appears to indicate embarrassment through laughter (line 18) and smiling (line 24) (Chang and Haugh 2011a; Heath 1988; Sandlund 2004; cf. Goffman 1956). Yet at the same time he also appears to display bemusement through shaking his head, and attempting to hold her accountable for this complaining by making reference to what she has been "saying" (line 24). In this way, it appears he disaffiliates with her stance that his prior questions were offensive. In other words, Gurmeet does not appear to regard her construal of his prior questions as occasioning offence as warranted, given his initial implicated premises were based on what she "said".

However, he is interrupted by the elder at point not recognisable as transition relevance place, and in emphatic speech style, which thereby treats Gurmeet's counter-claims as inappropriate or unjustified (Couper-Kuhlen 2012; Selting 1994). She then consequently moves to cast Gurmeet as an outsider (i.e. non-member) who there does not have any epistemic authority to be judging the situation of indigenous Australians, or the elder's account of it (line 26) (Heritage and Raymond 2005; Raymond and Heritage 2006; Sidnell 2012). Notably, Radhika elects into sharing a co-principal footing with the elder vis-à-vis this stance through an affiliative fall-pitch on an elongated negative (line 27). The elder continues this line, where Gurmeet's implicit judgement of her is treated as illegimate due to his outsider status (lines 28–29, 31–33), a line with which Joe also elects into sharing a co-principal footing with as well through his display of an affiliative stance in line 30.

In sum, while Gurmeet attempts to hold the elder accountable for unjustified complaining, this is treated as an impropriety by the elder. This is accomplished by the elder through recycling Gurmeet's claims (for which authorship is attributed to Gurmeet), but about which the elder indicates her stance that what has been implicated by Gurmeet is offensive. Other side participants elect to take recipient footings as addressees, as well as to share co-principal footing with respect to her stance that Gurmeet's line of questioning is offensive. Gurmeet, on the other hand, resists the construal of his questioning as offensive in attempting to appeal to what the elder has previously said, and so maintains his stance that she was complaining and that those complaints were not justified. The elder then finally moves to remove particular entitlements from Gurmeet, namely, the right to judge the situation of indigenous Australians, and the elder's account of it, by claiming he has his insufficient epistemic access, thereby undermining his right to any form of speakership on such issues. The above discussion thus illustrates how a more nuanced account of participation footings is required in order to analyse evaluations of im/politeness as they arise in multi-party interaction, although, as we shall see in the subsequent chapter, complex arrays of participation footings can even be invoked in dyadic interactions.

There is, of course, yet another layer of complexity in regards to the participation order relevant to this particular interaction given it was from a documentary broadcast on national television in Australia. While the participants here are tailoring their talk to each other, the viewing audience constitutes an overhearing audience to this interaction. Given the participants in question are aware of this overhearing audience there is some degree of ambivalence in regard to who these utterances are designed for: the addressee, the side participants, or the overhearing audience? There is thus another layer of "quasi-ratified" participants, namely, the overhearing audience, amongst whom evaluations of the im/politeness or im/propriety of Gurmeet's line of question can arise. Examples such as these illustrate the importance of acknowledging that im/politeness implicatures can, in some instances, involve multiple understandings (Kádár and Haugh 2013). Careful analytic attention thus needs to be paid to the participation order being instantiated through a particular interaction in order to tease out these multiple understandings.

In summary, then, to treat im/politeness as an attitudinal evaluation, rather than as an implicature, arguably necessitates a move to a broader treatment of im/politeness as social practice. In this view, im/politeness evaluations are reflexively occasioned by social actions and meanings, and are necessarily grounded in the moral order and participation order through which they are constituted. In the course of this discussion, reference has also been made to implicatures on numerous occasions. We have observed that not only can im/politeness evaluations arise through implicatures, but that "offence" can be receipted through implicatures. In the following chapter, building on the account of im/politeness as social practice outlined in this chapter, and the conceptualisation of implicature as a social action for which participants can be held accountable outlined in the previous chapter, we move to tease out the relationship between im/politeness and implicatures in greater detail.

However, before doing so, it is important to briefly acknowledge that throughout this chapter inferences about participant evaluations vis-à-vis im/politeness have been made (by the analyst). These represent second order (i.e. *observer*) understandings of im/politeness, which can, of course, be grounded in different theories of im/politeness. Here, the theoretical backdrop to the analysis has been a theorisation of im/politeness as social practice (Haugh 2007c, 2013c; Kádár and Haugh 2013), which draws, in turn, from research in ethnomethodology more broadly. The aim of such an approach is to ensure that such observer understandings are consonant with the first order understandings of the *users* themselves (Haugh 2007c). However, rather than simply reporting these user understandings, the aim here has been to systematically examine the moral grounding of evaluations of im/politeness, and the ways in which they arise within particular, locally situated participation orders. In this way, the analyst is arguably better placed to examine what participants are accomplishing through such evaluations.

Chapter Five:
Situating im/politeness implicatures in interaction

In our discussion of implicatures thus far their contingent, relatively indeterminate, and locally situated character has been emphasised. And in the previous chapter, in moving to examine im/politeness and its relationship with implicatures, it was argued that im/politeness is more productively theorised as an evaluative social practice than as simply a type of implicature. These discussions have laid the groundwork for the two key questions that underpin this chapter, namely, how and when do implicatures give rise to evaluations of im/politeness? In the first half of this chapter, the investigation of the moral underpinnings of implicatures begun in the previous chapter is extended by characterising in more detail how im/politeness implicatures themselves constitute a form of social practice. It is suggested that im/politeness implicatures not only encompass instances whereby evaluations of im/politeness are occasioned through implicating (i.e. im/politeness-as-occasioned-by-implicatures) (Haugh 2007a), but also encompass the broader evaluative field that can be constituted through scalar implicatures (i.e. implicatures-as-constitutive-of-im/politeness), as well as instances where evaluations of im/politeness can themselves subsequently occasion implicatures (i.e. implicatures-as-occasioned-by-im/politeness). Given the complex roles im/politeness implicatures can play in interaction, it is argued that they are more productively analysed with respect to the locally situated interactions in which they arise.

However, to emphasise the interactional grounding of im/politeness implicatures is not to suggest that the processes by which they arise are themselves ad hoc or impervious to systematic study. Indeed, in order for participants themselves to reach understandings of particular talk and conduct as implicating something, and thereby occasioning an evaluation of im/politeness, they inevitably draw from normative interpretative, or more broadly pragmatic, orders. It is thus one of the key tasks for the analyst to tease out the nature of the pragmatic orders whereby participants are able to make sense of the world, given they are largely opaque to conscious reflection by those participants (Garfinkel 1967; Heritage 1984a).

In working towards an interactionally-grounded and morally-imbued theory of im/politeness implicature, we will be drawing together a number of analytical threads that were highlighted in our discussion of indirectness and relationality more generally in Chapter One. In particular, we will be building on the observation that while such interpersonal and moral concerns very often arise in the course of highly localised, situated interactions, where the trajectory of the interaction is consequently inherently unpredictable in many respects, the mechanisms by which such concerns themselves are oriented to by participants are, at least in many respects, regular, predictable and ordered (Wrong 1995). In this way, the argument that im/politeness implicatures arise as a form of social practice outlined in the previous chapter will be fleshed out. That is to say, it is proposed here that im/politeness implicatures are underpinned by what Rouse (2001: 198) terms "regularities of behaviour or belief" (i.e. practices as regularities), as well as "arrays of activities that answer to norms of behaviour" (i.e. practices as normative) that arise as emergent systems across relational or social networks over time.

The second half of this chapter thus moves to consider the nature of the pragmatic orders than underpin im/politeness implicatures in more detail. There are four interpretive orders that are argued to be of particular importance for the analysis of im/politeness implicatures in interaction: the *moral order*, which refers to the sets of "seen but unnoticed" intersubjective expectancies through which members ground their understandings of im/politeness implicatures in interaction (Garfinkel 1967); the *participation order*, which encompasses the multiple participation footings relative to which im/politeness implicatures can arise in interaction (Goffman 1981); the *temporal-sequential order*, which underpins the inherently temporal nature of understandings of im/politeness implicatures in interaction (Sacks, Schegloff and Jefferson 1974; Schegloff 2007); and the *socio-inferential order*, which includes the complex arrays of intentional state-processes and inferential mechanisms by which im/politeness implicatures arise in interaction (Gumperz 1982).

We have already introduced the moral order and participation order in our discussion of im/politeness as evaluative social practice in the previous chapter. In this chapter, we thus focus on the latter two interpretive orders, namely, the temporal-sequential order and the socio-inferential order. In doing so, we also return to consider in more detail some of the issues raised in our discussion of different approaches to implicature in Chapter Two, including debates about the place of conventions or defaults as well as speaker intentions, vis-a-vis implicatures. The chapter concludes by drawing together the various threads from both this chapter and the previous one into an overall theoretical framework, which then grounds the analysis of im/politeness implicatures that follows in the subsequent two chapters.

1 Im/politeness implicatures as social practice

In introducing the notion of "politeness implicature", Haugh (2007a) initially suggested that they encompass "instances where by virtue of implying something politeness arises" (p.84; cf. Huang 2012: 225), building, in turn, on earlier observations by Brown and Levinson (1987) and Leech (1983). This was subsequently extended to the notion of "impoliteness implicatures" which were argued to encompass instances where by virtue of implying something impoliteness arises

(Haugh 2008d: 434; cf. Huang 2012: 151). However, in the course of arguing against the neo-Gricean position that im/politeness itself constitutes an implicature, and in proposing that it is better conceptualised as an evaluation, and thus as a form of social practice in the preceding chapter, it has become apparent that the relationship between implicature and im/politeness is somewhat more complex and nuanced than was outlined in my original account of im/politeness implicatures outlined in Haugh (2007a, 2008d). In this section, therefore, building on this preliminary sketch of im/politeness implicatures, we move to consider this relationship in more detail. It is suggested that im/politeness implicatures not only encompass instances where evaluations of im/politeness are occasioned by implicatures, but also instances where implicatures can be observed to be constitutive of im/politeness, and vice-versa, that is, where evaluations of im/politeness can be observed to be constitutive of implicatures. It is suggested that by focusing on these three ways in which im/politeness and implicatures are inter-related that we can more productively analyse im/politeness implicatures as a form of social practice.

1.1 Im/politeness as occasioned by implicatures

Im/politeness implicatures encompass, first and foremost, instances where evaluations of im/politeness are occasioned through the interactional achievement of implicatures. More specifically, through implicating the reflexively intentional object of a social action, participants invoke particular aspects of the moral order, thereby giving rise to an evaluation of im/politeness. Invoking the moral order is achieved by modulating the degree of *indeterminacy* of the said social action or the degree of participant *commitment* to, and thus their degree of accountability for that social action through these implicatures. It is in this way, then, that evaluations of politeness, impoliteness and so on arise.

In the following interaction, for instance, where Michael is visiting Mary who is his old music teacher, we can see how what is ostensibly framed as a noticing and offer from Mary is also accomplishing another social action, namely, an implicated request.

(76) DS300007: 4:23

    1   Mary: have a <u>bi</u>:scuit.

    2   Michael: ↑o:h okay↑ yeah. ↑<u>thank</u> you.

    3   Mary: you've gotta have a (.) <u>bi[k:kie]</u>

    4   Michael: [hava] squiggle=

5   Mary: =they're <u>lo:</u>vely squiggles?

6   Michael: I <u>l</u>ove squiggles=

7   Mary: =<u>m</u>:m.=

8   Michael: =<u>ye</u>:ah. hhh.

9   (0.6)

10 Mary: ((while eating)) ↑<u>o</u>:h.

11   (0.8)

12 Michael: [°<u>m</u>:m°

13 Mary: [I haven't gotten y'a bread 'n butter plate but (0.4)

14   there's <u>o</u>ne in the cupboard if you want one.

15 Michael: mm? o::h ↑<u>sho</u>:uld be okay? I'll j[u-

16 Mary: [<u>yo</u> [:u alright?]

17 Michael: [d'yu d'yu]

18   do you <u>wan</u>t one?

19 Mary: u::m yea- (.) well it's le- less <u>mess</u>ier <u>act</u>ually.

20 Michael: okay.

21 Mary: u:m. on the bottom shelf,

22 Michael: mhm.

23 MP: just above the stove.

In disguising this implicated request through a noticing and offer, Mary is arguably positioning Michael to make a pre-emptive offer, that is to say, she is soliciting an offer through an implicature. This interpretation of the upshot of her initial offer is one which Michael does not immediately display in his initial response, but once he does, this line of interpretation is confirmed by Mary herself, albeit with some qualification. Given this implicature is oriented towards a concern on the part of the participants that they are not perceived as impolite, as well as an orientation to being seen as polite, it arguably constitutes an instance of a politeness implicature.

However, in arguing that politeness and impoliteness arise as a form of social practice, as has been in the course of the previous chapter, it is important to show how such a claim is consonant with the understandings of the participants themselves. This entails, in turn, that careful analytic attention be directed first towards examining the way in which the participants' understandings of what is implicated (cf. implicatum) arise coordinate with their understandings of social actions, and then second, to justify the analyst's claim that in doing so the participants are invoking particular dimensions of the moral order, such that evaluations of politeness arise. It is to this detailed analysis that we now turn.

In lines 1–2, an offer of biscuits is made by Mary to Michael, followed by a repeat of the offer (line 3), oriented not to Michael's verbal response in line 2, but rather to his (as yet) incipient physical movement to take a biscuit. This is then followed by a positive assessment of the biscuit (line 5), an affiliative response from Michael (line 6), and an expression of enjoyment in eating the biscuit from Mary (line 7), and yet another affiliative response from Michael (line 8).

It is at that point, when they are both starting to eat the biscuits, that Mary formulates an oh-prefaced noticing and proposal, namely, that she hasn't got a plate for Michael but there are some in cupboard, thereby implicating that he can go and get one for himself (lines 10, 13–14).[56] The latter part of the turn counts as projecting an offer in the sense that Mary is giving Michael permission to use one of her plates. The particulars of this offer arise from the contingencies of the situation at play here, namely, that Mary and Michael both know it is much easier for Michael to go and actually get the plate, since it is not easy for Mary to move around. The offer thus orients here to a contingently relevant problem, namely, a noticing that Mary has not taken out a plate for Michael to use while eating the biscuit, followed by an offer formulated using an inverted conditional + main clause construction, that is, *(then) Y, if X* (cf. Curl 2006: 1259). Michael's subsequently orients to it as an offer through a declination, which is achieved here through indicating a plate won't be necessary (line 15).

However, the fact that the offer in lines 13–14 is oh-prefaced turns out to be interactionally significant. Bolden (2006) argues that "oh" is almost always used to preface self-attentive action sequences that benefit the speaker rather than the addressee, such as requests:

> 'oh' prefacing provides a means of advancing a temporarily stalled conversation, characterises the upcoming matter as 'just remembered,' and is apparently used for launching self-attentive sequences. (Bolden 2006: 674)

---

56 The apparent lack of contiguity between turns 10 and 13 is a matter of the contingencies of talking while eating a biscuit. Given those contingencies the "oh" in turn 10 is hearable as prefacing the subsequent proposal in turn 13.

In this case, by oh-prefacing what appears to be an other-attentive course of action, that is, making an offer, Mary implicitly orients to an unstated upshot of her noticing that Michael does not have a plate, namely, that she does not have a plate either. However, Michael does not initially orient to this related contingently relevant problem in declining Mary's offer that he get himself a plate.

Mary subsequently expresses concern for the problem at hand in line 16 in asking whether Michael is "alright" (i.e. without a plate), the implicated upshot of which coincides with an overlapping offer from Michael in lines 17–18, where he proposes getting a plate for Mary. The overlap itself may here constitute a form of recognitional onset (Jefferson 1986), that is, where the next speaker (i.e. Michael) feels he can recognise what current speaker (i.e. Mary) is likely to say and so can project its completion, even though this is launched before the end of Mary's current turn, or it may constitute evidence of a rethinking on Michael's part in regards to his prior response to her offer. Either way, the offer itself is also formulated using the DYW (*do you want me to X*) syntactic format, which frames it as responsive to a problem educed from previous talk (Curl 2006: 1276), namely, that if Michael does not have a plate (line 13), then neither does Mary. Finally, in constituting an indirect response to Mary's inquiry in line 16, Michael's offer here appears designed to "uncover the prior turn's agenda" (Walker, Drew and Local 2011: 2434), namely, to display what he takes Mary to really want. In other words, Michael's indirect response orients to "something like the motivation behind the question that is asked" (p.2441). In this case, that Mary wants Michael to get her a plate even if he doesn't want one. The oh-prefacing of Mary's prior offer that Michael can get himself a plate thus turns out to be indicating that the initial offer is not as straightforwardly other-attentive as might first appear. And Michael's subsequent pre-emptive offer thereby treats Mary's prior offer, which he initially treated as simply as an offer for him to go and get himself a plate, as also implicating a request that Michael go and get her a plate. In other words, Mary ends up soliciting a pre-emptive offer from Michael to get her a plate, although this is itself "disguised" as offer that Michael is free to go and get himself a plate.

Mary's subsequent response in line 19 indicates acceptance of Michael's pre-emptive offer. However, as Schegloff (1996a) points out, "*agreeing* with another's explication of an inexplicit 'message' may not always indicate a prior orientation to conveying it" (p.184), and so Mary's acceptance of the pre-emptive offer here does not, on its own at least, constitute evidence that the participants are orienting to this as a prior agenda on Mary's part. Yet there is evidence in the way in which Mary's response is formulated that is indicative of an orientation on her part to an unstated line of interpretation here, namely, that the agenda of her prior offer in lines 13–14 has been uncovered. Mary initially responds with the projectable beginning of a type-conforming response (i.e. 'yeah'), but this is subsequently abandoned in favour of a non-type-conforming response (Raymond 2003), namely, an account as to why using a plate is a good idea ("it's less messier"), which is not only well-prefaced but also followed by a turn-final attitudinal adverb "actually".

The non-type conforming formulation of Mary's response is indicative of resistance to the one of the presuppositions underpinning the formulation of Michael's pre-emptive offer in lines 17–18, namely, the implicit claim that her wanting Michael to get her a plate can be educed from her prior talk (i.e., her noticing and offer in lines 10, 13–14). In other words, the non-type confirming response by Mary is indicative of an orientation to the way in which Michael's pre-emptive response (in lines 17–18) does the interactional work of "uncovering" her prior turn's agenda (in lines 13–14). The well-prefacing here, which is typically used to indicate that the response being formulated is somehow dispreferred (Pomerantz 1984a) or non-straightforward in some sense (Schegloff and Lerner 2009), indicates an orientation to the fact that she is not straightforwardly accepting Michael's pre-emptive offer. The non-straightforwardness of her response arises from the fact that she is offering an alternative account for Michael's offer, namely, that it is not because she wants the plate for herself, but because it will avoid the troubles arising from both of them dropping biscuit crumbs, a stance towards which she increases her degree of commitment through the deployment of "actually". However, given it appears in turn-final position, "actually" also marks that this stance on Mary's part is contrary to what she perceives Michael to be expecting here (Clift 2001). It thereby implicates that Michael has not necessarily appreciated the trouble alluded to in bringing up the issue of the plates, namely, that without them they will end up dropping biscuit crumbs. It is thus to their different expectations as to the trouble caused by eating the biscuits without a plate, given that Michael declined Mary's prior proposal that he use a plate, to which Mary orients through her use of "actually" here.

In this way, then, we can see that while Michael has correctly educed that Mary wanted him to get a plate for her (and indeed she also wants him to get one for himself), he has not correctly educed the reasons for this, or at least Mary resists his construal of that warrant. Through the formulation of Mary's response it becomes apparent that the reason for Mary's implicated request is not simply that Mary prefers to use a plate, but can in fact be traced to the troubles alluded to by Mary's original noticing that she hadn't got a plate for Michael in lines 13–14, namely, not using a plate could result in them making a mess. The noticing that precedes Mary's original offer that he can get himself a plate turns out to be critical for the understanding that emerges, namely, Mary is soliciting a pre-emptive offer from Michael that he get her a plate.

It is apparent in this short excerpt that a considerable amount of interactional positioning has taken place on the part of both Michael and Mary. While not initially responded to, Mary's noticing and offer of a plate to Michael eventually turns out to be "disguising" an implicated request, through which Mary solicits an offer from Michael to get them both a plate. In constituting an offer that is solicited rather than Mary herself making a request (Lerner 1996; Schegloff 2007), Mary reduces her degree of commitment to that course of action by leaving it up to Michael to figure out the possible unstated upshot here. However, this not only decreases her degree of accountability for making a request, but more importantly in this case, reduces Michael's degree of accountability vis-à-vis complying with a the request in question.

It appears, then, that Mary is orienting to a relatively low entitlement to be making such a request (i.e. that Michael get her a plate as well as for himself in order to avoid making a mess) through this implicature, in spite of the evident contingencies (i.e. that she is relatively immobile and so it is much more practical for Michael to get the plates than her). It is in this sense that it constitutes not just an implicature, but a politeness implicature, that is, an implicature which occasions evaluations of politeness. Here it is important to note how the interactional roles Mary and Michael play here, as host and guest respectively, and the attendant expectations vis-à-vis those roles, are brought into play by this orientation to the entitlements relating to the request. One might normally expect that it lies within the host's realm of duties or obligations to provide plates and cutlery for guests, and indeed it is to this subsequently low entitlement that Mary appears to orient to through only *hinting* at a desired course of action on the part of her guest, Michael. In other words, through *hinting* Mary is orienting to a concern for being seen as "polite", or at least to avoid being seen as "impolite", in accomplishing an implicated request by soliciting a pre-emptive offer.

The more general claim that displaying an orientation to the entitlements vis-à-vis implicating a request through soliciting an offer pertains to "politeness", at least amongst (Anglo-New Zealand) speakers of English, amongst whom the prior conversation took place, can be further evidenced by another conversation where such issues were explicitly commented upon. In the following excerpt, Cheryl is being teased by her husband Larry about trying to accomplish a similar thing, namely, solicit a pre-emptive proposal. The interaction arises when Cheryl is visiting her aunty along with Larry and their son Mark. They have been talking for some time, and late afternoon has passed into early evening. Thus, when Cheryl brings up the issue of what they should do next, it is clear to the participants present that she is alluding to the issue of dinner, given they cannot have it with their aunty (whose unit, which is in a retirement village, is too small to host guests for dinner).

(77) 1 C: So what do you want to do?

  2 L: ((to Mark)) We all know that she's really already got

  3   something in mind.

  4   (2.0)

  5 C: I'm just being polite. You don't just come out with what

  6   <u>you</u> want to do all the time.

  7 L: [I'm just pullin' ya leg.

  8 C: [It's just what you do.
    (Field notes, Auckland, April 2008)

Here Larry makes a side remark to Mark, thereby treating Cheryl as an overhearer, suggesting that Cheryl already has an agenda in mind, namely, heading off to dinner. Cheryl then responds after a long pause, and visibly upset by Larry attributing an underlying agenda to her prior question, by claiming that she was "just being polite" by not "coming out with what she wants" (lines 5–6). While Larry backs off from the comment, claiming it was meant non-seriously (line 7), Cheryl frames "not coming out with what you want to do all the time" as an inherently moral concern through upgrading her claim through notionalisation (Deppermann 2011b), in this case through the generic use of "you". That is, Cheryl treats "not coming out with what you want" as something people in general do (line 8), because it's "polite" to avoid coming out what you (in the generic sense) want (line 5).

In the prior interaction between Mary and Michael, then, Mary is arguably orienting to the same underlying moral concern, namely, that not making explicit (i.e. "coming out with") what one wants is *polite*. Such an interpretation can also be warranted by the fact that Mary and Michael are reciprocating concern for their respective deontic rights and obligations (as host and guest) (Haugh 2007c: 213), in this case in regards to Mary's degree of entitlement to make this request. Through the course of the back-and-forth positioning vis-à-vis those entitlements in the latter half of the excerpt, as well as in the preceding first half, where Mary shows concern for Michael's comfort as a guest through repeating her offer of biscuits, and Michael's reciprocation of concern through affiliative responses to her offer and assessments of the biscuits, we can infer that both participants are indeed indicating concern for how the other is evaluating them vis-à-vis (im)politeness in the course of that particular interactional sequence. On those grounds, then, it can be claimed that what has arisen here is not simply an implicature, but a *politeness* implicature.

As we noted in the introduction to this book, however, implicatures are not limited to occasioning evaluations of politeness. In some instances, they can also occasion evaluations of "impoliteness" or "mock impoliteness", where the latter encompasses instances where what is ostensibly "impolite" is evaluated relative to the non-serious or jocular interpretative frame in which it is embedded as "not impolite" by at least some of the participants (Haugh and Bousfield 2012; cf. Culpeper 1996, 2011a; Leech 1983).

In the following excerpt from a conversation after lunch between four family members in a suburban home in Australia, for instance, we can observe how an implicature occasions evaluations of (mock) impoliteness. The sequence begins as four family members are sitting around the table after a meal talking about an unusual present that Melissa has given to Cindy and Bryan (which is apparently a mosquito coil holder as it turns out). The latter two have been trying to guess what it is along with Tim. This, in turn, has occasioned a joint evaluative activity where they are all implicitly invited to comment on the gift. However, rather than responding with positive assessments as one might generally expect (Good and Beach 2005; Robles 2012), this joint evaluative activity shifts into a teasing sequence when Bryan and Tim start mocking the present as an object open to derision (cf. Haugh 2013c).

(78) GCSAusE03: 1:29

> 66 M: it was only ↓three dollars so I thought o::h=
>
> 67 B: =I mean, is that a <u>crap</u> paint job? or is it-
>
> 68   is that art [istic.]
>
> 69 M: [<u>o</u>:hh,] <u>I</u> just pulled the (.) <u>price</u>
>
> 70   tag off it.
>
> 61 T: it looks like [it's been done-]
>
> 72 B: [<u>no</u>: I'm talking] about the
>
> 73   paint job in <u>gen</u>eral=like it looks it looks
>
> 74   like obviously they were holding this bit
>
> 75   here because they haven't <u>p</u>ainted that bit.
>
> 76   (0.2) [where they]=
>
> 77 T: [o:h right.]

78 B: =were holding it.

79 M: [o: :: h.]

80 T: [it looks] like it w's done with a pen.

81 B: does it?

82   (.)

83 T: yeah it [looks-]

84 M: [↑O::H,] I didn't notice that?

85 B: it looks like Joanna's painted it.

86 C: .hhh he [hehe]

87 M: [°no,] I didn't notice that.°

The excerpt itself begins when Melissa attempts to offer an account for the unsophisticated nature of the present by casting it as something that cost "only three dollars" (line 66). Bryan does not, however, align with Melissa's proffered account in his response (lines 67–68), which thus is, potentially at least, disaffiliative. Instead, by formulating an alternative question Bryan implicates a negative assessment of the present. What is notable here is that offering two alternatives, rather than presupposing a candidate answer in the form of a polar question (Pomerantz 1988), enables Bryan to display recognition of greater epistemic authority on Melissa's part to be evaluating the present by ostensibly increasing the epistemic gradient in favour of Melissa (Stivers 2010; Stivers and Rossano 2012). In other words, Bryan appears to be signalling to Melissa, and the others present, that Melissa is more knowledgeable than him in regards to the item being assessed here (i.e. the epistemic gradient is inclined in her favour), and so she has greater rights to be evaluating it than him (i.e. she has greater epistemic authority). However, this recognition of Melissa's epistemic authority by Bryan is only ostensible, because the latter option ("is that artistic") is framed as an ironic alternative, with respect to which Bryan is the producer but not the principal. In practice, then, Bryan in fact asserts epistemic authority over Melissa through his ironic formulation of the question. In this way, not only does Bryan find fault with its appearance (i.e., it has a "crap paint job"), and so it can be interpreted as criticising the gift, he also achieves a concurrent shift in speaker footing through this ironic framing (Clift 1999), whereby he detaches himself from commitment as principal of that second alternative (i.e. a positive assessment of the object as "artistic"), to a mocking evaluation of that assessment (i.e. something like, what kind of person would consider this artistic?). Through this footing shift Bryan thus implies a negative assessment of not only the object itself but also Melissa herself for purchasing the present in the first place, and also implicitly invites the side participants here (Cindy and Tim) to share in this mocking stance (Clift 1999).

Melissa's subsequent response in lines 69–70, where she offers an account for the "crap paint job", indicates that she is treating Bryan's prior utterance as implicating a negative assessment rather than as a straightforward information-seeking question. An understanding of Bryan's question as implicating a negative assessment is also apparent from Tim's subsequent formulation of an incipient tease in line 71 (which is interrupted by Bryan in line 72), where he attempts to further this overall teasing project.

The teasing of Melissa about the present then continues in lines 72–75 and 78 (by Bryan), and in lines 80, 83 and 85 (by Tim). What is notable, however, is the way in which Melissa responds to these mocking negative assessments. In lines 69–70 and 84, she proffers oh-prefaced accounts for the "crap paint job" of the present. In lines 69–80, the claim is that the attested problem with the paint job may have been caused by her ripping off the price tag, while in line 84, she claims to have not noticed that the paint job was poor overall. Oh-prefacing an account, according to Heritage (2002a), constitutes a possible resource by means of which Melissa claims epistemic independence for her stance compared to that proffered by Bryan in his sequentially first negative assessment. In other words, Melissa "conveys that the opinion that follows the *oh*-preface is independent of the 'here-and-now' of current experience and the prior speaker's evaluation" (Heritage 2002a: 201), by proffering "not noticing" at the time of purchase as an account for buying what appears to be a defective gift. The negative assessment from which Melissa claims epistemic independence, and thus disaffiliates, is the one that has been implicated here by Bryan, namely, the casting of her as someone who purchases presents that are defective and unsophisticated. Melissa then proceeds to a prototypical po-faced response to the tease, where she "treat[s] something about the tease, despite its humour, as requiring a serious response" (Drew 1987: 230), through explicit rejection of Bryan's stance in line 87.

However, while this implicated negative assessment by Bryan is recognised as non-serious by the participants, it does nevertheless invoke particular aspects of the moral order. For instance, by offering a present, Melissa implicitly displays an epistemic claim as to what she thinks the gift receivers (i.e. Cindy and Bryan) would want, like or need (Robles 2012: 767). In making assessments (on Byran and Tim's part), and offering accounts as to why the present itself might be evaluated negatively but not her person (on Melissa's part), the participants are implicitly claiming some degree of knowledge about the assessable itself (Pomerantz 1984a). Significantly, however, these negative assessments of the gift, and thus of Melissa for buying it in the first place, are not in accord with the moral expectation that a gift-giver is entitled to receive positive assessments from the gift-receiver(s) and other side participants (Good and Beach 2005; Robles 2012). Robles (2012), for instance, claims that in the normal course of things

> what 'everyone knows' is what everyone must pretend *not* to know – which is that gifts are socially and relationally loaded, that you cannot react badly to a gift even if it is undesirable, and that gifts must be assumed to have been selected in good faith, with positive intention, and aided by close knowledge of the recipient. (Robles 2012: 774, original emphasis)

In this case, then, Bryan has flouted expectations as to how a gift recipient might be expected to behave, and so the implicated negative assessment can be evaluated as "not polite" or even "impolite". For the target and direct addressee (i.e. Melissa), who is disaffiliating with the negative assessments of her person through her oh-prefaced accounts, we have evidence that she may be in fact be evaluating the implicated negative assessments as "not polite", or at least as undesirable. This latter inference seems further warranted by a subsequent positive assessment of the gift by Cindy (who says "I love it" in line 110), whereby she disaffiliates from the prior negative assessments of the gift, and thus from the implicated negative assessments of Melissa for buying the gift in the first place.

(79)   GCSAusE03: 2:25

    107   C: °oh, [that's funny.°   ]

    108   M: [°we:ll° I thought] it was a joke really,

    109   ?:   that's what he said

    110   C: I: ↑love it.

    111   M: .hhehehe

In this way, then, by invoking aspects of the deontic order through a positive assessment (i.e. how one is expected to respond to gifts), Cindy orients to the previous (implicated) negative assessments as potentially "not polite". It is in that sense, then, that these implicated negative assessments (by Byran and Tim) are likely treated as impoliteness implicatures (specifically, "not polite"), at least from the perspective of Melissa, and possibly Cindy as well.

However, given it is framed as non-serious or jocular teasing, it is evident that Bryan and Tim are treating these implicated negative assessments as "not impolite", and so as occasioning evaluations of mock impoliteness (Haugh and

Bousfield 2012). In that regard, these implicated negative assessments can also be characterised as instances of mock impoliteness implicatures. Indeed, because the (implicated) negative assessments are framed as jocular by Bryan and Tim, there is a strong normative expectation at play here that Melissa treat them as made in jest, and thus "not impolite", at least on the surface, which is exactly what she does. However, she evidently resists, at least implicitly, the implicated negative assessments about her person, as opposed to the gift, by offering accounts as to why she bought the gift (including that it was "a joke" in line 108).

In this section, we have seen how implicatures can occasion evaluations of politeness, impoliteness (cf. "not polite") and mock impoliteness (cf. "not impolite"). In examining how implicatures can occasion evaluations of im/politeness, one point that has been alluded to is that an evaluation of something as "polite" necessarily proceeds against the evaluative backdrop of what counts as "impolite", and vice-versa. Indeed, invoking the moral order through implicating can give to various im/politeness evaluations, ranging from (very) polite, not particularly polite, not polite, neither polite nor impolite, not impolite, (very) impolite, over-polite, and so and so forth.

In the following section, it is argued that these evaluations are situated within an evaluative field constituted in part via implicatures, more specifically, through scalar implicatures, which we briefly discussed in Chapter Two (section 1.2.2).

1.2 Implicatures as constitutive of im/politeness

While implicatures can evidently occasion evaluations of im/politeness, in this section it is argued that these evaluations themselves are related to one another via scalar implicatures. It is important to note that this does not amount to the claim that politeness itself constitutes an implicature (Brown and Levinson 1987; Kallia 2004; Leech 1983; cf. Terkourafi 2001, 2003, 2005). As we discussed in the previous chapter, im/politeness constitutes an attitudinal evaluation not an implicature per se (see Chapter Four, sections 2 and 3). Yet these attitudinal evaluations themselves can nevertheless be observed to be related in some instances through scalar implicatures. An evaluation of a social action or meaning as "impolite", for instance, can be interpreted by participants as scalar implicating that they evaluate it as "not polite", while evaluating a social action or meaning as "polite", can be interpreted by participants as scalar implicating that they evaluate it as "not impolite". Evaluations of im/politeness can thus arguably be productively analysed from the perspective of neo-Gricean work on scalar implicatures, in particular, drawing from Horn's (1989, 2009) work on oppositions and neg-raising. In this sense, then, while im/politeness does not constitute an implicature itself, (scalar) implicatures are nevertheless recognised in this account to be constitutive of evaluations of im/politeness in some cases.

Consider, for instance, the following excerpt from an interview with an informant about his views on how he would rate a particular apology vis-à-vis im/politeness (Chang and Haugh 2011b).[57]

(80) AM4: 5:13

  69 A: maybe it'd- he'd be placing towards the neither polite

  70   nor impolite or <u>verging</u> (.) on the polite, cer- certainly

  71   not very polite?

  72 W: mhm?

  73 A: not obsequiously polite or not any not- not- not-

  74   overly polite in any other sense, but (.)

  75   nor was he particularly impolite, I thought.

The informant starts by claiming that he would evaluate the apology as "neither polite nor impolite". What is notable here, however, is that informant subsequently attempts to characterise how he evaluates the apology both in terms of how it might be evaluated ("verging on polite"), as well as how it would not be evaluated by him ("not polite", "not obsequiously polite", "not overly polite", "not particularly impolite"). On the one hand, he accounts for his evaluation of the apology as "not (particularly) polite", through observing that the person apologising "wasn't very forthcoming with a justification or a reason or a motive for not having gone or attended you know" (data not shown). On the other hand, he accounts for his evaluation of the apology as "not (very) impolite", by suggesting the person apologising "went about retrieving by asking about the family ... you know he asked about Taiwan and the grandma and your mum, so he made a bit of an effort" (data not shown). In this way, then, the informant attempts to clarify what he means by his evaluation of the apology as "neither polite nor impolite".

---

57 This excerpt occurred in an interview with one of the informants, which formed part of a larger project on intercultural apologies. See Chang and Haugh (2011b) for further details of this study, including the process by which the informants' evaluations of the apology vis-à-vis im/politeness were elicited.

What we can see here, then, is that the informant is here implicitly invoking the so-called Apuleian or post-Aristotelian Square of Opposition (Horn 1989, 2009) in characterisating his evaluation of the apology vis-à-vis im/politeness. The Square of Opposition summarises two key types of opposition in natural language, namely, contrariety between two directions or positions, such as *good* versus *bad*, and contradiction between a position of affirmation and negation, such as *good* versus *not good*. These relationships are summarised in Figure 5 below.

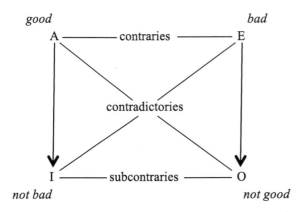

Figure 5: The post-Aristotelian/Apuleian Square of Opposition (adapted from Horn 2009: 6)

According to the Square of Opposition, A and E (e.g. *good* and *bad*) are contraries, which means they cannot be held to be simultaneously true, although they may be held to simultaneously false, that is, "neither good nor bad". Both A and O (e.g. *good* and *not good*) and E and I (e.g. *bad* and *not bad*), on the other hand, are contradictories, which means they cannot be simultaneously true or simultaneously false, and thus adhere to the Law of Excluded Middle.[58] Finally, due to the tendency in natural language to maximise contrariety, we also see the appearance of "subcontraries" (e.g. *not good* and *not bad*), which can be held to be simultaneously false, but not simultaneously true. Notably, while these subcontraries are entailed by their contraries (e.g. *good* entails *not bad*), the subcontraries only implicate their contraries (e.g. *not bad* implicates *good*). Horn (1972, 1989,

---

[58] Of course, one could say about something or someone that they are "both good and bad", "both good and not good" or "neither good nor not good" and so on. But in this case one is referring to different *aspects* of that same thing or person, and so such a claim does not negate Horn's (1989, 2009) claims about contraries in the Square of Opposition.

2012a) has focused primarily on quantity implicatures in relation to the Square of Opposition, specifically scalar implicatures, which arise vis-à-vis determiners and quantifiers (e.g. some +> not all). The key claim made by neo-Griceans is that asserting a relatively weak value implicates the speaker was not in an epistemic position to have asserted any stronger value, as we discussed in Chapter Two (see section 1.2.2).

While such analyses can be extended to deontic reasoning more generally (Beller 2008), what has not been noted to date is that evaluations of *im/politeness* themselves also fall under the scope of the Square of Opposition, as summarised in Figure 6 below.

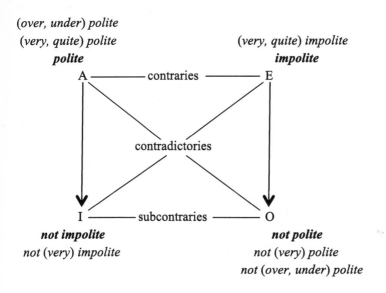

(over, under) polite
(very, quite) polite
polite

(very, quite) impolite
impolite

A ———— contraries ———— E

contradictories

I ———— subcontraries ———— O

not impolite
not (very) impolite

not polite
not (very) polite
not (over, under) polite

Figure 6: Evaluations of *im/politeness* in English and the Square of Opposition

With respect to the Square of Opposition, *polite* and *impolite* are contraries, given (the same aspect of) a social action or meaning can be evaluated ceteris paribus as *polite, impolite,* or *neither polite nor impolite,* but not as *polite and impolite.* In other words, the contrary opposition between *polite* and *impolite* allows for the existence of an unexcluded middle, namely, evaluations of something/someone as *neither polite nor impolite* (or what is sometimes termed "non-polite").[59] It thus

---

[59] Locher and Watts (2005: 12; cf. Locher 2004: 90; Watts 2005: xliii) propose that evaluations vis-à-vis im/politeness include those that are "over-polite" (negatively marked), "polite" (positively marked), "non-polite" (unmarked) and "impolite" (negatively marked). However, this

follows that social actions or meanings do not necessarily always have to be evaluated as either *polite* or *impolite*. In other words, there are a range of evaluations that can fall between "politeness" and "impoliteness".

Furthermore, as neo-Griceans point out, while contraries entail their sub-contraries, sub-contraries only implicate their contraries. It follows, then, that while to evaluate a social action or meaning as *polite* entails one evaluates it as *not impolite* (and in the same way an evaluation of something as *impolite* entails an evaluation of it as *not polite*), an evaluation of a social action or meaning as *not impolite* only implicates an evaluation of something as *polite*, and an evaluation of a social action or meaning as *not polite* only implicates an evaluation of it as *impolite*. In other words, an evaluation of a social action or meaning as *not impolite* scalar implicates an evaluation of it as *polite*, while an evaluation of a social action or meaning as *not polite* scalar implicates an evaluation of it as *impolite*. Yet because the latter are only implicated they are, of course, plausibly deniable. It follows, therefore, that one can evaluate a social action or meaning as *not impolite*, but not necessarily be held accountable for evaluating it is *polite* per se (and vice-versa, that one can evaluate something as *not polite* but not necessarily be held as evaluating it as *impolite*). However, the latter implicated evaluations might nevertheless be assumed as implicated by participants given the former (i.e. *not polite* and *not impolite*) are weaker scalar alternatives for the latter (i.e. *impolite* and *polite*, respectively). It also is important to note that given the existence of scalar implicatures vis-à-vis quantifiers, it follows that an evaluation of something as *not very polite* can implicate that it can be evaluated as *impolite*, and an evaluation of something as *not very impolite* can implicate that it can be evaluated as *polite*, and so on and so forth. Yet in being implicated, the latter evaluations are, of course, also plausibly deniable.

Another important point to note is that given both evaluations of *polite* and *not polite*, as well as evaluations of *impolite* and *not impolite*, are contradictories, one cannot ceteris paribus evaluate the same aspect of a social action or meaning as simultaneously "polite and not polite", or as simultaneously "impolite and not impolite". Thus, in cases where there are so-called mixed messages,

---

leaves open the question as to why they don't also include an evaluation of something as "non-impolite" or even "not polite" (as opposed to "non-polite") and "not impolite" (as opposed to "non-impolite"). It also leaves unanswered serious questions as to why something that is evaluated as "polite" is always "positively marked" (cf. Kádár and Haugh 2013: 63–65), and evaluating something as "impolite" or "overpolite" is always negatively marked (Haugh 2007c; see also Watts 2005, 2008). Appealing to the existence of other evaluative lexemes (e.g. *considerate*, *well-mannered*) does not readily solve these problems either (cf. Locher 2012: 13), nor does it recognise the way in which such accounts do not systematically examine the characteristics of the evaluative field in question.

that is, where features that point towards a "polite" interpretation are mixed with features that point towards an "impolite" interpretation (Culpeper 2011a), as in the case of mock impoliteness (Bousfield 2008; Culpeper 1996, 2011a; Haugh and Bousfield 2012; Leech 1983) or mock politeness (Bousfield 2008; Culpeper 1996, 2005, 2011a; Leech 1983), the importance of subcontraries for understanding evaluations of im/politeness comes to the fore. This is because subcontraries open the door to two kinds of "not impolite" or "not polite" evaluations via what Horn (1989) refers to as neg-raising.

It has long been noted that negation can be interpreted in two ways. For example, saying "I don't want to do it" can be interpreted as meaning either "I'm not-wanting to do it", or as "I'm wanting not to do it". In other words, the focus of negation can be on the speaker *not wanting* something or *not doing* something. The former is termed the outer-neg reading, and the latter the inner-neg reading. In the case of evaluations of something or someone as *not impolite* or *not polite* the so-called concessive pitch contour (Horn 2010), which involves a falling-rising (or sometimes a rising-falling) intonational contour, can be utilised to differentiate between these two senses of *not impolite* and *not polite*, depending on where intonational stress is placed. This falling-rising (or rising-falling) can involve increased amplitude or higher pitch (or both), and so can be represented as "not impoli:te" or "not poli:te" (following CA transcription conventions), or "not impoˇlite"/"not impoˆlite" or "not poˇlite"/"not poˆlite" (following more detailed GAT transcription conventions). Through intonational contour, then, speakers can differentitate between an outer neg reading and inner neg reading of *not impolite* and *not polite*. In the former case, which is generally marked with an even pitch contour (i.e. "not impolite_" or "not polite_"), the focus is on what the object of the evaluation is not taken to be. In this case, the evaluation is straightforwardly of what the social action or meaning is taken not to be, and the scalar implicated evaluation (i.e. *polite* or *impolite*, respectively) is allowed through. However, in the latter case, generally marked with some kind of concessive pitch contour (e.g. "not impoli:te" or "not poli:te"), the implicated evaluation is somewhat more nuanced, as the focus is on what the object of the evaluation could be taken to be, but is nevertheless not taken to be in that particular case. Thus, instead of "not impoli:te" scalar implicating *polite*, what is implicated instead is that the social action or meaning in question could legitimately be evaluated as *impolite*, and participants are aware of this, but it is not on this occasion evaluated as *impolite*. For this reason it can be glossed by the analyst as an evaluation of something as "non-impolite" (cf. Haugh and Bousfield 2012: 1103). And instead of "not poli:te" scalar implicating *impolite*, what is implicated instead is that the social action or meaning in question could legitimately be evaluated as *polite*, and participants are aware of this, but on this occasion it is not evaluated as *polite*. Once again, for this reason it can be glossed by the analyst as an evaluation of something as "non-polite".

These nuances in evaluations of im/politeness, which are enabled by scalar implicatures and neg-raising, are important because they allow participants, and thus analysts, to go beyond a simple binary categorisation of social actions and meanings as either "polite" or "impolite". Indeed, they allow us to go beyond even a three-way categorisation between "polite", "impolite" and "neither polite nor impolite". Instead, we have a rich set of im/politeness evaluations that collectively constitute a field in which participants themselves situate their evaluations of social actions and meanings vis-à-vis im/politeness. As we can saw in example (80) above, it is relative to this rich evaluative field this that particular informant could be seen to evaluating the apology in question vis-à-vis im/politeness. Thus, while an analysis of evaluations of im/politeness that draws from the relationships between contradictories, contraries and subcontraries might seem somewhat unnecessarily complex, the nuanced field of im/politeness evaluations that it gives rise to is a resource that we can observe participants themselves to be drawing upon in some cases. To evaluate anything vis-à-vis "politeness" or "impoliteness" necessarily invokes a broad and nuanced evaluative field. We therefore need to move beyond a simplistic approach to analysis where we classify the phenomena in question as either simply instances of "politeness" or "impoliteness", and acknowledge the broader set of evaluations that are inevitably invoked or implicated by participants themselves.

There are, of course, other relevant evaluative lexemes in English, such as *courteous, considerate, well-mannered* as well as *discourteous, inconsiderate* and *badly-mannered*, all of which can also be analysed with reference to the Square of Opposition. Even the evaluative lexemes *rude* and *offensive* can be analysed vis-à-vis *polite* with reference to the Square of Opposition, although it remains an open question as to what nuances in meaning differentiate *rude, offensive* and *impolite*, if indeed they can be systematically differentiated at all (Culpeper 2009; Watts 2008; cf. Bousfield 2010; Culpeper 2008; Terkourafi 2008).

The constitution of an evaluative field vis-à-vis im/politeness is also not, of course, limited to English, as there are analogous lexemes in other languages (Kádár and Haugh 2013: 190). Let us consider the lexeme *lǐmào* in Mandarin Chinese. When analysed with reference to the Square of Opposition, it can be argued that *bùlǐmào* constitutes the contrary of *lǐmào*, while *méilǐmào* constitutes its contradictory. However, while *búshì bùlǐmào* is logically possible as the contradictory of *bùlǐmào*, it appears that *búshì méilǐmào* is more commonly used. This potential field of evaluations directly related to *lǐmào* can thus be represented as follows:

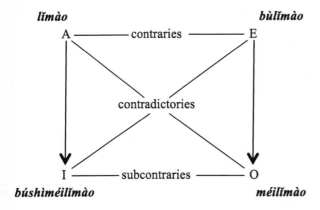

Figure 7: Evaluations of im/politeness in Chinese and the Square of Opposition

Following the same principles, we find that implicatures do not always have to be evaluated as either *lǐmào* or *bùlǐmào* given the existence of an unexcluded middle. Such an analysis also suggests that while an evaluation of the person responsible for what has been implicated as *bùlǐmào* entails that person is *méilǐmào*, an evaluation of a person as *méilǐmào* only implicates that person is *bùlǐmào*. The difference between these two evaluations is one of degree. To be *bùlǐmào* might be glossed as being "deliberately or overtly rude", while to be evaluated as *méilǐmào* constitutes a means of registering offence given it literally means "to have no *lǐmào*".

However, it is worth remembering that while is through such scalar implicatures the evaluative field vis-à-vis im/politeness can be constituted, at least in part, a number of different "politeness"-related lexemes can be invoked by participants in evaluating implicatures. In other words, scalar implicatures offer only a partial explanation of the evaluative field(s) that can be invoked by members.

Consider, for instance, the following invitation that was reported as delivered by the husband of Mei-Lin's sister with a flat and compressed intonation, when Mei-Lin went to drop off some items for her sister around dinnertime:

(81) *nǐ   yào-bu-yào   lai   chī fàn.*
      you want-Neg-want come   eat dinner
      you want Neg want come eat dinner
      ('Do you want to stay for dinner?')
      (Field notes, Brisbane, April 2013)

The first thing to note here is the expectation amongst Taiwanese (and indeed Chinese more generally) that one will invite family or friends who are visiting one's house around mealtimes to show one is "polite" (*yǒu kèqì*), as part of the broader "manners" vis-à-vis offering guests food and drinks (*shēnghuólǐyí*). However, while Mei-Lin's brother-in-law avoided an evaluation of himself as *méilǐmào* here, which would likely arise were he not to invite Mei-Lin as might be expected, the delivery of this particular invitation indicated that he was not concerned whether she would actually accept the invitation or not. The informant thus reported evaluating him as *méiyǒu chéngyì* (lit. does not have sincerity) in this instance.

It is also worth reiterating that to characterise implicatures, on some occasions at least, as constitutive of im/politeness does not amount to the claim that im/politeness itself constitutes an implicature. Instead, it draws attention to the way in which evaluations of im/politeness can be productively analysed from the perspective of neo-Gricean work on scalar implicatures. Indeed, it is these scalar implicatures that enable, in part, alongside the underpinning principles of the Square of Opposition and neg-raising, the complex and nuanced evaluative field within which such evaluations are often situated by participants.

1.3 Implicatures as occasioned by im/politeness

In the preceding two sections we have seen that not only can implicatures occasion evaluations of im/politeness in some instances, but that these evaluations themselves may be occasioned in some instances via scalar implicatures. In this section, it is proposed that there are also cases where evaluations of im/politeness may occasion the interactional achievement of implicatures. It is in this latter sense that it can be argued that evaluations of im/politeness may also be, at times, constitutive of implicatures.

Such an observation has, in fact, been made in passing in early work on speaker meaning (Leech 1983; Bertuccelli Papi 2001). Leech (1983), for instance, noted that in order for participants to readily understand what has been implicated, they must also orient to issues of im/politeness. In the following excerpt, which was briefly noted in the previous chapter (see section 2), the second interactant is responding to the accusation implicated by the first speaker.

(82)　P:　Someone's eaten the icing off the cake.

　　　　C:　It wasn't *me*.
　　　　(Leech 1983: 80, original emphasis)

However, as Leech (1983) points out, the second speaker figures out what is being implicated with respect to not only the Cooperative Principle, but also through an orientation to a concern for politeness as well: "the apparent relevance of *C*'s reply is due to an implicature of *P*'s utterance. *C* responds to that implicature [an indirect accusation], the indirectness of which is motivated by politeness, rather than to what is actually said" (Leech 1983: 81). In other words, in order to figure out what is being implicated by P, C is necessarily assuming that P is taking a more "polite" stance through impersonalisation (i.e. "someone") than could otherwise have been taken. Such an example also illustrates that evaluations of (im) propriety, (im)politeness and so on, can occasion implicatures. In other words, the implicature arising through P's initial utterance is a consequence, in turn, of P's evaluation of someone (most likely C) having "eaten the icing off the cake" as an impropriety, and C's inference that P is treating that as an impropriety.

In subsequent work, Bertuccelli Papi (2001) also argued that "attitudes and emotions may represent alternative options which most strongly inhere the notion of speaker's meaning, and ... lead the search for implicit meaning in different directions" (p.247). She offers the example of interpreting what is meant by someone saying, "You are an academic". She suggests that what is taken to be meant by the speaker depends on the presumed attitude of the speaker, which can range, for instance, from deferential through to sceptical or even scornful. In cases where the recipient presumes a "deferential" attitude, the speaker can be taken to mean something like, "Your knowledge is vast, what you say is influential, you are very intelligent, you hold an important position, you are reliable ... therefore, I respect you" (*ibid.*: 259). In cases where the recipient presumes a "scornful" attitude on the part of the speaker, in contrast, the speaker can be taken to mean something like, "You are interested in power, you can deceive, you are a narcissist ... therefore, I dislike you" (*ibid.*: 260). In other words, inferences by the recipient about the stance of the speaker vis-à-vis im/politeness plays a part in figuring out what is meant by that speaker. It is for this reason that Bertuccelli Papi (2001) argues that "if what we are looking for is the *speaker's* meaning ... [we] must integrate some representation of the speaker him/herself within the utterance" (p.248, original emphasis). It follows, then, that in many cases when analysing implicatures we must necessarily consider the attitudinal stance of the speaker him or herself.

A series of experiments on the interpretation of implicatures has also demonstrated that an orientation to "politeness" can influence the way in which scalar implicatures are interpreted by participants (e.g. Bonnefon and Villejoubert 2006; Bonnefon, Feeney and Villejoubert 2009; Demeure 2010; Demeure, Bonnefon and Raufaste 2008, 2009; Feeney and Bonnefon 2013; Pighin and Bonnefon 2011) or "indirect meanings" more generally (Holtgraves 1998b, 2000). For instance, Bonnefon and Villejoubert (2006) found that the more severe a medical condition was judged to be, the more likely participants were to interpret the use of "possibly" as a hedge, and thus the more likely they would be to interpret the prospect of the medical condition arising. While "possibly" is generally understood to mean something around 55% probability, given it scalar implicates "not probable", it was found amongst many participants that they assessed the probability as rising to up to 70% when the medical condition was judged to be severe. Bonnefon and Villejoubert's (2006) thus concluded that the quantifier "possibly" was being construed as a politeness marker rather than as an uncertainty marker by the participants, and it is this interpretation which blocked "not probable" being scalar implicated.

The question, then, is in what way or ways can an orientation to (im)politeness on the part of participants contribute to those participants figuring out what has been implicated? Here it is argued that there are at least two key ways in which (im)politeness may be constitutive of implicatures. The first is that an orientation on the part of the speaker to being evaluated as polite, or to avoid being evaluated as impolite, can occasion implicatures. The second is that evaluation of an impropriety or inapposite action on the part of another person or group of persons can also occasion implicatures.

We can see how evaluations of im/politeness can be constitutive of the participants' understanding of what has been implicated in the following interaction, where what has been left unsaid through an utterance-final "or" is interpreted with respect to their evident concern about avoiding potential evaluations of impoliteness. The excerpt is from part of a larger sequence where Chris and Emma have been talking about Emma's acupuncture business.[60]

(83) ERCH: 11:07

    304 C: how do you go generally with most of your

    305   customers °are they happy or°

    306   (0.8)

    307 E: ↑YEAH

    308 C: yeah?

    309 E: yeah. I've been getting (0.6) most of my business

    310   actually <u>now</u> (0.2) now that it's gaining (0.2)

---

60 cf. the analysis of this example in Haugh (2008c: 59–60, 2011b: 207).

311   momentum is um word of mouth

312 C: mmm

313 E: from (.) patients telling other patients.

314 C: right.

As Haugh (2011b) argues, through the use of utterance-final "or" in interrogatives, speakers are able to indicate greater epistemic uncertainty about the candidate answer than what is standardly taken to be indicated through polar questions. This is because interrogatives formulated as "*p* or?" can be interpreted as either polar questions (i.e. *p* or not *p*?), or as alternative questions (i.e. *p* or *q*?). It is through this interpretative equivocality that greater epistemic uncertainty is indicated:

> While utterances of the form *p?* are interpreted as the speaker not knowing whether *p* is the case (i.e., $\neg K_a(p)$), the utterance-type examined here, *p* or?, [can be] interpreted by recipients as the speaker indicating he does not know that *p or not p* ($\neg K_a(p) \wedge \neg K_a(\neg p)$) or alternatively, he does not know that *p or q* ($\neg K_a(p) \wedge \neg K_a(q)$). (Haugh 2011b: 215)

This means that through an utterance-final "or" in line 305, Chris is able to implicate a greater degree of epistemic uncertainty as to the level of happiness or satisfaction of Emma's customers. This utterance-final disjunctive particle thus constitutes evidence that Chris is orienting to the negative assessment that potentially arises as an implicated premise from the content of the question itself, that is, the supposition that some customers may not be happy or satisfied with the treatment that Emma offers. This is because it constitutes an attempt to background this potentially "impolite" implicated premise by increasing the epistemic gradient through an implicature of uncertainty. We can also see evidence that Emma also orients to the potential impoliteness of this implicated premise, as while she opts for a treatment of Chris's interrogative as instantiating a polar question through responding "yeah" (lines 307, 309), these affirmative responses are delivered with a rising tone and louder volume accompanied by an account or warrant for this affirmative response (lines 309–311, 313). The discourse particle "actually" in line 310 here also indexes that her response is contrary to what she perceives to be Chris's expectations (Clift 2001), once again implicitly orienting to the negative assessment (i.e. that the customers are unhappy or dissatisfied) that potentially arises as an implicated premise through Chris's initial query. Once again, then, we can observe how incipient evaluations of impoliteness can be oriented to by participants, and thereby occasion implicatures. It is in this sense, then, that we can analyse im/politeness as constitutive of implicatures on some occasions.

The way in which evaluations of impropriety, offence or impoliteness in regard to the actions of another party can occasion implicatures can be observed in the following conversation between two sisters who are talking over dinner. The excerpt begins when Adriana suddenly interrupts what Bianca is saying to inquire about the whereabouts of the coke.

(84)   ICE-AUS: S1A-007: 8:39

    193 B: and I thought- I was thinking oh I wonder

    194   if Brian's [ring-

    195 A: [whe:re's the ↑CO:ke.

    196 B: been ringing.

    197 B: I <u>had</u> it.

    198   (0.4)

    199 A: °wha:t?° <u>a</u>:ll of it.

    200   (1.0)

    201 B: there's some co:rdial in the- (.) in the u:m (0.7) <u>pan</u>try.

    202   have some co:ld <u>wat</u>er an' cordial.

    203 A: °thanks for having the coke°

    204   (2.5)

    205 B: can you get me a glass <u>too</u>?

While formulated syntactically as an interrogative, Adriana's utterance in line 195 evidently functions as a question seeking an explanation or account as to what has happened to the coke that she evidently expected to find in the fridge. Thus, through reporting an "unhappy incident" (Pomerantz 1978b), namely, the coke no longer being in the fridge, and seeking an account for that state of affairs through a *why*-interrogative (Bolden and Robinson 2011), Adriana is implicating an accusation that Bianca may be the one responsible for this unhappy incident. Upon hearing Bianca admit that she finished off the coke (line 197), Adriana subsequently indexes a stance of shocked surprise with a faintly uttered "what" token (line 199), which functions here as a self-directed response cry (Goffman 1978[1981]).

This is followed by another utterance in the same turn that is syntactically formulated as a polar question, but here implicates that finishing off the coke constitutes an "impropriety". This claim implicitly invokes aspects of the deontic order, specifically Adriana's perceived high entitlement to be the one to finish off the coke, and Bianca's low entitlement to be doing so, and thus the latter's attendant obligation to *ask* before finishing it off. The sense that Adriana does indeed perceive an impropriety on Bianca's part is further evidenced by her subsequent response in line 203 to Bianca's suggestion that she get some cordial instead (lines 201–202), namely, an ironically formulated thanks, which here functions as a possible complaint (Drew 1998). Through the incongruity of thanking in this context, where she is implicating accusations and complaints, Adriana thereby implicates a strongly negative evaluation of the alleged target of this thanking, and so it is hearable as sarcasm (Clift 1999), or what has been characterised as a "mock politeness" in the literature (Culpeper 1996). In this case, then, it is an evaluation of an impropriety on the part of Adriana (i.e. finishing off Bianca's coke) which evidently occasions evaluative social actions (i.e. accusing/blaming, complaining, sarcasm), which are achieved, in turn, through implicatures. In other words, evaluations of impoliteness or impropriety on Bianca's part by Adriana are here constitutive of the implicatures that subsequently arise.

In sum, it has been argued here in analysing im/politeness implicatures as social practice that not only can implicatures occasion evaluations of im/politeness, but that evaluations of im/politeness can be constituted through scalar implicatures in some instances, and that such evaluations can occasion implicatures in other cases. The relationship between im/politeness and implicatures is thus more complex than previous accounts of (im)politeness-as-implicature would have it.

One point that has been repeatedly alluded to in analysing im/politeness implicatures in this chapter thus far, is that close attention needs to be directed at the sequential environment in which they arise. It is thus to a consideration of the import of the locally situated sequential environment in which im/politeness implicatures arise that we now turn.

2 Im/politeness implicatures and the temporal-sequential order

It has long been recognised that time is fundamentally constitutive of social action in interaction as they arise through and across sequences of turns formulated by different participants (Garfinkel [1964]1967; Heritage 1984a; Schegloff 2007; Sacks, Schegloff and Jefferson 1974). Close examination of implicatures in interaction indicates that they can also emerge across turns (i.e. from a sequence of utterances), and so the same temporal constraints and affordances on participants' interpretations of social actions apply equally to participants' understandings of implicatures. As we have seen from numerous examples discussed thus far, an implicature does not necessarily always belong to any single one utterance, a point which lies in stark contrast to the way in which implicatures have traditionally been analysed as tied to or arising from single utterances or speaker turns. It follows that tying the interpretation of implicatures to the speaker's communicative intention is overly constraining for our analyses of them (Haugh 2008c, 2009a), and in some cases may even be potentially misleading (Haugh 2012b; cf. Wedgwood 2011). It is thus claimed in this section that im/politeness implicatures need to be situated relative to the sequential, and thus oft-time, emergent contexts in which they arise. As Schegloff (1988a) argues, "it is clear that temporality and sequentiality are inescapable; utterances are in turns, and turns are parts of sequences; sequences and the projects done through them enter constitutively into utterances like the warp in a woven fabric" (p.61). The temporal affordances and constraints on the ways in which im/politeness implicatures arise in interaction all form part of what is termed here the temporal-sequential order. In this section, two key dimensions of the temporal-sequential order are claimed to be of particular importance to the analysis of im/politeness implicatures: temporality, in the sense of time in both the here-and-now and the there-and-then (section 1.1), and sequential position (section 1.2). It is suggested that the temporal-sequential order affords the way in which interpretations of im/politeness implicatures are inevitably contingent, and so are "recalculable" by participants, and yet are also constrained by the very same order, and so are also "calculable" by those participants (Sanders 1987).

2.1 Temporality: adjacency, incrementality and emergence

In early work, Garfinkel ([1964]1967) argued that the temporal nature of interaction constrains and affords the interpretations of participants through what he termed the "retrospective-prospective sense of a present occurrence", which involves participants "waiting for something later in order to see what was meant before" (p.41). This is now generally analysed in terms of adjacency in CA, where "next turns are understood by co-participants to display their speaker's understanding of the just-prior turn and to embody an action responsive to the just-prior turn so understood" (Schegloff 2007: 15). In other words, through the normative force of adjacency, present turns constrain and afford interpretations of the actions, meanings and evaluations occasioned by both prior and prospective talk. Retrospectively, current turns offer indications of a "speaker's understanding of the prior" turn, while prospectively, current turns set "some of the terms by which a next turn will be understood" (Schegloff 2007: 16). Given the simultaneously retrospective-prospective orientation of participants, it has been observed that talk itself develops incrementally. In other words, speakers adjust or modify their talk in light of how the progressive uttering of units of talk is received by other participants both within (Goodwin 1979), and across turns (Nevile and Rendle-Short 2009). The fact that social actions and meanings are produced incrementally in interaction also means they are inevitably subject to ongoing evaluation as they are produced, and so they can be adjusted accordingly in real time. This is particularly pertinent in the case of im/politeness implicatures, where participants are often actively inferring or even anticipating what others are taken to be incipiently implicating.

The importance of adjacency and incrementality for the analysis of social actions and meanings in social interaction more generally has been formalised through three principles in the Conjoint Co-Constituting Model of Communication (CCM) (Arundale 1999, 2005, 2008, 2010a): the Recipient Design Principle (RDP), the Sequential Interpreting Principle (SIP), and the Adjacent Placement Principle (APP). The first principle, the RDP (Recipient Design Principle), refers to the ways in which speakers take into account the perspective of other participants in formulating meanings that are implicated through talk (and conduct):

> Speakers *frame* an utterance to be produced on the basis of expectations arising in prior producing and interpreting, recipient meanings and actions to be engendered, and expectations regarding recipient uptake; they *attribute* to the future recipient certain knowledge of evolving interpretings and of resources and practices for interpreting; they *presume* the recipient will ascribe to him/her the interpreting the recipient formulates, and will hold him/her accountable for it; they *anticipate* the recipient's interpreting, ascribing, assessing, and invoking in formulating meanings and actions for the utterance being designed; and they *produce* the utterance by selecting and articulating components. (Arundale 2010a: 2082–2083, original emphasis; cf. Arundale 1999: 135)

According to the RDP, then, speakers draw from particular design features that take into account their understanding of the recipients' expectations, knowledge, and the like, when implicating something in interaction. In other words, speakers presume they will be held accountable (albeit to varying degrees) for implicatures that arise through *implying, hinting, alluding* and so on.

The second principle, the SIP (Sequential Interpreting Principle), refers to the ways in which recipients take into account prior and possible subsequent talk in forming their understandings of what might be implicated by current talk:

> Recipients *interpret* the utterance currently being produced using both knowledge and expectations arising in designing and interpreting prior utterances; they *ascribe* their current interpreting to the producer of the utterance as the producer's meaning or action, holding him/her accountable for it; they *assess* consistency between their current provisional interpreting and evolving prior interpreting, forming operative interpretings; and they *invoke* expectations for designing and interpreting subsequent utterances. (Arundale 2010a: 2082, original emphasis; cf. Arundale 1999: 131)

According to the SIP, then, understandings displayed through next turns have the potential to engender both "retroactive modifying" and "retroactive confirming" (Arundale 2010a: 2082) of what is taken to have been implicated by participants. In other words, recipients can hold speakers accountable for implicatures arising through *implying, hinting, alluding* and so on, through their responses.

Finally, the APP (Adjacent Placement Principle) refers to the way in which participants treat current talk as closely related to talk that is contiguous, that is, talk that is immediately prior or subsequent to current talk:

> Unless the speaker indicates otherwise, *recipients interpret* the utterance currently being produced on the presumption that it is designed in view of the immediately prior utterance (and others that may have preceded it), and is grounds for designing the immediately subsequent utterance (and others that follow). Reciprocally, unless they indicate otherwise, *speakers design* the utterance currently being produced on the presumption that it will be interpreted in view of the immediately prior utterance (and others that may have preceded it), and is grounds for interpreting the immediately subsequent utterance (and others that follow). (Arundale 2010a: 2081, original emphasis; cf. Arundale 1999: 139)

The APP is what affords a speaker's understanding of what has been implicated contingent on a recipient indicating what he or she understands to have been implicated, and vice-versa. It is this simultaneously retrospective and prospective operation of current turns of talk that ultimately confers emergent properties on social actions and meanings in talk-in-interaction (Arundale 2010a; Haugh 2012a).

The utility of the three key principles of the Conjoint Co-Constituting Model of Communication in relation to the analysis of politeness implicatures has already been explored at length in Haugh (2007a), where it is argued that im/politeness implicatures emerge as joint products of turn design (cf. RDP) and interpretative work (cf. SIP) undertaken by speakers and recipients, as participants' utterances or turns are produced incrementally over time (cf. APP). It is argued that only through examining at least three adjacent turns of talk can it be formally established that an implicature has indeed arisen. According to this view, an (im)politeness implicature emerges as a conjoint understanding that is dependent on the design and interpretation of adjacent turns at talk. Specifically, it is an *emergent* understanding because the design and interpretation of each turn is reciprocally linked and conditional upon those that proceed and follow it (Arundale 2010a; Haugh 2012a: 260).

The incremental emergence of understandings of im/politeness implicatures means it is thus critical that the analysis of im/politeness implicatures is grounded in the locally situated interactions in which they arise. Indeed, the incremental emergence of im/politeness implicatures over sequences of turns of talk is why they are inevitably treated as contingent understandings by participants, as was noted in relation to implicatures more generally in Chapter Three. In other words, the oft contingency of im/politeness implicatures is a consequence of the way in which they emerge over sequences of talk.

Yet while the sequential order has often been studied at the level of adjacent turns of talk, it is important to note that there is a second key way in which the temporal nature of interaction constrains and affords the interpretations of participants. This involves what Garfinkel ([1964]1967) refers to as the "occasionality of expressions" (p.41), in which their "sense" cannot be understood unless a participant "knows or assumes something about the biography and the purposes of the speaker, the circumstances of the utterance, the previous course of the conversation, or the particular relationship of actual or potential interaction that exists between user and auditor" (Garfinkel [1964]1967: 40; cf. Levinson 2013: 127). Consistent with arguments made by Sifianou (2012) and others, then, im/politeness, and thus im/politeness implicatures, cannot be analysed without reference being made to time in a somewhat different sense, where we talk of interactions as "turns in an ongoing exchange interspersed with 'pauses' of minutes, hours or days" (Sifianou 2012: 1561), since, as was suggested in the previous chapter, while evaluations of im/politeness are occasioned by social actions/meanings, they can also in themselves occasion social actions/meanings. In other words, analyses of im/politeness implicatures must ultimately be grounded both in the locally situated sequential contexts in which they are occasioned, as well as situated with respect to the broader relational histories of those participants.

The importance of taking into account the potential non-summativity or reciprocal conditionality of interpretings by participants, alongside the broader relational history of those participants in analysing im/politeness implicatures can be illustrated with reference to the following excerpt from an interaction where the two participants are getting acquainted. What is notable here is that there are (at least) two possible understandings that might be implemented by Chris's enquiry about whether Emma is able to treat a particular condition using acupuncture, namely, as a teasing challenge or as request implicative (Haugh 2008c: 62–64, 2009a: 103–104, 2012b: 178–185), as we briefly discussed in Chapter Three (see example [57], section 3.1). Here, we consider this example in more detail from the perspective of time both as punctuated (i.e. the here-and-now) and as emergent (i.e. with respect to the then-and-there), in conjunction with the three principles of Arundale's (1999, 2006, 2010a) CCM.

(85)   ERCH: 8:18

    216 E: SO: (0.2) the:y (0.5) aim to learn to understand it [an:d]=

    217 C: [right]

    218 E: =grow sensitive to it you know, I'm like [(   )]

    219 C: [yeah]

    220   (0.6)

    221 C: °mmm°

    222   (0.2)

    223 E: and the needles happen to be one of the most

    224   effective ways to (0.6) manipulate it

    225 C: yea:h?

    226 E: mmmm

    227 C: can you fix patellar tendonitis? °heh°

    228   (1.7)

    229 E: ↑maybe ↑ye:ah

    230 C: yeah?

    231   (0.3)

    232 E: yeah you got that?

    233 C: I have yeah
(adapted from Haugh 2012b: 178)

Emma initially treats Chris's utterance in line 227 as implementing a request for information through her subsequent response (line 229). More specifically, Emma appears to orient to the second possible understanding of Chris's question in line 227, namely, as potentially pre-request implicative through a go-ahead response to Chris's pre-asking. However, Chris does not initiate a request subsequent to Emma's possible go-ahead response, but rather seeks confirmation of this affirmative response (line 230), occasioned perhaps by the hedged response Emma has given to this prior question, when she initially indicates some uncertainty ("maybe"), although subsequently upgrades her degree of certainly through a self-initiated self-repair in the same turn ("ye:ah"). Emma then orients to the possibility that this interactional project (i.e. that Chris would like to seek acupuncture treatment from her) might be in play by inquiring whether Chris has such a condition (line 232). In other words, while Chris's utterance in line 227 is hearable as implementing two distinct actions (RDP), that is, as implicating a teasing challenge or as pre-request implicative, Emma response in line 229 is consistent with a provisional interpreting of it as implementing the latter (SIP). Chris's subsequent response in line 230 is consistent with Emma's apparent interpreting of his prior utterance as pre-request implicative (APP), and thus an operative interpreting of Chris's utterance in line 227 as implementing a pre-request is conjointly co-constituted.

Chris subsequently withholds such a request, however, as they move into a line of questioning initiated by Emma about Chris's condition (data not shown). It is more than one and a half minutes, then, before the participants return to what has been possibly implicated by Chris's initial query in turn 226, namely, a request for acupuncture treatment from Emma. At this point in the interaction Emma implements an offer, which here still counts as pre-emptive given Chris has not actually made a request for any such treatment thus far in the conversation.

(86)   ERCH: 9:40

    288 E: [BUT] I don't know how (0.3) u::h

    289 C: [oh]

    290   (1.0)

    291 E: like (0.5) I don't know if I could get a

    292   lasting result I don't know if I could cure

    293   it but I could [certainly] probably improve it

    294 C: [yeah]

    295   (0.5)

    296 C: yeah (0.2) ( ) your card [or a::h]

    297 E: [↑YEAH] I'll give ya a card

    298 C: yeah

299 E: I'll give ya a card [now   ]

300 C: [willing] to give anything a go

Notably, the offer here in lines 291–293 is not formulated with a "do you want X" syntactic structure. In this way, Emma avoids the implication that she has understood Chris's prior raising of his condition in line 227 as a "fishing device" (Curl 2006: 1274; see also Pomerantz 1980), or even an attempt to solicit an offer of treatment from her. In other words, through implementing the offer indirectly through implicature rather than through an explicitly formulated offer, Emma avoids an unwanted, potentially impolite implication.

Yet while an understanding of Chris's utterance in line 227 as pre-request implicative becomes the focus of the official business of this interaction (i.e. what is oriented to by the participants in the action trajectory that subsequently develops turn-by-turn), there are nevertheless grounds nevertheless claim that another possible understanding of Chris's utterance is that it unofficially implements a teasing challenge (i.e. implicating something like, but could you really treat something like this?). It is important to note first of all that the design of the utterance itself is consistent with such an understanding, as was briefly noted in Chapter Three. It is delivered with a compressed intonation, consistent with other studies of the intonation of mockery (Attardo et al. 2003; Haugh 2010a, 2014; Haugh and Bousfield 2012), as well as being appended with a post-utterance completion laughter particle, which here invites Emma to join in with laughter (Glenn 2003; Jefferson 1979; Jefferson, Sacks and Schegloff 1987; Schenkein 1972), as well as orienting to the incipient trouble such a teasing challenge might engender (Shaw, Hepburn and Potter 2013). In other words, in being designed as a potentially non-serious question, an understanding of Chris's utterance as implementing a teasing challenge is made available to Emma. The availability of this possible understanding to the participants is further evident from a sequence that occurs more than one minute prior to Chris's utterance in line 227, where Emma displays an understanding of Chris's question about how acupuncture works as implying a teasing challenge.

(87)   ERCH: 7:03

181 C: so what's the basic idea behind acupuncture?

182   I mean [I know a little about] it but, [you know]

183 E: [OH COME ON HEH]   [.hhhhh   ]

184   (0.3)

185 C: I mean

186   (0.4)

187 E: u::m=

188 C: =does it wo(hh)rk? kheh

189 E: ye:ah it works=

190 C: =ye(hh)h?

191 E: yeah yeah it really works (0.3) there's no

192   (.) no question about it working (0.5) but

193   nobody knows exactly what the mechanism is (0.5)

194   [scientifically]

195 C: [yeah it's a bit] mysterious.

The beginning of a new action sequence is indicated here by *so*-prefacing of the question turn-construction unit in line 181, which, as Bolden (2009), argues is used to mark it as "'emerging from incipiency' rather than being contingent on the immediately preceding talk" (p.974). In this way, the question is interactionally positioned as "having been 'on the speaker's mind' or 'on agenda' for some time" (*ibid.*: 976). Emma orients to this incipient agenda as one of scepticism or doubt about the efficacy of acupuncture by responding in line 183 with a display of possible exasperation ("oh come on") delivered in a markedly louder voice in overlapping talk that lies outside a recognisable transition relevance place (Sacks, Schegloff and Jefferson 1974). Chris's implicated challenge is subsequently made more explicit in an *I mean*-prefaced self-repair (lines 185, 188), whereby he "encourage[s] alignment to the action that [the] connected-to utterance projects", here a question-answer sequence in the context of seemingly "dispreferred and inapposite talk" (Maynard 2013: 227). Notably, interpolated particles of aspiration (IPAs) occur in "work" (line 188), thereby "softening the action" (Potter and Hepburn 2010: 1552), which is here perceived to be a teasing challenge, alongside the post-utterance completion laughter particle by which Chris invites Emma to see the challenge as non-serious, as well as to indicate an orientation to the incipient trouble occasioned by this teasing challenge (Shaw, Hepburn and Potter 2013). In this way, Chris appears to attend to the potential impropriety of such a challenge. While Emma emphatically responds in the affirmative (line 189), Chris pursues further confirmation (lines 190), which is also indicative of his apparent scepticism (see also line 195). Notably, this pursuit of confirmation is delivered with IPAs (i.e. "ye(hh)h?"), thereby marking this action as potentially problematic for Emma (Potter and Hepburn 2010), and so yet again Chris can be seen to be attending to the potential impropriety of his implicated scepticism. Yet while the teasing challenge here is oriented to as ostensibly non-serious, and so "not impoli:te"/"not impo˘lite" (i.e. mock impolite) (see section 1.2 this chapter), at least from Chris's perspective, but given that acupuncture is Emma's livelihood an interpretation of the question as challenging the legitimacy of her occupation is almost inevitable from her perspective. In light of this preceding sequence, then, Chris's question in line 227 is hearable as implicating a teasing challenge, although this is not an understanding that Emma orients to in subsequent talk as it turns out.

What this analysis of talk prior to and subsequent to that initial turn – and which is thus sequentially distanced from that talk – shows is that participants can entertain multiple possible understandings of current talk that are dependent on the broader, evolving sequential context instantiated in the course of the participants ongoing relationship. In this case, one possible understanding of Chris's utterance in line 227 as pre-request implicative is treated as the official business of the interaction, while another possible understanding, an implicated teasing challenge, remains unofficial business as it does not change "the nature of the sequential action type now due" (Levinson 2013: 107). In analysing im/politeness implicatures, then, it is important to remember they can work at both the official and unofficial levels of understanding in interaction.

2.2 Sequential position and accountability

The critical role sequentiality plays in the analysis of im/politeness implicature can be further explored along other lines. One productive line of investigation is to carefully examine the sequential position in which implicatures arise. More specifically, it can be observed that im/politeness implicatures arise as either *first*-positioned (i.e initiating) or *next*-positioned (i.e. responsive) relative to a particular action trajectory. This turns out to be critical as this sequential positioning is in some cases constitutive of what these im/politeness implicatures are taken by participants to be doing in interaction, and so can be particularly important for evaluating the degree of accountability of participants for the implicatures in question.

A first-positioned im/politeness implicature is one which is oriented towards accomplishing an incipient or nascent social action trajectory. It is thus fundamentally projective in character, albeit contingent on the possible understanding(s) that are oriented to by next speaker(s). In being first-positioned, implicatures can thereby afford the pursuit of multiple possible understandings by participants. However, given there is more than one possible understanding at play, this modulates the degree to which the first speaker can be held accountable for this incipient upshot, allusion and the like (see Chapter 3), and also the degree to which he or she can be held accountable for mobilising a particular (set of) response(s) (Schegloff 2010; cf. Stivers and Rossano 2010). In other words, first-positioned implicatures allow speakers to decrease their degree of accountability for this incipient upshot, allusion and so on, and thus renders them less accountable for mobilising a particular (set of) contingently relevant response(s). Initiating social actions through incipient upshots and the like in this way also allows participants to orient to salient aspects of the moral order, thereby occasioning evaluations of im/politeness.

In the following excerpt, for instance, from a telephone call in which Skip has called Jim, a request is achieved through Skip alluding to the conditions for fulfilling the said request.

(88) Holt 2:14

```
1   Jim:   J.P. Blenkinsop good morning,

2          (.)

3   Skip:  Good morning Ji:m,

4          (0.5)

5   Skip:  Uh it's Skip.

6   Jim:   ↑Hiyuh,

7   Skip:  You coming past the doo:r,

8   Jim:   Certainly?

9          (0.8)

10  Jim:   What time wouldju like the car Sah.=

11  Skip:  =Uh ↓well ehhh hhehh hhhehh hhehh .hh Oh that's

12         m:ost unexpected of you hhh::: n(h)o it's v(h)ery

13         nice'v you to offer huhh uh-↑heh huh-u-hu-.ehhh

14         £Thanks very much.£ .hh [h

15  Jim:                          [Eh:m I wz planning tih

16         leave here at just about twenty ...
```
(Drew 1995: 118)

In this excerpt, Skip's inquiry in line 7 is treated by Jim as a recognisable pre-asking (Schegloff 2007), which makes a go-ahead or blocking response conditionally relevant. However, while Jim initially responds with a go-ahead response (line 8), thereby affording a subsequent request from Skip, Jim subsequently issues a reformulated response to the pre-asking, namely, a pre-emptive offer (line 10). The latter potentially constitutes the preferred response to this pre-request, as it "pre-empts the need for a request altogether by offering that which is to be requested" (Schegloff 2007: 90). However, there are two features of this reformulated response by Jim that mark this interaction as somewhat more than a simply a straightforward case of a pre-request occasioning a pre-emptive offer (Drew 1995: 119).

First of all, Jim's reformulated response constitutes an instance of responding indirectly in that it is non-type-conforming (i.e. it is not yes/no in this case), and also requires some form of inference in order for it be understood as a response to Skip's prior turn (Walker, Drew and Local 2011: 2340). Through couching his response as responding indirectly, then, not only does Jim implement a pre-emptive offer, but does so in such a way that "uncovers the perceived purpose or 'agenda' displayed in the prior turn", or what Jim takes Skip to "'really' want to know" (p.2441), namely, whether Jim can give him a ride. In other words, through responding indirectly, Jim draws attention to their respective benefactive status (Heritage 2013). This next-positioned response thus constitutes a social action in itself beyond what is projected as contingently relevant through the design of Skip's prior turn.

Second, through his response, Jim mimics the voice of a chauffeur (Drew 1995: 118–119), a jocular framing which then elicits laughing acceptance and appreciation of the offer by Skip (line 11). In framing the pre-emptive offer in this way, Jim takes a position of "deontic subordination" (Heritage 2013: 571), to which Skip responds in turn with an overdone expression of gratitude, thereby highlighting incongruities between this non-serious or jocular invoking of deontic status (i.e. Jim should be giving Skip a ride), and their respective benefactive status (i.e. Skip is the one who is benefiting given Jim is not obligated to give Skip a ride). Given Heritage (2013) argues this interactional sequence is "most likely part of a regular pattern of car sharing" (p.571), it appears that the two participants are orienting to an "over-polite" routine. While this is interactionally achieved within a mocking frame, it does nevertheless indicate that this request, here achieved through an implicated upshot, does indeed involve an orientation on the part of the participants to issues of politeness.

What we can see from both this example, then, is that first-positioned im/politeness implicatures enable speakers to place some degree of responsibility for the development of the incipient action trajectory on the recipient, who is not only interpreting what has been implicated by the producer of the prior talk, but is also afforded the opportunity to decide upon which course of action to take in response.

While a first-positioned im/politeness implicature initiates a particular action trajectory, a next-positioned im/politeness implicature is one which is responsive to an action trajectory already in progress. A key feature of next-positioned im/politeness implicatures is that they implement social actions that are responsive to this trajectory, and so are analysable (to participants) as occasioned by prior actions. This means that next-positioned im/politeness implicatures arise not only through *implying*, *hinting*, and not-saying and the like, but can also arise through withholding a response in such a way that it constitutes a "noticeable" or "relevant" absence (Schegloff 1968: 1083, 2007: 20, 2010: 39–40), as we alluded to in discussing example (60) at the beginning of Chapter Four. Yet despite being responsive to an ongoing action trajectory, they also constitute social actions in themselves, as through them (prior) speakers can be held morally accountable for a particular (set of) understanding(s), as noted by Walker, Drew and Local (2011). At the same time, just as in the case of first-positioned implicatures, the speaker positions him or herself as less than fully accountable through this incipient upshot, allusion and so on, thereby invoking aspects of the moral order.

In the following example, which we discussed briefly in Chapter One, the two speakers are talking about an ESL (English Second Language) program in an American university. A has been talking up until this point about how they have been spending quite a bit of money upgrading the facilities at the ESL centre at his university

(89)   IND77 CHAm4247

8   B: do they have any scholarships for foreign students

9   A: .hhhhhh I- I'm- I've never heard of a scholarship

10   for an English language program personally

11   b[ut I think

12   B: [>we never did< either but I keep thinking

13   I'm going to fin::d one one of these days uh huh

14   ((laughter))
(adapted from Walker, Drew and Local 2011: 2446)

As was previously noted, A's response in lines 9–11 to B's inquiry about scholarships for foreign students in line 8 implicates that they do not have such scholarships. However, it not only implies a negative response, but also constitutes an instance of responding indirectly (Walker, Drew and Local 2011), whereby A displays an understanding of B's question as inapposite. In other words, A indicates through indirectly responding that B should already know this, given their presumed shared knowledge of the area, and so the prior question is seemingly redundant. Indeed, B herself acknowledges the possible inappropriateness of her question in the subsequent turn, when she admits that she was pretty sure that such scholarships don't exist. In this case, then, A orients to the implicated premise implemented through B's prior question – specifically the existential presupposition that there are scholarships for English language programs in existence – as inapposite by responding indirectly. However, given A only implicates that such a presupposition is not sound and that B should already know this, he treats this apparent lapse as a delicacy. In other words, A treats an outright correction of B's (apparently mistaken) presupposition as something that cannot be properly said here in this interaction, and so any such explicit correction could potentially constitute an impropriety (Lerner 2013: 95). On those grounds, then, it can be argued that this next-positioned implicature involves an orientation to a concern for avoiding impropriety, thereby occasioning politeness. However, while B orients to what has been implicated in her next turn, this lapse remains at the unofficial level (Drew 1984: 132, 1995; Levinson 2013: 107), thereby reducing the degree to which both participants are holding themselves morally accountable for displaying an understanding of B's initial question as inapposite.

In examining more carefully the temporal-sequential order relative to which im/politeness implicatures arise it has become clear, then, that

> meaning lies not with the speaker nor the addressee nor the utterance alone as many philosophical arguments have considered, but rather with the interactional past, current, and projected next moment. The meaning of an entire utterance is a complex, not well understood, algorithm of these emergent, non-linear, sense-making interactions. (Schegloff, Ochs and Thompson 1996: 40).

In this section it has been argued that im/politeness implicatures are constrained and afforded by the temporality of interaction in two senses: both in the sense of time as punctuated and time as emergent (Haugh 2012a). In this way, we can account for how im/politeness implicatures are not only calculable (i.e. participants are able to develop plausible interpretings of what is meant on this occasion at this point), but also recalculable (i.e. those interpretings of what is meant are contingent, and so can change in light of subsequent talk, or by invoking additional contextual assumptions) (see also Sanders 1987).

In the following section, we move to consider the way in which the socioinferential order that underpins the generation of im/politeness implicatures affords their (re)calculability.

3 Im/politeness implicatures and the socio-inferential order

The sociocognitive work that underpins im/politeness implicatures involves a complex array of intentional state-processes, including attention/attending, intention/intending, belief/believing, desire/wanting, thought/thinking, inference/inferring and so on (Haugh 2012b; Kádár and Haugh 2013: 209–211). Various frameworks have thus been developed to account for the dynamic nature of socio-cognitive work that underpins communicative interaction (e.g. Arundale 1999, 2010a; Arundale and Good 2002; Kecskes 2010; Levinson 2006; Sanders 1987). However, given the focus of this book is primarily on what interactional and interpersonal work is accomplished through im/politeness implicatures, a comprehensive account of the underpinning socio-inferential order must be deferred for the moment. Instead, the discussion in this section will focus primarily on the distinction between default (or presumptive) and nonce (or particularised) inference, and how these can give rise to default im/politeness implicatures and nonce im/politeness implicatures, respectively (cf. Haugh 2008c: 57–67). It is suggested that by drawing such a distinction we can account the way in which im/politeness implicatures that appear to arise in minimal contexts (see footnote 19) unless otherwise blocked, and those that appear to require locally, situated contextual information in order to arise, modulate the (speaker's) accountability for what has been implicated in systematically different ways. These two main categories of inference, default and nonce, and subtypes of them are summarised in Figure 8 below (see Haugh 2013e for further discussion).

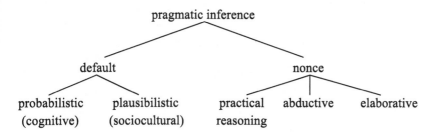

Figure 8: Types of pragmatic inference

3.1 Default im/politeness implicatures

Numerous scholars have emphasised the important role default inferences or conventions play in communicative interaction (e.g. Arundale 1999; Bach 1984, 1995; Davies 1998; Grice 2001; Jasczcolt 2005; Levinson 1995, 2000; Mazzone 2011; Recanati 2004; Terkourafi 2003, 2005), as we discussed in Chapter Two. Different definitions of default, standardised or associative inference abound, but here default im/politeness implicatures are broadly defined as encompassing those instances where im/politeness is occasioned by an utterance-type that is standardly taken to implicate x by members of a particular speech community. An utterance-type is taken to encompass particular expressions, or linguistic resources, that are recurrently deployed in particular sequential environments to implicate particular social action trajectories. In other words, a default im/politeness implicature is identified by the way in which an implicature arises through inference that has been compressed by precedent, as formalised in Arundale's (1999) "default interpreting principle":

> If an expectation for default interpreting is currently invoked, and if no conflicting interpreting is present, recipients formulate the presumed interpreting(s) for any current constituent consistent with th[at] expectation. (Arundale 1999: 143)

It is important to note that this does not amount to the claim that an evaluation of im/politeness is necessarily occasioned by such utterance-types, but rather that what is implicated recurrently arises when this utterance-type arises in particular sequential environments. A default implicature may, in turn, depending on local contingencies, also give rise to an evaluation of im/politeness, and it is only in these cases that it can be characterised as a default im/politeness implicature.[61] In other words, a default im/politeness implicature is characterised as such because what is implicated by the utterance-type in question standardly arises, not because such an utterance-type necessarily gives rise to evaluations of im/politeness.

Thus far we have alluded in passing to a number of examples of default implicatures that can occasion evaluations of im/politeness. In Chapters Two and Three, for instance, we briefly discussed how asking what someone is doing or planning is standardly taken to be pre-invitation implicative (see examples 30 and 45), and in some instances at least can be perceived as indicating a "polite" attitude on the part of the speaker. And in this chapter, we briefly discussed

---

61 It thus differs from the distinction drawn between im/politeness being anticipated by participants as opposed to inferred (Haugh 2003; cf. Fraser 2005; Jary 1998; Terkourafi 2001, 2003, 2005).

another example, namely, the occurrence of trailing-off "or" in utterance-final position in information-seeking questions (example 84). The latter involves an implicature of epistemic uncertainty on the part of the speaker which standardly arises in this sequential environment (Haugh 2011b), and which can also be perceived as indicating a "polite" attitude on the part of the speaker on some occasions (see also Haugh 2008c: 60–61). Instances of what neo-Griceans term short-circuited implicatures thus appear to constitute one potential type of default (im/politeness) implicature.

There is arguably an array of so-called conventionalised expressions, some of which may be specific to particular languages, that can occasion default im/politeness implicatures. In the following interaction, for instance, we can observe how the expression *kangaete okimashō* (lit. 'I'll think about it'), which standardly implicates a refusal, is deployed in an exchange where a salesperson (S) is trying to convince a potential customer, Ms Tanaka (T), to purchase a subscription to the Maiasa newspaper.

(90)   (A lady picks up the intercom phone after the doorbell rings)

1   S: *konnichiwaa. Maiasa-shinbun   na-n-desu   ga,*
          good day   Maiasa newpaper Cop-Nomi-Cop(Pol) but

2   *ima, shinbun   nani   o-tori-ninat-te-i-masu   ka.*
     now newspaper which Hon-subscribe-Hon-Te-Prog-Pol Q
     ('Good day. I am from the Maiasa newspaper. Which paper are you subscribing to at the moment?')

3   T: *sumimasen, uchi wa   zutto   hibi   na-n-desu   yo.*
          excuse me   we   Top always daily Cop-Nomi-Cop(Pol) M
          ('Sorry, we already have a daily at our place')

4   S: *sō desu   ka. Kondo   uchi no shinbun   o*
          that wayCop(Pol) Q   next time you of newspaper Acc

5   *tot-te-mora-e-mas-en   ka, sankagetsu de*
     subscribe-Te-receive-Pot-Pol-Neg Q three months with

6   *ii-n-desu   yo. Ima nara, iroiro   saabisu*
     good Nomi-Cop(Pol) M   now if   various extras

7   *shi-masu yo.*
     do-Pol   M
     ('Really? Won't you try our newspaper for just three months? If you subscribe now we have various specials and extras we can offer')

8 H: *sō*   *desu*   *ne, kangae-te-oki-mashō.*
      that way Cop(Pol) M think-Te-leave-Aux(Pol)
      ('Sure...let me think about it')
(adapted from Hashimoto 1992: 149)

In lines 1–2, there is a recognisable pre-sequence that is designed to lead into a proposal that the lady, Tanaka, purchase a subscription to a different newspaper. The response in line 3 from Tanaka is pre-refusal implicative, in part because she frames it as a dispreferred response through a turn-initial "apology" (*sumimasen*), and in part because she does not name the newspaper she subscribes to, thereby resisting the terms of the salespersons prior question (Stivers and Hayashi 2010). This potential pre-refusal is not, however, oriented to by the salesperson, who goes on to formulate a proposal (lines 4–7). Tanaka then responds that she will "think about it" (line 8). However, given the prior pre-refusal implicative turn, the default implicature, namely, that she is not interested, is here triggered, alongside a closing of the sequence. This is clear from the fact that the salesperson does not engage in any further attempts to persuade the lady. However, since this refusal is only implicated, the lady ostensibly orients to the salesperson's deontic entitlement vis-à-vis his role (i.e. *tachiba*) to have such offers taken seriously. In this way, a polite attitude is indicated through her claim that she will "think about it". Yet, on the other hand, it is clear to both participants that a refusal has been implicated, or at least it has been for the moment.

    A feature of default im/politeness implicatures more generally, then, is that the degree of indeterminacy vis-à-vis what is implicated is relatively low. In other words, the object of the implicature is more or less determinate (albeit contextually sensitive), and so there is a low degree of type 1 indeterminacy (see section 4.1 in Chapter Three). However, the degree to which the speaker is committed to that implicature is somewhat more indeterminate, and so there is potentially a high degree of type 2 indeterminacy. In other words, what is implicated is fairly clear (i.e. there is a low degree of type 1 indeterminacy), but whether the speaker is fully committed to that is less clear (i.e. there is potentially a high degree of type 2 indeterminacy). It is through maintaining some degree of indeterminacy vis-à-vis the speaker's commitment to what is standardly implicated by the expression in question, that the speaker modulates his or her degree of accountability for what has been implicated. In the example above, for instance, what remains indeterminate is the extent to which Tanaka is committing herself to her implicated refusal of the salesperson's offer. There always remains the possibility that she could decide later on to subscribe to the newspaper in question, and, importantly, this would not be a choice that is incoherent with what she has previously said.

This feature of default im/politeness implicatures also explains why there is no indeterminacy in regards to the evaluative field co-constituted through scalar implicatures. For example, an evaluation of something as "not impolite" can scalar implicate an evaluation of it as "polite", while an evaluation of something as "not polite" can scalar implicate and evaluation of it as "impolite", as we discussed earlier in this chapter (section 1.2). Yet it is apparent that these scalar-implicated im/politeness evaluations are not necessarily oriented to by participants in locally, situated interactions. Given default im/politeness implicatures are not type 1 indeterminate, but only type 2 indeterminate, what is implicated may remain clear (e.g. "not impolite" implicates "polite"), but whether the participant(s) in question is committed at that time to the evaluation in question that has been scalar implicated remains indeterminate. In other words, saying someone is "not impolite" standardly implicates that person is "polite", but whether the speaker in question is committed to that which has been scalar-implicated may can remain relatively indeterminate.

In the following section, we shall see that nonce im/politeness implicatures, in contrast, may be either type 1 indeterminate or type 2 indeterminate, or even both in some cases.

3.2 Nonce im/politeness implicatures

Nonce im/politeness implicatures arise through inferences specific to particular situated contexts, and so are largely analogous in scope to what Grice identified as particularised conversational implicatures, or what Relevance theorists simply term implicatures. The way in which nonce im/politeness implicatures arise through reflective inferences, that is, through inferences that require a meta-representational process of reasoning (albeit not necessarily consciously experienced) (Mercier and Sperber 2009), is formalised in Arundale's (1999) "nonce interpreting principle":

> If an expectation for nonce interpreting is currently invoked, whether because default interpreting was terminated, because no expectation for default interpreting was invoked, or because the expectation for nonce interpreting was invoked explicitly, recipients formulate a particularised interpreting for any constituent consistent with th[at] expectation. (Arundale 1999: 143)

Nonce im/politeness implicatures thus differ from default im/politeness implicatures in that they can be both type 1 and type 2 indeterminate. In other words, either what is implicated or how committed the speaker is to that which is taken to be implicated can be indeterminate, and as a consequence is recalculable.

If we recall example (87), for instance, which we discussed earlier in this chapter, what Chris meant by asking "Can you fix patellar tendonitis?" was initially potentially ambiguous between being understood as pre-request implicative or as implicating a teasing challenge. What was implicated by this question on this occasion was subsequently conjointly co-constituted by the two participants. This jointly accomplished understanding of what Chris had implicated drew, in turn, on the two participants' contingent interpretings of Chris's overall project (cf. higher-order intention; see section 1.4 in Chapter 3), which it emerged, in this case, involved seeking treatment for that condition.

The inevitable contingency of participants' understandings of nonce im/politeness implicatures, and default im/politeness implicatures on occasion, also underpins the existence of what Arundale (2008, 2010a) terms non-summative or emergent interpretings. A non-summative interpreting in relation to a (nonce) im/politeness implicature is where the participants' understanding of this implicature arises through inferences on their part that are formally interdependent. In other words, what one participant understands to have been implicated depends not only on what she perceives the other participant to have understood to have been implicated, but also on what she perceives the other participant to perceive she has perceived to have been implicated, and vice-versa.

The interdependency of inferences underpinning the interactional achievement of im/politeness implicatures can be illustrated by returning to the example mentioned above, and tracing how the inferences underpinning Chris and Emma's interpretings of what has been implicated through him asking "Can you fix patellar tendonitis" become interdependent over a number of turns. The relevant part of example (85) has been reproduced in a simplified form in order to make tracing these inferences more tractable.[62]

(91)   Chris: can you fix patellar tendonitis?   [utterance a]

      Emma: maybe yeah   [utterance b]

      Chris: yeah?   [utterance c]

      Emma: yeah you got that?   [utterance d]

      Chris: I have yeah   [utterance e]

As was previously argued in section 2.1 of this chapter, Chris and Emma indicate to each other through their subsequent turns, utterance c in the case of Chris, and

---

62 This analysis draws from that outlined in Haugh (2012b: 186–188).

utterance d in the case of Emma, that they have reached an understanding that Chris's original question (utterance a) is pre-request implicative. The question, then, is how do Chris and Emma not only infer that Chris's question (utterance a) can be interpreted as pre-request implicative, but also infer that the other person has inferred this?

In order to trace the inferences that underpin their respective understandings, we can draw from Arundale's (2010a) distinction between provisional and operative interpretings. This distinction is a formal one based on whether or not the degree of fit or aptness of an interpreting of a particular locally situated utterance (or other unit of talk) with the overall trajectory of the talk has been considered in light of understandings displayed by others. A provisional interpreting of an utterance, according to Arundale (2010a), is an understanding on the part of one participant that is "not yet assessed in view of uptake" by the other participant (or participants) (p.2080). This does not mean that a participant is necessarily uncertain about his or her understanding at that point, but simply that it has not yet been considered in light of the responses of others to that particular utterance. An operative interpreting of an utterance, according to Arundale (2010a), is an understanding of one participant that has been "assessed in view of uptake" by other participants (p.2080). However, this does not mean to say that a participant cannot subsequently change his or her understanding in light of further interaction. Both provisional and operative interpretings are always contingent. The difference lies in whether or not the interpretings are grounded in subsequent uptake by other participants.

Building on these distinctions, the main inferences that can be hypothesised to underpin their respective understandings of not only Chris's question itself, but also, more importantly, their understandings of each other's understandings of Chris's question, are outlined below:

C1: Chris's inference of Emma's projected interpreting of his *utterance a*.
E1: Emma's inference of Chris's provisional interpreting of his *utterance a*.
C2: Chris's inference of Emma's provisional interpreting of his *utterance a* in light of her *utterance b*.
E2: Emma's inference of Chris's operative interpreting of his *utterance a* in light of his *utterance c*.
C3: Chris's inference of Emma's operative interpreting of his *utterance a* in light of her *utterance d*.

The inferential work required for them to achieve operative interpretings of utterance a (i.e. understandings that have been assessed for their fit with subsequent displays of understanding of that utterance) can be described in three inferential steps for each participant: C1–C3 represents the three inferences made by Chris, and E1–E3 represent the three inferences made by Emma. What is most important to note here is how these inferences progressively become interlocked and so formally interdependent.

Chris's inference about Emma's operative interpreting of *utterance a* (C3), for instance, is dependent, in part, on Emma's indication through *utterance d* of her interpreting of Chris's operative interpreting of *utterance a* (E2), as well his inference about Emma's provisional interpreting of *utterance a* (C2), which is dependent, in turn, on Emma's indication through *utterance b* of her inferred interpreting of Chris's provisional interpreting of *utterance a* (E1), as well as on Chris's initial inference about Emma's projected interpreting of *utterance a* (C1). We can see, then, that Chris's inference at this point in the sequence (C3) is afforded and constrained by his own prior inferences (C2, C1), as well as inferences made evident by Emma (E2, E1) through her responses to *utterance a*, which are in turn, afforded and constrained by inferences that Chris has made evident (C2) through his subsequent response in *utterance c*. Chris's inference about Emma's operative interpreting of *utterance a* at this point is thus formally interdependent with displays of inferences by Emma, which are formally interdependent, in turn, with displays of inferences made by Chris (Haugh 2012b: 187).

This kind of cognitive interdependence is achieved over a number of turns at talk rather than at any single one turn. For this reason, it appears that im/politeness implicatures not only require inferences that arise independently of the cognitive processes of others (e.g. those leading to C1), but also inferences that are interdependent with the cognitive processes of others(e.g. those leading to C3) (see Arundale and Good 2002 for a similar point). The typology of inferential work underpinning im/politeness implicatures presented in Figure 8 thus needs to be expanded to include such interdependent or dyadic inferences. This is not to say that such interdependent inferencing is always required in order for nonce im/politeness implicatures to arise. But as we shall see in the subsequent two chapters, im/politeness implicatures often arise over the course of a number of turns involving two or more different participants. In such cases, the inferential work on the part of each participant, and displays of that work through their respective utterances, becomes entwined such that one can no longer trace an individual participant's understanding of that im/politeness implicature without also considering how it fits with the understandings of others. It is for this reason that the inferential work underpinning im/politeness implicatures is best studied as situated in interaction.

4 The pragmatics of im/politeness implicatures

In this chapter, building on the prior observation that implicatures can arise due to a concern for interpersonal relations on the part of participants (see section 1 in Chapter 4.), it has been suggested that implicatures and im/politeness have a complex and nuanced relationship. Not only are evaluations of im/politeness occasioned by implicatures in some instances, but, implicatures themselves may also be constitutive of evaluations of im/politeness, and vice-versa, evaluations of im/politeness can, in some instances, be constitutive of implicatures. It has thus been suggested that im/politeness implicatures are more productively ana-lysed as a form of social practice, given the complex and nuanced relationship that exists between im/politeness and implicature.

In analysing im/politeness as social practice in the course of this chapter we have also alluded to the way in which the degree of indeterminacy of an impli-cature is interactionally achieved by participants relative to the transparency of its overall purpose (cf. illocutionary point), its intentional direction (cf. proposi-tional content), and its target (cf. figure). The degree of participant commitment to or accountability for an implicature is interactionally achieved by participants, in turn, vis-à-vis the perceived force or strength of the lexico-semantic composi-tion of the talk in question, its sequential position, and the participation footing relative to which it arises.

This view of im/politeness implicatures is summarised in Figure 9 below. According to this hypothesised model, it is through modulating the degree of indeterminacy of pragmatic meanings, or modulating the degree of participant (i.e. speaker or recipient) commitment to pragmatic meaning by implicating that participants are able to invoke particular aspects of the moral order. And it is invoking aspects of moral order in this way that can occasion, in turn, evalu-ations of im/politeness. To analyse im/politeness implicatures we thus need to consider both their interactional and moral grounding.

In this chapter, we have focused on the importance of situating the analy-sis of im/politeness implicatures in time, and how participants do so in regular, recurrent ways vis-à-vis the temporal-interactional order. In particular, it has been suggested that im/politeness implicatures have both summative and non-summative properties given the understandings of participants themselves are sequentially-grounded. It has been further argued that im/politeness implica-tures can be either first-positioned or next-positioned, and that this sequential positioning relative to the overall action trajectory is constitutive, in part, of what such im/politeness implicatures are taken by participants to be doing in interac-tion. This finding is critical to the analysis of politeness and impoliteness implica-tures, as the discussion in the following two chapters will illustrate.

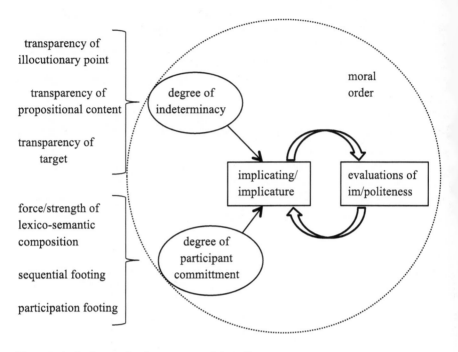

Figure 9: Im/politeness implicatures as social practice

We have also considered how understandings of im/politeness implicatures arise relative to what Agha (2003) terms "socially locatable persons" (p.242). In other words, im/politeness implicatures do not exist in the abstract, but rather relative to persons situated in social space, which leads us into a consideration of the questions of *for whom* certain implicatures are taken to be occasioning im/politeness, and on *what grounds* these implicatures are interpreted and evaluated in that way (Haugh 2013c). It is argued that the former can be formally approached vis-à-vis the participation order, the complex array of production and reception footings relative to which im/politeness implicatures arise (see Chapter 4: section 4.2), while the latter can be systematically studied vis-à-vis the moral order, the complex sets of seen but unnoticed intersubjective expectancies relative to which participants ground their understandings of im/politeness implicatures (see Chapter 4: section 4.1). And while there has not been sufficient space to develop this line of argument here, it has been implicitly suggested throughout these analyses that our understanding of the moral order can be extended through systematic consideration of the metapragmatics of im/politeness implicatures, that is, an analysis of various forms of awareness on the part of participants themselves vis-à-vis im/politeness (Kádár and Haugh 2013: Chp.9; Haugh and Kádár forthcoming).

Finally, the socio-inferential processes by which im/politeness implicatures arise have been briefly considered. It has been suggested that we need to acknowledge, but also go beyond traditional accounts, in order to account for the dynamic socio-inferential grounding of understandings of im/politeness implicatures. In other words, the socio-inferential order that underpins the interpretive and evaluative processes through which im/politeness implicatures are (conjointly) co-constituted must be one which is grounded in a cognition *for* interaction (Arundale and Good 2002; Haugh 2009a, 2012b; Levinson 2006). In doing so, we have returned to consider in more detail some of the issues that were raised in our discussion of different approaches to implicature in Chapter Two, including debates about the place of conventions or defaults as well as speaker intentions, vis-a-vis implicatures.

In the following two chapters, we move to analyse examples of politeness implicatures and impoliteness implicatures in greater detail, building on various elements of this analytical framework.

Chapter Six:
Politeness implicatures and social action

1 Analysing politeness implicatures vis-à-vis social action

A politeness implicature has been broadly defined as an instance where through implicating rather than saying, a polite stance on the part of the speaker is occasioned. In the previous two chapters, it has been argued, more specifically, that through implicating the participants can unofficially invoke aspects of the moral order, thereby occasioning an evaluation that the current speaker is orienting to a concern for "politeness" or "propriety". The various ways in which implicating can invoke aspects of the moral order has only been alluded to in the course of that discussion, although we have briefly touched upon the ways in which it can involve negotiating the respective epistemic, deontic or benefactives stances of participants. It has been suggested that it is by orienting to these aspects of the moral order through politeness implicatures that participants are able to accomplish particular moral dimensions of the interactional projects in progress in unofficial ways. To be accomplished unofficially means that the "sequential action type now due" is not overtly constrained by that which has been implicated (Levinson 2013: 107), and so that aspect of the interactional project in question remains open to deniability, or at the very least, there is some room to move left in which further negotiations about what exactly the participants are taken to be committing themselves to meaning can continue. This is important because it suggests that politeness implicatures are not simply a means of being polite, but rather can be analysed from the perspective of what participants are *doing* through such implicatures in interaction.

In the following excerpt, for instance, which is taken from a discussion between two colleagues in a Japanese importing company based in Australia, Matthew and Satomi are considering what information to include on the label of a fruit juice product. Matthew has been suggesting they should include information about how much lycopene the fruit juice contains. However, Satomi has countered that this could prove difficult, as they do not have detailed information about the amount of lycopene in the lemon content of the juice. This then leads into the following discussion about what they should include in the contents of the label.

(92)   Office Day: 11:02AM

33   S: *ja: remon wa   tte   koto   ni nat-ta   toki   ni*
          then lemon Top Quot thing to become-Past time in
          ('when we are asked, "well, how about lemon?"')

34   M: *un*
          ('yeah')

35   S: *nante (   ) shi-tara*
          how   do-if
          ('how can we (   )')

36   M: *shiraberu?*
          find out
          ('[should we] find it out?')

37   (2.5)

38   S: *dō   shi-yō   ka*
          how do-Vol Q
          ('<u>what</u> should we do...?')

39   (3.0)

40   S: *un   sō.   dakara   atashi koko no   e   ni   wa*
          hmm that way therefore I   here Nomi to in   Top

41   *kaka-nakat-ta-n-da   yo=*
          write-Neg-Past-Nomi-Cop M
          ('hmm, yeah. That's why I didn't put it on this picture')

42   M: *=u::n*
          ('ye::ah')

43   S: *bunshō   de hidari-gawa ni kaitoi-ta-n-da   yo*
          paragraph at left-side   in put-Past-Nomi-Cop M
          ('I put that in a <u>para</u>graph on the left')

44   M: *u::n*
          ('we::ll')

45   (20.0)

46   M: *at-ta   hō   ga   ii   to   omou-n-dat-tara*
          have-Past way Nom good Quot think-Nomi-Cop-if

47   *kantan-ni shirabereru to   omou-n-da   kedo*
        easily   find   Quot think-Nomi-Cop but

48   <*hitsuyō   nano kana:*> *kore mo*
        necessary thing wonder this also
        ('if you think [that information] should be there, then I can easily
        find it out, but I wonder if this is really necessary)

49 S: *HONto-ni chotto desho* (.) *go-paasento miman dakara ne*
        really   little   probably 5 percent   under so   M
        ('it's really a small amount, isn't it? It's under 5%')

50 M: *iya iya iya motto* (.) *motto aru   motto aru*
        no no no more   more have more have
        ('no, no, no, more. It has more. It has more')

51 S: ↑*a sō*↓   *na   no?*
        oh that way COP Nomi
        ('ah, is that really?')

52 M: %they are organic%

53 S: *a   sō   na   no*
        oh that way COP Nomi
        ('ah, is that so?')

54 M: *desho* (.) *ja:*
        probably then
        ('it is, isn't is? so:')

55 S: *a: sō   da ne ja: shirabete   sa:*
        oh that way Cop M then find out-Te M
        ('ah, that's right. Then you find it out, and')

56 M: *un*
        ('yeah')

(adapted from Watanabe 2009: 178–181)

By outlining this potential problem more explicitly (lines 33–34), and then raising the question of what they should do (lines 35), specifically in the form of an "asking conditional" (Stevanovic 2013), Satomi implicitly challenges Matthew's position that they should include lycopene content in the label, and yet simultaneously invites him to "engage in joint decision-making about the proposed plan" (Stevanovic 2013: 519). The upshot itself is, however, left attenuated (Schegloff 2007: 83). This allows Satomi to signal that she is, at least ostensibly, leaving it open to Matthew to make a decision about the label by leaving the completion of her turn "designedly ambiguous" (Mori and Nakamura 2008: 53), thereby orienting to her lower deontic entitlement to be making such a decision (Stevanovic and Peräkylä 2012). Their respective deontic entitlements reflect, in turn, thir perceived role-status (i.e. *tachiba*) of each participant up to this point, both of which are being interactionally negotiated and achieved in this particular situated context (Haugh and Obana 2011). In other words, by implicating this upshot, and consequently indexing deontic aspects of the moral order, Satomi's response is open to evaluation as "polite".

Matthew subsequently suggests that they can find out the lycopene content of the lemon in the juice (line 36), thereby maintaining, here through an implicated premise, at least some degree of commitment to his position thus far that they should include the lycopene content on the label. However, rather than answering his query directly, Satomi repeats the question of what they should do (line 38) after somewhat of a pause (line 37). This delayed repetition is not only framed as a dispreferred (Mori 1999; Mori and Nakamura 2008; Pomerantz 1984b), but also constitutes an instance of "indirectly responding" (Walker, Drew and Local 2011), given it is a non-type-conforming answer (i.e. it is neither a yes or no response despite the formulation of prior Matthew's turn as a polar question), and thereby indicates that Matthew's question is somehow inapposite. In other words, through indirectly responding, Satomi is able to implicate disagreement with Matthew's position, but in such a way that once again ostensibly indicates a lower deontic entitlement in regards to making the final decision. This therefore constitutes yet candidate politeness implicature.

Satomi next offers an account for her design of the label (lines 40–41, 43). The upshot of this account, namely, that they shouldn't include lycopene content on the label, is once again left attenuated, although she does this time index a concern that her account be "acknowledged and acted upon" through the deployment of turn-final *yo* (Morita 2012b: 1721) (cf. lines 29–32). In other words, the implicated proposal is implemented through a turn design that makes a response to this proposal contingently relevant in contrast to the design of the previous upshots (cf. lines 35, 38). In that sense, Satomi is positioning herself as more accountable for this implicated upshot, shifting from an implicated expression of doubt to an implicated expression of incipient disagreement.

A relatively long period of silence then follows, which is finally broken when Matthew proposes that if including the lycopene content of the lemons in the juice is necessary (line 46), then they should find out this information (line 47), although he subsequently weakens his commitment to this proposal when he questions whether it is really necessary to include the information (line 48).

Satomi then implicitly suggests that it is not worth finding out the information because lemons only contain a negligible amount of lycopene (line 49), but this assumption is subsequently strongly challenged by Matthew (line 50). Matthew's counter-claim that the amount of lycopene is more than 5%, and thus not negligible, is subsequently treated by Satomi as constituting new information (line 51), although this receipting is done through a question design format, rather than a straightforward assertion, thereby implicating some uncertainty about the veracity of this claim.

After Matthew provides an account for this claim, namely the lemons are "organic" (line 52), which Satomi once again receipts as new information (line 53), he then implicates that Satomi should accede to his suggestion through an utterance final epistemic particle, *deshō* ('it is, isn't is?') in line 54. This particle indicates, according to Kamio (1994, 1997), epistemic certainty on the part of the speaker about the information in question, but also indicates the speaker's assumption that the recipient is also aware of this information, albeit with a lesser degree of certainty. In other words, through this particle Matthew indexes a positive epistemic gradient between himself and Satomi (i.e. that he knows more than her, but she knows enough to know he is right), thereby implicating that they should agree on his suggested course of action. However, in attributing some degree of knowledge to Satomi, Matthew thereby also indexes a lower degree of deontic entitlement to make the final decision about the label. In this way, then, Matthew mirrors the concern that Satomi has previously displayed towards their respective situated role-status (i.e. *tachiba*) through implicating her disagreement with his suggested course of action. An orientation to a concern for their respective role-status on the part of both participants is thus reciprocated, and so evaluations of politeness are here arguably interactionally achieved (Haugh 2007c), specifically, a concern for avoiding being seen as making unwarranted claims to deontic authority in relation to making decisions and thus "impolite" by the other.

Satomi herself also acknowledges that this positive epistemic gradient lies in Matthew's favour through the formulation of her subsequent response (line 55), where she expresses agreement with Matthew's initial suggestion that they find out the necessary information about the lycopene content of lemons, as well as indicating this action trajectory is prospectively "non-negotiable" through the utterance-final *sa* (Morita 2005: 26). In other words, Satomi strongly affiliates with Matthew's stance here, thereby reciprocating his concern for her epistemic status vis-à-vis this professional, work-related knowledge.

It is evident from this analysis, then, that participants are able to accomplish things in interaction through politeness implicatures. In this case, politeness implicatures arise in the course of negotiating a proposal about what course of action to take in a workplace. As Chang (1999) argues, implicatures afford "inter-actants considerable flexibility in negotiating relational position and role behaviour within the confines of a relational system" (p.535). Here the relational system in question is the relative role-status (*tachiba*) of Matthew and Satomi in the company for which they work. Through these politeness implicatures such negotiations can proceed in unofficial ways, whereby these participants can (ostensibly) "manage to disguise an object's strategic use" (Drew 1995: 134). This means in effect that "by not being responsible for formulating an upshot, and thus *not being committed to a position*, speakers can subsequently revise a position attributed to them" (Drew 1984: 138–139, emphasis added), while at the same time allowing the current speaker to position the recipient as themselves contingently committed to a particular position should they indicate or formulate a particular interpretation of any such upshot through their subsequent uptake.

This observation leads us to a consideration, in turn, of the various practices by which participants can frame a social action (or set of social actions) as "attenuated" through withholding an upshot (Schegloff 1995, 2007: 83), "avoided" through indexing hesitation or delaying mention of this upshot (Lerner 2013: 98), or "masked" through accomplishing the said action in the guise of another action (Schegloff 2007: 84). Indeed, as Drew (2013) argues, "*withholding* a response, and *implying that one disagrees* without doing so explicitly, are both actions" (p.140, emphasis added). In this chapter, then, we analyse in more detail the practices by which participants recognise such "attenuated", "avoided" or "masked" social actions, thereby providing the grounds for examining what participants are *doing* through politeness implicatures in interaction. While there are more than likely many such practices, in this chapter we will consider just six of them here in order to sample the range of such practices available to participants, and to demonstrate how through politeness implicatures, participants can accomplish social actions in unofficial ways.

In addition, while most of the examples considered up until this point have been from English, in this chapter examples from other languages, specifically, Chinese and Japanese, are also considered in order to make the point that while implicatures may arise in similar ways across languages, whether these are treated as indicating an orientation on the part of participants to "politeness", that is, as *politeness* implicatures can vary across languages. In other words, whether implicating is taken by participants to indicate an orientation to "politeness" depends not only on the particulars of the locally situated interaction, but also the practices by which the moral order is implemented and sustained by its members, as we discussed in Chapter Four (see section 4.1). Given the latter is something which can systematically vary across groups of speakers, including those groups marked by the use of different languages, whether an implicature counts as a politeness implicature is something that inevitably draws on members' understandings of aspects of the moral order in which their evaluation of "politeness" is grounded. For this reason, the analysis of politeness implicatures vis-à-vis social action in this chapter necessarily makes reference to aspects of the moral order being implemented and sustained by speakers of the language in question through these implicatures. This should not be taken to indicate implicit claims about so-called cultural differences given the limited number of examples considered in this chapter, but rather an attempt to take seriously the understandings of participants not simply as individuals, but as members vis-à-vis particular aspects of the moral order from which they are inevitably drawing in interacting with other members.

We start, in the following section, by considering instances of "attenuating" and "withholding" whereby speakers not only implicate upshots (cf. *implying, imparting*), but also position the formulation of that upshot as contingently relevant for subsequent talk. We then move on to examine instances of "pre-empting" (cf. *supposing, construing*) where recipients attribute an incipient agenda to a prior turn, thereby making as if it has already been implicated, followed by an analysis of "soliciting" (cf. *hinting*), where by making a pre-emptive response contingently relevant, speakers position recipients as responsible for that action. We next consider instances of "disattending" which is accomplished through either transformative or sequentially irrelevant responses to that which has been made contingently relevant in the prior turn. Finally, we discuss instances of doing "delicacy" (cf. *not-saying, alluding*) that arise through delaying or hesitating in saying, thereby orienting to what is not said as a potential impropriety.

It is concluded from this analysis, albeit only a partial one, of some of the different practices through which politeness implicatures arise that they involve much more than simply indirectly conveying information, as the traditional pragmatic account might have it. Instead, it is suggested that through politeness implicatures participants are able to negotiate the trajectory of interactions in ways that orient to their locally situated sensitivity or delicacy by framing (and sometimes even masking or disguising) actions in the guise of other actions. It is also argued that while analysing meaning-actions such as *implying, hinting* and even *not-saying* is indeed important for furthering our understanding of politeness implicatures, as was proposed in Chapter Three, the practices by which politeness implicatures arise are evidently not exhausted by these.[63]

---

63 There are arguably other meaning-actions, which are not, due to constraints of space, explored in any detail in this chapter on politeness implicatures. However, some of these meaning-actions are considered further in the following chapter on (mock) impoliteness implicatures, including instances of *alluding, supposing* and *misconstruing*.

2 Attenuating and withholding

The focus in studies of implicature to date in pragmatics, as we discussed in Chapter Two, has been primarily on those cases of implicature that arise through *implying*, that is, where speakers 'convey' particular information, or some stance vis-à-vis that information, without expressly stating or saying this information or stance. One analytical limitation of the notion of *implying*, however, is that it is first and foremost something achieved by the speaker. In other words, a focus on *implying* naturally leads us to focus primarily on what the current speaker is (taken to be) doing, without adequately acknowledging either the incipient nature of that which is being implicated (i.e. what is here referred to as the "upshot", but which might more generally be termed an implicatum), or the way in which implicatures position particular (sets of) responses by recipients as contingently relevant.[64] In other words, analysing implicatures through the lens of *implying* potentially neglects the ways in which implicatures can arise as either first-positioned or next-positioned (see section 5.1.2), and the ways in which these mobilise potentially different (sets of) responses from other participants. It is proposed in this section that upshots can be implicated in two key ways: through participants either "attenuating" a contingently relevant incipient upshot in first-position, or "withholding" a contingently relevant response in next-position. In doing so, the current speaker positions the formulation of that upshot by another participant – sometimes but not always the addressee – as contingently relevant.

As Schegloff (2007) has argued, a dispreferred first-pair part "may be *attenuated* to the point of actual non-articulation" (p.83, emphasis added). He cites an example of the way in which a request, which we discussed at the beginning of Chapter Four (see example 60), is achieved through making "a remedy or help or the offer of a remedy or help" (Schegloff 1995: 198) contingently relevant through "incrementally constructed discourse" that constitutes "a multiply renewed effort (or series of efforts) to elicit help from Marcia, without ever requesting it (as we say in the vernacular) *explicitly*" (ibid.: 199). Notably, then, despite an "offer of help" being projected as a contingently relevant response, Donnie attenuates formulation of this request itself. In other words, pleading for help in getting to the bank is implicated as the object of a request that is never explicitly made.

In the same example we also saw how Marcia withheld an offer of help or a remedy in spite of Donnie's evident troubles. In *withholding* a response that was projected as contingently relevant by Donnie's prior turns, Marcia was able to

---

64 The term "upshot" is preferred here over what Sperber and Wilson (1995) term "implicated conclusions" as it allows for the way in which upshots can arise through either attenuating or withholding.

indicate difficulty or interactional trouble in offering such a response (Schegloff 1968: 1073, 2007: 51, 92; Sidnell 2010: 9–12). In other words, withholding a contingently relevant response, and in this case formulating it as a dispreferred second-pair part through delay and hesitation, constitutes a "noticeable" or "accountable" absence (Pomerantz 1984a Schegloff 2007: 20), thereby imparting a particular upshot, in this case an "indirect" refusal of Donnie's "indirect" request. Notably, by only reporting her situation, Marcia "leave[s] it to the recipient [Donnie] to extract the upshot and the consequent appropriate response" (Schegloff 1995: 206, fn.16; cf. Drew 1984: 137–139).

Two ways in which implicatures can thus arise are either through attenuating upshots (in first position) or withholding upshots (in next position). In both cases, it is difficult (albeit not impossible) for the speaker to dispute having *imparted* an upshot, but the reflexively intentional object of that upshot is, of course, to some degree indeterminate. In other words, *imparting* an upshot through either attenuating or withholding is characterised by type 1 indeterminacy (see Chapter 3: section 4.1). In attenuating or withholding upshots in a way that decreases their accountability for the object of the social action trajectory in question, speakers thereby invoke particular aspects of the moral order, and in some instances, can also occasion evaluations of politeness.

In the following example, for instance, a first-positioned politeness implicature appears to arise when a cooking instructor (T), who is instructing one of the students (S), attenuates a contingently relevant upshot through a confirmation-seeking question. The student, however, does not initially respond, which occasions a repetition by the teacher of the question reformulated as information-seeking (rather than confirmation-seeking). The student subsequently undertakes that which has been implicated by the instructor, namely, that she add some chilli pepper to the dish she is making.

(93) 1 T: *hai, ano tōgarashi   mo soko ni ari-masu deshō?*
         yes um chilli pepper also there in exist-Pol probably(Pol)

2 *watakushi mot-te-ki-ta-no   ga   ne.*
  I(Pol)   carry-Te-come-Past-Nomi Nom M
  ('there's a bottle of chilli pepper there too, isn't there?
  I mean the one I brought')

3 S: *sensei, zenbu ire-chat-te   saisho maze-te*
     teacher all   put in-finish-Te first   mix-Te

4   *ii-n-desu*   *ka?*
       good-Nomi-Cop(Pol) Q
       ('Teacher, is it okay to put everything into the pan and stir first?')

5   T: *hai, ii-desu   yo. sō   desu.*
       yes good-Pol M   that way Cop(Pol)

6   *sono hen ni tōgarashi   nai?*
       that area in chilli pepper none
       ('yes, it's okay. that's right. Isn't there any chilli pepper there?')

7   ((the student puts some red pepper into the dish))

8   T: *a, hai, arigatō.*
       oh yes thanks
       ('oh, thanks')
(adapted from Ikuta 1988: 112–113)

The teacher appears to design her utterance in line 1 as a question seeking confirmation of a particular state of affairs given the utterance-final tag question marker (*deshō*), which is commonly used in seeking agreement or confirmation from a recipient (Hosoda 2006: 108; Ikeda 2004: 24). The turn-final particle in line 2 (*ne*) also marks alignment with the current turn's action as a relevant next, and so indicates a request for affiliative action in subsequent turn (Morita 2005: 148; cf. Tanaka 2000). However, the object of this affiliative next action is attenuated here by the teacher, thereby leaving it up to the student to infer the relevant upshot, which is that if the red pepper has not yet been added, the student needs to add some. However, while such a directive is licensed by the teacher's role-status (*tachiba*), it is nevertheless attenuated. In other words, despite orienting to her (deontic) entitlement to make such a directive, by attenuating the upshot, and so construing it as a "suggestion" rather than a "request", the teacher also orients to the student's entitlement to prepare the dish according to her liking. In that sense it constitutes an instance of an implicature that indicates a "polite" stance on the part of the teacher towards the student.

In this case, however, the attenuated upshot is not attended to by the student (line 3), who appears to be engaged in another task competing for her attention. After attending to the student's question (line 4), the teacher pursues a response (Pomerantz 1984b) through reformulating her prior confirmatory question from line 1 in the form of an information seeking question (line 5), and thus, in effect repeats the question (Kasper 2006). This reformulated question constitutes a third-position repair through which the teacher signals that the student's understanding of her prior turn was problematic (Hayashi, Raymond and Sidnell 2013:

15), and so treats the student's response as inadequate (Jefferson 1981; Pomerantz 1984b; Stivers and Rossano 2010). This move by the teacher is notable in two respects. First, through this turn design she tips the epistemic gradient in favour of the student (Heritage 2012a, 2012b; Heritage and Raymond 2012), thereby more explicitly mobilising a response from the student that attends to the implicated action trajectory. Second, the teacher "reasserts her position in a way that simply renews the relevance of a response, without orienting to a possible problem a delay in responding might adumbrate" (Bolden, Mandelbaum and Wilkinson 2012: 139), which, in effect, gives the student a second chance to formulate a response to the attenuated upshot without bringing attention to the potentially embarrassing implications of the student having not properly attended to the teacher's prior implicated instructions. In this way, a "polite" stance is indicated not only through attenuation of the upshot (see above), but also through not explicitly attending to the student's prior failure to furnish an adequate response to the teacher's prior implicated directive.

The student subsequently attends to the attenuated upshot of this reformulated through nonverbal action (i.e. putting some red pepper in the dish) (line 7), to which the teacher responds with "thanking" in line 8, in order to signal closing of the request sequence (Goldberg 2004: 285; Kuroshima 2010: 864; cf. Kumatoridani 1999: 640). In this way, the teacher also frames compliance with the attenuated upshot as something which also benefits the teacher, rather than simply the student, thereby orienting to their respective benefactive statuses (Heritage 2013), and so reiterating the "polite" stance on the teacher's part towards the student.

In the following excerpt, between Yusuke and Jun who are friends talking about soccer, a next-positioned politeness implicature can be observed to arise through Jun withholding a response that was positioned as contingently relevant through Yusuke's prior turn.

(94)   Field notes: Tokyo, February 2000

    1   Y: *Zerokussu Sūpā Kappu o   mi-ni   ika-nai?*
           Xerox Super Cup   Acc watch-to go-Neg
           ('do you want to go and see the Xerox Super Cup?')

    2   J: *dono   chiimu?*
           which team
           ('which teams [are playing]?')

    3   Y: *Jubiro tai   Guranpasu*
           (Jubiro versus Guranpasu)

4 J: *zen   Nippon   dat-tara   tobitsuku-n-da   kedo   ne*::
    all   Japan   Cop-if   jump at-Nomi-Cop   but   M
    ('if it were a national league game, I might be grabbed but ...')

5 Y: *a,   sō   ka.*
    oh   that way   Q
    ('oh really?')
(adapted from Haugh 2008d: 438).

In response to an invitation from Yusuke to attend a soccer match (line 1), which itself is implemented through a recognisable default politeness implicature (i.e. a negatively valenced formulation that standardly occasions an invitation), an insert expansion is occasioned in lines 2–3 (Schegloff 2007), when Jun asks which teams are playing. The delay in responding to the said invitation, which this post-first insert expansion creates, raises the possibility that Jun's response to the invitation is contingent on the nature of that forthcoming information. In returning to the issue of responding to the invitation itself in line 4, Jun signals that an upshot has been withheld through a trailing-off utterance-final 'but' (*kedo*) and turn-final *ne*. The turn-final *ne* in response position, which constitutes an implicit invitation to "co-construct the utterance's meaning" (Morita 2005: 148), indicates that an upshot has been withheld, while the occurrence of utterance-final *kedo* sets up an implicit contrast between what is said and the withheld upshot, as well as indicating that the current turn is being yielded to the other participant (Haugh 2008d; Ono, Thompson and Sasaki 2012). The contrast here is, of course, between what Jun would do if a particular team were playing (but happens to not be playing on this occasion), and the upshot, namely, his declination of the invitation given that team is not playing. In withholding a response made contingently relevant by Yusuke's prior invitation, Jun thereby imparts an upshot. However, the inclusion of the clause-final *kedo* here mitigates this refusal (Mori 1999) by "claiming to agree with the prior while marking, and accompanying, a shift in the assessed parameters which partially contrasts with the prior" (Pomerantz 1984a: 63). In other words, Jun implicates that he would accept the invitation if the terms of it were different. Notably, the turn-final *ne* here also works to highlight his "'concerns' with the current actions being instantiated by [his] talk" (Morita 2012a: 304; cf. Tanaka 2000: 1141), in particular, to express his "due regard of social disquietude regarding these actions", including his "disquietude with the possibility that one has caused harm or disalignment to the harmony of the relationship" (Morita 2012a: 304).

In this case, then, a polite stance, at least on Jun's part, is arguably occasioned through imparting this "concern" through withholding an upshot, because in that way Jun indicates his "disquietude" about refusing the invitation, and so indexes an orientation to their relationship as friends, and the (moral) expectancy that one should show consideration (*hairyo*) for the "feelings" (or "heart-mind" (*kokoro*) more broadly) of one's friends (Intachakra 2012).[65] Indeed, it is in that sense that this implicature is recognisable to the participants in the first place. This orientation to showing concern for Yusuke's "feelings" also intersects with what Stevanovic and Peräkylä (2014) have recently termed the "emotional order", where the latter refers to the participants' orientation to the expression of affect. The emotional order encompasses both "emotional status", namely, "socially shared expectations regarding experiencing, expressing, and sharing of emotions" (*ibid.*: 192), as well as "emotional stance", namely, "the valence and the relative strength of emotional expression directed to a co-present or absent target" (*ibid.*: 192). In this case, Jun is orienting to the potential for inconsistency between the emotional stance enacted through a refusal and the emotional status that has been co-constituted thus far in their interaction by implicating the said refusal. Of course whether Yusuke himself evaluated Jun's implicated refusal as sufficiently "polite" on this occasion remains open to question, as he did not reciprocate Jun's "polite" stance", although there was no evidence from his subsequent responses to suggest that he evaluated it as either "impolite" or "not polite".

In the following example, reported by Yang (2009), a next-positioned politeness implicature also arises through a participant withholding a contingently relevant response, here agreement with the course of action suggested in the prior turn. The example begins when Zhang, who is driving to the airport to pick someone up, realises they need to get some more petrol, and so reports this to Li and Wang, who are both accompanying him.

(95) 1 Zhang: *chēzi   kǒnpà   děi   jiāyóu   le.*
              car   afraid need petrol   PRT
              ('I'm afraid we need [some] petrol')

      2 Li: *pángbiān   bú   jiù   yǒu   ge   jiāyóuzhàn   ma.*
              next   not PRT   have one petrol station Q

---

65 While in earlier work I invoked 'place' (*tachiba*) as what underpins evaluations of politeness in Japanese (Haugh 2005, 2008d: 438), in this case, it appears what is most salient is their relationship (Arundale 2006, 2010a, 2010b), and, in particular, an orientation to their respective "heart-minds" (*kokoro*) (see also Intachakra 2012). As Haugh and Obana (2011) acknowledge, the notion of 'place' or 'role' (*tachiba*) only goes part of the way in explaining the moral grounding of evaluations of politeness in Japanese, and so needs to be complemented by other aspects of the moral order (cf. O'Driscoll 2007: 487, fn.9).

3		qù nàr	[jiā	bú		jiù	xíng	le.
		go there	add	not		PRT	okay	PRT

('isn't there a petrol station over there? can't we go there and fill up?')

4	Wang:		[qiánmiàn	kěndìng	hái	yǒu	jiāyóuzhàn,
			ahead	definitely	also	have	petrol station

5		nàr	bú	shùn	lù.
		there	not	along	road

('there will definitely be a petrol station ahead. [the one] over there is not on our way')

6	Zhang:	nn,	yīnggāi	hái	yǒu	jiāyóuzhàn	de.
		mm	probably	also	have	petrol station	PRT

('mm, they probably have a petrol station [ahead]')

(adapted from Yang 2009: 84)

Li responds to Zhang's informing in line 1 by suggesting a course of action, namely, filling up at a petrol station on the other side of the road (line 3). This suggestion is preceded by an utterance in line 2 formulated as a question seeking confirmation of the information asserted, namely, that there is a petrol station across the road where they can fill up. Through the utterance-final *ma*, Li frames the information as something which the recipient (here, ostensibly Zhang) has the "right and obligation to confirm" (Kendrik 2010: 92). It thus functions as "preparatory confirmation" that "establish[es] the relevant preparatory information and secur[es] alignment to the course of action to which the pre-sequence belongs" (*ibid.* 120) for the suggestion that follows in line 3. However, the negative particle that precedes it creates a shallower epistemic gradient through which Li signals that he knows there is a petrol station across the road, but nevertheless leaves it to Zhang to confirm its relevance to the activity in question, namely, stopping for petrol (cf. Kendrik 2010: 19). Through this negatively formulated question, then, agreement with the suggested course of action is positioned as preferred (Heritage 2002b).

However, rather than waiting for Zhang to respond, Wang, ostensibly a side participant, elects to take an addressee footing in implicitly confirming Li's assertion (i.e., that there is a petrol station across the road). Yet Wang does so in a way that challenges its relevance to the overall interactional project in claiming there is likely to be another petrol station on their way to the airport (line 4). The subsequent claim by Wang that the one Li pointed out is not on their way (line 5) thus functions as an account that implicates rejection of Li's suggested course of action, given accounts frequently mark responses to suggestions as dispreferred (Davidson

1984; Heritage 1984a). Zhang himself then subsequently confirms Wang's claim (line 6), thereby also indicating that he is rejecting Li's suggested course of action.

Notably, the rejection of Li's suggestion itself remains attenuated, thereby orienting to Li's "relational entitlement" (Chang forthcoming; Haugh and Kádár forthcoming) to be making such a suggestion to Zhang in the first place. In other words, Wang indicates a "polite" stance through attenuating the upshot. This "polite" stance is echoed by Zhang in the subsequent turn when the upshot of Zhang's confirmation of Wang's prior claim in line 3 is left attenuated, namely, they won't be stopping at the petrol station across the road as Li has suggested. By attenuating this upshot, Zhang also orients to Li's relational entitlement to be making this suggestion. In other words, it is through this orientation to Li's entitlements vis-à-vis his relationship with Zhang that a concern for issues of "politeness" (*kèqì*) in maintaining their ongoing relationship is indicated.

Politeness implicatures can also arise through withholding a contingently relevant pre-emptive response or upshot. In the following excerpt from a phone conversation between two friends, for instance, we can observe how politeness implicatures arise through withholding upshots and contingently relevant pre-emptive responses, as they negotiate off-record the possibility of a visit by Oscar.

(96) (Oscar and Martin are friends talking on the phone)

1. O: so- (.) ↑we'll be in Canberra this: (.) comin' weekend

2. of cou::r [se,

3. M: [ye:::s,

4. (0.7)

5. ?: .hh

6. O: an:: (0.4) goin' t' th' <u>gam</u>e on Sat'rday ni:ght,

7. M: ri::ght¿

8. (1.0)

9. O: a- (.) an (0.5) and (.) <u>we</u> had sort of planned on seeing

10. you (0.2) on our retu:rn¿ (0.3) [to <u>Syd</u>ney¿ (.) on <u>Sun</u>day.

11. M: [.hh

12. (0.4)

13. M: o:ka:y¿

14   O: is that (0.4) okay with you?=[or or:

15   M: [.hh eh-eh-w-we-well look,

16   uh uh (.)pr<u>o</u>bably it's okay, .hh a- we- we've been

17   d'invited for a bir-a fiftieth bi<u>rth</u>[da:y ah:, (0.2)]

18   O: [*a:::h¿*   ]

19   M: <<u>ce</u>lebra:tion:> at tw<u>e</u>lve th<u>ir</u>ty on <u>Sun</u>da::[y?

20   O: [aah::.

21   (0.5)

22   M: [right?

23   O: [(ook) it's::::: <u>not</u> gonna work¿ <u>i</u>s it.
(Nevile and Rendle-Short 2009: 79)

The proposal itself develops over the course of a number of turns. The excerpt in question begins with an allusion by Oscar to previously known information (here indicated through "of course" in line 2), namely, that they are visiting Canberra that weekend (lines 1–2), thereby opening up the possibility that he would like to visit Martin (Nevile and Rendle-Short 2009: 80). Notably, until the proposal itself emerges in lines 9–10, there are a number of relatively long pauses (lines 4 and 8), which is not only indicative of possible uncertainty in regards to the trajectory of the interactional project at play here (Jefferson 1988), but also constitutes instances where Martin noticeably withholds a response, namely, a pre-emptive invitation (Nevile and Rendle-Short 2009: 80). Given that such a pre-emptive invitation is likely expectable in light of the framing of Oscar's visit as previously known to both parties (lines 1–2), as well as potentially constituting a preferred response given the dispreferred formulation of Oscar's attenuated proposal (Schegloff 2007: 90), the minimal sequence-forwarding responses (lines 3 and 7) and subsequent "silences" (lines 4 and 8) on Martin's part are analysable as a "noticeable" or "relevant" absences (Schegloff 2007: 20). Such a withholding of a response, and thus "noticeable" absence, is indicative of possible difficulty on Martin's part in furnishing such a pre-emptive invitation.

Indeed, Oscar himself orients to this potential difficulty both in the tentative formulation of the proposal itself in lines 9–10 ,when a pre-emptive invitation from Martin is not forthcoming (Davidson 1990), and in the subsequent increase in tentativeness achieved through a trailing-off "or" interrogative formulation in line 14 (Haugh 2011b; cf. Walker 2012). More specifically, through this utterance-final disjunction interrogative Oscar decreases his level of commitment to the candidate answer in question (Pomerantz 1988), namely, that it is "okay" to visit, because he relinquishes his right to determine whether it should be interpreted as a polar (i.e. "okay or not") or alternative question (i.e. "okay or maybe okay/not sure" etc.), and so implicates greater epistemic uncertainty than would be indicated through implementing a polar or alternative question formulation (Haugh 2011b) (see also example [84] in section 1.3, Chapter Five). This implicature of epistemic uncertainty thereby increases the epistemic gradient between Oscar and Martin, since through it Oscar indicates greater uncertainty about what might possible (than would otherwise be indicated through the candidate answer that is implicit in a polar question formulation). In this way, he arguably invokes relational aspects of the epistemic order, because he decreases the likelihood of eliciting a disaffiliative response (Steensig and Drew 2008), as well as acknowledging Martin's greater claim to epistemic primacy here (Heritage 2012a, 2012b, 2013), thereby indicating an orientation to issues of propriety (Haugh 2011b). Critically, then, the trajectory of Oscar's proposal develops incrementally over a number of turns in a way that appears responsive to the pauses and noticeable withholding of a pre-emptive invitation by Martin, and is ultimately implemented through a reformulation of the proposal made more tentative, and so open to evaluation as "polite, through an utterance-final disjunctive.

Martin's subsequent response in lines 15–17 furthers an understanding of there being possible difficulty in progressing the proposed visit by framing his response as dispreferred through disfluencies and well-prefacing that thereby delay it (Davidson 1984). Notably, while Martin indicates that "probably it's okay" for such a visit to take place, the well-prefacing here alerts Oscar to the non-straightforwardness of this response (Schegloff and Lerner 2009), which in this case implicates incipient refusal. Indeed, Oscar treats the birthday celebration as new information with change-of-state tokens in lines 18 and 20 (Heritage 1984b), and then makes explicit his understanding that a visit is not possible (line 23), thus treating Martin's response as having attenuated a likely upshot, namely, a refusal of Oscar's proposed visit. In this way, Oscar anticipates and thus pre-empts the necessity of Martin having to make explicit a refusal of the proposed visit, thereby reciprocating the concern displayed through Martin's dispreferred formulation of an incipient refusal. This mutual orientation to displaying "reciprocal approval" (Arundale 2006: 206) constitutes evidence of an orientation on the part of the participants to issues of politeness, alongside a concern for their maintenance of their ongoing relation al connection more broadly.

In this section, we have seen how politeness implicatures can arise through both attenuating and withholding upshots, thereby allowing an action trajectory to be negotiated off-record. Examples of implicatures arising through attenuating and withholding were examined in interactions involving different language data, namely, Chinese, English and Japanese. An interesting suggestive finding was that while these implicatures arose in similar ways, their relevance as *politeness* implicatures was grounded in different moral concerns on the part of participants, ranging from a concern for 'place'/'role' (*tachiba*) and 'feelings/heart-mind' (*kokoro*) through to an orientation to 'relational entitlements' and 'reciprocal approval.'

In the last example we also saw how participants can recognisably withhold not only an upshot, but also a contingently relevant pre-emptive response, thereby positioning a likely upshot (e.g. an incipient refusal) as attenuated. In addition, we observed how participants can interactionally achieve a particular social action through a pre-emptive response, whereby one participant attributes a particular action as meant (but not said) by the other. It is thus to politeness implicatures that arise through pre-empting that we now turn.

3 Pre-empting

A pre-emptive response is one that is produced before a turn that recognisably implements a particular action that construes the pre-emptive action as contingently relevant has been fully produced. Pre-empting is not, however, simply a matter of a participant anticipating or *supposing* what another participant might be about to say. As Drew (2011) argues, "when a recipient treats the prior speaker as having done something, *they* are doing something (i.e. 'ascribing an action' is itself an action)" (p.1, original emphasis). In other words, through a pre-emptive response, a participant is *construing* a prior speaker as having a particular agenda. Pre-emptive responses also forestall the production of the action to which it is responsive. In some cases, such forestalling might be analysable as preferred with respect to the action trajectory it forwards. Schegloff (2007) argues that pre-emptive responses are preferred when the turn to which they are responsive is formulated as a dispreferred first pair part (p.90). He claims, for instance, that "when possible, the preferred response to the pre-request is a pre-emptive offer" (*ibid.*: 90–91). However, in cases where the turn to which they are responsive are formulated as preferred first pair parts, a pre-emptive response is analysable as dispreferred. A pre-emptive response to a pre-announcement, for instance, is generally oriented to as dispreferred by participants (*ibid.*: 90).

Implicatures can thus arise through a pre-emptive response that attributes an incipient agenda to a prior speaker. That speaker can in some cases dispute his/her commitment to that incipient agenda, as well as the reflexively intentional object of the unstated agenda that is attributed to him/her, and so implicatures that arise through pre-empting are characterised by both type 1 and type 2 indeterminacy (see Chapter 3: section 4.1). In pre-empting an incipient agenda in this way, thereby blurring their respective accountability for the implicature in question, participants can invoke particular aspects of the moral order, and in some instances this also occasion evaluations of politeness.

In the following excerpt, for instance, Sayuri and Kumiko are discussing a handout from a class Sayuri missed. However, before Sayuri formulates a request to borrow the handout in question from Kumiko, Kumiko's implements a pre-emptive response that construes a request as having already been launched (cf. Haugh 2007b: 667).

(97)   Xie 2000: R45

    1 S: *Kumiko-chan, konoaida no jugyō no purinto mot-te-ru?*
            Kumiko-Dim   recent   of class of handout have-Te-Prog
            ('Kumiko, do you have the handout from the last class?')

    2 K: *e,   dono   jugyō desu   ka?*
            um which class Cop(Pol) Q
            ('um, which class?')

    3 S: *ano ne, getsuyō sangen,   ano jugyō.*
            um M Monday third period that class
            ('um, the class third period on Monday')

    4 K: *getsuyō sangen   tte   iū   to, watashi wa,*
            Monday third period Quot say if I   Top

    5   *are-desu ne, ano eigo   desu   ne.*
            that-Pol M   that English Cop(Pol) M
            ('Monday third period huh … I … um … that English [class] huh')

    6 S: *konoaida yasun-jat-te   sā*
            recently absent-completely-Te M
            ('I missed the class recently')

    7 K: *ā.*
            ('oh')

    8 S: *purinto, morat-ta   mitai   na-n-da   kedo...*
            handout receive-Past seems Cop-Nomi-Cop but
            (and it seems you got a handout but ...)

    9 K: *a, ii-desu   yo.*
            oh good-Pol M

10   *kopī   shimasu   ka?*
        copy   do(Pol)   Q
        ('Oh, that's fine. Will you make a copy?')

Sayuri has called Kumiko on the phone, and after a preamble where they exchange greetings (data not shown), Sayuri launches what turns out to be a request sequence through an information-seeking question in line 1 that checks a preparatory condition for making a request (namely that Kumiko has the handout in question). It is thus interpretable here as pre-request implicative. An insert expansion then follows in lines 2–5, where they clarify which class and so which handout Sayuri is talking about. Kumiko indicates she knows which one, thereby implicitly providing a go ahead response for the sequence to progress (Schegloff 2007), although notably Kumiko does not actually indicate whether or not she was present in the class.

Sayuri then implements an informing in line 6, which functions as an account for an incipient request. However, the deployment of the utterance-final particle *sa* also indicates Sayuri's assumption of Kumiko's "tacit collaboration in temporarily closing down the next immediate possible negotiation space so that the projected trajectory of the action being advanced can be accomplished unimpeded" (Morita 2005: 216). In other words, Sayuri indicates more is to be added to this account, the progressivity of which is forwarded through a continuer deployed by Kumiko (line 7). This account then expanded in line 8, when Sayuri moves from reporting her own circumstances to reporting hearsay that Kumiko attended that class. However, while this is designed as seeking confirmation that Kumiko did indeed attend the class in question, the turn-final "trailing" *kedo* ('but') indicates an upshot of this reporting has been attenuated (Haugh 2008d; Mori 1999), namely, that Sayuri would like to borrow the handout in question.

The subsequent response by Kumiko constitutes a pre-emptive offer as it is formulated as if a request has already been accomplished through an utterance-final *yo* attached to an adjective (*ii*), which thereby "makes the utterance an action of giving permission" (Morita 2012b: 1722). Notably, such "yo-marked turns [also] more explicitly implicate participants in the co-construction of talk" (ibid: 1727). Here, then, Kumiko is formulating the offer as if the request has already been made, a stance that is furthered through her subsequent progression in line 10 to makinge arrangements for lending the handout. Given Sayuri never actually formulates a turn that is recognisably implementing a request, Kumiko's giving permission for Sayuri to borrow the handout in line 9 thus counts as a pre-emptive response, whereby she treats Sayuri's prior turns as pre-request implicative.

In this case, a polite stance is indicated through the way in which Kumiko demonstrates attentiveness (*kikubari*) towards the implied needs of Sayuri (Fukushima 2004, 2009, 2011, 2013). In other words, the pre-emptive offer made by Kumiko is recognisably "polite" because it shows concern for the well-being of the beneficiary. In that sense it invokes aspects of the "benefactive order", as through pre-empting Kumiko is indicating an orientation to benefits, advantages, gains and so on accrued through future action(s) (Clayman and Heritage forthcoming; Heritage 2013). More specifically, she enacts their respective benefactive stances in a way that downplays the "cost" to herself through her pre-emptive response, and thereby indicates a concern for being seen as "polite". She also reciprocates the initial "polite" stance on Sayuri's part that was accomplished through attenuation of the upshot of the latter's account, which had indicated an orientation to a relatively low deontic entitlement on the latter's part vis-à-vis their respective 'places' as fellow students (i.e. *tachiba*) to be making such a request in the first place. In this case, then, an orientation to "politeness" appears to have been interactionally achieved by the participants through reciprocation of "polite" stances accomplished via their respective actions of attenuating (an upshot) and pre-empting.

In the following example, an orientation to "politeness" is also accomplished through a pre-emptive offer. Here Zhang has called Ma on the phone to talk about a visitor coming to Ma's school.

(98)   1   Z: *wéi   nínghǎo,   shì   Mǎ yuànzhǎng ma?*
                 hello   good-day(Pol) Cop   Ma   principal   Q

       2   *wǒ shì   Zhāng Míng.*
                 I   Cop   Zhang Ming
                 ('hello, is this principal Ma?, it's Zhang Ming')

       3   M: *o,   Zhāng Míng a,   yǒu   shénme shì   ma?*
                 PRT   Zhang Ming PRT   have what   matter   Q
                 ('oh Zhang Ming, you have some matter [to discuss]?')

       4   Z: *míngtiān Thomas dào   nǐmen   xuéyuàn zuò   jiǎngzuò,*
                 tomorrow Thomas arrive your(PL) school   do   lecture

       5   *wǒ dǎtīng yíxià   wǎncān zěnme ānpái?*
                 I   like to ask a little dinner   how   arrange
                 ('Thomas is arriving tomorrow at your school to give a lecture. I wanted to ask about the arrangements for dinner')

       6   M: *o,   zuò wán   bàogào jiù   yào   wǔdiǎn   duō   le*
                 PRT   do   finish report then   will five o'clock more PRT

7		*zài*	*wǒmen*	*zhèlǐ*	*qù*	*ba,*	*wǒ*	*qǐngkè*	*nǐ*	*gùo*	*lái*	*ba*
		at	our	here	go	PRT	I	shout	you	pass	come	PRT

('oh [he] will finish the lecture [just] after five, [so] we
can go there, and I will shout you [dinner]')

8	Z:	*nà*	*hǎo*	*ba.*	*zhè*	*cì*	*tā*	*lái*	*fǎng*	*shì*
		then	good	PRT	this	time	he	come	visit	COP

9		*wài*	*bàn*	*chū*	*qián*	*dànshì*	*nǐmen*
		outside	organisation	spend	money	but	you(PL)

10		*xuéyuàn*	*yàoshì*	*néng*	*qǐng*	*tā*	*chī*	*dùn*	*fàn*
		school	if	can	shout	he	eat	C	meal

11		*nà*	*tā*	*shìhuì*	*hěn*	*gāoxìng*	*de.*
		then	he	will	very	pleased	PRT

('okay, his visit this time is from outside [meaning you]
spend money [on him], but if your school can shout him
a meal he will be happy')
(adapted from Yang 2009: 85)

Here Zhang asks about arrangements for the visitor in lines 4–5, in response to which Ma pre-emptively offers that he will be able to pay for the guest's dinner (lines 6–7), an offer which is subsequently accepted by Zhang as a joint decision (line 8), and subsequently the object of a positive assessment (lines 9–11).

Notably, by formulating this offer with turn-final *ba*, Ma indicates "incomplete or insufficient access to the information in question" (Kendrik 2010: 44). However, given Ma does appear to have some degree of certainty about this information, the *ba*-suffixing of his response about the guest's likely movements, as well as of the subsequent offer to buy him dinner, implements these as "noncommittal and equivocal" (p.45). The second occurrence of *ba* is particularly critical as through it Ma displays "a lack of commitment ... to the course of action to which the question belongs" (Kendrik 2010: 52). In other words, an offer is made, but it is made tentatively.

This turns out to be important because by making an offer, Ma is arguably pre-empting an incipient request from Zhang that Ma pay for the dinner. He thus construes Zhang's prior question in line 3 as indirectly bringing up the issue of who will be paying for the dinner, and supposes that Zhang is most likely wanting him to pay. We can thus observe here an orientation on the part of Ma to the unstated needs of Zhang, which is achieved through pre-empting an incipient request with a pre-emptive offer. This pre-emptive offer itself likely counts as "polite" (for these participants) because Ma is here demonstrating "attentiveness" (*tǐtiē*)[66] towards Zhang's implied, but nevertheless unsaid, needs (Fukushima and Haugh forthcoming; Haugh and Kádár forthcoming). In this way, he orients to the potential inconsistency between what Zhang might be expecting (benefactive status) and what would be enacted if Ma were not to pre-emptively make this offer (benefactive stance) (Clayman and Heritage forthcoming). It also helps Zhang avoid a potentially delicate action, that is, requesting that Ma pay for dinner, and so, in this way, Ma allows Zhang to maintain a "polite" (*kèqì*) stance. Nevertheless, in framing his offer as tentative, Ma orients to the possibility that such an offer was not what Zhang was after. In other words, Ma also orients to the potential delicacy of construing Zhang's prior question as alluding to the issue of who will be paying for the dinner.

In this section, it has been argued that construing another participant as doing something before they have recognisably done it, and forestalling production of a turn that recognisably implements the action attributed to that participant through pre-empting has important interpersonal implications, among which an orientation to politeness is arguably one. However, it is worth remembering that a pre-emptive response does not necessarily construe that action in the same way that it might have been formulated by the prior speaker (Hayashi 2001: 323), and so the unofficial business accomplished through pre-emptive responses may be resisted or challenged by the target of that construal. We have already discussed such an example in Chapter Five (see example 76, section 1.1), when we observed in passing how the terms of the pre-emptive offer by Michael were resisted by the other participant, Mary. It is thus to an examination of soliciting vis-à-vis politeness implicatures that we now turn.

4 Soliciting

Soliciting involves a speaker interactionally positioning another participant to pre-emptively initiate an action sequence for which that other person is thus held primarily responsible (cf. Terasaki [1976]2004: 180). It is generally accomplished by the speaker creating a warrant for the other person to infer that something is being treated as "better left unsaid though not undone" (Pomerantz 1980: 195). The warrant for initiating an action sequence can be implemented by speakers through a number of inter-related practices.

One way in which such a warrant is implemented is through a "my side telling" (or "fishing"), whereby the assertion of something that should already be

---

66 *Tǐtiē* (體貼) can be glossed broadly as thorough consideration of the other's mood or showing care by standing in someone else's shoes.

self-evident to the recipient is treated as grounds for that participant to "volunteer information, make an offer, extend an invitation, remedy an offense, answer an accusation, and so forth without his *directly* being asked, requested, accused, or complained against" (Pomerantz 1980: 193, original emphasis). As Pomerantz (1980) argues, "a 'my side telling' is intended to be heard in terms of an unformulated event that is being treated as appropriately referred to in that manner, that is, as better unsaid" (p.194). This means that the inference warranted by the "my side telling" is guided, in part, by "the fact that it has not been said" (p.194), and so likely involves a relationally "sensitive" action that is better "delicately and circuitiously handled" (p.197). It also allows for the speaker to occasion a response from another participant without being held accountable for doing so, given it is left up to the other participant whether or not he or she elects to proffer this response. We have addressed an example of this practice in passing in section 2, when we examined an instance of a participant withholding a contingently relevant pre-emptive invitation in response to an attenuated proposal that is formulated as dispreferred, in part through its construal as a my-side telling (see example 96).

A second practice by which a speaker implements a warrant for another participant to infer that a particular social action is being afforded by the prior speaker's talk is through "reportings" that make the formulation of a particular social action "relevant, but not obligatory" (Drew 1984: 136). Notably, the formulation of this social action as an "upshot" also "displays what the report [of the prior speaker] is taken to implicate" (p.135) by the current speaker. We have already discussed an instance of this practice in Chapter 3 (see example 48, cf. example 58).

A third, related way in which such a warrant is implemented is by "topicalising troubles" through either reporting or asking questions. In this way, the speaker can hint that he or she would like some form of help, which often takes the form of a pre-emptive offer. We discussed an example of this in Chapter 3 (see example 47), but also briefly alluded to this possibility in discussing example (96) in particularly section 2, whereby asking about arrangements for dinner, the speaker topicalises those arrangements as a possible source of trouble.

A fourth practice by which a speaker implements a warrant that provides for inferences about what social actions are being afforded by the prior speaker's talk is through "noticing a deficiency".[67] This practice involves a speaker treating some state of affairs as somehow deficient or undesirable, but one which has only just been "noticed", thereby hinting that another participant is in a position to do something about remedying this state of affairs. We have already discussed one instance of this in Chapter 5 (see example 76).

---

[67] My sincere thanks to Anita Pomerantz and Bob Sanders for this observation, and their comments on the analysis of such examples.

However, whether soliciting through "my side tellings", "reportings", "topi-calising troubles", or "noticing a deficiency", the participants are orienting in all cases to "what is *not* being said as preferably not said" (Pomerantz 1980: 197). And it is this orientation to "the fact that it has not been said" (Pomerantz 1980: 194) that underpins, in part, the inference of which action trajectory is likely being solicited on this occasion. Such implicatures are characterised primarily by indeterminacy in regards to the speaker's degree of commitment to occasioning that social action (type 2 indeterminacy), although type 1 indeterminacy is possible on occasion, as the speaker's ambivalence in regards to whether this social action is carried out is the *raison d'être* of soliciting. In other words, by only *hinting* that he or she would like another participant to pre-emptively enact a particular social action, the speaker is, by definition, avoiding responsibility for that social action through leaving it up to the recipient to enact. In this way, participants thereby invoke particular aspects of the moral order, and in some instances, can also occasion evaluations of politeness.

In the following excerpt, a politeness implicature arises when a mother, who is walking with her daughter down the street towards the local train station, does a noticing namely, that she has forgotten to bring a handkerchief (see also Haugh 2007a: 95).

(99)   Field notes, Tokyo, August 2000

    1   M: *Mama,   hankachi   mot-te-ki-ta*
           mother   handkerchief   carry-Te-come-Past

    2   *to   omot-ta-n-da   kedo ...*
           Quot   think-Past-Nomi-Cop   but
           ('I thought I had brought a hankie along but ...')

    3   D: ((passes her handkerchief to her mother))

    4   M: *a, dōmo.*
           ('oh, thanks')

By raising the issue of a handkerchief through noticing it as a deficiency (lines 1–2), the mother thereby opens up the possibility that she is hinting she would like something to be done by her daughter to remedy that deficiency. This possibility is further raised through the trailing-off utterance-final *kedo* ('but ...'), whereby the attenuation of an upshot is indicated (Haugh 2008d; Mori 1999). Through offering her handkerchief, the daughter treats the prior noticing by her mother as soliciting such an offer.

The way in which this implicature arises through soliciting on the part of the mother, and pre-empting on the part of the daughter, also indicates an orientation here in this particular interaction to issues of "politeness". On the one hand, soliciting an offer of her daughter's handkerchief rather than requesting it enables the mother to indicate her low deontic entitlement to be making such a request in the first place. On the other hand, this pre-emptive offer demonstrates attentiveness (*kikubari*) towards the implied needs of her mother, which is recognisably "polite" because it shows concern for her well-being (Fukushima 2004, 2009, 2011, 2013). It also reciprocates the "polite" stance on her mother's part (which was indicated through soliciting), and so, in this case, an orientation to a concern for "politeness" is arguably interactionally achieved by the two participants.

However, while in the above example, the informant reported that this was a frequent practice on the part of her mother, and that this type of soliciting/pre-empting sequence is a recognisable part of the way in which they co-constitute their ongoing relationship, soliciting need not necessarily be grounded in that kind of well-established relationship. In the following excerpt, for instance, a cooking instructor (I) solicits an offer from one of the students (S) through noting a possible deficiency.

(100) 1 I: *kyō   o-tōban   no kata   irassharu?*
today Hon-turn of person(Pol) present(Hon)

2 *koko n naka   ni.*
here of amongst in
('is the person whose turn it is today here among us?')

3 S: *i-mas-en,   Sasagawa-san ga.*
present-Pol-Neg Sasagawa-Pol Nom
('Miss Sasagawa is not here')

4 I: *i-mas-en   ka? chotto o-nasu   kono gurai*
present-Pol-Neg Q   a little Hon-eggplant this amount

5 *hoshii-n-da   kedo ...*
want-Nomi-Cop but
('she's not? I just wanted to have about this many eggplants, but ...')

6 S: *yaoyasan it-te-ki-mashō   ka?*
grocer   go-Te-come-Vol(Pol)   Q
('shall I go to the grocery store?')
(adapted from Ikuta 1988: 86)

The excerpt begins when the instructor asks whether the person whose turn it is to get ingredients is present (lines 1–2), to which one of the student responds in the negative (line 3). The instructor then implements a noticing of a particular deficiency or trouble, namely, that they don't have any eggplant (lines 4–5). The possibility is thus raised that the instructor would like one of the students to do something about remedying this deficiency. This possible understanding is also oriented to by the instructor indicating that an upshot has been attenuated through a trailing-off utterance-final *kedo* ('but ...') (Haugh 2008d; Mori 1999). One of the students then offers to go and buy some eggplant for the class (line 6).

The way in which an implicature arises through soliciting indicates an orientation to issues of "politeness" on the instructor's part in the same way as example (99) above, as through soliciting an offer, rather than requesting it, the instructor orients to her low entitlement to be making such a request, in spite of her 'role' (*tachiba*) as the teacher, and the attendant entitlements such a role is assumed to confer. The student also reciprocates this "polite" stance through a pre-emptive offer that demonstrates "attentiveness" (*kikubari*) towards the implied needs of the instructor, and thus the class more broadly.

It is worth noting, however, that since soliciting leaves it up to the other participant whether they elect to proffer the social action in question, in some cases while a noticing by the prior speaker may be registered by a participant, it may nevertheless not be acted upon. The following interaction was reported by an informant, Mei, as one where she was aware that her sister, Yu, was trying to solicit an offer through topicalising troubles, yet she chose in this instance to not make such a pre-emptive offer, but rather to let it pass.

(101)   Field notes, Brisbane, March 2013

>1   M: *nǐmen   jīntiān   zùo   shénme?*
>   you(PL)   today   do   what
>   ('what did you do today?')

>2   Y: *wǒmen   jīntiān   qù   kàn   Yáng   Jiā   Jiàng,*
>   we   today   go   watch (surname) family general

>3   *Xiángxiáng   chǎo   zhe   yào   qù   kàn.*
>   Xiangxiang   hassle Cop   want   go   watch
>   ('we went to see "Yang Family General". Xiangxiang was hassling to go as well')

>4   M: *nà   mèimèi   ne?*
>   then   younger sister   Q
>   ('how about his sister?')

5 Y: *tā   yě   yìqǐ   qù   a,   yàobùrán   zěnme bàn.*
       she   also together go PRT otherwise how   do
       ('she went with us, otherwise what could we do [with her]?')

6 M: *xiá, tā   kàn   de   dǒng   ma?*
       PRT   she watch PRT understand Q
       ('huh, did she understand?')

7 Y: *yīnggāi kàn   bù   dǒng   ne.*
       probably watch not understand PRT

8   *méibànfǎ   wǒ yòu bù   néng fàng tā   yí   ge rén.*
       can't be helped I   also Neg can   leave her one C person

9   *wǒ běnlái   xiǎng shūo jiào nǐ   bāng wǒ kàn   xiǎohái.*
       I   originally want say ask you help me watch children
       ('[she] probably didn't understand [but] it can't be helped.
       I can't leave her on her own. I originally thought of asking you to
       help look after her')

10 M: *o,   kěshì tāmen liǎng ge kàn   de   dǒng   ma?*
       PRT but   they two   C watch PRT understand Q
       ('oh, but did the two of them understand [the film]?')

11   ((a topic shift was initiated by Yu))

The interaction begins when Yu, who has two young children (Xiangxiang and
his sister Tingxuan), is reporting that they went to see a movie (line 2). However,
that going to this movie was problematic or troublesome in some sense is alluded
to by the way in which she reports her son as "hassling" to go (line 3), as through
this formulation she thereby supposes that there was resistance on her part about
her son going to see the movie. The allusion to potential troubles is oriented to by
Mei in line 4 when she inquires whether Xiangxiang's younger sister, Tingxuan,
also went. Notably, Yu's subsequent response that Tingxuan also went to see the
movie (line 5) is marked with an utterance-final *a*-particle, which indicates her
stance that "the information provided in the *a*-suffixed utterance is something
that the recipient should have known" (Wu 2004: 224), and is followed by an
expression of helplessness to be doing otherwise. The troubles that have been
alluded to thus far are then explicitly raised by Mei in line 6, when she expresses
a stance of surprise at the fact that Tingxuan also went through turn-initial *xia*,
and then asks whether she could understand the movie (which was one aimed
at adult viewers). Yu then orients to Mei's expectation that Tingxuan wouldn't
have been able to properly understand the movie (and so would not have enjoyed

watching it) in line 7, through marking confirmation of Mei's candidate answer with an utterance-final *ne* particle (Li and Thompson 1981: 300).

The interaction thus far motivates the subsequent reporting by Yu of a baulked intention to ask Mei for help looking after the kids (lines 8–9). Through this baulked intention (Edwards 2008), Yu indicates, on the one hand, a "polite" (*kèqì*) stance by displaying her reluctance to ask Mei for help and ostensibly low relational entitlement to be doing so, but raises the possibility, on the other hand, that she might need such help in the future. In this way, then, Yu attempts to solicit a pre-emptive offer from Mei. The latter reported thinking the following at the time:

(102)   Field notes, Brisbane, March 2013

      Mei: The reason I thought about 'fishing', was she was kind of waiting for an offer for next time... if I had said yes, that it would be okay for me to look after the kids ... she would be more inclined to ask me next time if something happens like this again. She was fishing for an agreement that she will have more authority to make another request next time.

In other words, Yu was perceived by Mei to be reporting on troubles in order to solicit a pre-emptive offer to look after Yu's children next time Yu wanted to go to a movie that was not suitable for her children. On this occasion, Mei avoided responding to this attempted solicitation through recycling a prior question about whether the children understood the movie (line 10), and the conversation subsequently shifted to another topic. In this way, then, Mei recognisably disattended that which had been hinted at by Yu, and so implicated, in turn, a refusal to make such a pre-emptive offer. Disattending prior implicatures through this kind of "irrelevant response" constitutes another practice by which politeness implicatures can arise, a practice to which we will now move to consider in more detail.

5 Disattending

While practices such as attenuating and withholding upshots, soliciting and doing delicacy may, in turn, occasion pre-emptive responses by participants, in other cases, participants may, on occasion, disattend that which has been implicated. This is, of course, not surprising given the *raison d'être* of implicatures is that not only speakers, but also other participants reduce their degree of accountability for the social actions, and the 'object' or 'content' of those social actions, when they are implicated. Yet this is not to say that disattending implicatures is not an interactional move in itself. Indeed, in instances where there is little indeterminacy in regards to the speaker's commitment to something having been implicated then a lack of orientation to that which has been implicated may itself be construed as an "accountable" or "noticeable absence" (Schegloff 1968, 2007).[68] In this case, a further implicature arises through an accountable with-holding of a response that would otherwise interactionally fit the action trajectory that has been made conditionally relevant by the prior turn. In other cases, however, disattending a prior implicature is a recognisable practice by which the action trajectory being implemented through that implicature can be blocked or resisted. And on some occasions, blocking or resisting that prior implicature through disattending can indicate an orientation on the part of participants to issues of "politeness".

We have already briefly alluded to such a case in discussing example (101) vis-à-vis soliciting in the previous section. As we discussed, Mei's sister, Yu, was trying to solicit an offer from Mei to look after Yu's children next time she goes to the movies through topicalising troubles vis-à-vis the children's ability to understand and enjoy the kind of movie Yu and her husband like to go and watch. Here the last few lines of that excerpt are reproduced in order to focus in more detail on the way in which Mei responded to what she perceived as an attempt by Yu to solicit a commitment from Mei to look after the children the next time a similar situation arises.

(103)   Field notes, Brisbane, March 2013

9   *wǒ běnlái   xiǎng shūo jiào nǐ   bāng wǒ kàn   xiǎohái.*
       I   originally want say   ask you help me watch children
       ('[she] probably didn't understand [but] it can't be helped.
       I can't leave her on her own. I originally thought of asking you to
       help look after her')

10 M: *o,   kěshì tāmen liǎng ge kàn   de   dǒng   ma?*
       PRT but   they   two   C   watch PRT understand Q
       ('oh, but did the two of them understand [the film]?')

11   ((a topic shift was initiated by Yu))

---

68 A "noticeable" or "official absence" is a term used in CA to refer to instances where an expected response (often, but not always a second pair part) is not forthcoming, and so is accountably absent (Schegloff 2007: 20).

To briefly reiterate, through reporting a baulked intention (line 9), Yu raised the possibility that she might need help from Mei in the future. On this occasion, however, Mei avoided responding to this as soliciting through recycling a prior question about whether the children understood the movie (line 10), and the conversation subsequently shifted to another topic. In this way, then, Mei recognisably disattended that which had been hinted at by Yu, and so implicated, in turn, a refusal to make such a pre-emptive offer. However, by shifting the focus away from this refusal through this sequentially "irrelevant response" that curtails further development of that action trajectory, Mei reduced any potential "embarrassment" or "ill-feeling" (*bùhǎoyìsi*) on Yu's part that might arise from such a rejection, thereby indicating concern for her ongoing relationship with Yu. As we have previously noted, negotiating courses of action through implicatures allows participants "considerable flexibility in negotiating relational position and role behaviour within the confines of a relational system" (Chang 1999: 535). In this case, while it is part and parcel of this younger sister's relationship with her older sister to be called upon for favours, Mei was able to block the move by Yu on this occasion to establish a further entitlement within her relationship with Mei, which would legitimise Yu asking Mei in the future to look after Yu's children when she goes to movies that might not be interesting for children to watch. Yet in doing so unofficially, Mei was able to preserve the official assumption that Yu has entitlements within her relationship with Mei to ask for favours, and in that way indicates concern for Yu's "feelings" (*xīn*, 'heart-mind'). Given displaying concern for the "feelings" of others constitutes another way in which a "polite" stance can be instantiated (Intachakra 2012), disattending prior implicatures through this kind of "irrelevant response" arguably constitutes another practice by which politeness implicatures can arise.

Irrelevant responses can also be used in recognisably disattending to an "impolite" stance instantiated in a prior turn. In this way, that offence has been taken is receipted, and yet it is done in such a way so as to avoid this receipting of offence itself being open to evaluation as "impolite". In the following excerpt, the participants are negotiating whether the cost of dental implants should be paid to the people who were injured in a car accident. The representative from the insurance company with whom the at-fault party are insured, Ying, has just repeated his position that their company is not able to pay for this, in response to the appeal from the chair of the mediation committee (CM) to consider whether there is not something his company can offer in that regard. This refusal to pay for the dental implants occasions a critical comment from the committee vice-chair (CVC) of the mediation committee, who is representing the victim party.

(104)   Yi-Lan mediation committee 100727001

22   CM: >ÁN-NE<   LI   BÔ-HUAT-TOŌ   OOH=
            this   you   Neg-solution   PRT
            ('You can't do anything [about it]?')

23   Ying: =<u>bô-huat-tōo</u>=
             Neg-solution
             ('I have no solution')

24   CVC: *ah hiau-hīng ah   bô-huat-tōo beh-án-náh*
            ah terrible   PRT   n-solution how

25   *tshòng āu-pái pó   pát-king bô pó   Daxing*
             do   future insure   other C Neg insure company name
             ('It's terrible. What [can we] do if you can't do anything.
             [Let's] not insure with *Daxing* and insure with another
             [company] next time')

26   ((someone sniggers))

27   Ying: *hong-piān   tioh hó   lah hong-piān khah hó   lah-*
             convenient   then good PRT convenient more good PRT
             ('It's better to be more convenient')
(Chang and Haugh 2011a: 2959)

In response to the CVC's negative assessment of Ying's company (lines 24–25) and suggestion that everyone present choose to insure with another company (line 25), there is laughter, indicating that this is indeed embarrassing for Ying. However, rather than orienting to this threat to the reputation of his company through offering some kind of account, Ying responds with an assertion that here appears sequentially irrelevant with respect to what is made conditionally relevant by the CVC's prior turn. In this way, Ying is able implicate his stance that the CVC's remarks are "offensive", and yet nevertheless resists the preference structure occasioned through the prior turn, namely, "raising the stakes" through a counter-challenge (Reynolds 2011: 423). In this way, he avoids an unwanted evaluation that he is "not polite" or even "impolite", which could arise through instantiating such a counter-challenge.

In some cases, then, an implicature can occasion politeness through indicating a participant's concern that he or she not be seen as "impolite" or "not polite". This orientation towards avoiding an "impolite" stance can also be accomplished through treating a matter as a "delicacy", as discussed in the following section.

6 Doing delicacy

A matter is formulated, or an action implemented, as "delicate" when there are speech perturbations, delays, trail-offs, *sotto voce* delivery, and speech-obscuring laughter in articulating what is being said at a point of imminent possible completion in a turn (Chevalier 2009; Lerner 2013; Pillet-Shore 2012).[69] In this way, the speaker indicates his or her reluctance or hesitance to voice that which is being treated as a delicacy through such practices. More broadly, doing delicacy can be characterised as a way of indicating that something is being left unsaid. Through *not-saying*, the speaker positions the recipient as responsible for either articulating that part which has not been said, often with an alternative formulation, or signalling understanding of that which has not been said, in subsequent talk. In this way, the implementation of a particular action or the formulation of a matter, and the attendant unwanted implications that would arise through its implementation or formulation, can be avoided by a speaker who leaves it up to the recipient to "find" and "enact" (Drew 2011). Politeness can be occasioned in some instances through doing delicacy in this way, as through it, participants display recognition of the potential impropriety of *saying* something.[70]

In the following exchange between female acquaintances, for instance, a politeness implicature arises through the way in which delicacy is signalled by Mayuko in formulating her response to Kumiko's invitation to go and play tennis.

(105) 1   K: *eeto   ne,   jitsuwa   ne,   tenisu   no   menbā   ga*
                 well M   actually   M   tennis   of   member   Nom

       2   *hitori   tari-naku-te,   ima   komat-te-iru   no.*
                 one person enough-Neg-Te   now   trouble-Te-Prog   M
                 ('well, actually, we are short one person for tennis, and
                 now we're in trouble')

       3   M: *hā*
                 ('oh')

---

69 The potential for hesitation to be deployed by speakers in order to accomplish some interactional goal, alongside its role as an indicator of cognitive load for the speaker, was noted in passing in earlier work by Good and Butterworth (1980)

70 We briefly alluded to this in discussing an instance in the previous chapter (see example 83), where a trailing-off utterance final *or* is deployed by a speaker to treat what is left unsaid as a potential delicacy.

4 K: *sorede, mō   kōto   mo   toc-chat-te-iru   shi*
      and   already court also take-Past-Te-Prog and
      ('and we've already booked a court and')

5 M: *ee*
      ('yes')

6 K: *deki-tara, Mayuko-san ni   ki-te-itadakeru   to*
      can-if   Mayuko-Pol by   come-Te-receive(Hon)   Quot

7   *tasukaru-n-da   kedo.*
      help-Nomi-Cop   but
      ('if you can, it would help if you could come')

8 M: *aa, tenisu desu   ka, ii   desu   ne.*
      oh tennis Cop(Pol) Q   good Cop(Pol) M

9   *tada, chotto doyōbi   wa...*
      just   a little Saturday Cont
      ('oh, tennis? That sounds nice, but Saturday is a bit ...')

10   *nan-ji   kara desu   ka.*
      what-time from Cop(Pol) Q
      ('what time will it start?')

11 K: *eeto ne, 10 ji   gurai   kara yar-ō   kana*
      well M 10 o'clock   around   from do-Vol wonder

12   *to   omot-te-iru-n-da   kedo ne.*
      Quot think-Te-Prog-Nomi-Cop   but   M
      ('um, I think we'll start from around 10 but')

13 M: *aa, chotto yotei ga   hait-te-shimat-te-*
      oh a little plan   Nom   enter-Te-complete-Te-

14   *iru-n-de,   mōshiwake-nai-n-desu   kedo*
      Prog-Nomi-Cop(Te)   excuse(Pol)-Neg-Nomi-Cop(Pol)   but
      ('oh, unfortunately I already have plans, so I am really
      sorry but')

15 K: *aa, sō.*
      ('oh really')

16 M: *mata tsugi no kikai   ni demo ...*
      again next of chance   in even
      ('if there is a chance next time ...')

17   K: *aa,*   *hontō ni.*
            ('oh,   really')

18   M: *ee.*
            ('yes')
(adapted from Date 2005: 307–308)

Kumiko formulates her invitation to Mayuko to play tennis as a favour (that is, of benefit to Kumiko) (lines 1–7), thereby positioning acceptance of that invitation as the preferred response (Davidson 1984, 1990). The way in which Mayuko initially delays specifically addressing this invitation by commenting in line 8 that tennis in general is a good thing is thus indicative of an incipient dispreferred response, that is, where she refuses the said invitation. The likelihood of a forthcoming refusal is further signalled through a trail-off in line 9, whereby Mayuko's readiness (or not) to accept the invitation to play on Saturday is treated as a delicacy (Lerner 2013). Mayuko then alludes to the possible trouble in readily accepting the invitation by checking a preparatory condition for accepting the invitation, namely, her availability at the time the tennis match will be played (line 10). After hearing Kumiko indicate the time the match is planned for (lines 11–12), Mayuko responds that she herself has plans at that time (lines 13–14), and then apologises (line 14). While the upshot here is left attenuated (see section 2, this chapter), there is also an orientation on Mayuko's part to the upshot itself constituting a delicacy, as she explicitly treats it as an impropriety through an apology (Robinson 2004). Overall, then, the refusal is accomplished not only through attenuating an upshot, but by delaying the implementation of this implicated refusal over a number of turns, in the course of which Mayuko orients to both the troubles in accepting the invitation as a delicacy, as well as the incipient refusal itself.

In this interaction, then, we can observe the reciprocation of a concern for "politeness" by both participants. In the case of Kumiko, while her invitation is formulated in a way that indicates acceptance is the preferred response, it is nevertheless sensitive to Mayuko's willingness and ability to accept (lines 6–7), and also affords a dispreferred response through the turn-final *kedo* ('but'). In this way, Kumiko orients to a low deontic entitlement vis-à-vis her relationship with Mayuko that the latter necessarily comply with Kumiko's wishes, and so indicates a "polite" stance. In response to this invitation, Mayuko treats an incipient refusal as a delicacy through delays and trail-offs (lines 8–9), as well as through an apology for the relational transgression a refusal potentially creates (line 14). In this way, then, Mayuko orients to the articulation of the incipient (and eventually implicated) refusal as an impropriety (Lerner 2013; Pomerantz 1980).

Politeness implicatures can also arise through treating the formulation of a matter as a delicacy. In the following excerpt from negotiations about the amount of compensation that should be paid by the party at fault for the death of someone in a car accident, for instance, the matter of asking for more or less money to be paid as compensation is treated as a delicacy.

(106) 10 Lin: ah *tān-sī huat-sing tsit-tsióng ì-guā*   *tak-ke*   *mā   long*
                   PRT but   occur   this kind   accident everyone also all

        11   *bô-guān-ì lah*   (.)   *%shei yuan-yi kan dao zhi yangzi%*
                   Neg   willing PRT who   willing see CP   this kind

        12   (.) hònn ( ) *tsóng-sī heh-leh:* (.) *bô   uân-siān lah   ah*
                       PRT   invariably   that Neg perfect PRT PRT

        13   *mā-sī ai   lāi* (.) *tsò   tsit ê mí-póo   ah   hònn*
                   still   need CP   make one C compensation PRT PRT

        14   *tak-ke   tuì   tse-ê mí-póo   heh-leh °hong-bīn*
                   everyone ASP this compensation that   aspect

        15   *sī   m   sī   lan tshiann:: heh-leh: lan* (.) *siū-hāi-tsia*
                   be Neg be   we ask   that   our   victim

        16   *tsit-pîng hònn* (.) *lái thé-liōng tsit-ê   khuànn ē-thang°*
                   this side PRT   CP consider a little see   able
                   ('but no-one wanted to see this accident [happen], who would
                   have wanted to see it happen? [The compensation] is not ideal,
                   but [we] still need to redeem [the loss], can we ask ... the side
                   of the victim to show more consideration
                   [towards the people at fault]?)

        17 Chen: *bô   lah* (.) *tsit-má mā-sī kāng–khuán lah   lí   it-tit kóng:*
                   Neg PRT   now   also   the same   PRT you keep say

        18   (1.0) *lâng   í-king   bô-tī   ah* (.) *tsit-ma m-sī   kong*
                       person already deceased PRT   now   Neg-be say

        19   *iōng kè-tsînn lái* >*kóng an-na*< *tsuè-khí-má lí   mā*
                   use price CP say this   at least   you also

        20   *ài   piáu-sī tsit-ê kóng lí   ū   siánn-mah* (.) *mí-póo*
                   need show a little say you have what   compensation

21	ê	hong-sik (.)	kóng	lái	tsò	tsham-khó	khuànn (.)
	Nom	way	say	CP	as	reference	CP

22	°hònn°
	PRT

('no, now it's the same. You keep saying that [we are] not negotiate [over a life] with a price, but at least you need to show a
little bit, saying what compensation [you can provide] for our
reference')

(adapted from Chang forthcoming)

At this point in the negotiations, Lin, who is representing the at-fault party,
implements a request (lines 10–16), namely, that the victim party accept the
amount of compensation that has already been offered in prior turns (data not
shown). Mention of a reduction in the amount of money to be paid in compensation is avoided, however, through the euphemistic expression, thé-liōng ('consideration'). In this way, talking about money as compensation for the death of
someone is treated as a delicacy (Lerner 2013: 97–98). Chen, however, steps in
and argues that the victim's side can also ask for the same "consideration" to be
shown (line 17), and then alludes to what has been treated as a delicacy here,
namely, negotiating the "price" of someone's life (lines 17–18). It is claimed by
Chen that treating this matter as a delicacy is obstructing the progress of the
negotiations (lines 19–22).

However, while Chen construes regarding the amount of money to be paid in
compensation to be a delicacy as problematic vis-à-vis the ongoing progressivity
of the negotiations themselves, Lin later comments that explicit talk about this
matter is "not polite" (bô lé-māu).

(107)	28	Lin:	>án-ne	hit-lō-ah	lah	hònn<	lán	tī	kóng	ê	tī	hia
			this	that	PRT	PRT	we	just	say	PRT	ASP	there

29	khiú	lái	khiú	khì	°hònn° ( )	siūnn	kóng	duì	hit-lō-ah
	pull	CP	pull	CP	PRT	think	CP	for	that

30	khah	bô	lé-māu	lah	°hònn°(.)	ah
	more	Neg	polite	PRT	PRT	PRT

('Well, we think it's not polite towards the deceased while we are
bargaining there')

(adapted from Chang forthcoming)

In this way, then, we find evidence in later talk that Lin, at least, is treating the mention of money in these negotiations as a delicacy, and so mention of it constitutes an impropriety. In other words, Lin claims to be avoiding the mention of money in these negotiations over the amount to be paid in compensation due to his concerns for matters of "politeness" (*lé-māu*). For this reason, his construal of the matter of reducing this amount of money as a delicacy through the euphemistic term "consideration" (*thé-liōng*) in the context of his prior implicated request arguably indicates a "polite" stance on his part.

In sum, then, we have seen in the course of this chapter that implicatures arise through various practices, including attenuating and withholding, preempting, soliciting, disattending, and doing delicacy. Through these practices participants are able to mask or even disguise what has been implicated in a way that can reduce not only their degree of accountability for the masked or disguised action trajectory, but also allows them to treat the interactional and relational work that is accomplished through implicatures as unofficial business of interaction. In other words, politeness implicatures are not simply a means of being "polite", but are a means of accomplishing various kinds of interactional business. It was also observed in passing that while the way in which participants can indicate a concern for "politeness" through these various practices is a locally situated in the particulars of the interaction in question, participants nevertheless draw upon aspects of the broader moral order that are implemented and sustained through accomplishing actions and broader interactional projects in unofficial ways. Notably, these aspects of the moral order were varied, ranging from a concern for 'place'/'role' (*tachiba*) and feelings/heart-mind (*kokoro*) through to an orientation to relational entitlements and reciprocal approval. Underpinning these, in turn, was an orientation to the respective benefactive, deontic and epistemic status of the participants. An investigation of politeness implicatures as a form of social action thus arguably offers insight into the moral order itself as an object of study (Haugh 2013c, 2013d).

One point that has only been alluded to in the course of this discussion is not only can evaluations of politeness be occasioned through implicatures in some instances (or what are termed politeness implicatures), but that an orientation to issues of impoliteness and relationships amongst participants can also be indicated through implicatures. It is thus to a consideration of implicatures vis-à-vis impoliteness, and relationality more broadly, that we now turn.

Chapter Seven:
Impoliteness implicatures and offence

An impoliteness implicature has been broadly defined as an instance where through implicating rather than saying, an impolite stance on the part of the speaker is occasioned. However, it is important to note from the outset that impoliteness implicatures do not arise simply through an absence of politeness. As Culpeper (2011a, 2012) argues, impoliteness is associated with different emotions (e.g. *anger, hurt, disgust* in English), and different sets of conventionalised formulae. And while there is some overlap with politeness, the metalanguage that evaluations of impoliteness draw from is also ultimately quite distinct in many respects (e.g. *rude, patronising, aggressive* do not have counterparts in the politeness metalanguage in English). Yet while such metalinguistic distinctions are clearly important, in this chapter, the focus will be primarily on how impoliteness implicatures differ from politeness implicatures as forms of social action.

One key difference in that respect is the intimate relationship that holds between impoliteness implicatures and phenomena such as irony or sarcasm. This relationship leads us, in turn, to a consideration of mock impoliteness implicatures and mock politeness implicatures, two phenomena which we briefly introduced in Chapter 1 (see section 1). In the case of mock impoliteness implicatures what is implicated *could* legitimately or conceivably be evaluated as "impolite", and participants are aware of this, but is in this instance framed (or treated) as "non-impolite".[71] In the case of mock politeness implicatures, in contrast, an ostensibly "polite" stance, which is indicated through the occurrence of a (non-)linguistic form or practice that would in other circumstances be associated with a polite attitude, masks or disguises an "impolite" stance that arises through implicature.[72] While impoliteness implicatures are distinct from both mock impoliteness implicatures and mock politeness implicatures, they are nevertheless clearly

---

[71] The term "mock impoliteness" was coined by Leech (1983). It was originally regarded as interchangeable with the term "banter" (see also Culpeper 1996). However, following Haugh and Bousfield (2012), it will be argued in this chapter that mock impoliteness constitutes an evaluation that is occasioned through various social actions, including teasing, mockery and banter. According to that view, mock impoliteness and banter constitute distinct objects of analysis.

[72] The term "mock politeness" was also coined by Leech (1983). It was originally treated as interchangeable with the terms irony or sarcasm (see also Culpeper 1996). However, it will be presumed in this chapter that irony and sarcasm involve a different level and mode of analysis, and so while clearly inter-related, they are better analysed as distinct phenomena (see Dynel [2013] for a recent neo-Gricean analysis of irony). After all, being interpreted as being ironic or sarcastic does not necessarily mean one will be evaluated as mock polite or even impolite.

inter-related practices given they all involve invoking evaluations of impoliteness in one way or another, albeit an ostensibly impolite stance (in the case of mock impoliteness implicatures), or in a way that ostensibly masks an impolite stance (in the case of mock politeness implicatures).

Another important difference is that impoliteness implicatures, mock impoliteness implicatures, and mock politeness implicatures arise through a largely distinct range of practices to those underpinning politeness implicatures. Of course, in the same way that politeness implicatures allow for some degree of indeterminacy in regards to what exactly participants are taken to be committing themselves to be meaning in interaction, (mock) impoliteness implicatures and mock politeness implicatures can also allow participants to position themselves as less accountable for that which has been implicated, or at least as having not *said* it, and in that way, decrease the (perceived) degree of offence in some cases. However, as we shall see, in some instances, what is implicated is largely tractable, even if the participant's degree of commitment to that implicature is not totally determinate, and in such cases, the offence that can be taken by recipients, in particular, the target, may even be amplified. Through various practices, then, the degree to which offence is designed to be taken can be modulated, as well as the range of response types afforded to recipients. These three types of implicature consequently accomplish rather different kinds of interactional and relational work than that accomplished through politeness implicatures.

In this chapter, we will thus examine some of the practices by which such implicatures can arise, as well as the sorts of interactional and relational work that can be accomplished by them.[73] We begin, in the first section, by examining how offence can be occasioned through implicating negative assessments. We then move, in the second section, to examine how participants can register and sanction (perceived) offence through implicatures. This is followed in section three by a discussion of how "mock offence" can be occasioned through implicatures. However, given implicatures designed to occasion mock offence can, in some instances, nevertheless be taken as offensive by one or more recipients (and in some cases may actually be designed to do so through disguising an impolite stance in the guise of an ostensibly mock impolite stance), this leads in the final section to a consideration of the ways in which implicated offence can be disputed.

---

73 This survey is, however, envisaged as indicative rather than definitive, due to reasons of space.

1 Implicating negative assessments

There are various ways in which an "impolite" stance can be indicated and perceived offence disputed, as the growing literature on impoliteness suggests (e.g. Bousfield 2008, 2013; Bousfield and Culpeper 2008; Bousfield and Locher 2008; Culpeper 1996, 2005, 2011a; Garcés-Conejos Blitvich 2009, 2010; Graham 2007; Harris 2001; Haugh 2010c; Locher 2011; Mills 2009). However, with the exception of work by Bousfield (2008) and Culpeper (2011a), there has been much less said about sarcasm (cf. "mock politeness") and what in Brown and Levinson's terms might be called "off record impoliteness", namely, ambiguous insults, insinuations, innuendo and so on (cf. "implicational impoliteness"). We briefly reviewed such work in Chapter 4 (see section 2), when we outlined Culpeper's (2011a) claim that impoliteness can be implicated through (1) marked surface forms or semantic content in the behaviour (form-driven implicational impoliteness), (2) mismatches between the context projected by the behaviour and either the context of use or the context projected by another part of the same speaker's behaviour (convention-driven implicational impoliteness), or (3) invoking expectations from the context (context-driven implicational impoliteness).

In this section, it will be argued that what lies at the heart of many, if not most, instances of these three different types of "implicational impoliteness" proposed by Culpeper, are negative assessments of one or more recipients that are implemented through implicatures. Assessments involve social actions that "espouse a stance or evaluation" (Robles 2012: 757), more specifically, "describing something as good or bad" (Potter 1998: 250). Notably, in producing assessments, the speaker is implicitly claiming some knowledge of the assessable (Pomerantz 1984a). In the case of negative assessments, this description casts a person (or group of persons) into a valenced category that is undesirable, objectionable or disagreeable to that person (or group of persons) with respect to the locally situated context and interactional trajectory of its occurrence. While the assessable might, in the first instance, be an object, place or particular event/situation rather than a person (or set of persons), such assessments can nevertheless be directed at persons who might align themselves with that object, place or situation/event (for instance, through ownership of the object being assessed, a long-term affiliation with the place being assessed, or direct involvement with the situation or event being assessed). A negative assessment is, of course, not an objective description of that person, object, place or situation/event, but rather constitutes a subjective evaluation:

assessments show a view of the assessable as something perceived by an actor who both takes up a particular alignment to it and sees the assessable from a particular perspective, one that may be quite different from that of a co-participant who is simultaneously assessing the same event (Goodwin and Goodwin 1992: 165).

For this reason, different participants may legitimately construe or otherwise respond to negative assessments in different ways.

Yet no matter how the negative assessment in question is construed by participants, it inevitably evokes aspects of the "epistemic order", specifically, the participants' orientation to knowledge, namely, who knows what and who knows better (Heritage 2011, 2012a, 2012b; Heritage and Raymond 2005; Raymond and Heritage 2006). The epistemic order encompasses both "epistemic status", that is, the expectations of participants in relation to a certain domain of knowledge with respect to their co-participant(s), as well as "epistemic stance", which refers to the displays by participants in talk-in-interaction of how knowledgable they are (Stevanovic and Peräkylä 2014). Notably, a negative assessment is open to evaluation as "impolite" in cases when one or more participants take that assessment to be enacting an epistemic stance on the part of the producer that is inconsistent with their (perceived) epistemic rights to be making that negative assessment.

One key finding from studies of assessments in situated interactions is that assessments regularly occasion second assessments (Goodwin and Goodwin 1987, 1992; Pomerantz 1984a). In other words, when one person makes an assessment of him/herself or someone else, another co-present participant may generally offer his/her own assessment. Instances where a second assessment is not produced, then, can be construed as an "accountable absence", and so warrant an inference that a disaffiliative stance (e.g. disagreement with the negative assessment) is being withheld, particularly in instances where a negative assessment is targeted at a particular recipient (or set of recipients).[74] It follows that the activity of performing assessments is "intrinsically social in that it can provide for the collaborative, but differentiated, participation of multiple actors" (Goodwin and Goodwin 1992: 181).

A second key finding is that the design of turns that implement assessments generally fall into two broad patterns. On the one hand, they may be performed with a minimum of delay and early in the turn or they can involve some kind of upgrade. This is generally characterised as a preferred turn design with respect

---

74 cf. McKinlay and McVittie (2006) who claim "assessments made in a multi-party context ordinarily are available to all members rather than directed to individual recipients. In consequence, responses subsequently provided by speakers who disagree with the initial assessment will not necessarily adopt the turn shapes found in the two-party situation" (p.812).

to assessments (Pomerantz 1984a), whether in response to, or in initiating an assessment (Pomerantz and Heritage 2013). On the other hand, assessments may be performed after some delay, and so later in turn, and may be "softened" or "qualified", in which case they are characterised as involving a dispreferred turn design (Pomerantz 1984a; Pomerantz and Heritage 2013). This is not to say, of course, that the same turn cannot involve features of both types of preference structure, as is the case for compliment responses, for instance (Pomerantz 1978a; Schegloff 2007). In the case of assessments, this preference design is important given "assessments are morally implicative", and thus "socially and relationally consequential, dealing with the shared (or unshared) understandings and values assumed between" participants (Robles 2012: 757). It is through the preference design of assessments that participants open up "linkages between talk and the social construction of solidarity" (Lindström and Mondada 2009: 299; see also Pomerantz 1984a: 76; Heritage 1984a: 275), and in the case of multi-party interactions, allow participants to "construct and enact shared experiences and collective affect" (Robles 2012: 757).

Finally, it has been demonstrated that the sequential positioning of assessments involves issues of epistemic authority and rights (Heritage 2002a; Heritage and Raymond 2005). Heritage (2002a), for instance, claims that "going first can have a greater impact in establishing superior access, expertise, authority and rights to assess the matter in question, if only because the relative access and expertise of the parties to the state of affairs may remain to be negotiated" (p.200). It follows that "the positioning of first and second assessments contributes to the display of epistemic authority" (Lindström and Mondada 2009: 300). In other words, it matters whether a negative assessment is positioned as a first (i.e. initiating) or a second (i.e. responsive) assessment.

One phenomenon that has received less attention thus far, however, is the way in which a negative assessment can be implicated through a preferred turn design in first-position. In such cases, the negative assessment is implemented with a minimum of delay early in the turn and without any overt "softening" or "mitigation" of its inferable formulation. In other words, the implicated object of the negative assessment can be readily inferred, and so is largely tractable to the recipients. Implicating a negative assessment in this way thus exacerbates the potential offence for the target, and underpins the ready characterisation of such instances as impoliteness implicatures. At the same time this turn design also affords, alongside constraining, a particular range of responses from the target of the negative assessment, as well as other recipients if present, given the implicit claim to epistemic authority implemented when a negative assessment is first-positioned. In other words, implicating a negative assessment can in fact exacerbate the degree of potential offence for the target, because it is accomplished with a turn design that delivers the inferable formulation of the negative assessment in an unmitigated manner, positions agreement with the negative assessment by other recipients as the preferred response, and also carries with it implicit claims to epistemic authority on the part of the producer of that negative assessment. It is for these reasons we can account for Culpeper's (2011a) rather astute observation that "off-recordness in contexts where the impoliteness interpretation is clear seems not to mollify the offence: if anything, it might exacerbate it" (p.160).

Let us first consider an example where a negative assessment is implicated in a small-group discussion amongst high school children who are comparing their homework, for which they had to write poems or letters about the Great Depression. The excerpt in question begins with a claim by Tiffany about the way in which all their poems had something "sad" included.

(108) 1 T: oh well, we all put something sad in our poems, I guess.

    2 E: it's the <u>Gr</u>eat Depression.

    3   [you think there are going to be   ] pa:rtie:s:.=

    4 J: [of course. you had to put something sad.]

    5 T: =yeah, of course! I'm just kidding.
    (adapted from Dobs and Garcés-Conejos Blitvich 2013: 118)

A negative assessment is implicated by Elijah in lines 2–3 in response to Tiffany's claim, namely, "that Tiffany's original contribution to the discussion is pointless" (Dobs and Garcés-Conejos Blitvich 2013: 118) given it states the obvious. This is obviousness of her claim is emphasised through the intonational stress on "great" (line 2), and the subsequent suggestion in line 3, which Elijah attributes to Tiffany as principal, thereby indicating a mocking stance towards it. In this way, he implicates that it is not an apt or intelligent thing to be saying, and so implicitly casts her as "dumb" or at least "not sufficiently intelligent" for this class (*ibid.*: 118).

There are number of things to note about the way in which the utterances through which this negative assessment is implicated by Elijah are formulated. First, the inferable formulation of the negative assessment itself is delivered unmitigated, and indeed is upgraded through the intonational stress in line 2. In other words, it is not suggested that Tiffany's contribution *might* be too obvious, or that she *might* be being a little stupid in making, but rather a negative asssement is implemented through a turn design where the assessment itself is delivered without delay or being mitigated per se, thereby implicating that her contribution is *clearly* pointless, and construing her as *obviously* stupid or dumb for having made it. Second, agreement with this implicated negative assessment is projected through the design of his turn. This is most evident from the way in which his utterance in line 3 is formulated as a "reversed polarity question" that is not seeking information, but rather asserts a position that challenges the relevance of Tiffany's prior claim (Koshik 2005). Third, in implementing the negative assessment in first position, Elijah is implicitly claiming superior epistemic authority and rights to judge Tiffany's contribution to the discussion (Heritage 2002a; Heritage and Raymond 2005). In order to contest the implicated negative assessment, then, the target, Tiffany, must also design her turn in way that undermines or resists that claim to epistemic authority.

Jessica, a side participant here, implicates a negative assessment in line 4 in overlap with Elijah's reversed polarity question in line 3, thereby affiliating with his stance that Tiffany's contribution was so obvious that it wasn't worth mentioning, and so was dumb. In this way, she creates a relational coalition where she and Elijah are evaluating Tiffany in the same way, thereby instantiating solidarity with Elijah, on the one hand, and excluding Tiffany from that grouping, on the other. This reinforces the negative assessment, thereby exacerbating the potential offence for Tiffany.

It is evident from Tiffany's subsequent response in line 5, where she attempts to reframe her footing vis-à-vis her prior claim in line 1, that this implicated negative assessment is indeed undesirable and objectionable to her. She resists the way in which Elijah and Jessica have held her accountably committed to this prior claim as principal by attempting to position herself as its author but not its principal ("I'm just kidding"), thereby allowing her to also affiliate with Elijah's mocking stance. However, the inclusion of "of course" in her ostensibly affiliative response also contests, at the same time, what Stivers (2011) terms the "presupposition of askability" in relation to Elijah's prior question in line 3. In this way, Tiffany implicates that she is "not 'the kind of person' the questioner [Elijah] had suggested with [his] question" (p.105), thereby implicitly resisting the implicated negative assessment that she was "dumb" in making that prior claim. In sum, then, the design of Tiffany's response suggests that this implicated negative assessment is indeed undesirable and objectionable for her, and thus offensive, although she works to minimise this offence by implicitly contesting the implicated premise that occasions it.

In some cases, negative assessments can also be implicated through talk that is formulated as ostensibly indicating a polite stance on the part of the speaker. In such instances, the negative assessment is disguised or masked in the form of a mock politeness implicature. We discussed just such an example in Chapter Four (example 67), which is reproduced here in order to facilitate further discussion of it.

(109) NJGR: 8:00

    210 G: U:M I haven't got any questions to ask you actually.

    211   (1.2)

    212 N: ↑you must be fun at parties.

    213 G: .hhh don't like parties

    214 N: no: I can imagine. ahe parties probably don't like you

    215   either(h)

    216   (0.6)

    217 G: I guess so. ↑OH NO. (0.8) people always like

    218   someone they can saddle up to (2.1) talk to.

    219   at least someone in the corner they can talk to.

As was previously noted, Natalie responded to Gary's claim that he doesn't have any questions to ask her with an ostensibly positive assessment (line 212). However, the occurrence of a positive assessment does not fit with the interactional trajectory here, in which Natalie has been exhorting Gary to ask her some questions. This incongruity triggers the inference that Natalie is taking a mocking stance towards that positive assessment, and thereby implicating a negative assessment of Gary, namely, that he is socially inept. This is implicated negative assessment is then upgraded in her subsequent turn (lines 214–215) to an outright insult in which "parties" metonymically stands for "people".

In this case, while the implicated negative assessment is ostensibly mitigated by a positive assessment, the mocking stance that Natalie takes towards the latter (hence the hearably sarcastic tone), alongside the claim to epistemic authority to judge Gary's person outside of the context of their current conversation (bearing in mind this is the first time Natalie has talked with Gary), intensifies the illocutionary force of this insult. A mock politeness implicature can thus accomplish a negative assessment in a way that exacerbates the potential offence for the target.

As we earlier noted, however, Gary does not orient to this potential offence in this response, but rather contests Natalie's assumption that he would want to go to parties in the first place (line 213), thereby undermining the relevance of her claim. He then subsequently contests her implicated claim that no one would want to talk to him at parties (lines 217–219). It is also evident from subsequent talk that Gary interprets Natalie's implicated negative assessment as registering offence on her part (see example 69, chapter 4), because he had previously declined to ask her questions despite her exhorting him to do so.

In this section, it has been argued that implicatures can be designed to deliver negative assessments not as mitigated or softened, but rather as attenuated upshots for which the recipient is positioned as partly responsible for identifying. The reflexively intentional object of the attenuated upshot is itself largely unmitigated in its anticipated formulation by the recipient, and so offence on the part of the recipient(s) can be occasioned. Such instances therefore constitute examples of impoliteness implicature. In other cases, however, an impolite stance arising through what is implicated may be masked by an ostensibly polite stance that is indicated through the formulation of what is said, in which case a mock politeness implicature arises. Thus, while it has traditionally been assumed that indirectness is a means of softening or mitigating negative assessments (see sections 2 and 3 in Chapter One), in this section we have illustrated exactly the opposite. Implicatures can also allow speakers to deliver negative assessments in a relatively unmitigated inferable formulation in which the object of the negative assessment is largely tractable to the participants. Yet the speaker is nevertheless positioned as less accountable for that negative assessment than they would have otherwise been if delivered as said (even if mitigated), given the way in which the speaker's degree of commitment to that negative assessment can be positioned as more or less indeterminate through implicature.

2 Registering and sanctioning offence

In the previous section we briefly alluded to the way in which through impoliteness implicatures and mock politeness implicatures participants may not only accomplish particular situated relational work amongst themselves, but can also contribute to renewing, sustaining, and sometimes challenging the moral substrate that underpins evaluations of im/politeness (see Chapter 4: section 4.1). In this section, we develop this observation further in suggesting that implicating negative assessments can, in some instances, register and sanction perceived offence on the part of participants. In this way, we can observe an orientation on the part of participants to the moral order, an orientation that affords the recognisability of im/politeness implicatures in the first place.

In the following interaction, for instance, which is also situated within a high school discussion group, one of the participants, Sara, draws the attention of others to a potentially embarrassing situation involving one of the other participants, Devonte, namely, that there is a "booger" hanging out of his nose.

(110) 8 S: there's some [thing inside] your nose.

        9 J: [the milkman]

    10 S: you have a big booger [hanging] [out of your   ] nose.

    11 J: [milkman]

    12 C: [no, you don't.]

    13 D: ((to Jason)) awright.

    14 S: ((gasp)) Carrie::: ((squeaky voice))

    15 C: the way you're supposed to do it, is do it discreetly

    16   so if someone's itching.

(adapted from Dobs and Garcés-Conejos Blitvich 2013: 123)

The noticing here by Sara is directed at Devonte, but given the presence of other side participants, it is evidently an attempt to "elicit a reaction from Devonte and entertain her group" (Dobs and Garcés-Conejos Blitvich 2013: 124). There is no response, however, and Sara upgrades the reference from "something" (line 8) to "a big booger" (line 10), and thus increases the embarrassment it potentially occasions. In response to this second noticing, Carrie counters Sara's claim on behalf of Devonte (line 12), while Devonte himself, and the other side participants, continue to disattend Sara's noticings (cf. Chapter 6: section 5). Sara's prior noticings are evidently projecting a defensive move on the part of the target, Devonte, and a negative assessment of Devonte on the part of the other participants as contingently relevant next moves. Yet it is not the target, but a side participant, Carrie, who elects to counter the noticing with a reprimand. Devonte, on the other hand, offers no response to Sara's noticing. As we have already noted, withholding a response in next position can implicate an upshot, here that the noticing does not need to be attended to because it is in some way inapposite.

While Sara appears to indicate disappointment in line 14 at the lack of a reaction from the group, in particular, from Carrie in her subsequent turn, Carrie offers an account for the lack of the desired response from Sara's perspective (lines 15–16). This account, as Dobs and Garcés-Conejos Blitvich (2013) argue, "functions as an indirect reprimand as it implies that Sara's behaviour was inappropriate" (p.124). We can see here how implicating a negative assessment registers offence at Sara's prior noticings of a potentially embarrassing situation for Devonte, and construes them as uncalled for. She also sanctions this behaviour, by formulating this account at a more generalised level through abstraction (Deppermann 2011a) than is warranted in the locally situated context in which the noticings take place. In this way, deontic aspects of the moral order are invoked, namely, that members should know that one should not explicitly point out such embarrassing matters, but rather should subtly indicate that situation to the person in question. Consequently, Sara is implicitly cast as someone with an inadequate understanding of the "'seen but unnoticed', expected, background features of everyday scenes" (Garfinkel 1967: 35–36), which also implicitly renews and sustains a particular set of expectancies as part of the moral substrate that underpins evaluations of im/politeness. Through implicated negative assessments, then, we can observe how members construe not only what behaviour is perceived as "impolite" or "offensive", but also what behaviour counts as "polite".

Offence can also be registered and sanctioned through mock politeness implicatures. As we saw from example 83 (see Chapter 5: section 1.3), offence can be registered by mock politeness implicatures that arise through conventionalised politeness formulae (Culpeper 2011a), namely, thankings. They may also arise through honorifics that index social distance (so-called *desu-masu* forms), which although standardly associated with "politeness", can be used in situations where they do not fit the overall tenor of the interaction. They thus constitute an instance of the so-called "sarcastic" use of honorifics (Brown 2013; Okamoto 2002, 2007). In the following excerpt, for instance, this sarcastic use of honorifics along with an ostensible apology gives rise to mock politeness implicatures (see also Haugh 2007b: 668–669; Haugh and Obana 2011: 172).

(111) 1 F: *gochisō-sama.*
          feast-Hon
          ('thanks for dinner')

       2 G: *ara, mō   tabe-nai no?*
             oh   longer eat-Neg M
             ('oh, you're not eating any more?')

       3 F: *kō-iu   abura-kkoi ryōri wa   su-kan.*
             this kind oil-thick   food Cont like-Neg
             ('I don't like this kind of oily food')

       4   ((grandmother takes the dish away))

       5 G: *ara sō   desu   ka. suimasen-deshi-ta.*
             oh that way Cop(Pol) Q excuse me-Pol-Past
             ('oh, is that right? [Well] sorry [then]')

       6   ((grandmother washes the dishes noisily))

7　F:　*okot-ta?*
　　　angry-Past
　　　('are you angry?')

8　G:　*betsuni*　　　　　　*okocchai-ma-sen yo.*
　　　not particularly　angry-Pol-Neg　　M
　　　('no, I'm not angry')
　　(Ueda 1998: 117)

The excerpt begins just as Kobo-chan's father (F) indicated he has finished dinner (line 1). Kobo-chan's grandmother (G) subsequently seeks an account as to why Kobo-chan's father is not going to eat more (line 2), to which the father responds with a negative assessment of the meal (i.e. it was too oily) (line 3). At this point there is a marked upshift in speech level to addressee honorifics that indicate social distance, as the grandmother ostensibly apologises for the meal (line 5). While the apology and the addressee honorifics through which the utterance is formulated are ostensibly indicators of a "polite" stance, here they implicate that she has taken offence at the negative assessment of the meal (evidently she was the cook). This becomes even more apparent as the father maintains the use of plain-forms (line 7), in contrast to the continued use of addressee honorifics by the grandmother in formulating her denial that she is upset (line 8). In this way, then, offence is registered through a mock politeness implicature.

Mock impoliteness implicatures can also, on occasion, register offence on the part of one or more participants. In the following excerpt, an insurance agent is trying to persuade his client, who is the at-fault party in a mediation about how much compensation should be paid to the victim's party, to bear some of the cost himself rather than trying to get the insurance company to pay the full amount. The insurance agent suggests that his client needs to be more "serious" (*tsìng-king*) and "sincere" (*yao you nage xin*) in making an effort to pay part of the compensation to the victim's party himself (lines 17–28).

(112)　17　IA:　*hònn tse　sī　sū-sit oh*(.) *TIÓH BÔ* (.) *M SĪ* (.) *NĀ-BÉ*
　　　　　　　PRT　this　be　fact　PRT　right　PRT　Neg be　if want

　　　　18　　　*HÚ-LĪ LÁN KÓNG TSÌNG-KING LÍ　TŌ- >GUÁ Ê*
　　　　　　　　deal　we　say　seriously　you　then　I　Nom

　　　　19　　　*Ì-SÙ　　SĪ　KÓNG* (.) *LÍ　TŌ　BĒ　TSHÂN　BĒ　HŇG*
　　　　　　　　meaning　be　say　　you　need sell farmland sell property

　　　　20　　　*MĀ　ÀI　TSHÚ-LÍ LAH< HÒNN:* (.) %a *yào　yǒu　nàge*
　　　　　　　　also　need　deal　　PRT　PRT　　PRT　need have that

21   *xīn* *la* (.) *yào* *yǒu* *nàge xīn*   A: *jiǎng nántīng*   *yìdiǎn*
        heart PRT need have that heart PRT say   unpleasant a little

22   *zhēnde méi yǒu qián jiào nǐ   qù shā rén   fànghuǒ*
        really Neg have money ask you go kill people set on fire

23   *zhège yě   bù   kěnéng*% (.) *hònn*: (.) %*nǐ zìjǐ kǎoliáng*
        this   also Neg possible   PRT   you self consider

24   *yíxià* (.) *wǒ běnshēn yǒu   dūoshǎo*% *nénglì*   %*shìbúshì*%
        a little I   self   have how much capability be-Neg-be

25   (.) *hònn* (.)*ē-sái tam   tsit-ē   bô* (.) >*ah tsīn-liōng*
             PRT   able shoulder a little Q   PRT as far as possible

26   *tam   tsit-ē*< (.) *lí* (.) *siūnn khuànn māi ah   tsit-ē* (.)
        shoulder a little   you think CP   CP PRT a little

27   *hònn ah: lán nng ê tshut-lâi guā-kháu gián-kiù tsit-ē*
        PRT PRT we two C come CP outside   discuss a little

28   *ā-sī* >*kah lán tāi-piáu   gián-kiù khuànn māi tsit-ē*<=
        or   with our representative discuss see   CP a little
        ('this is fact, right? No. If [you] want to deal with [it], to be
        serious, you then, I mean [that you] need to deal with [it even
        you need to] sell farmland or land. [You] need to have the heart.
        [You] need to have the heart. [It's] unpleasant to say [that]
        asking you to kill people or set places on fire is also impossible
        if you don't have money. Is that right? You need to consider a
        bit. "How much capability do I have ?", "Am I able to shoulder
        [the extra indemnity] a bit?" Try your best to shoulder some
        [extra indemnity]. Think about it. We two come outside to
        discuss or discuss with our representative')

29 Lin: = *bo* [*lah*   ]
         Neg PRT
         ('no')

30 IA: %[*bìjìng*] *lái   zhèbiān háishì yào   tán   yíxià la*%
             after all come here   still   need talk CP   PRT
        ('after all [we] come here for negotiation')

31 Lin: *guā kah sûn-mn-g* [*tsìt-ē*]
         I   CP   ask   CP
         ('I ask [him first]')

32 IA: [*án-ne*] *hó   bô   hònn*
                                            this   good Neg   Q
        (is this okay?')

33 Chen: *lín   sing tâm khuànn lah::*
          you first talk CP   PRT
          ('you [guys]talk first')

34 Peng: *kóng tsit-ē kah   tsìng-king*
          talk CP   more serious
          ('be more serious')

35 Wu: *lán   guá sī tsin tsìng-king*
         person I   be very serious
         ('I am very serious.')

36 Peng: hhhehhheh
         ((laughter))

37   ((Kuo, Kong, Lin, IA and Wu stepped outside to discuss
           the amount of indemnity))
        (adapted from Chang forthcoming)

In the course of this turn, the insurance agent invokes a somewhat extreme analogy for how sincere his client needs to be by ironically proposing that one who is truly sincere would go to any lengths to obtain the necessary funds (lines 22–23). The insurance agent then concludes his turn by proposing that the at-fault party step outside to discuss in private the amount of compensation they will offer to the victim's party (lines 27–28).

However, just as they are about to move out of the room, Peng, who is a member of the party representing the victim, self-selects and admonishes the insurance agent that *he* should be more serious (line 34). Wu, who is a member of the at-fault party, then elects to respond to that admonishment in place of the insurance agent who was nominally the addressee by claiming they are serious (line 35), which then occasions laughter from Peng (line 36). That the admonishment itself is framed by Peng as mock or not-serious is evident from the way in which it does not fit with the interactional trajectory (namely, the at – fault party moving out of the room to discuss the amount of compensation to be offered in private), and from Peng's subsequent laughter (Glenn 2003; Holt 2010; Jefferson, Sacks and Schegloff 1987). However, while it ostensibly occasions "mock impoliteness" through the formulation of an admonishment with an unmitigated imperative, in this case, Peng is also alluding to the insurance agent's prior analogy, and thereby also implicating that it was indicative of an insufficiently serious attitude on his part, and so was potentially offensive in the context of these negotiations (Chang forthcoming). It further implicates a request, within a jocular frame, that the at-fault party take seriously their private discussions about how much compensation to offer, thereby also supposing (i.e., as an implicated premise) that they have not been sufficiently serious, and thus sincere, in their discussions thus far. In this way, then, a mock impoliteness implicature can be used to not only register perceived offence, but can also be used to accomplish serious interactional business in the guise of a nominally jocular side sequence.

In this section, we have discussed how implicatures can register and sanction perceived offence(s). Notably, in registering and sanctioning such offences, participants invariably invoke the "'seen but unnoticed', expected, background features of everyday scenes" that constitute the moral order (Garfinkel 1967: 35–36), and thereby highlight the "understandings and values" that are assumed to be shared amongst members (Robles 2012: 757). An important feature of impoliteness implicatures, mock politeness implicatures and mock impoliteness implicatures, then, is that through attending to them in interactions where they arise, or in reporting on them in subsequent discourse, aspects of the moral order that ground evaluations of social actions and meanings as "polite" or "impolite" can be renewed, sustained, and in some cases challenged. In this way, an analysis of impoliteness implicatures offers us a window into the workings of the moral substrate that grounds evaluations of im/politeness, given the moral order does not exist outside of the interpretive work of the members that sustain it.

However, in the latter part of this discussion it has also become evident that through such implicatures, participants can accomplish particular interactional projects in unofficial ways. In the following section, we will thus turn to examine in more detail how such interactional and relational work can accomplished concurrently through mock impoliteness implicatures.

3 Mock impoliteness implicatures and relationality

It has long been noted that jocular or non-serious teasing, mockery and improprieties more generally can be used to instantiate solidarity or rapport amongst participants (e.g. Bousfield 2008; Boxer and Cortés-Conde 1997; Brown and Levinson 1987; Culpeper 2011a; Kotthoff 1996; Leech 1983; Norrick 1993; Straehle 1993) or can be treated as affiliative by those participants (e.g. Antaki 1998; Beach and Glenn 2011; Holt 2007; Jefferson, Sacks and Schegloff 1987; Sidnell 2011). While such work has traditionally come under the banner of "mock impoliteness" or "banter" in politeness research (e.g. Bousfield 2008; Culpeper 1996, 2011a; Furman 2013; Leech 1983; Sinkeviciute 2014), it has subsequently been argued that the analysis of the actions by which jocular teasing, mockery, insults and the like arise should be distinguished from the relational connection instantiated through such actions (Haugh 2010a), on the one hand, and evaluations of such actions as indicating a "mock impolite" stance, on the other (Haugh and Bousfield 2012).

The term mock impoliteness was originally coined by Leech (1983) to refer to instances "where a speaker says something which is obviously 'untrue' and 'impolite' in order to convey by implicature something which is 'true' – often the opposite of what is said – and 'polite' to the addressee" (Haugh and Bousfield 2012: 1100). However, close examination of instances of mock impoliteness has since suggested that mock impoliteness does not constitute an evaluation of politeness nor of impoliteness per se, but rather something conceptually distinct. Haugh and Bousfield (2012) propose that mock impoliteness involves "evaluations of talk or conduct that are potentially open to evaluation as impolite by at least one of the participants in an interaction, and/or as non-impolite by at least two participants" (Haugh and Bousfield 2012: 1103). What is meant by "non-impolite" is something that is "evaluated as neither polite nor impolite, but in being potentially open to evaluation as impolite is closer in some respects, of course, to the latter" (*ibid.*: 1103).

In order to better understand what is meant by something to be evaluated as "non-impolite", the previous discussion of how im/politeness evaluations can be constituted through scalar implicatures proves relevant (see Chapter 5: section 1.2). To reiterate, it was previously suggested that an evaluation of something as "not impolite" has two possible interpretations, namely, an "outer neg reading" and an "inner neg reading", where the focus of negation is different. An outer neg reading is signalled through an even pitch contour (i.e. "not impolite_"), and on that reading, evaluating something as "not impolite" implicates that it is also potentially open to evaluation as "polite". An inner neg reading, which can be signalled through a concessive pitch contour (i.e. "not impoli:te"), shifts the focus of negation. Accordingly, on an inner neg reading, "not impolite" implicates that something could be evaluated as "impolite", and participants are aware of this, but on this occasion it is being treated as "non-impolite" (i.e. neither "polite" nor "impolite"). This is important because it retains the intuition that while mock impoliteness is framed so as to avoid offence, the door is still open to an evaluation of the action in question by some participants as disguising an "impolite" stance on the part of the speaker. In the case of mock impoliteness implicatures, an ostensibly "impolite" stance is occasioned by an implicature, but is framed on that occasion as jocular or non-serious.[75]

It is worth noting, in passing at least, that some scholars have critiqued the notion of "mock impoliteness" as a morally relative term that conceals an analyst's evaluation of behaviour that would not be considered "mock impolite" by those concerned. Eelen (2001), for instance, focuses on the practice of ritualised insults or "sounding" amongst African American adolescents, which were originally noted by Labov (1972), in arguing that

> banter is not a form of politeness1 at all … it is not a case of classificatory politeness1, since the speaker's behaviour is obviously not evaluated by the hearer as genuinely impolite or rude. If it were, it would no longer qualify as 'banter' but would rather become 'insult' … it cannot be expressive politeness1 either (where the speaker aims at being impolite), since one of the characteristics of banter is exactly that the 'insults' used are not sincere. Since it is neither intended nor perceived as impoliteness, banter does not seem to qualify as politeness1; it is only a form of (im)politeness according to the scientist's classification. (Eelen 2001: 36)

Eelen (2001) consequently suggests that the qualification of impoliteness as *mock* impoliteness "derives from the ethical reality of the researcher" (p.181). However, while Eelen's (2001) point that im/politeness is inherently a morally-imbued judgement is one that rings true (see Chapter 4: section 4.1; see also Haugh 2011c), his claim that ritualised banter should not be considered a form of im/politeness, at least from the perspective of participants, deserves further scrutiny. On closer examination, it appears that Eelen (2001) neglects to consider two key arguments, which follow from his own work, that would actually support the view that such ritualised banter is indeed open to evaluation as impolite from a participant's perspective. The first is the broader discourse on insults as *rude* or *impolite* at the societal level, of which most if not all speakers of American English would be aware, including African American adolescents (i.e., what Eelen terms "metapragmatic politeness1"). The second is that the whole point of such rituals is that they constitute a kind of competition where one scores 'points' by creating insults that would be incredibly offensive if taken seriously; although in framing them as non-serious, treating them seriously is positioned as a sanctionable matter in such contexts. Yet there is no competition possible if the insults could not be at least *potentially* evaluated as impolite or offensive by at least one of the participants. These two points undermine Eelen's (2001) overly simplistic claim

---

75 Brown (2013) also recently notes how sarcastic honorifics (ostensibly mock impoliteness) can also be used in teasing and banter, and thereby can also occasion evaluations of mock impoliteness.

that mock impoliteness does not count as an evaluation open to lay participants, and so is an analyst's fiction. The term mock impoliteness itself is a quasi-technical term to be sure. However, the evaluation it represents, namely, the inner neg reading of "not impolite" signalled through a "concessive" pitch contour (i.e. "not impoli:te") is indeed available to lay participants.

Culpeper (2011a: 215), in discussing the role of mock impoliteness more broadly in interaction suggests that is has three main functions: (1) reinforcing solidarity, (2) disguising coercion, and (3) exploitative entertainment. We can observe instances of the first, namely, reinforcing solidarity in the following interaction, where two young Taiwanese female friends, Chen and Lin, are debating who did more shopping on their recent trip to a department store.

(113) MSC of Taiwanese Mandarin: Shopping: 1:30

> 10 C: *hòu   hǔochēzhàn shéi mǎi de   bǐjiào   dūo.*
>   back   train station who   buy   PRT   relatively   more
>   ('who did the most shopping at the back of the train station?')
>
> 11 L: *hahaha.*
>   ('ha ha ha')
>
> 12 C: *xiǎngdào zhège jìu hěn lìhài.*
>   think   this C   PRT   very   amazing
>   ('when [I] think of this, [I think you] are amazing')
>
> 13 L: *wǒ yě   shì   bībùdéyǐ   de.*
>   I   also Cop   compelled   PRT
>   ('I'm compelled [to do it]')
>
> 14 C: *nǐ   yīnggāi yào   kàn yīshēng ba*
>   you   should   need   see   doctor   PRT
>   ('you should see a doctor')
>
> 15 L: *haha.*
>   ('haha')

While both Chen and Lin have teasingly accused the other of doing more shopping up until this point, when Chen raises the question of who did more shopping on their recent trip (line 10), it is evident from Lin's laughter that she did more, a point she subsequently concedes in offering an account for this, namely, she just can't help herself (line 13). This occasions a mock suggestion by Chen that Lin go to see a doctor (line 14), which implicates that Lin has some kind of sickness or mental issue. While casting someone as suffering from a sickness is potentially offensive (*méilǐmào*), here it is clearly framed through exaggeration, and receipted through laughter, as jocular (Haugh 2014). It can thus be characterised as an instance of a mock impoliteness implicature.

However, while the three functions outlined by Culpeper (2011a) are largely borne out, it becomes clear on closer examination that mock impoliteness implicatures can actually accomplish a much wider range of different kinds of relational and interactional work. In the following interaction, for instance, while the mock impoliteness implicature that arises evidently contributes to reinforcing solidarity amongst this group of friends who regularly meet for gaming sessions, the way in which James is made the butt of the mockery, not only occasions amusement for the others (and ostensibly for James), but also constitutes part of a semi-competitive ongoing game of scoring 'points' against others in the group. The instance of jocular mockery here is occasioned when James reaches for a biscuit and then proceeds to consume most of it in a single bite.

(114)   12:10:08: 0:46

    31   B: so that'll make it about, four hundred

    32   and seventy five will it?

    33   (0.8)

    34   J: m(h)m. (0.2) I'd say so.

    33   (0.4)

    33   S: <u>ba</u>:sically that run you went on this

    34   morning James you might as well've

    35   not bothered. ((laughs loudly))

    36   M: ((laughs))

    37   B: ((laughs))

    38   J: ((pulls face, shakes head, then

    39   shrugs and smiles whilst eating))

    40   D: ((laughs))

    41 Se: ((laughs))
(Haugh and Bousfield 2012: 1107)

The excerpt begins when Baz draws attention to fact that James is taking a biscuit, and alluding to James's prior claim to be actually trying to lose weight by referencing the alleged calories contained in that biscuit (lines 31–32). Simon then suggests James wasted his time going for a run (lines 33–35), thereby implicating that he does not have sufficient will-power to lose weight, and that he is likely to fail in that endeavour. In that sense, then, it constitutes an implicated negative assessment, although it is framed and treated as jocular by Simon and the other side participants through laughter (lines 36–37, 40–41), as well as by James himself, at least nominally (lines 38–39) (Glenn 2003; Holt 2010; Jefferson, Sacks and Schegloff 1987). However, given James indicates such an implicated negative assessment is undesirable to him through initially pulling a face, and so it could be evaluated as offensive, and yet subsequently treats it as meant in jest, it appears to have occasioned an evaluation of mock impoliteness in this instance (i.e. as "not impoli:te").

However, while relational connection or solidarity is indeed reinforced amongst this group through such mock impoliteness implicatures, Simon has also evidently scored a point at James's expense. Indeed, over time such point-scoring can become a source of discontent. As Bousfield reports (2009, personal communication), "shortly after these recordings were made, James temporarily left the group citing work commitments which were later amended to include the 'pissing about' the group engaged in ... which was sometimes 'hurtful'". It is evident, then, that mock impoliteness implicatures do not simply reinforce solidarity or relational connection. In some cases, they can also contribute to the development of a semi-competitive game of scoring points, which, in such cases may be resisted or challenged as undermining solidarity across the group (see also Butler 2007).

Mock impoliteness implicatures may also be deployed to accomplish serious interactional business in an unofficial manner alongside occasioning amusement amongst participants. In the following example, for instance, which is taken from a national radio broadcast where members of the public have been invited to call-in and ask Australian author Tim Winton questions about his (then) new novel "Cloudstreet", a caller announces she is a year 12 high student.

(115)　ART: ABCnat2: 25:34

　　　1　R:　I'm Ramona Koval? um (.) talking with Tim <u>Wi</u>nton?

　　　2　　　and Sandy McCutcheon? .hhh and ↑let's go: um tsk

　　　3　　　to Sydney again to <u>J</u>ennifer, hi <u>J</u>ennifer.

　　　4　J:　↑hi:(.) um: tsk .hhh I'm <u>cu</u>rrently studying year

5   twelve at the moment? .hh and we've just

6   started (.) <u>Cl</u>oudstree:t and I was just wondering

7   if I could: ask a f- few quick questions.

8   S: are you doing homework [here. he he he he   ]

9   R: [are you writing an e(h)ssay?]

10   S: [ha ha ha]

11   J: [n(h)o. heh] .hh [I'm not-]

12   R: [we're not] w(h)riting your essay

13   for you.

14   J: £no um we just wrote an essay on why we thought

15   Tim Winton should have <u>wo</u>n the prize last yea:r

16   so I've already done my essa:y.£ hh but I was

17   wondering um: tsk (.) Tim what was the purpose

18   of including magic realism (.)

19   like why- why did you include it hh.
(Haugh 2014: 108)

Jennifer begins her call with a recognisable pre-asking (Schegloff 2007), where she not only indicates a low entitlement to be making such a request for information through a conventional "I was wondering if" formula (Drew and Curl 2008), combined with a conventionally indirect modal form (lines 6–7), she also minimises the projected forthcoming request with "disarmers" (line 7). There thus appears to be an orientation on her part to displaying a "polite" stance by formulating her request in this way. However, rather than occasioning the projected go-ahead response, one of the presenters responds with a tease that construes Jennifer's request as one for help with her homework (line 8), along with turn-final laughter particles that serve to invite the participants to laugh (Glenn 2003; Jefferson 1979; Jefferson, Sacks and Schegloff 1987; Schenkein 1972), thereby framing the tease as non-serious. The other presenter, Ramona, affiliates with this mocking stance with another tease where she attributes the same agenda to Jennifer in line 9, although this tease is somewhat softened through the interpolated aspiration particle in "essay" (Potter and Hepburn 2010). This is followed by an unmitigated rejection of the request, at least as it is construed by the two presenters (lines 12–13). Yet while (mis)construing Jennifer's request in this way, and then proceeding to reject it outright, is potentially open to evaluation as offensive or impolite, particularly in light of the way it jars with the polite stance instantiated through Jennifer's initial formulation of the pre-request, it is evident that these teases and the rejection are framed as jocular. The teases are also treated as non-serious through subsequent laughter by Sandy (line 10), and the target herself (line 11). A mock impolite stance is thus apparently occasioned through the way in which the presenters implicate that Jennifer has an inappropriate agenda in making the call-in. This mock impoliteness implicature arises by them *supposing* such an agenda (i.e. in the form of implicated premises) through the formulation of the respective candidate answers (Pomerantz 1988) in their teasing questions.

However, the target, Jennifer subsequently rejects the attributed agenda with a "smile voice" (i.e. with suppressed laughter) in lines 14–16, whereby she acknowledges the prior laughter on the part of others (Jefferson 2004b), and so treats the suggestion of an underlying agenda as a laughable (Holt 2011), and yet simultaneously displays that her response is disaffiliative with that stance (Greer et al. 2005). Through her po-faced rejection of this tease (Drew 1987), then, Jennifer thereby orients to the implicated agenda as undesirable or objectionable to her. She then returns to the interactional project foreshadowed in the pre-asking, namely, the request for information (lines 16–19).

Yet while these mock impoliteness implicatures, and the instances of jocular mockery through which they arise, constitute a discernible jocular or non-serious insert sequence (Schegloff 2001, 2007) relative to the main serious interactional trajectory, namely, Jennifer seeking information from Tim Winton, the boundaries of what is allowable for Jennifer to request are nevertheless being implicitly negotiated through this ostensibly non-serious insert sequence (Holt 2013). In other words, while framed and treated as non-serious by the participants, this jocular insert sequence nevertheless allows the participants to negotiate these boundaries as part of the unofficial business of this interaction. Thus, while the mock impoliteness implicatures that arise here clearly generate amusement for the other participants, and are seemingly designed for the entertainment of the over-hearing audience as well, they also accomplish particular interactional business.

As we have seen from the examples discussed in this section, while mock impoliteness implicatures arise in ostensibly jocular or non-serious sequences, they can nevertheless sometimes run a thin line between "bonding" and "biting" (Boxer and Cortés-Conde 1997), and in such situations multiple understandings amongst participants can emerge. Indeed, as Haugh and Bousfield (2012) point out, "the target, or any participants sympathising with the target, may actually (covertly or overtly) evaluate the talk or conduct as impolite" (p.1103). In the following section, we thus move to discuss instances where participants dispute whether or not so-called genuine impoliteness as opposed to mock impoliteness has arisen.

4 Disputing implicated offence

There can be instances in which participants dispute their degree of accountability for the impoliteness implicature, either through disputing the implicature itself or disputing the grounds on which the recipient(s) in question has taken offence. Disputing the implicature that occasions the perceived offence involves challenging the other participant's claimed interpretation of the object of implicature or disavowing commitment to what is assumed to have been implicated in the first place by that participant. Participants who have been held accountable for implicated offence may also challenge the way in which other participant(s) have taken offence in the first place. Disputing offence that has been occasioned by implicatures often involves a claim on the part of the participant being held accountable for it that it was part of a non-serious or jocular sequence, and so should not have been taken seriously. On the other hand, participants may also challenge the grounds on which offence itself has been taken, suggesting that the offence being taken is not warranted. The latter involves recourse to particular understandings of the moral order, and, in that sense, also represents another instance of where the moral substrate that underpins im/politeness implicatures can itself be renewed, negotiated, and sometimes challenged by members.

In this final section, we will be exploring how participants claim impoliteness implicatures have been *misinterpreted, misconstrued* or constitute a *misfiring*. It is important to note at the outset that such metalinguistic labels are not meant to be taken to be in any way as objective analytical categories, but rather represent the practices that participants themselves employ to dispute impoliteness implicatures. In other words, for a participant to (implicitly) claim something has been misinterpreted, misconstrued or is a misfire constitutes a social action in and of itself.

In some cases, participants attempt to position an impoliteness implicatures as having arisen through a misinterpretation, either of the broader discourse context (e.g. the framing of the sequence in question as serious versus non-serious) or of the claimed *intentions* of the participant being held accountable for that implicated offence (Gibbs 1999a; Haugh 2012b; Haugh and Jaszczolt 2012). For instance, implicatures that are perceived to occasion offence can also be disputed as "unwanted", and in this way, the perceived offence can also be construed as arising through misinterpretation.

In the following example, Jenny has been joking just prior to this excerpt that if she hadn't come then Edith and Viola wouldn't have had anything to talk about. Edith then subsequently asks Viola where she is from, but given this followed by laughter on her part, which invites the other participants to laugh (Glenn 2003; Jefferson 1979; Jefferson, Sacks and Schegloff 1987), it indicates a jocular stance here, namely, an orientation to the stereotypical formulation of this "getting to know you" question. In this way, Edith implicitly orients to Jenny's prior claim that she and Viola would have nothing to talk about were Jenny not present.

(116) 15 E: so Viola where are you from hhhhhh [h   ]h?

16 J: [(no)]

17 V: ((pushes the cup of tea away from herself, tilts her head

18   and averts her gaze)) so bad of me.

19 J: [(some)] (nice)

20 V: [I   ]

21 V: just [reali]sed,

22 J: [(   )]

23 V: that I have to-

24 E: I'll shut it. ((rises and walks to shut banging door))

25   (0.8)

26 V: be on the video with two native speakers (0.5) definitely

27   I will be the ((air quotes)) stupid ((air quotes)) o(h)ne

28   y(h)ou kn(h)ow? hh

29 J: why would you be the stupid one.

30 V: (.) because you as-

31   (0.3)

32 J: technically we're the stupid ones cause we don't speak

33   Finnish h (0.3) or [Hungarian?]

34 E: [aagh   ]

35 V: [nn   ]

36   (1.3)

37 J: it's often your perspective we're the stupid ones cause we

38   don't speak your language.

39 V: hhhhhhhhh yes °of course°
(adapted from Yu 2013: 4–5)

However, it becomes apparent as the interaction progresses that Viola has taken offence. This is indicated through both non-verbal signals (e.g. tilting the head and averting her gaze) that display possible embarrassment or discomfort (Chang and Haugh 2011; Goffman 1956; Heath 1988; Sandlund 2004), as well as through the way in which Viola projects a forthcoming negative assessment of herself (lines 17–18). That offence has been taken is then implicated through the negative assessment itself (line 27), that she is "stupid", and the account she offers for this, namely, that she is not a "native speaker" (lines 26–27), which she construes as a "realisation" (lines 21, 23). Jenny first orients to this construal on Viola's part as not justified (line 29), and then implements a negative assessment of herself and Edith (lines 32–33, 37–38), which Viola treats as a laughable (line 39). In doing so, Jenny construes what Viola has apparently taken to have been implicated by Edith's initial question in line 15, namely, "Viola's status of inequality in speaking English" (Yu 2013: 7) as a misinterpretation, given she construes herself and Edith as actually having the 'lower status' here as speakers of (presumably) just one language, English. The implicated offence is thus framed as unwanted by Jenny, although she also appears to orient to the offence perceived by Viola through pre-emptive negative assessments directed at herself and Edith.

Impoliteness implicatures can also be disputed through participants claiming they have been misconstrued. We have already discussed an example of this at length in Chapter 3 (see example 44). As we previously noted, Sally is here offering an account as to why kangaroo meat is not commonly eaten in Australia.

(117)   AmAus02: 4:15

113 S: I guess [because] (0.2) it's a bit of a <u>cul</u>tural thing?

114 P: [he hem?]

115   like where I'm from people feed kangaroo meat to <u>dogs</u>?

116   so: (0.2) <u>ye</u>:ah.

117 P: °I guess I'm a dog.°

118 S: [I- <u>no</u>: I don't mean dogs] <u>eat</u> it

119 P: [I like dogs so that's okay]

120   I just mean because [(I   know   )] that my fath-

121 P: [>that's okay<]

122 S: you know like my stepdad's a farmer? and that's what he

123   does? it's just (0.2) I wouldn't °even° (0.2) like I would <u>eat</u>

124   it, but I just wouldn't go out of my way to °eat it°

125   sort of thing

To briefly reiterate, Peter first construes Sally's prior explanation as implicating that he is a dog (line 117), and also displays "mock offence" at this implicated negative assessment. While Sally appeals to her *intentions* and what she *meant* here, thereby disputing this impoliteness implicature (lines 118, 120), Peter resists her attempt to block his construal of what she has implicated through her account by only absolving her of having caused offence (lines 119, 121), but implicitly maintaining that she has indeed implicated he is a dog. Sally then works to reframe what she has implicated to a claim that Australians (at least in rural areas) are not enthusiastic about eating kangaroo meat because it is fed to dogs (lines 122–125). She thereby treats Peter's understanding of what has been implicated as a miscontrual, and, in that way attempts to distance herself from the offence that this misconstrual occasions.

Finally, in some instances, perceived offence can be construed as the result of the "misfiring" of a mock impoliteness implicature. This misfiring is attributed to a participant taking offence that is not warranted. Consider, for instance, the following excerpt from an interview between the radio jock, Mojo, and the singer, Justin Bieber, which was broadcast on a Detroit-based radio show.

(118)   (Mojo in the Morning, 28th June 2012)

1   M: do you <u>wo</u>rry about Harry [Styles], uh, you know when

2   he's around your mom, since it seems he likes older

3   women?

4   B: do I wonder (.) <u>wh</u>at?

5   M: do you worry Harry around your mum, since he (.)

6   u:h (.) he likes older women?

7   B: I think you should worry about yo- your mom bro.

8   M: .hhhHahhh I should worry about my mum?

9   B: <u>ye</u>:a(hh)h

10   M: Justin, my mum's d[ead so unfortunately (.) that

11   B: [jeez

12   M: wouldn't work.

13   (10.0)

14   ((line goes dead))
("Mojo in the Morning", *Channel 95.5*, Detroit, 28th June 2012)

The excerpt here begins when the interviewer, Mojo, teases Bieber by implicating that Harry Styles might be interested in going out with Bieber's mother
(line 1–3), thereby alluding to the (then) recent news that Styles has been dating
older women. Bieber initially responds with an open class repair initiator (line 4),
through which he indicates the "repairable trouble" is related to the "propriety of
the prior turn" (Drew 1997: 95), and thus that he is treating this question as potentially offensive. The repair initiator also implements a pre-disagreement, which is
here arguably designed to "elicit a self-correction, or a backdown" (Koshik 2005:
28). However, Mojo subsequently repeats the tease (lines 5–6), thereby raising
the stakes (Reynolds 2011), in response to which Bieber responds with a counter-
tease (line 7), when he implicates that Styles may be wanting to go out with Mojo's
mother. In this way, the interaction develops into a "banter" sequence, although
whether this mock impoliteness implicature is disguising a hostile intent on
Bieber's part remains a distinct possibility. While Mojo subsequently orients to
this implicated tease as a laughable in line 8 (Drew 1987; Everts 2003; Glenn 2003;
Holt 2010; Jefferson, Sacks and Schegloff 1987), it subsequently emerges that this
is because it falls out flat, as Mojo's mother has already passed away (lines 10, 12).
Bieber's counter tease is thus construed by Mojo as a misfiring, and, in this way,
he implicates that Bieber has (inadvertently) become the butt of his own tease. A
long silence then follows and then the phone line goes dead. It was subsequently
reported that when the technician tried to get Bieber back on the line to continue
the interview that "He [Bieber] got a little upset with the question".

In a subsequent broadcast, Mojo talks with fellow radio jocks, Rachael and
Spike, about the offence that Bieber took at the misfiring of the mock impoliteness implicatures in question.

(119) ("Justin Bieber HANGS UP on interviewer: Mojo in the morning",
       Channel 95.5, Detroit, 30th June 2012)

1   R: but even (.) even the <u>way</u> he said it back to you

2   ↓you got watch out for yer m- uhm yer mum↓

3   M: mm

4   R: like you could tell, at <u>that</u> point he was pissed already

5   M: ye:ah

6   S: here's the thing I'm kinda getting bummed out because,

7   you know (0.2) I don't listen to his <u>mu</u>sic but I always

8   thought Justin was pretty cool but

9   R: he <u>i:s</u>.

10 S: he ['s

11 R: [he usually [is

12 S: [he- he's starting to take himself <u>way</u>

13   too seriously.

Rachael implicates here that while Bieber's counter-tease was ostensibly framed as non-serious or jocular it actually masked a hostile intent (lines 1–2, 4), where Bieber was trying to get back at Mojo for offence perceived as arising from Mojo's initial tease. Spike then implicates that Bieber was "not cool" on this occasion (lines 6–8), a claim that Rachael initially rejects on the grounds that he is "cool" in general (line 9), but subsequently concedes through a self-repair that Bieber was not being "cool" on this occasion (line 11). In this way, interactional work is done to avoid the unwanted implication that they, the radio jocks, think that Bieber is "not cool" in general. Spike then characterises Bieber as taking himself "too seriously", thereby casting the way in which he took offence from the misfiring as not warranted. Through such metapragmatic talk the participants invoke elements of the moral order for the overhearing audience. However, this particular example also indicates that disputing impoliteness implicatures may involve recourse not only to the locally situated interaction in which it arose, but can also be mediated through perceptions of that person and their relationships with others that are co-constituted over time and across relational networks.

In this section, we have discussed the practices by which participants may dispute implicated offence. It has been suggested that speakers can dispute their degree of accountability for impoliteness implicatures, either through disputing the interpretation of the implicature itself or disputing the grounds on which the recipient(s) in question has taken offence. Disputing the implicature that occasions the perceived offence involves challenging the other participant's claimed interpretation of the reflexively intentional object of implicature or disavowing commitment to what is assumed to have been implicated by that participant. Participants who have been held accountable for implicated offence may also challenge the way in which other participant(s) having taken offence in the first place. Disputing offence that has been occasioned by implicatures often involves a claim on the part of the participant being held accountable for it that it was part of a non-serious or jocular sequence, and so should not have been taken seriously. On the other hand, participants may also challenge the grounds on which offence itself has been taken, suggesting that the offence is not warranted. The latter involves recourse to understandings of the moral order, and, in that sense, also represents another instance of where the moral substrate that underpins im/politeness implicatures is itself renewed, negotiated, and sometimes challenged by members through interaction. Given the moral order is a complex set of expectancies that is sustained through interaction over time and across intersecting relational networks (Kádár and Haugh 2013), it is perhaps not surprising that in some situations participants do not invoke or appeal to aspects of it in the same way. The study of impoliteness implicatures thus arguably offers valuable insights into the moral substrate underpinning interpersonal interaction and the ideological disputes that can arise in relation to it.

Chapter Eight:
Conclusion

1 Im/politeness implicatures, social action and social practice

At the beginning of this volume, an im/politeness implicature was broadly defined as an instance where through implicating rather than saying, im/politeness is occasioned. However, this gave rise to an analytical and practical puzzle: why is it that implicatures occasion im/politeness in some instances but in other cases they do not? In this book it has been proposed that in order to explain the relationship between implicature and im/politeness, we need to examine more carefully the interactional and moral underpinnings of them both. The interactional grounding of im/politeness implicatures has been suggested to encompass the ways in which participants' understandings of implicatures and evaluations of im/politeness arise with respect to locally situated sequential environments, while the moral grounding of im/politeness implicatures has been said to refer to the ways in which participants' understandings of implicatures and evaluations of im/politeness arise with respect to a complex moral substrate of seen but unnoticed expectancies. In order to analyse im/politeness implicatures, then, we need to examine the ways in which particular, locally situated interactional and relational work is accomplished through them.

Implicatures have been characterised here as a form of pragmatic meaning where participants are held accountable for implicating (e.g. *implying, hinting at, alluding to, supposing* and so on) reflexively intentional state-processes (e.g. thought/thinking, belief/believing, intention/intending, desire/wanting, attitude/evaluating, inference/inferring, perception/perceiving, attention/attending) that constitute the object of a (set of) social action(s) achieved through talk. Im/politeness implicatures have consequently been defined as instances where by implicating something, a participant (or set of participants) is taken to be orienting to particular (sets of) moral concerns. In the case of politeness implicatures, the participant(s) – more often than not the speaker – are taken to be orienting toward a concern that one be seen as "polite" or that oneself or others avoid being seen as "impolite" (or "not polite"). In the case of impoliteness implicatures and mock politeness implicatures, the participant(s) are taken to be orienting toward a concern that one's "impolite" stance remains (ostensibly) unofficial or that the "impolite" stance of other(s) is unofficially registered. Finally, in the case of mock impoliteness implicatures, the participant(s) are taken to be orienting toward a concern that one's ostensibly "impolite" stance be regarded as "not impolite" (i.e. "non-impolite") or that the "impolite" stance of other(s) is unofficially registered. It was thus argued that not only can implicatures occasion evaluations of (mock) im/politeness, but that evaluations of (mock) im/politeness can themselves be constituted through implicatures in some instances, and that such evaluations can occasion implicatures in other cases.

In characterising im/politeness as involving an orientation on the part of participants to particular (sets of) moral concerns it was initially proposed in Chapter Three that these involve issues of interpersonal rights, obligations, responsibilities, permissibility and the like. In the course of analysing examples of im/politeness implicatures, however, it has been found that these rights, obligations and so on are intimately interconnected with a concern on the part of participants for interpersonal "roles", "feelings", "relationships" and "reciprocity", alongside a concern for "face". In other words, an implicature can be characterised as an *im/politeness* implicature in cases where the participants are indicating through the said implicature an orientation to particular dimensions of the moral order. These were found to include the deontic order, the benefactive order, the epistemic order, and the emotional order.[76] In each case, im/politeness was found to arise by participants orienting to (potential) inconsistencies between *moral status* (i.e. the situtionally-relevant expectations of participants vis-à-vis some aspect of the moral order) and *moral stance* (i.e. the interactional enactment or display of moral rights, entitlements, obligations and so on) through implicatures.[77] What lies at the core of im/politeness implicatures, then, is the renewal, negotiation and chal-

---

76 Stevanovic and Peräkylä (2014: 203, fn.6) argue that matters of benefit are subordinate to the epistemic, deontic and emotional orders. Indeed, Clayman and Heritage (forthcoming) suggest as much when they claim that there is a hierarchy with respect to these orders:

> Perhaps most pervasive is the epistemic 'ticker' argued by Heritage (2012a) to be universally applicable when speakers produce or understand declarative or interrogative utterances. The deontic 'ticker' by contrast may be relevant when the talk represents future (and perhaps some past) courses of action. The benefactive 'ticker' applies still more narrowly only to that subset of the latter in which costs and benefits are relevantly apportioned. (Clayman and Heritage forthcoming)

However, while this may well prove to be the case when considering the relationship between different dimensions of the moral substrate with respect to the broader analytical and practical problem of action ascription (Levinson 2013), in relation to the analysis of *im/politeness* it appears that all four orders are equally as important. Indeed, it may well be that there are further orders within the moral substrate that remain to be identified and further explored in im/politeness research.

77 In earlier work this was glossed as the degree of consistency between what participants think others should show they think of them (e.g. "what B thinks A should show A thinks of B") and what they think others are showing they think of them (e.g. "what B thinks A shows thinks of B", "what A thinks A shows A thinks of B") (Haugh and Hinze 2003).

lenging of particular dimensions of the moral order by participants through the various practices by which implicatures are interactionally achieved.

Given the importance of the moral order to the analysis of im/politeness implicatures it is worth recapping those dimensions of the moral order that have proven especially critical to this analysis. The deontic order encompasses the participants' orientation to performing future action(s) (Heritage 2013; Stevanovic and Peräkylä 2012, 2014), in particular, their rights and obligations with respect to determining actions, including "requesting for, deciding about, and performing actions in the world" (Stevanovic and Peräkylä 2014: 190). It thus involves deontic status, which refers to the expectations of participants in relation to a certain domain of action with respect to their co-participant(s), as well as deontic stance, namely, displays by participants in talk-in-interaction of their respective deontic rights. To request something of someone, for instance, implicitly indicates some entitlement to be making the said request (Curl and Drew 2008; Heinemann 2006). Such a request is thus open to evaluation as "impolite" or "not polite" in cases where one or more participants regard the implementation of that request to be enacting a deontic stance on the part of the producer that is (potentially) inconsistent with their (perceived) deontic rights to be making that request.

The benefactive order encompasses the participants' orientation to benefits, advantages, gains and so on accrued through future action(s) (Clayman and Heritage forthcoming; Heritage 2013), such as "whether a service will be rendered that is of actual benefit to its recipient", "whether the cost to the performer is high or low", or "whether the performer of the service is able and willing to perform it" (Clayman and Heritage forthcoming). Benefactive status thus encompasses the expectations of participants about the underlying benefits and possible costs of a projected future action, while benefactive stance encompasses the "the distribution of benefits and/or costs associated with a projected future action" (Clayman and Heritage forthcoming). To offer something, whether material goods or advice/ suggestions, involves implicitly claiming that this course of action is of benefit to the recipient (who is thereby construed as a beneficiary) (Heritage 2013). An offer, for instance, is thus open to evaluation as "impolite" or "not polite" in cases when one or more participants regard the production of that offer to be enacting respective benefactive stances that are (potentially) inconsistent with their perceived expectations about who will really benefit or whether the service in question is of actual benefit to the recipient.

The epistemic order encompasses the participants' orientation to knowledge, namely, who knows what and who knows better (Heritage 2012a, 2012b; Heritage and Raymond 2005; Raymond and Heritage 2006). It thus involves epistemic status, namely, the expectations of participants in relation to a certain domain of knowledge with respect to their co-participant(s), as well as epistemic stance, which refers to displays by participants in talk-in-interaction of how knowledgable they are. To assess someone or something, for instance, involves implicitly claiming some knowledge of the assessable (Pomerantz 1984a), and, potentially, the claim that one knows better than others in relation to that assessable. A negative assessment is therefore open to evaluation as "impolite" in cases when one or more participants take that assessment to be enacting an epistemic stance on the part of the producer that is inconsistent with their perceived epistemic rights to be making that negative assessment.

Finally, the emotional order refers to the participants' orientation to the expression of affect (Stevanovic and Peräkylä 2014). It thus encompasses emotional status, namely, "socially shared expectations regarding experiencing, expressing, and sharing of emotions" (*ibid.*: 192), as well as emotional stance, which refers to "the valence and the relative strength of emotional expression directed to a co-present or absent target" (*ibid.*: 192). Refusing an inviation, for instance, can be interpreted, depending on the design of invitation itself, as indicating one does not (sufficiently) like or esteem the recipient in question, and so is potentially disaffiliative (Davidson 1984; Pomerantz and Heritage 2013: 215). A refusal of an invitation is therefore open to evaluation as "impolite" in cases when one or more participants take that refusal to be enacting an emotional stance on the part of the producer that is inconsistent with the expected expression of affect (i.e. emotional status) in that locally situated interaction.

These four dimensions of the moral order are summarised in Table 1 below:

Table 1: Key dimensions of the moral order

Deontic order	Orientation to determining performance of future action: – deontic status: expectations of entitlements in relation to certain domain of action – deontic stance: displays of deontic entitlements
Benefactive order	Orientation to benefits of future action: – benefactive status: expectations in relation to benefits of a course of certain action – benefactive stance: displays of (distribution of) benefits
Epistemic order	Orientation to knowledge: – epistemic status: expectations in relation to certain domain of knowledge – epistemic stance: displays of knowledge
Emotional order	Orientation to expression of affect: – emotional status: expectations in relation to experiencing, expressing, and sharing of emotions – emotional stance: displays of emotions

What counts as an instance of "deontic entitlements", "benefits" or "costs", "knowledge" and "affect/emotions", and the moral basis for such expectations is, of course, grounded in a particular cultural-relational network in which this moral order is renewed, negotiated and sometimes challenged by members.

Im/politeness, in this view, involves an orientation to aspects of the moral order such as these in the course of interactionally achieving social actions and meanings (Haugh 2013c; Kádár and Haugh 2013: Chapter 4). This is because in the course of accomplishing social actions, not only is the recognisability of those actions rooted in the seen but unnoticed expectancies of the moral order (Clayman and Heritage forthcoming; Heritage 2012a, 2013; Stevanovic and Peräkylä 2012, 2014), but this recognisability is rooted in "familiar scenes of everyday affairs" that are regarded by members as familiar scenes "because it is morally right or wrong that they are so" (Garfinkel 1967: 35). In other words, the ascription of social action and construal of pragmatic meanings is an inherently moral activity because they are inevitably open to evaluation as good/bad, appropriate/inappropriate, polite/impolite and so on (Haugh 2013c; Kádár and Haugh 2013). Im/politeness itself arguably involves an orientation on the part of participants to potential inconsistencies between (expected) moral status and (enacted) moral stance with respect to the deontic, benefactive, epistemic and emotional orders, and perhaps other dimensions of the moral order yet to be identified.

Through implicating, as we have discussed, participants can position social actions, such as requests or negative assessments, as ostensibly avoided, disguised, masked, open to deniability and so on. In this way, participants thereby indicate an orientation to *unofficially* enacting a deontic, benefactive, epistemic or emotional stance that is (potentially) inconsistent with their respective (perceived) deontic, benefactive, epistemic or emotional status. Given an orientation to such aspects of the moral order is the basis by which participants recognise a concern on the part of others (and themselves) for being seen as "polite", avoiding being seen as "impolite"/"not polite" (at least ostensibly) and so on, it follows, then, that through implicating participants can occasion evaluations of im/politeness. In other words, an implicature occasions im/politeness in those cases where by implicating the participants are unofficially indicating an orientation to enacting a deontic, benefactive, epistemic and emotional stance that is (potentially) inconsistent with their (perceived) deontic, benefactive, epistemic and emotional status.

In the course of the preceding analysis, politeness implicatures were largely found to involve an orientation on the part of participants to aspects of the deontic order (e.g. orienting to role-status entitlements/obligations or relational entitlements/obligations) and the benefactive order (e.g. displaying attentiveness), as well as the emotional order (e.g. indicating empathy and reciprocal approval). In doing so, participants accomplished particular interactional work in unofficial ways. This, as we discussed in Chapter One, may not only involve fostering affiliation and interpersonal harmony, as well as avoiding disaffiliation and interpersonal conflict, but may also involve co-constituting persons/identities and relationships in particular, located situated ways (e.g. positioning the self vis-à-vis other as powerful or ostensibly less powerful. (re)negotiating relational entitlements and so on).

In contrast, impoliteness implicatures, and to some extent mock politeness implicatures and mock impoliteness implicatures as well, were found to involve an orientation on the part of participants to aspects of the epistemic order in that the negative assessments involved were implicated, and so, ostensibly at least, accomplished unofficially. However, in implicating these negative assessments, the force of the mocking or ridiculing of the target was in some respects exacerbated, thereby invoking aspects of the emotional order. They also involved an orientation to the emotional order in cases where the participants registered their offence at the (perceived) perceived transgressions of others through such implicatures. These perceived transgressions could, in turn, involve implicit claims about the deontic, benefactive or epistemic orders, alongside the emotional order. In doing so, participants thereby not only accomplish particular interactional work in unofficial ways, but in the course of doing so provide for the affective, coercive and entertaining functions of impoliteness (Culpeper 2011a).

In examining mock im/politeness implicatures, however, yet another dimension of the moral order also proved critical, namely, the orientation of participants to the current social action or activity-in-progress as "serious" or "non-serious" (Glenn 2003; Holt 2013; Sacks 1992; Schegloff 2001; Schenkein 1972). To be framed as non-serious can involve claims that the social action (e.g. mockery) or social activity (e.g. banter) in question is meant to be taken as jocular or playful. Such claims are inherently moral because participants are expected to understand or recognise that social actions or activities that are framed as non-serious play or jocularity are not meant to be taken seriously. However, the distinction between seriousness and non-seriousness is not always clear-cut (Glenn 2003; Holt 2013), which can lead to divergences amongst participants in regards to how implicatures are evaluated vis-à-vis (mock) im/politeness, as we have seen.

From this analysis a more nuanced view of the relationship between implicature and im/politeness has arguably emerged. It has been proposed that im/politeness implicatures arise in a broader relational milieu in which indicating politeness, impoliteness, mock politeness, mock impoliteness and so on, is just one of the myriad of interpersonal functions of implicatures (recall Figure 1, Chapter 1). It would appear, then, that im/politeness implicatures are a subset of a much broader category of *relational* implicatures. Yet while the interpersonal dimensions of implicatures are not exhausted by an investigation of im/politeness implicatures, it has become evident from the analyses undertaken in the course of this volume that they nevertheless form an important cornerstone of the moral substrate that underpins interpersonal interaction. Im/politeness implicatures are not simply a means of conveying information indirectly, and thereby indicating a polite or impolite stance on the part of speakers, as traditional accounts would have it. Instead, they constitute social actions in their own right through which interactional and relational business can be accomplished in various unofficial ways that position social actions as withheld, forestalled, attenuated, avoided, masked, or even disguised. In so doing, participants renew, as well as sometimes challenge, the moral substrate of interpersonal interaction.

An examination of the practices through which im/politeness implicatures arise thus gives us critical insights into the complex sets of seen but unnoticed expectancies that collectively constitute the moral order. It thereby affords an analysis of the moral order as an object of empirical research in and of itself. The theorisation of im/politeness implicatures as a form of social practice that has been developed in this volume also has implications for the theorisation of implicatures and im/politeness more broadly. It is therefore to a consideration of these broader theoretical implications that we now turn.

2 Theoretical implications

2.1 Implications for theorising implicature

In research on implicature to date most of the work that has developed out of the Gricean programme, or as an alternative to it, has focused either on the linguistic aspects of implicatures (e.g. Levinson's GCI theory), or on the cognitive processing of implicatures at the utterance-level (e.g. Relevance theory). While these are clearly important areas of research, it has been argued here that Grice's initial insights into the ways in which implicatures arise through a range of normative practices in communicative interaction have remained somewhat neglected in subsequent accounts of implicature.

We noted earlier that in Grice's original account he coined the terms implicate (cf. *imply, mean*), implicature (cf. *implying*) and implicatum (cf. *what is implied*). The care with which Grice introduced the notions of implicate, implicature and implicatum has three important implications for the way in which we theorise implicature, all of which have been discussed in the course of this volume. The first is that the notion of implicature itself was arguably conceptualised by Grice as an inherently normative notion, namely, what a speaker can in normal cirumstances be held to be *implying*. While the appropriateness of the Cooperative Principle and associated conversational maxims has since become the subject of considerable controversy, Grice's initial claim that conversational implicatures are not necessarily what may have actually been implicat*ed* on a particular occasion but rather are what the speaker can normatively be taken to be implicat*ing*, is consistent with his broader claims about speaker meaning. It is commonly assumed in pragmatics that speaker meaning is determined by a particular kind of intention, namely, the so-called communicative intention ("*A* intended the utterance of *x* to produce some effect in an audience by means of the recognition of this intention", Grice [1957]1989: 220). What is less commonly recognised is that Grice ([1957]1989) went on to note that "an utterer is held to intend to convey what is normally conveyed (or normally intended to be conveyed), and we require a good reason for accepting that a particular use diverges from the general usage (e.g. he never knew or had forgotten the general usage)" (p.222). In other words, speaker meaning, and so implicatures, are inherently normative notions that reflect what members commonly understand speakers to be implicating, rather than reflecting what the actual private and potentially idiosyncratic intentions of the speaker in question might be (Arundale 2008; Sanders 2012, 2013, forthcoming). The question is, then, just how do participants figure out what is "normally conveyed" or "normally intended to be conveyed"?

In the interactional account of implicatures developed in this book it has been proposed that this recognisability is predicated on sets of inter-related practices that are torqued to fit the particulars of locally situated contexts. We have discussed, for example, how doing a "noticing" of something that lies within the epistemic domain of the recipient can be taken to be doing something in addition to simply informing the said recipient of the object of that noticing, because noticing what someone already likely knows seems to beg the question of what then is the relevance of that noticing in this particular situated context? In this way, speakers are normally taken to be implicating – often construed as *hinting* – something through such a noticing (unless something in the context otherwise blocks such an inference). An important focus of ongoing analysis should thus be on better understanding the various practices by which speakers are held to be recognisably implicating something.

This leads us to the second key implication of Grice's original proposals, namely, that implicatures are not simply "indirect" or "unsaid" meanings, which are determined by either the intentions of the speaker or the hearer's perceptions of the speaker's intentions, but are also social actions in their own right. This is what is arguably alluded to in Grice's distinction between implicature and implicate. However, in this volume we have taken Grice's initial proposal that "implicate" function as a cover term for *imply, suggest, indicate* and *hint* much further by examining implicatures as a form of social action in interaction. In this way, we have opened up a whole range of practices for investigation that go beyond simply *implying, hinting* and *alluding* to include withholding, attenuating, soliciting and so on. Yet we have also gone beyond cases of meaning-actions where the agency of the speaker is foregrounded to cases where the agency of the recipient is foregrounded, such as in the case of pre-empting, construing or (dis) attending. We have also touched upon cases of *supposing* where the extent to which speakers (in *presuming, assuming* and so on) and recipients (in *presuming, assuming, educing, deducing, inferring* and so on) contribute to the interactional achievement of the implicature in question can be regarded as somewhat equivocal. Thus, while coining the term implicate to act as a cover term for various ways in which we can *imply, suggest, hint, allude, insinuate, withhold, attenuate, construe, (dis)attend, suppose, presume, educe* and so on did allow Grice to "avoid having, on each occasion, to choose between this or that member of the family verbs for which *implicate* is to do general duty" (Grice [1975]1989: 24), this is not to say that there are not important differences between them, as Grice himself admitted. Indeed, we have examined in considerable detail how participants can position themselves as accountable to varying degrees for implicatures through these different meaning-actions. The fact that the focus here has been primarily on meaning-actions in English, albeit extended to cases in Chinese and Japanese to a limited extent, begs the question, of course, as to whether these meaning practices are necessarily the same across different languages. Another focus of ongoing analysis in theorising implicature should thus be on examining the ways in which participants position themselves as more or less accountable for particular social action trajectories through implicatures.

This leads us to a consideration of the third key implication of Grice's original proposals about implicature, namely, how should we theorise implicatures vis-à-vis actual communicative interaction? In proposing the notion of "implicatum", Grice arguably recognised the existence of both speaker and recipient understandings of implicature. Yet in much of the work on implicature to date there has been an emphasis on either speaker understandings of implicature (i.e. what the speaker intended to implicate) or recipient understandings of implicature (i.e. what the recipient understands the speaker to have intended to implicate) to the exclusion of the other. However, as Keckses (2010) points out, speaker meanings do not arise in a vacuum where either only speaker understandings or only recipient understandings of implicature are at play. In addition, we have also seen that participants' – whether speakers or recipients – understandings of implicature often emerge over a sequence of utterances, and so implicatures are not necessarily tied to single utterances. What this suggests is that we need to theorise implicatures within an alternative model of communicative interaction that goes beyond an account of recipients inferring the putative intentions of speakers (Arundale 2005, 2008). Instead, implicatures should be theorised with respect to the interactions in which they arise. In doing so, we can see that participants themselves take into account the sequential environment in which implicatures arise vis-à-vis specific action trajectories and particular activities or frames.

Whether one take seriously such claims depends, of course, on one's broader epistemological position vis-à-vis implicature. There is arguably an ongoing tension between accounts of implicatures as what people are (taken to be) *thinking* (i.e. implicature as speaker intended thought) and what people are (taken to be) *communicating* (i.e. implicature as what participants are held accountable for implicating), a tension that has been alluded to throughout this book. If one elects to pursue the former course, then this book has been largely a study of *implicating* and *implicatum* rather than *implicature* per se. Yet even if one prefers to approach implicature in the form of an abstracted analysis of speaker intended thoughts, it should be evident from the analyses of (im/politeness) implicatures undertaken here that reading off the putative thoughts of speakers from what they say is no simple matter. Indeed, one might conclude from these analyses that if one is to treat implicature as a form of speaker intended thought, then quoting relatively decontextualised examples of language use is a rather limited, if not outright flawed, way of evidencing such putative thoughts. An account of implicature as a cognitive object – as opposed to the account of implicature as a communicative object that has been advanced here – necessarily requires a different set of methods by which one taps into the object of study.

However, in spite of these apparent differences, an analysis of implicatures as they arise in communicative interaction is nevertheless highly suggestive for more cognitively focused accounts. One case in point is the analysis of default implicatures. While defaults vis-à-vis implicatures have been attached to particular expressions in some accounts (e.g. Levinson 2000), more recently it has been proposed that these defaults are not context-free in their operation (e.g. Jaszczolt 2005; Terkourafi 2003, 2005). Instead, we need to be examining defaults for contexts, that is, the regular occurrence of expressions in particular sequential environments relative to particular action trajectories.

Another important implication for developing an account of cognition *for* interaction (Levinson 2006) is that it is simply not plausible to tie the analysis of implicatures to communicative intentions in isolation. While participants may indeed at times entertain inferences about what a speaker intended an utterance to mean by recognition of this intention (cf. communicative intention), such inferences often do not arise without a consideration of the social action trajectory relative to which the utterance in question arises (cf. higher order intention), or the broader activity or frame with respect to which this action trajectory is accomplished (cf. we-intention) (Haugh 2012b; Haugh and Jaszczolt 2012).

Indeed, it has become evident in the course of this analysis of im/politeness implicatures that not only intentions, but other intentional state-processes, such as thoughts, beliefs, attitudes and so on are also potentially of relevance to participants' understandings of implicatures. It is these multiple loci of inference that give rise to the apparent indeterminacy of implicatures, either with respect to their object (i.e. the reflexively intentional state-process in question), or the degree of speaker commitment to that reflexively intentional object. It is important to remember, however, that this relative indeterminacy does not mean that implicatures are not calculable by participants per se, but rather affords the way in which they are recalculable. Thus, while the degree of plausible deniability of implicatures may vary, the raison d'être of implicatures is that they very often involve a disjunction, or even conjunction, of possible inferences. Implicatures therefore not only afford plausible deniability, but may also afford multiple meanings on occasion. It is for this reason that we must move beyond an overly reductive account of implicatures that emphasises speaker intentions over other intentional state-processes, given the latter are evidently just as important in many instances.

Finally, it is worth reiterating that while im/politeness has generally been treated as a fairly peripheral concern in theorising implicature, such a position has arguably neglected the importance of the user him/herself in understanding pragmatic meaning. As Bertuccelli Papi (2001) has pointed out, "if what we are looking for is the *speaker's* meaning ... [we] must integrate some representation of the speaker him/herself within the utterance" (p.248, original emphasis). Given the way in which an account of im/politeness implicatures necessitates an account of participants vis-à-vis those implicatures, an analysis of im/politeness implicatures should therefore not be treated as a peripheral, optional add-on to implicature theory, as it has often been treated to date, but as central to the pursuit of a comprehensive theory of implicature.

2.2 Implications for theorising im/politeness

The theorisation and analysis of politeness, and more recently impoliteness, has traditionally fallen with the purview of pragmatics. The first wave of theories of politeness drew heavily from core notions in pragmatics, including speech acts and implicatures (e.g. Brown and Levinson 1978, 1987; Leech 1983; Lakoff 1973; see also Bousfield 2008; Culpeper 1996). These approaches were subsequently the focus of sustained critique in a second wave of theorisation where it was argued that im/politeness should be re-conceptualised from the perspective of social theory (e.g. Eelen 2001; Mills 2003; Watts 2003). However, as Kádár and Haugh (2013) point out, the second wave in im/politeness research has not yet yielded a coherent theory of im/politeness. Indeed, there are some discursive theorists who argue that a theory of im/politeness may not be desirable (Mills 2011) or even possible (Watts 2005), given the extent to which evaluations of im/politeness can be contested. Yet while a *predictive* theory of im/politeness may not be feasible given that evaluating something or someone as im/polite can constitute a social action in and of itself, and thus the agency of participants themselves may play a role in evaluations of im/politeness in some instances, the analysis undertaken in this volume would suggest that the pendulum has swung too far in the direction of an exclusively social theorisation of im/politeness.

It is important, of course, to be always cognisant of the fact that evaluations of im/politeness can over time sustain implicit ideologically-imbued social structures, and thus im/politeness is a resource that may be called upon by people to influence or even coerce others. In that sense, a social theorisation of im/politeness is both desirable and necessary. However, what we also need is a detailed theoretical account not only of how im/politeness arises, but how evaluations of im/politeness can contribute to a multitude of different interpersonal dimensions of interaction, ranging from positioning the self vis-à-vis others and negotiating relationships, through to accomplishing particular interactional goals or projects and engaging in interactional play. It is thus not enough to say that im/politeness is a contested ideological construct, nor to assume that im/politeness can be equated with the various metalinguistic labels used by participants, as advocated in various discursive approaches to im/politeness. Here it has been suggested that by close examination of the moral order in which evaluations of im/politeness are grounded, we can gain insight not only into how im/politeness itself arises, but into the role it plays in the broader interpersonal milieu that is accomplished through ongoing interaction.

In this volume, then, it has been argued that through im/politeness participants can accomplish a range of interactional and interpersonal work (see Figure 1). Yet many of these practices lie below the purview of conscious reflection by participants. This naturally begs the question: what then do participants understand by im/politeness, not only as a social, and thus ideological, concept, but as a complex set of social practices? It has been proposed here that in attempting to answer this critical analytical question we need to move back to the pragmatic roots of im/politeness research. It has been argued that im/politeness arises through participants orienting to particular dimensions of the moral order in the course of interactionally achieving social actions and pragmatic meanings, including, of course, implicatures. In doing so, a framework for analysing im/

politeness has emerged that respectfully alludes to traditional pragmatic notions such as speech acts, speaker intentions and Gricean implicatures, yet also reconfigures them in quite different ways as forms of social action, and thus ultimately as social practice. The analysis of im/politeness implicatures undertaken here has also attempted to move the theorisation of im/politeness away from an over-reliance on the notion of face, and towards an empirical analysis of participant understandings of the moral order in which im/politeness as social practice is grounded.

A move towards examining the understandings of participants themselves has, of course, been underway for more than a decade in politeness research, following the so-called discursive turn (Mills 2011). However, in the vast majority of theoretical frameworks that have been subsequently developed, with the notable exception of Arundale's (2006, 2010a) Face Constituting Theory, the notion of face as a claimed social image or identity has remained at the core of the analysis of im/politeness (e.g. Bousfield 2008; Culpeper 2011a; Locher and Watts 2005; Spencer-Oatey 2005), with recourse still being made to the avoidance of imposition (cf. negative face) and showing approval of others (cf. positive face) in many of these analyses. However, the analysis of im/politeness implicatures here has indicated that this is overly reductive. In analysing how through implicating participants can occasion evaluations of im/politeness, recourse has been made to the orientation of participants to their respective epistemic rights and authority, deontic entitlements, benefactive status, interactional roles, relationships, feelings, reciprocal approval, and attentiveness/consideration, among other things. The notion of face thus offers, at best, only a partial account of the rich moral substrate in which evaluations of im/politeness are grounded.

This point is, of course, implicitly recognised in Culpeper's (2011a: 68) recent socio-cognitive model of impoliteness, where the face of self and others is located within a broader mileu of social norms, morality and attitudes/ideology. However, it has been argued here that we must take this implicit recognition much further, and start to systematically analyse the moral grounds in which evaluations of im/politeness are grounded as an important object of ongoing study in its own right. It has been suggested here that through the lens of im/politeness implicatures we can gain useful insights into the moral order. Yet ultimately, given moral orders are renewed, negotiated and challenged by members across relational networks over time, any theorisation of im/politeness as social practice necessitates many more studies of im/politeness implicatures not only across various languages, but perhaps more critically, from different *emic* viewpoints. In that sense, the analysis in this volume represents a starting point, not an end-point, for a larger programme investigating the (meta)pragmatics of interpersonal interaction.

3 Towards an interactional pragmatics

In the course of this volume, an analytical framework for grounding the analysis of im/politeness implicatures as social practice has been developed. It has been proposed that the analysis of im/politeness implicatures needs to be situated relative to four interpenetrating pragmatic orders: the moral order, the participation order, the temporal-sequential order, and the socio-inferential order. The moral order refers to the sets of seen but unnoticed intersubjective expectancies through which members ground their understandings of such pragmatic phenomena in interaction; the participation order involves the multiple participation footings relative to which such pragmatic phenomena can arise in interaction; the temporal-sequential order encompasses the inherently temporal and sequentially situated nature of interpretations of pragmatic meanings, social actions and attitudinal evaluations in interaction; and the socio-inferential order encompasses the sets of intentional state-processes and inferential mechanisms by which such pragmatic phenomena arise in interaction. While the relative importance of each of these orders for the analysis of im/politeness implicatures will naturally vary depending on one's research question, it has been proposed here that what has been most lacking in accounts of implicature vis-à-vis im/politeness to date has been an account of the moral order that treats it as an important object of study in its own right.

It has also been implicitly suggested, albeit in passing, that that our understanding of these four inter-related orders, in particular the moral order, can be furthered through systematic consideration of the metapragmatics of im/politeness implicatures, that is, an analysis of various forms of reflexive awareness on the part of participants themselves vis-à-vis im/politeness. These forms of reflexive awareness include metalinguistic, metacognitive, metacommunicative, and metadiscursive awareness. Metalinguistic awareness encompasses reflexive representations of pragmatic phenomena (e.g. awareness of differences between *implying* and *insinuating*); metacognitive awareness involves reflexive presentations of cognitive state-processes (e.g. awareness of expectations amongst members about what a particular expression would commonly imply); metacommunicative awareness refers to reflexive interpretations and evaluations of pragmatic meanings, social actions and attitudinal evaluations (e.g. debates amongst participants about what was not said but nevertheless meant by the speaker); and metadiscursive awareness encompasses reflexive social discourses on pragmatic meanings, social actions and attitudinal evaluations (e.g. claims amongst lay users that Chinese and Japanese favour "indirect" forms of communication). (Kádár and Haugh 2013: Chp.9; see Haugh and Kádár forthcoming for further details).

This underlying analytical framework is summarised in Figure 10 below.

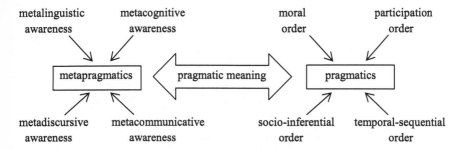

Figure 10: The (meta)pragmatics of im/politeness implicatures

Yet while im/politeness implicatures are pragmatic phenomena through and through, here an approach that draws from research in ethnomethodology and conversation analysis has been explicitly advocated. Thus, although interactional pragmatics is an approach to the analysis of pragmatic phenomena, such as politeness, implicature, and im/politeness implicatures that is informed by methods and research in ethnomethodological conversation analysis (Arundale 2005, 2010a; Haugh 2012a), it is by no means restricted to such methods. Interactional pragmatics is not a covert form of CA, but rather a distinct programme in its own right, with its own analytical foci, and its own distinct set of methodological approaches and theoretical assumptions. While, similar to CA, interactional pragmatics places critical emphasis on the understandings of participants themselves as they arise in naturally occurring discourse and interaction, it also emphasises the analysis of participants' *awareness* of such understandings. In other words, interactional pragmatics focuses not only on how im/politeness implicatures arise in interaction (i.e. the pragmatics of im/politeness implicatures), but also the perceptions and awareness of those users with respect to those im/politeness implicatures (i.e. the metapragmatics of im/politeness implicatures). Without careful examination of the metapragmatics of phenomena such as im/politeness implicatures, we are left without a clear explanation of their recognisability to members.

In conclusion, the approach to im/politeness implicatures outlined in this book has been grounded in the understandings of participants rather than the formal distinctions of theorists, although the latter have been drawn upon when they were found to be consonant with the understandings of participants. To borrow from Schegloff (1996a), then, underpinning the analysis im/politeness implicatures developed in this volume has been the assumption that

> the relevant senses of 'explicit' and 'implicit' or 'inexplicit' [should] *not* [be] those of the professional student of logic, semantics, pragmatics, or rhetoric, but those of the participants themselves; and the level of detail worth working out is given by the concerns of the participants' lives, not those of professional students ... We are here getting at the *members' then-relevant* sense and practice of explicitness [and implicitness]. (Schgeloff 1996a: 191, original emphasis)

Yet while the understandings of participants have been the primary focus of the analysis in this volume, this is not to say that a role for the analyst no longer exists. Indeed, the analyses of im/politeness implicatures developed here have tapped into sets of practices, many if not most of which remain largely out of the purview of conscious, detailed reflection by those members. While these analyses have thus highlighted a number of limitations in the ways in which implicature and im/politeness have been theorised in pragmatics to date, they have also mapped out new, potentially fruitful areas for further empirical analysis.

There nevertheless remains considerable work to be done in further reconciling cognitive-philosophical approaches with sociocultural-interactional perspectives on implicature and im/politeness. Most importantly, there still remains work to develop an account of cognition for interaction that is able to account for the dynamic, locally situated character of im/politeness implicatures, and yet can also account for the recurrent and ordered practices by which they evidently arise. There also remains significant work to better understand the role im/politeness implicatures play in the broader relational milieu in which they arise. The account of im/politeness implicatures developed here is intended as a modest contribution toward that broader endeavour.

References

Agha, Asif. 2003. The social life of cultural value. *Language and Communication* 23. 231–273.

Antaki, Charles. 1998. Identity ascriptions in their time and place: 'Fagin' and 'The terminally dim'. In Charles Antaki & Sue Widdicombe (eds.) *Identities in Talk*, 71–86. London: Sage.

Ariel, Mira. 2002. Privileged interactional interpretations. *Journal of Pragmatics* 34 (8). 1003–1044.

Arundale, Robert B. 1999. An alternative model and ideology of communication for an alternative to politeness theory. *Pragmatics* 9 (1). 119–154.

Arundale, Robert B. 2005. Pragmatics, conversational implicature and conversation. In Kristine Fitch & Robert Sanders (eds.) *Handbook of Language and Social Interaction*, 41–63. Mahwah, NJ: Lawrence Erlbaum.

Arundale, Robert B. 2006. Face as relational and interactional: a communication framework for research on face, facework, and politeness. *Journal of Politeness Research* 2 (2). 193–216.

Arundale, Robert B. 2008. Against (Gricean) intentions at the heart of human interaction. *Intercultural Pragmatics* 5 (2). 229–258.

Arundale, Robert B. 2010a. Constituting face in conversation: face, facework and interactional achievement. *Journal of Pragmatics* 42 (8). 2078–2105.

Arundale, Robert B. 2010b. Relating. In Miriam Locher & Sage L. Graham (eds.) *Interpersonal Pragmatics*, 137–166. Berlin: Mouton de Gruyter.

Arundale, Robert B. & David Good. 2002. Boundaries and sequences in studying conversation. In Anita Fetzer & Christine Meierkord (eds.) *Rethinking Sequentiality. Linguistics Meets Conversational Interaction*, 121–150. Amsterdam: John Benjamins.

Arsenault, Madeleine. 2014. An implicature account of idioms. *International Review of Pragmatics* 6 (1). 59–77.

Asher, Nicholas & Alex Lascarides. 2001. Indirect speech acts. *Synthese* 128 (1/2). 183–228.

Attardo, Salvatore, Jodi Eisterhold, Jennifer Hay & Isabella Poggi. 2003. Multimodal markers of irony and sarcasm. *Humor* 16 (2). 243–260.

Augoustinos, Martha, Iain Walker & Ngaire Donaghue. 2006. *Social Cognition*. London: Sage.

Austin, J L. 1962. *How to Do Things with Words*. Oxford: Clarendon Press.

Bach, Kent. 1984. Default reasoning: jumping to conclusions and knowing when to think twice. *Pacific Philosophical Quarterly* 65. 37–58.

Bach, Kent. 1994. Conversational impliciture. *Mind and Language* 9 (2). 124–162.

Bach, Kent. 1995. Standardization and conventionalization. *Linguistics and Philosophy* 18. 677–686.

Bach, Kent. 1998. Standardization revisited. In Asa Kasher (ed.) *Pragmatics. Critical Concepts. Volume 4, Presupposition, Implicature and Indirect Speech Acts*, 713–722. London: Routledge.

Bach, Kent. 1999. The myth of conventional implicature. *Linguistics and Philosophy* 22. 327–366.

Bach, Kent. 2001. You don't say? *Synthese* 128 (1/2). 15–44.

Bach, Kent. 2002. Seemingly semantic intuitions. In Joseph Campbell, Michael O'Rourke & David Shier (eds.) *Meaning and Truth: Investigations in Philosophical Semantics*, 21–33. New York: Seven Bridges Press.

Bach, Kent. 2004. Pragmatics and the philosophy of language. In Laurence Horn & Gregory Ward (eds.) *Handbook of Pragmatics*, 463–487. Oxford: Blackwell.

Bach, Kent. 2006. The top 10 misconceptions about implicature. In Betty Birner & Gregory Ward (eds.) *Drawing the Boundaries of Meaning. Neo-Gricean Studies in Pragmatics and Semantics in Honor of Laurence R. Horn*, 21–30. Amsterdam: John Benjamins.

Bach, Kent. 2012. Saying, meaning, and implicating. In Keith Allan & Kasia M. Jaszczolt (eds.) *The Cambridge Handbook of Pragmatics*, 47–67. Cambridge: Cambridge University Press.

Bach, Kent & Robert Harnish. 1979. *Linguistic Communication and Speech Acts*. Cambridge, MA: MIT Press.

Bara, Bruno G. 2010. *Cognitive Pragmatics*. Cambridge, MA: MIT Press.

Bayraktaroğlu, Arin, and Maria Sifianou. 2012. The iron fist in a velvet glove: how politeness can contribute to impoliteness. *Journal of Politeness Research* 8 (2). 143–160.

Bazzanella, Carla. 2011. Indeterminacy in dialogue. *Language and Dialogue* 1. 21–43.

Beach, Wayne A. 1994. Relevance and consequentiality. *Western Journal of Communication*, 58. 51–57.

Beach, Wayne A. & Phillip Glenn. 2011. Bids and responses to intimacy as 'gendered' enactments. In Susan Speer & Elizabeth Stokoe (eds.) *Conversation and Gender*, 210–228. Cambridge: Cambridge University Press.

Bell, David M. 1997. Innuendo. *Journal of Pragmatics* 27 (1). 35–59.

Beller, Sieghard. 2008. Deontic norms, deontic reasoning, and deontic conditions. *Thinking & Reasoning* 14 (4). 305–341.

Berg, Jonathan. 2002. Is semantics still possible?. *Journal of Pragmatics* 34 (4). 349–359.

Bertuccelli Papi, Marcella. 1996. Insinuating: the seduction of unsaying. *Pragmatics* 6 (2). 191–204.

Bertuccelli Papi, Marcella. 1999. Implicitness to whom? In Jef Verschueren (ed.) *Pragmatics in 1998. Selected Papers from the 6th International Pragmatics Conference, Vol. 2*, 57–72. Antwerp: International Pragmatics Association.

Bertuccelli Papi, Marcella. 2000. *Implicitness in Text and Discourse*. Pisa: Edizoni ETS.

Bertuccelli Papi, Marcella. 2001. Where Grice feared to tread: inferring attitudes and emotions. In Giovanni Consenza (ed.) *Paul Grice's Heritage*, 247–281. Turnhout: Brepols.

Bertuccelli Papi, Marcella. 2014. The pragmatics of insinuation. *Intercultural Pragmatics* 11 (1). 1–29.

Bezuidenhout, Anne & J. Cooper Cutting. 2002. Literal meaning, miminal propositions and pragmatic processing. *Journal of Pragmatics* 34 (4). 433–456.

Bezuidenhout, Anne & Robin Morris. 2004. Implicature, relevance and default inferences. In Dan Sperber & Ira Noveck (eds.) *Experimental Pragmatics*, 257–282. Basingstoke: Palgrave Press.

Bianchi, Claudia. 2013a. Implicating. In Maria Sbisà & Ken Turner (eds.) *Pragmatics of Speech Actions*, 107–142. Berlin: Mouton de Gruyter.

Bianchi, Claudia. 2013b. Writing letters in the age of Grice. In Alessandro Capone, Franco Lo Piparo & Marco Carapezza (eds.) *Foundations of Philosophical Pragmatics*, 189–202. New York: Springer.

Bilmes, Jack. 1993. Ethnomethodology, culture and implicature: toward an empirical pragmatics. *Pragmatics* 3 (4). 387–410.

Bilmes, Jack. 2011. Occasioned semantics: a systematic approach to meaning in talk. *Human Studies* 34. 129–153.

Birner, Betty. 2013. *Introduction to Pragmatics*. Malden, MA: Wiley-Blackwell.

Blakemore, Diane. 1987. *Semantic Constraints on Relevance*. Oxford: Blackwell.

Blakemore, Diane. 2000. Indicators and procedures: *nevertheless* and *but*. *Journal of Linguistics* 36. 463–486.

Blakemore, Diane. 2002. *Relevance and Linguistic Meaning*. Cambridge: Cambridge University Press.

Blome-Tillmann, Michael. 2008. Conversational implicature and the cancellability test. *Analysis* 68 (2). 156–160.

Blum-Kulka, Shoshana. 1987. Indirectness and politeness in requests: same or different? *Journal of Pragmatics* 11. 131–146.

Blum-Kulka, Shoshana & Elite Olshtain. 1984. Requests and apologies: a cross-cultural study of speech act realization patterns (CCSARP). *Applied Linguistics* 5. 196–213.

Blum-Kulka, Shoshana & Elda Weizman. 1988. The inevitability of discourse ambiguities. *Text* 8 (3). 219–241.

Bolden, Galina B. 2006. Little words that matter: Discourse markers "so" and "oh" and the doing of other-attentiveness in social interaction. *Journal of Communication* 56 (4). 661–688.

Bolden, Galina B. 2009. Implementing incipient actions: the discourse marker 'so' in English conversation. *Journal of Pragmatics* 41 (5). 974–998.

Bolden, Galina B., Jenny Mandelbaum & Sue Wilkinson. 2012. Pursuing a response by repairing an indexical reference. *Research on Language in Social Interaction* 45 (2). 137–155.

Bolden, Galina B. & Jeffrey D. Robinson. 2011. Soliciting accounts with *why*-interrogatives in conversation. *Journal of Communication* 61 (1). 94–119.

Bonnefon, Jean-Francois, Aidan Feeney & Gaelle Villejoubert. 2009. When some is actually all: scalar inferences in face-threatening contexts. *Cognition* 112 (2). 249–258.

Bonnefon, Jean-Francois & Gaelle Villejoubert. 2006. Tactful or doubtful? Expectations of politeness explain the severity bias in the interpretation of probability phrases. *Psychological Science* 17 (9). 747–751.

Börjesson, Kristin. 2012. The role of context in interpreting implicit meaning aspects. In Rita Finkbeiner, Jörg Meibauer & Petra B. Schumacher (eds.) *What is a Context?: Linguistic Approaches and Challenges*, 175–198. Amsterdam: John Benjamins.

Börjesson, Kristin. 2014. *The Semantics-Pragmatics Controversy*. Berlin: Mouton de Gruyter.

Bott, Lewis & Ira Noveck. 2004. Some utterances are underinformative: the onset and time course of scalar inferences. *Journal of Memory and Language* 51 (3). 437–457.

Bousfield, Derek. 2008. *Impoliteness in Interaction*. Amsterdam: John Benjamins.

Bousfield, Derek. 2010. Researching impoliteness and rudeness: issues and definitions. In Miriam A. Locher & Sage L. Graham (eds.) *Interpersonal Pragmatics*, 101–134. Berlin: Mouton de Gruyter.

Bousfield, Derek. 2013. Face in conflict. *Journal of Language Aggression and Conflict* 1 (1). 37–57.

Bousfield, Derek & Jonathan Culpeper (eds.). 2008. Impoliteness: eclecticism and diaspora. [Special issue]. *Journal of Politeness Research* 4 (2).

Bousfield, Derek & Miriam Locher (eds.). 2008. *Impoliteness in Language*. Berlin: Mouton de Gruyter.

Boxer, Diana. 1993. Social distance and speech behaviour: the case of indirect complaints. *Journal of Pragmatics* 19 (2). 103–125.

Boxer, Diana & Florencia Cortés-Conde. 1997. From bonding to biting: conversational joking and identity display. *Journal of Pragmatics* 27 (3). 275–294.

Bratman, Michael. 1987. *Intention, Plans, and Practical Reason*. Cambridge, MA: Harvard University Press.

Breheny, Richard. 2002. The current state of (radical) pragmatics in the cognitive sciences. *Mind and Language* 17 (1/2). 169–187.

Breheny, Richard, Napoleon Katsos & John Williams. 2006. Are generalised scalar implicatures generated by default? An on-line investigation into the role of context in generating pragmatic inferences. *Cognition* 100 (3). 434–463.

Brenneis, Donald. 1986. Shared territory: audience, indirection and meaning. *Text* 6 (3). 339–347.

Brown, Lucien. 2013. Mind your esteemed business: sarcastic honorifics use and impoliteness in Korean TV dramas. *Journal of Politeness Research* 9 (2). 159–186.

Brown, Penelope. 1995. Politeness strategies and the attribution of intentions: the case of Tzeltal irony. In Esther Goody (ed.) *Social Intelligence and Interaction*, 153–174. Cambridge: Cambridge University Press.

Brown, Penelope. 2001. Politeness and language. In Neil Smelser & Paul Baltes (eds.) *International Encyclopedia of the Social and Behavioural Sciences*, 11620–11624. Oxford: Elsevier Science.

Brown, Penelope & Stephen C. Levinson. 1978. Universals in language usage: politeness phenomena. In Esther Goody (ed.) *Questions and Politeness*, 56–311. Cambridge: Cambridge University Press.

Brown, Penelope & Stephen C. Levinson. 1987. *Politeness: Some Universals in Language Usage*. Cambridge: Cambridge University Press.

Bultinck, Bert. 2005. *Numerous Meanings: The Meaning of English Cardinals and the Legacy of Paul Grice*. Oxford: Elsevier Science.

Burton-Roberts, Noel. 2010. Cancellation and intention. In Belén Soria & Esther Romero (eds.) *Explicit Communication. Robyn Carston's Pragmatics*, 138–155. London: Palgrave Macmillan.

Burton-Roberts, Noel. 2013. On Grice and cancellation. *Journal of Pragmatics* 48. 17–28.

Butler, Clay. 2007. From bite to nip: the dialogic construction of teases. *Texas Linguistic Forum* 50. 22–34.

Caffi, Claudia. 1999. On mitigation. *Journal of Pragmatics* 31 (7). 881–909.

Caffi, Claudia. 2007. *Mitigation*. Oxford: Elsevier Science.

Capone, Alessandro. 2009. Are explicatures cancellable? Towards a theory of the speaker's intentionality. *Intercultural Pragmatics* 6 (1). 55–83.

Carston, Robyn. 1988. Implicature, explicature, and truth-theoretic semantics. In Ruth Kempson (ed.) *Mental Representations: The Interface between Language and Reality*, 155–181. Cambridge: Cambridge University Press.

Carston, Robyn. 1995. Quantity maxims and generalised implicature. *Lingua* 96. 213–244.

Carston, Robyn. 1998. Informativeness, relevance and scalar implicature. In Robyn Carston & Seiichi Uchida (eds.) *Relevance Theory. Applications and Implications*, 179–236. Amsterdam: John Benjamins.

Carston, Robyn. 2002a. *Thoughts and Utterances: The Pragmatics of Explicit Communication*. Oxford: Blackwell.

Carston, Robyn. 2002b. Linguistic meaning, communicated meaning and cognitive pragmatics. *Mind and Language* 17 (1/2). 127–148.

Carston, Robyn. 2004. Relevance theory and the saying/implicating distinction. In Laurence Horn & Gregory Ward (eds.) *Handbook of Pragmatics*, 633–656. Oxford: Blackwell.

Carston, Robyn. 2005. Relevance theory, Grice and the neo-Griceans: a response to Laurence Horn's 'Current issues in neo-Gricean pragmatics'. *Intercultural Pragmatics* 2 (3). 303–319.

Carston, Robyn. 2010. Explicit communication and 'free' pragmatic enrichment. In Belén Soria & Esther Romero (eds.), *Explicit Communication. Robyn Carston's Pragmatics*, 217–285. Basingstoke: Palgrave Macmilla.

Carston, Robyn. 2012. Metaphor and the literal/nonliteral distinction. In Keith Allan & Kasia Jaszczolt (eds.) *The Cambridge Handbook of Pragmatics*, 469–492. Cambridge: Cambridge University Press.

Carston, Robyn & Alison Hall. 2012. Implicature and explicature. In Hans-Jörg Schmid (ed.) *Cognitive Pragmatics*, 47–84. Berlin: Mouton de Gruyter.

Chang, Hui-Ching. 1999. The 'well-defined' is 'ambiguous' – indeterminancy in Chinese conversation. *Journal of Pragmatics* 31 (4). 535–556.

Chang, Wei-Lin Melody. forthcoming. *Face and Face Practices in Chinese Interaction: A Study in Interactional Practices*. London: Equinox.

Chang, Wei-Lin Melody & Michael Haugh. 2011a. Strategic embarrassment and face threatening in business interactions. *Journal of Pragmatics* 43 (12). 2948–2963.

Chang, Wei-Lin Melody & Michael Haugh. 2011b. Evaluations of im/politeness of an intercultural apology. *Intercultural Pragmatics* 8 (3). 411–442.

Chaves, José E. 2010. Explicature, what is said, and Gricean factorisation criteria. In Belén Soria & Esther Romero (eds.) *Explicit Communication: Robyn Carston's Pragmatics*, 109–125. Houndmills: Palgrave Macmillan.

Cheng, Winnie & Martin Warren. 2003. Indirectness, inexplicitness and vagueness made clearer. *Pragmatics* 13 (3). 381–400.

Chevalier, Fabienne H. 2009. The facework of unfinished turns in French conversation. *Discourse Studies* 11 (3). 267–284.

Chevallier, Coralie, Ira Noveck, Tatjana Nazir, Lewis Bott, Valentina Lanzetti & Dan Sperber. 2008. Making disjunctions exclusive. *The Quarterly Journal of Experimental Psychology* 61 (11). 1741–1760.

Christie, Chris. 2007. Relevance theory and politeness. *Journal of Politeness Research* 3 (2). 269–294.

Clark, Billy. 2013. *Relevance Theory*. Cambridge: Cambridge University Press.

Clark, Herbert. 1979. Responding to indirect speech acts. *Cognitive Psychology* 11 (4). 430–477.

Clark, Herbert. 1997. Dogmas of understanding. *Discourse Processes* 23 (3). 567–598.

Clark, Herbert & Dale Schunk. 1980. Polite responses to polite requests. *Cognition* 8 (2). 111–143.

Clark, Herbert & Dale Schunk. 1981. Politeness in requests: a rejoinder to Kemper and Thissen. *Cognition* 9 (3). 311–315.

Clayman, Steven and John Heritage. Forthcoming. Benefactors and beneficiaries: benefactive status and stance in the management of offers and requests. In Paul Drew & Elizabeth Couper-Kuhlen (eds.) *Requesting in Interaction*. Amsterdam: John Benjamins.

Clift, Rebecca. 1999. Irony in conversation. *Language in Society* 28 (4). 523–553.

Clift, Rebecca. 2001. Meaning in interaction: the case of *actually*. *Language* 77 (2). 245–291.

Cook, Haruko Minegishi. 2006. Japanese politeness as an interactional achievement: academic consultation sessions in Japanese universities. *Multilingua* 25 (3). 269–291.

Cooren, François. 2005. The contribution of speech act theory to the analysis of conversation: how pre-sequences work. In Kristine Fitch & Robert Sanders (eds.) *Handbook of Language and Social Interaction*, 21–40. Mahwah, NJ: Lawrence Erlbaum.

Cooren, François & Robert Sanders. 2002. Implicatures: a schematic approach. *Journal of Pragmatics* 34 (8). 1045–1067.

Couper-Kuhlen, Elizabeth. 2012. On affectivity and preference in responses to rejection. *Text and Talk* 32 (4). 453–475

Culpeper, Jonathan. 1996. Towards an anatomy of impoliteness. *Journal of Pragmatics* 25 (3). 349–367.

Culpeper, Jonathan. 2005. Impoliteness and entertainment in the television quiz show: *The Weakest Link. Journal of Politeness Research* 1 (1). 35–72.

Culpeper, Jonathan. 2008. Reflections on impoliteness, relational work and power. In Derek Bousfield & Miriam Locher (eds.), *Impoliteness in Language*, 17–44. Berlin: Mouton de Gruyter.

Culpeper, Jonathan. 2009. The metalanguage of impoliteness: using sketch engine to explore the *Oxford English Corpus*. In Paul Baker (ed.) *Contemporary Corpus Linguistics*, 66–88. London: Continuum.

Culpeper, Jonathan. 2011a. *Impoliteness: Using Language to Cause Offence*. Cambridge: Cambridge University Press.

Culpeper, Jonathan 2011b. Politeness and impoliteness. In Karin Aijmer & Gisle Andersen (eds.) *Pragmatics of Society*, 393–438. Berlin: Mouton de Gruyter.

Culpeper, Jonathan. 2012. (Im)politeness: three issues. *Journal of Pragmatics* 44 (9). 1128–1133.

Culpeper, Jonathan & Michael Haugh. 2014. *Pragmatics and the English Language*. Basingstoke: Palgrave Macmillan.

Curl, Traci S. 2006. Offers of assistance: constraints on syntactic design. *Journal of Pragmatics* 38 (8). 1257–1280.

Curl, Traci S. & Paul Drew. 2008. Contingency and action: a comparison of two forms of requesting. *Research on Language and Social Interaction* 41 (2). 129–153.

Date, Kumiko. 2005. An Analysis of Japanese Language Learners' Communication Strategies: The Use of Indirect Expressions of Refusal. Unpublished PhD dissertation, University of Malaya.

Davidson, Judy. 1984. Subsequent versions of invitations, offers, requests, and proposals dealing with potential or actual rejection. In J. Maxwell Atkinson & John Heritage (eds.) *Structures of Social Action*, 102–128. Cambridge: Cambridge University Press.

Davidson, Judy. 1990. Modifications of invitations, offers and rejections. In George Psathas (ed.) *Interaction Competence*, 149–179. Washington, D.C.: University Press of America.

Davies, Bethan. 2007. Grice's cooperative principle: meaning and rationality. *Journal of Pragmatics* 39 (12). 2308–2331.

Davis, Wayne. 1992a. Speaker meaning. *Linguistics and Philosophy* 15 (3). 223–253.

Davis, Wayne. 1992b. Cogitative and cognitive speaker meaning. *Philosophical Studies* 67 (1). 71–88.

Davis, Wayne. 1998. *Implicature. Intention, Convention and Principle in the Failure of Gricean Theory*. Cambridge: Cambridge University Press.

Davis, Wayne. 2003. *Meaning, Expression and Thought*. Cambridge: Cambridge University Press.

Demeure, Virgine. 2010. Facework and utilitarian relevance in the disambiguation of statements with two indirect replies. *Journal of Language and Social Psychology* 29 (4). 443–457.

Demeure, Virgine, Jean-Francois Bonnefon & Eric Raufaste. 2008. Utilitarian relevance and face management in the interpretation of ambiguous question/request statements. *Memory and Cognition* 36 (4). 873–878.

Demeure, Virgine, Jean-Francois Bonnefon & Eric Raufaste. 2009. Politeness and conditional reasoning: interpersonal cues to the indirect suppression of deductive inferences. *Journal of Experimental Psychology* 35 (1). 260–266.

Deppermann, Arnulf. 2011a. The study of formulations as a key to an interactional semantics. *Human Studies* 34 (2). 115–128.

Deppermann, Arnulf. 2011b. Notionalization: the transformation of descriptions into categories. *Human Studies* 34 (2). 155–181.

Dillard, James, Steven Wilson, Kyle Tusing & Terry Kinney. 1997. Politeness judgements in personal relationships. *Journal of Language and Social Psychology* 16 (3). 297–325.

Dobs, Abby Mueller & Pilar Garcés-Conejos Blitvich. 2013. Impoliteness in polylogal interaction: accounting for face-threat witnesses' responses. *Journal of Pragmatics* 53. 112–130.

Drew, Paul. 1984. Speakers' reportings in invitation sequences. In J. Maxwell Atkinson & John Heritage (eds.) *Structures of Social Action*, 129–151. Cambridge: Cambridge University Press.

Drew, Paul. 1987. Po-faced receipts of teases. *Linguistics* 25 (1). 219–253.

Drew, Paul. 1995. Interaction sequences and anticipatory interactive planning. In Esther Goody (ed.) *Social Intelligence and Interaction*, 111–138. Cambridge: Cambridge University Press.

Drew, Paul. 1997. 'Open' class repair initiators in response to sequential sources of troubles in conversation. *Journal of Pragmatics* 28 (1). 69–101.

Drew, Paul. 1998. Complaints about transgressions and misconduct. *Research on Language and Social Interaction* 31 (3/4). 295–325.

Drew, Paul. 2005. Conversation analysis. In Kristine L. Fitch & Robert E. Sanders (eds.) *Handbook of Language and Social Interaction*, 71–102. Mahwah, NJ: Lawrence Erlbaum.

Drew, Paul. 2011. Reflections on the micro-politics of social action, in interaction. Paper presented at the 12th International Pragmatics Association Conference, University of Manchester, U.K., 3–8 July.

Drew, Paul. 2013. Turn design. In Jack Sidnell & Tanya Stivers (eds.) *The Handbook of Conversation Analysis*, 131–149. Malden, MA: Wiley-Blackwell.

Drew, Paul & Elizabeth Holt. 1988. Complainable matters: the use of idiomatic expressions in making complaints. *Social Problems* 35 (4). 398–417.

Drew, Paul & Traci Walker. 2009. *Going too far*: complaining, escalating and disaffiliation. *Journal of Pragmatics* 41 (12). 2400–2414.

Dynel, Marta. 2011. 'You talking to me?' The viewer as a ratified listener to film discourse. *Journal of Pragmatics* 43 (6). 1628–1644.

Dynel, Marta. 2012. Setting our House in order: the workings of impoliteness in multi-party film discourse. *Journal of Politeness Research* 8 (2). 161–194.

Dynel, Marta. 2013. Irony from a neo-Gricean perspective: on untruthfulness and evaluative implicature. *Intercultural Pragmatics* 10 (3). 403–431.

Edwards, Derek. 2008. Intentionality and *mens rea* in police interrogations: the production of actions as crimes. *Intercultural Pragmatics* 5 (2). 177–199.

Edwards, Derek & Alessandra Fasulo. 2006. 'To be honest': sequential uses of honesty phrases in talk-in-interaction. *Research on Language in Social Interaction* 39 (4). 343–76.

Eelen, Gino. 2001. *A Critique of Politeness Theories*. Manchester: St. Jerome.

Escandell-Vidal, Victoria. 1996. Towards a cognitive approach to politeness. *Language Sciences* 18 (3/4). 629–650.

Escandell-Vidal, Victoria. 1998. Politeness: a relevant issue for relevance theory. *Revista Alicantina de Estudios Ingleses* 11. 45–57.

Everts, Elisa. 2003. Identifying a particular family humour style: a sociolinguistic discourse analysis. *Humor* 16. 369–412.

Feeney, Aidan & Jean-Francois Bonnefon. 2013. Politeness and honesty contribute additively to the interpretation of scalar expressions. *Journal of Language and Social Psychology* 32 (2). 181–190.

Félix-Brasdefer, J. César (2005). Indirectness and politeness in Mexican Requests. In David Eddington (ed.), *Selected Proceedings of the 7th Hispanic Linguistic Symposium*, 66–78. Somerville, MA: Cascadilla Press.

Feng, Guangwu. 2010. *A Theory of Conventional Implicature and Pragmatic Markers in Chinese*. Bingley: Emerald Group.

Feng, Guangwu. 2013. Speaker's meaning and non-cancellability. *Pragmatics and Cognition* 21 (1). 117–138.

Ferenčík, Milan. 2007. Exercising politeness: membership categorisation in a radio phone-in programme. *Pragmatics* 17 (3). 351–370.

Field, Margaret. 1998 Politeness and indirection in Navajo directives. *Journal of Southwest Linguistics* 17 (2). 23–34.

Fisher, Lawrence E. 1976. Dropping remarks and the Barbadian audience. *American Ethnologist* 3 (2). 227–258.

Fraser, Bruce 1990. Perspectives on politeness. *Journal of Pragmatics* 14 (2). 219–236.

Fraser, Bruce. 2001. An account of innuendo. In Istvan Kenesei & Robert M Harnish (eds.) *Perspectives on Semantics, Pragmatics and Discourse. A Festschrift for Ferenc Kiefer*, 321–336. Amsterdam: John Benjamins.

Fraser, Bruce. 2005. Whither politeness. In Robin Lakoff & Sachiko Ide (eds.) *Broadening the Horizons of Linguistic Politeness*, 65–83. Amsterdam: John Benjamins.

Fukushima, Saeko. 2004. Evaluation of politeness: the case of attentiveness. *Multilingua* 23 (4). 365–388.

Fukushima, Saeko. 2009. Evaluation of politeness: Do the Japanese evaluate attentiveness more positively than the British? *Pragmatics* 19 (4). 501–518.

Fukushima, Saeko. 2011. A cross-generational and cross-cultural study on demonstration of attentiveness. *Pragmatics* 21 (4). 549–571.

Fukushima, Saeko. 2013. Evaluation of (im)politeness: A comparative study among Japanese students, Japanese parents and American students on evaluation of attentiveness. *Pragmatics* 23 (2). 275–299.

Fukushima, Saeko & Michael Haugh. Forthcoming. The role of emic understandings in theorizing im/politeness: the metapragmatics of attentiveness, empathy and anticipatory inference in Japanese and Chinese. *Journal of Pragmatics*.

Furman, Michael. 2013. Impoliteness and mock-impoliteness. A descriptive analysis. In Nadine Thielemann & Peter Kosta (eds.) *Approaches to Slavic Interaction*, 237–256. Amsterdam: John Benjamins.

Garcés-Conejos Blitvich, Pilar. 2009. Impoliteness and identity in the American news media: the 'culture wars'. *Journal of Politeness Research* 5 (2). 273–303.

Garcés-Conejos Blitvich, Pilar. 2010. A genre approach to the study of im-politeness. *International Review of Pragmatics* 2 (1). 46–94.

Garcés-Conejos Blitvich, Pilar. 2013. Introduction: face, identity and politeness. Looking backward, moving forward: from Goffman to practice theory. *Journal of Politeness Research 9* (1). 1–33.

Gardner, Rod. 2005. Acknowledging strong ties between utterances in talk: connections through right as a response token. In Ilana Mushin (ed.) *Proceedings of the 2004 Conference of the Australian Linguistic Society*, 1–12. http://hdl.handle.net/2123/115.

Garfinkel, Harold. 1956. Conditions of successful degradation ceremonies. *American Journal of Sociology 61* (5). 420–424.

Garfinkel, Harold. 1964. Studies of the routine grounds of everyday activities. *Social Problems* 11 (3). 225–250. Republished in Garfinkel 1967, 35–75.

Garfinkel, Harold. 1967. *Studies in Ethnomethodology*. Englewood Cliffs, NJ: Prentice-Hall.

Garrett, Merrill & Robert Harnish. 2009. Q-phenomena, I-phenomena and impliciture: some experimental pragmatics. *International Review of Pragmatics 1* (1). 84–117.

Gauker, Christopher. 2001. Situated inference versus conversational implicature. *Nous 35* (2). 163–189.

Gazdar, Gerald. 1979. *Pragmatics: Implicature, Presupposition and Logical Form*. New York: Academic Press.

Geis, Michael. 1995. *Speech Acts and Conversational Interaction*. Cambridge: Cambridge University Press.

Georgakopoulou, Alexandra. 2001. Arguing about the future: On indirect disagreements in conversations. *Journal of Pragmatics 33* (12). 1881–1900.

Geurts, Bart. 2009. Scalar implicature and local pragmatics. *Mind and Language 24* (1). 51–79.

Geurts, Bart. 2010. *Quantity Implicatures*. Cambridge: Cambridge University Press.

Geurts, Bart & Nausicaa Pouscoulous. 2009. Embedded implicatures?!?. *Semantics and Pragmatics 2* (article 4). 1–34.

Gibbs, Raymond, Jr. 1979. Contextual effects in understanding indirect requests. *Discourse Processes 2* (1). 1–10.

Gibbs, Raymond, Jr. 1981. Your wish is my command: convention and context in interpreting indirect requests. *Journal of Verbal Learning and Verbal Behavior 20* (4). 431–444.

Gibbs, Raymond, Jr. 1983. Do people always process the literal meanings of indirect requests? *Journal of Experimental Psychology: Learning, Memory and Cognition 9* (3). 524–533.

Gibbs, Raymond, Jr. 1986. What makes some indirect speech acts conventional? *Journal of Memory and Language 25* (2). 181–196.

Gibbs, Raymond, Jr. 1999a. *Intentions in the Experience of Meaning*. Cambridge: Cambridge University Press.

Gibbs, Raymond, Jr. 1999b. Interpreting what speakers say and implicate. *Brain and Language 68* (3). 466–485.

Gibbs, Raymond, Jr. 1999c. Speaking and thinking with metonymy. In Klaus-Uwe Panther & Günter Radden (eds.) *Metonymy in Language and Thought*, 61–76. Amsterdam: John Benjamins.

Gibbs, Raymond, Jr. 2002. A new look at literal meaning in understanding what is said and implicated. *Journal of Pragmatics 34* (4). 457–486.

Gibbs, Raymond, Jr. & Herbert L. Colston. 2012. *Interpreting Figurative Meaning*. Cambridge: Cambridge University Press.

Gibbs, Raymond, Jr. & Jessica Moise. 1997. Pragmatics in understanding what is said. *Cognition 62* (1). 51–74.

Gil, José María. 2011. Relevance theory and unintended transmission of information. *Intercultural Pragmatics* 8 (1). 1–40.

Glenn, Phillip. 1995. Laughing *at* and laughing *with*: negotiation of participant alignments through conversational laughter. In Paul ten Have & George Psathas (eds.) *Situated Order: Studies in the Social Organisation of Talk and Embodied Activities*, 43–56. Washington, D.C.: University Press of America.

Glenn, Phillip. 2003. *Laughter in Interaction*. Cambridge: Cambridge University Press.

Goddard, Cliff & Anna Wierzbicka. 2014. *Words and Meanings: Lexical Semantics across Domains, Languages and Cultures*. Oxford: Oxford University Press.

Goffman, Erving, 1956. Embarrassment and social organization. *American Journal of Sociology* 62 (3). 264–271.

Goffman, Erving. 1978. Response cries. *Language* 54 (4). 787–815. Republished in Goffman 1981, 78–123.

Goffman, Erving. 1979. Footing. *Semiotica* 25 (1). 1–29. Republished in Goffman 1981, 124–159.

Goffman, Erving. 1981. *Forms of Talk*. Philadelphia: University of Pennsylvania Press.

Goldberg, Jo Ann. 2004. The amplitude shift mechanism in conversational closing sequences. In Gene Lerner (ed.) *Conversation Analysis: Studies from the First Generation*, 257–298. Amsterdam: John Benjamins.

Good, David & Brian L Butterworth. 1980. Hesitancy as a conversational resource: some methodological implications. In Hans Dechert & Manfred Raupach (eds.) *Temporal Variables in Speech*, 145–152. The Hague: Mouton.

Good, Jeffrey S. & Wayne Beach. 2005. Opening up gift-openings: birthday parties as situated activity systems. *Text* 25 (5). 565–593.

Goodwin, Charles. 1979. The interactive construction of a sentence in natural conversation. In: Georg Psathas (ed.) *Everyday Language: Studies in Ethnomethodology*, 97–121. New York: Irvington.

Goodwin, Charles. 2007. Interactive footing. In Elizabeth Holt & Rebecca Clift (eds.) *Reporting Talk*, 16–46. Cambridge: Cambridge University Press.

Goodwin, Charles & Marjorie Harness Goodwin. 1987. Concurrent operations on talk: notes on the interactive organization of assessments. *IPrA Papers in Pragmatics* 1 (1). 1–54.

Goodwin, Charles & Marjorie Harness Goodwin. 1992. Assessments and the construction of context. In Alessandro Duranti & Charles Goodwin (eds.) *Rethinking Context: Language as an Interactive Phenomenon*, 151–189. Cambridge: Cambridge University Press.

Goodwin, Charles & Marjorie Harness Goodwin. 2004. Participation. In Alessandro Duranti (ed.) *A Companion to Linguistic Anthropology*, 222–244. Malden, MA: Blackwell.

Goodwin, Charles & John Heritage. 1990. Conversation analysis. *Annual Review of Anthropology* 19. 283–307.

Goodwin, Marjorie Harness. 1980. 'He-said-she-said': formal cultural procedures for the construction of a gossip dispute activity. *American Ethnologist* 7 (4). 674–695.

Goodwin, Marjorie Harness. 1990. *He-Said-She-Said: Talk as Social Organisation among Black Children*. Bloomington: Indiana University Press.

Graham, Sage Lambert. 2007. Disagreeing to agree: conflict, (im)politeness and identity in a computer-mediated community. *Journal of Pragmatics* 39 (4). 742–759.

Green, Mitchell. 1999. Illocutions, implicata, and what a conversation requires. *Pragmatics and Cognition* 7 (1). 65–92.

Green, Nancy & Sandra Carberry. 1993. A discourse-plan-based approach to a class of particu-larized conversational implicature. *Proceedings of the Eastern States Conference on Linguistics* 10. 117–128.

Green, Nancy & Sandra Carberry. 1999. Interpreting and generating indirect answers. *Computational Linguistics* 25 (3). 389–435.

Greer, Tim, Yoshiko Usui, Toki Kato and Hitomi Taniguchi. 2005. Suppressing laughter in the display of (dis)affiliation. *Kobe Daigakui Kokusai Komyunikeeshon Sentaa Ronshuu* [Kobe University International Communication Centre bulletin] 2. 27–42.

Grice, H. Paul. 1957. Meaning. *Philosophical Review* 66 (3). 377–388. Republished in Grice 1989, 213–223.

Grice, H. Paul. 1967. Logic and conversation. *William James Lectures.* Published in revised form as Grice, H. Paul. 1989.

Grice, H. Paul. 1969. Utterer's meaning and intention. *Philosophical Review* 78 (2). 147–177. Republished in Grice 1989, 86–116.

Grice, H. Paul. 1975. Logic and conversation. In Peter Cole & Jerry Morgan (eds.) *Syntax and Semantics, Volume 3. Speech Acts*, 41–58. New York: Academic Press. Republished in Grice 1989, 22–40.

Grice, H. Paul. 1978. Further notes on logic and conversation. In Peter Cole (ed.) *Syntax and Semantics Volume 9. Pragmatics*, 113–127. NY: Academic Press. Republished in Grice 1989, 41–57.

Grice, H. Paul. 1987. Retrospective epilogue. Published in Grice 1989, 339–385.

Grice, H. Paul. 1989. *Studies in the Way of Words.* Cambridge, Massachusetts: Harvard University Press.

Grice, H. Paul. 2001. *Aspects of Reason.* Oxford: Clarendon Press.

Groefsema, Marjolein. 1992. 'Can you pass the salt?': a short-circuited implicature. *Lingua* 87 (1–2). 103–135.

Gumperz, John. 1982. *Discourse Strategies.* Cambridge: Cambridge University Press.

Haddington, Pentiti. 2013. Pragmatics of stance. In Carol A. Chapelle (ed.), *The Encyclopedia of Applied Linguistics*, 4616–4622. Malden, MA: Blackwell.

Hamblin, Jennifer & Raymond Gibbs Jr. 2003. Processing the meanings of what speakers say and implicate. *Discourse Processes* 35 (1). 59–80.

Harris, Sandra. 2001. Being politically impolite: extending politeness theory to adversarial political discourse. *Discourse and Society* 12. 451–472.

Hashimoto, Yoshiaki. 1992. Enkyokuteki komyunikeeshon hooryaku no ibunkakan hikaku [An intercultural comparison of euphemistic communication strategies]. *Tokyo Daigaku Shakai Joohoo Kenkyuujo Choosa Kenkyuu Kiyoo* [The Research Bulletin of the Institute of Socio-Information and Communication Studies, The University of Tokyo] 1. 107–159.

Haugh, Michael. 2002. The intuitive basis of implicature: Relevance theoretic *implicitness* versus Gricean *implying. Pragmatics* 12 (2). 117–134.

Haugh, Michael. 2003. Anticipated versus inferred politeness. *Multilingua* 22 (4). 397–413.

Haugh, Michael. 2005. The importance of 'place' in Japanese politeness: implications for cross-cultural and intercultural analyses. *Intercultural Pragmatics* 2 (1). 41–68.

Haugh, Michael. 2007a. The co-constitution of politeness implicature in conversation. *Journal of Pragmatics* 39 (1). 84–110.

Haugh, Michael. 2007b. Emic conceptulisations of (im)politeness and face in Japanese: implications for the discursive negotiation of second language learner identities. *Journal of Pragmatics* 39 (4). 657–680.

Haugh, Michael. 2007c. The discursive challenge to politeness theory: an interactional alternative. *Journal of Politeness Research* 3 (2). 295–317.

Haugh, Michael. 2008a. Intention in pragmatics. *Intercultural Pragmatics* 5 (2). 99–110.

Haugh, Michael. 2008b. Intention and diverging interpretings of implicature in the "uncovered meat" sermon. *Intercultural Pragmatics* 5 (2). 201–228.

Haugh, Michael. 2008c. The place of intention in the interactional achievement of implicature. In Istvan Kecskes & Jacob Mey (eds.), *Intention, Common Ground and the Egocentric Speaker-Hearer*, 45–85. Berlin: Mouton de Gruyter.

Haugh, Michael. 2008d. Utterance-final conjunctive particles and implicature in Japanese conversation. *Pragmatics* 18 (4). 425–451.

Haugh, Michael. 2009a. Intention(ality) and the conceptualisation of communication in pragmatics. *Australian Journal of Linguistics* 29 (1). 91–113.

Haugh, Michael. 2009b. Face and interaction. In Francesca Bargiela-Chiappini & Michael Haugh (eds.), *Face, Communication and Social Interaction*, 1–30. London: Equinox.

Haugh, Michael. 2010a. Jocular mockery, (dis)affiliation and face. *Journal of Pragmatics* 42 (8). 2106–2119.

Haugh, Michael. 2010b. Co-constructing what is said in interaction. In Enikő Németh T. & Károly Bibok (eds.), *The Role of Data at the Semantics-Pragmatics Interface*, 349–380. Berlin: Mouton de Gruyter.

Haugh, Michael. 2010c. When is an email really offensive? Argumentativity and variability in evaluations of impoliteness. *Journal of Politeness Research* 6 (1). 7–31.

Haugh, Michael. 2011a. Humour, face and im/politeness in getting acquainted. In Bethan Davies, Michael Haugh & Andrew John Merrison (eds.), *Situated Politeness*, 165–184. London: Continuum.

Haugh, Michael. 2011b. Practices and defaults in interpreting disjunction. In Kasia M. Jaszczolt & Keith Allan (eds.), *Salience and Defaults in Utterance Processing*, 193–230. Berlin: Mouton de Gruyter.

Haugh, Michael. 2011c. Epilogue: culture and norms in politeness research. In Dániel Z. Kádár & Sara Mills (eds.), *Politeness in East Asia*, 252–264. Cambridge: Cambridge University Press

Haugh, Michael. 2012a. Conversational interaction. In Keith Allan & Kasia M. Jaszczolt (eds.) *The Cambridge Handbook of Pragmatics*, 251–273. Cambridge: Cambridge University Press.

Haugh, Michael. 2012b. On understandings of intention: a response to Wedgwood. *Intercultural Pragmatics* 9 (2). 161–194.

Haugh, Michael. 2012c. Epilogue: the first-second order distinction in face and politeness research. *Journal of Politeness Research* 8 (1). 111–134.

Haugh, Michael. 2013a. Speaker meaning and accountability in interaction. *Journal of Pragmatics* 48. 41–56.

Haugh, Michael. 2013b. Implicature, inference and cancellability. In Alessandro Capone, Franco Lo Piparo & Marco Carapezza (eds.), *Perspectives on Pragmatics and Philosophy*, 133–151. New York: Springer.

Haugh, Michael. 2013c. Im/politeness, social practice and the participation order. *Journal of Pragmatics* 58. 52–72.

Haugh, Michael 2013d. Disentangling face, facework and (im)politeness. *Sociocultural Pragmatics* 1 (1). 46–73.

Haugh, Michael. 2013e. Inference and implicature. In Carol A. Chapelle (ed.), *The Encyclopedia of Applied Linguistics*, 2658–2665. Oxford: Wiley-Blackwell.

Haugh, Michael. 2013f. Conversational implicature. In Carol A. Chapelle (ed.), *The Encyclopedia of Applied Linguistics*, 938–943. Oxford: Wiley-Blackwell.

Haugh, Michael. 2014. Jocular mockery as interactional practice in everyday Anglo-Australian conversation. *Australian Journal of Linguistics* 34 (1). 93–123.

Haugh, Michael & Derek Bousfield. 2012. Mock impoliteness, jocular mockery and jocular abuse in Australian and British English. *Journal of Pragmatics* 44 (9). 1099–1114.

Haugh, Michael, Bethan Davies, & Andrew John Merrison. 2011. Situating politeness. In Bethan Davies, Michael Haugh and Andrew John Merrison (eds.) *Situated Politeness*, 1–23. London: Continuum.

Haugh, Michael & Carl Hinze. 2003. A metalinguistic approach to deconstructing the concepts of 'face' and 'politeness' in Chinese, English and Japanese. *Journal of Pragmatics* 35 (10/11). 1581–1611.

Haugh, Michael & Kasia M. Jaszczolt. 2012. Speaker intentions and intentionality. In Keith Allan & Kasia M. Jaszczolt (eds.) *The Cambridge Handbook of Pragmatics*, 87–112. Cambridge: Cambridge University Press.

Haugh, Michael & Dániel Z. Kádár (forthcoming) *The Metapragmatics of (Im)Politeness*. Amsterdam: John Benjamins.

Haugh, Michael & Yasuko Obana. 2011. Politeness in Japanese. In Daniel Kádár & Sara Mills (eds.) *Politeness in East Asia*, 147–175. Cambridge: Cambridge University Press.

Haverkate, Henk. 1988. Politeness strategies in verbal interaction: An analysis of directness and indirectness in speech acts. *Semiotica* 71 (1/2). 59–71.

Haviland, John B. 1986. 'Con Buenos Chiles': talk, targets and teasing in Zinacantan. *Text* 6 (3). 249–282.

Hayashi, Makoto. 2001. Postposition-initiated utterances in Japanese conversation: an interactional account of a grammatical practice. In Margaret Selting & Elizabeth Couper-Kuhlen (eds.) *Studies in Interactional Linguistics*, 317–343. Amsterdam: John Benjamins.

Hayashi, Makoto, Geoffrey Raymond & Jack Sidnell. 2013. Conversational repair and human understanding: an introduction. In Makoto Hayashi, Geoffrey Raymond & Jack Sidnell (eds.) *Conversational Repair and Human Understanding*, 1–40. Cambridge: Cambridge University Press.

Heath, Christian, 1988. Embarrassment and interactional organization. In Paul Drew & Andrew Wootton (eds.) *Erving Goffman: Exploring the Interaction Order*, 136–160. Cambridge: Polity Press.

Heinemann, Trine. 2006. 'Will you or can't you?': Displaying entitlement in interrogative requests. *Journal of Pragmatics* 38 (7). 1081–1104.

Heritage, John. 1984a. *Garfinkel and Ethnomethodology*. Cambridge: Polity Press.

Heritage, John. 1984b. A change of state token and aspects of its sequential placement. In J. Maxwell Atkinson & John Heritage (eds.) *Structures of Social Action*, 299–345. Cambridge: Cambridge University Press.

Heritage, John. 2002a. *Oh*-prefaced responses to assessments. In Cecilia E. Ford & Sandra A. Thompson (eds.) *The Language of Turn and Sequence*, 196–224. Oxford: Oxford University Press.

Heritage, John. 2002b. The limits of questioning: negative interrogatives and hostile question content. *Journal of Pragmatics* 34 (10/11). 1427–1446.

Heritage, John. 2012a. Epistemics in action: action formation and territories of knowledge. *Research on Language and Social Interaction* 45 (1). 1–29.

Heritage, John. 2012b. The epistemic engine: sequence organization and territories of knowledge. *Research on Language and Social Interaction* 45 (1). 30–52.

Heritage, John. 2013. Action formation and its epistemic (and other) backgrounds. *Discourse Studies* 15 (5). 547–574.

Heritage, John & Geoffrey Raymond. 2005. The terms of agreement: indexing epistemic authority and subordination in talk-in-interaction. *Social Psychology Quarterly* 68 (1). 15–38.

Heritage, John & Geoffrey Raymond. 2012. Navigating epistemic landscapes: acquiescence, agency and resistance in responses to polar questions. In Jan P. de Ruiter (ed.) *Questions: Formal, Functional and Interactional Perspectives*, 179–192. Cambridge: Cambridge University Press.

Hickey, Leo. 1992. Politeness apart: why choose indirect speech acts? *Lingua e Stile* 27 (1). 77–87.

Higashimori, Isao & Deirdre Wilson. 1996. Questions on relevance. *UCL Working Papers in Linguistics* 8. 111–124.

Hirschberg, Julia. 1991. *A Theory of Scalar Implicature*. New York: Garland.

Hinkelman, Elizabeth and James Allen. 1989. Two constraints on speech act ambiguity. *Proceedings of the 27th Annual Meeting of the Association for Computational Linguistics*, 212–219. Association for Computational Linguistics.

Holdcroft, David. 1976. Forms of indirect communication: an outline. *Philosophy and Rhetoric* 9 (3). 147–161.

Holt, Elizabeth. 2007. 'I'm eyeing your chop up mind': reporting and enacting. In Elizabeth Holt & Rebecca Clift (eds.) *Reporting Talk: Reported Speech in Interaction*, 47–80. Cambridge: Cambridge University Press.

Holt, Elizabeth. 2010. The last laugh: shared laughter and topic termination. *Journal of Pragmatics* 42 (6). 1513–1525.

Holt, Elizabeth. 2011. On the nature of 'laughables': laughter as a response to overdone figurative phrases. *Pragmatics* 21 (3). 393–410.

Holt, Elizabeth. 2013. 'There's many a true word said in jest': seriousness and nonseriousness in interaction. In Phillip Glenn and Elizabeth Holt (eds.) *Studies of Laughter in Interaction*, 69–89. London: Bloomsbury.

Holtgraves, Thomas. 1997. Styles of language use: individual and cultural variability in conversational indirectness. *Journal of Personality and Social Psychology* 73 (3). 624–637.

Holtgraves, Thomas. 1998a. Interpreting indirect replies. *Cognitive Psychology* 37 (1). 1–27.

Holtgraves, Thomas. 1998b. Interpersonal foundations of conversational indirectness. In Susan Fussell & Roger Kreuz (eds.) *Social and Cognitive Approaches to Interpersonal Communication*, 71–89. Mahwah, NJ: Lawrence Erlbaum.

Holtgraves, Thomas. 1999. Comprehending indirect replies: when and how are their conveyed meanings activated? *Journal of Memory and Language* 41 (4). 519–540.

Holtgraves, Thomas. 2000. Preference organization and reply comprehension. *Discourse Processes* 30 (2). 87–106.

Holtgraves, Thomas. 2002. *Language as Social Action*. Mahwah, NJ: Lawrence Erlbaum.

Holtgraves, Thomas & Joong-Nam Yang. 1990. Politeness as universal: cross-cultural perceptions of request strategies and inferences based on their use. *Journal of Personality and Social Psychology* 59 (4). 719–729.

Horn, Laurence. 1972. On the Semantic Properties of Logical Operators in English. Unpublished PhD dissertation, University of California Los Angeles.

Horn, Laurence. 1984. Toward a new taxonomy for pragmatic inference: Q-based and R-based implicature. In Deborah Schiffrin (ed.) *Georgetown University Round Table on Languages and Linguistics. Meaning, Form, and Use in Context: Linguistic Applications*, 11–42. Washington, D.C.: Georgetown University Press.

Horn, Laurence. 1989. *A Natural History of Negation*. Chicago, IL: University of Chicago Press.

Horn, Laurence. 1999. Implicature. In Robert Wilson & Frank Keil (eds.) *The MIT Encyclopedia of the Cognitive Sciences*, 391–393. Cambridge, MA: MIT Press.

Horn, Laurence. 2004. Implicature. In Laurence Horn & Gregory Ward (eds.) *Handbook of Pragmatics*, 3–28. Oxford: Blackwell.

Horn, Laurence. 2005. Current issues in neo-Gricean pragmatics. *Intercultural Pragmatics* 2 (2). 191–204.

Horn, Laurence. 2009. Wj-40: Implicature, truth and meaning. *International Review of Pragmatics* 1 (1). 3–34.

Horn, Laurence. 2010. Multiple negation in English and other languages. In Laurence Horn (ed.) *The Expression of Negation*, 111–148. Berlin: Mouton de Gruyter.

Horn, Laurence. 2012. Implying and inferring. In Keith Allan & Kasia M Jaszczolt (eds.) *The Cambridge Handbook of Pragmatics*, 69–86. Cambridge: Cambridge University Press.

Horn, Laurence & Samuel Bayer. 1984. Short-circuited implicature: a negative contribution. *Linguistics and Philosophy* 7 (4). 397–414.

Hosoda, Yuri. 2006. Diluting disagreement in Japanese conversation. *Jinbun Kenkyuu* [Studies in the Humanities, Kanagawa University] 169: 87–117.

Housley, William & Richard Fitzgerald. 2009. Membership categorisation, culture and norms in action. *Discourse and Society* 20 (3). 345–362.

Huang, Yan. 2012. *The Oxford Dictionary of Pragmatics*. Oxford: Oxford University Press.

Huitink, Janneke, and Jennifer Spenader. 2004. Cancelation resistant PCIs. In Bart Geurts & Rob van der Sandt (eds.) *Proceedings of the Esslli 2004 Workshop on Implicature and Conversational Meaning*, 8–13. Nancy, France: University of Nijmegen.

Hutchby, Ian. 2008. Participants' orientations to interruptions, rudeness and other impolite acts in talk-in-interaction. *Journal of Politeness Research* 4 (2). 221–241.

Ikeda, Keiko. 2004. 'Listenership' in Japanese: an examination of overlapping listener response. *NFLRC NetWork #32*. Honolulu: National Foreign Language Resource Centre, University of Hawai'i at Manoa. http://nflrc.hawaii.edu/NetWorks/NW32.pdf.

Ikuta, Shoko. 1988. Strategies of Requesting in Japanese Conversational Discourse. Unpublished PhD dissertation, Cornell University.

Intachakra, Songthama. 2012. Politeness motivated by the 'heart' and 'binary rationality' in Thai culture. *Journal of Pragmatics* 44 (5). 619–635.

Iten, Corrine. 2005. *Linguistic Meaning, Truth Conditions and Relevance*. Basingstoke: Palgrave MacMillan.

Jary, Mark. 1998. Relevance theory and the communication of politeness. *Journal of Pragmatics* 30 (1). 1–19.

Jary, Mark. 2013. Two types of implicature: material and behavioural. *Mind & Language* 28 (5). 638–660.

Jaszczolt, Kasia M. 1999. *Discourse, Beliefs and Intentions*. Amsterdam: Elsevier.

Jaszczolt, Kasia M. 2005. *Default Semantics. Foundations of a Compositional Theory of Acts of Communication*. Oxford: Oxford University Press.

Jaszczolt, Kasia M. 2009a. *Representing Time: An Essay on Temporality as Modality*. Oxford: Oxford University Press.

Jaszczolt, Kasia M. 2009b. Cancellability and the primary/secondary meaning distinction. *Intercultural Pragmatics* 6 (3). 259–289.

Jayyusi, Lena. 1984. *Categorisation and Moral Order*. London: Routledge and Kegan Paul.

Jayyusi, Lena. 1991. Values and moral judgement. In Graham Button (ed.) *Ethnomethodology and the Human Sciences*, 227–251. Cambridge: Cambridge University Press.

Jefferson, Gail. 1979. A technique for inviting laughter and its subsequent acceptance-declination. In George Psathas (ed.) *Everyday Language. Studies in Ethnomethodology*, 79–95. New York: Irvington.

Jefferson, Gail. 1981. The abominable 'ne?' An exploration of post-response pursuit of response. In P. Shroder (ed.) *Sprache der Gegenwaart*, 53–88. Dusseldorf. BRD: Pedago-gischer Verlag Schwann.

Jefferson, Gail. 1986. Notes on 'latency' in overlap onset. *Human Studies* 9 (2/3). 153–183.

Jefferson, Gail. 1988. On the sequential organization of troubles talk in ordinary conversation. *Social Problems* 35 (4). 418–441.

Jefferson, Gail. 2004a. Glossary of transcript symbols with an introduction. In Gene Lerner (ed.) *Conversation Analysis: Studies from the First Generation*, 13–23. Amsterdam: John Benjamins.

Jefferson, Gail 2004b. A note on laughter in 'male-female' interaction. *Discourse Studies* 6 (1). 117–133.

Jefferson, Gail, Harvey Sacks & Emmanuel Schegloff. 1987. Notes on laughter in the pursuit of intimacy. In Graham Button & John R. E. Lee (eds.) *Talk and Social Organisation*, 152–205. Clevedon, UK: Multilingual Matters.

Jucker, Andreas. 2009. Speech act research between armchair, field and laboratory. The case of compliments. *Journal of Pragmatics* 41. 1611–1635.

Kádár, Dániel Z. & Michael Haugh. 2013. *Understanding Politeness*. Cambridge: Cambridge University Press.

Kallia, Alexandra. 2004. Linguistic politeness: the implicature approach. *Multilingua* 23 (1/2). 145–169.

Kamio, Akio. 1994. The theory of territory of information: the case of Japanese. *Journal of Pragmatics* 21 (1). 67–100.

Kamio, Akio. 1997. *Territory of Information*. Amsterdam: John Benjamins.

Kasper, Gabriele. 1990. Linguistic politeness: current research issues. *Journal of Pragmatics* 14 (2). 193–218.

Kasper, Gabriele. 2006. Speech acts in (inter)action: repeated questions. *Intercultural Pragmatic* 1 (1). 125–133.

Katsos, Napoleon. 2008. The semantics/pragmatics interface from an experimental perspective: the case of scalar implicature. *Synthese* 165 (3). 385–401.

Katsos, Napoleon. 2012. Empirical investigations and pragmatic theorising. In Keith Allan & Kasia M. Jaszczolt (eds.) *The Cambridge Handbook of Pragmatics*, 275–290. Cambridge: Cambridge University Press.

Kecskes, Istvan. 2010. The paradox of communication: socio-cognitive approach to pragmatics. *Pragmatics and Society* 1 (1). 50–73.

Keltner, Dacher, Lisa Capps, Ann Kring, Randall Young & Erin Heerey. 2001. Just teasing: a conceptual analysis and empirical review. *Psychological Bulletin* 127 (2). 229–248.

Kendrik, Kobin H. 2010. Epistemics and Action Formation in Mandarin Chinese. Unpublished PhD thesis, University of California Santa Barbara.

Kerbrat-Orecchioni, Catherine. 2004. Introducing polylogue. *Journal of Pragmatics* 36 (1). 1–24.

Kiefer, Ferenc. 1979. What do conversational maxims explain? *Lingvisticae Investigationes* 3 (1). 57–74.

Kiesling, Scott F. 2010. Introduction: rethinking indirection and the indexical cycle. *Journal of Pragmatics* 42 (2). 279–282.

Kiesling, Scott F. & Elka Ghosh Johnson. 2010. Four forms of interactional indirection. *Journal of Pragmatics* 42 (2). 292–306.

Kingswell, Mark. 1993. Is it rational to be polite? *The Journal of Philosophy* 90 (8). 387–404.

Kissine, Mikhail. 2013. *From Utterances to Speech Acts*. Cambridge: Cambridge University Press.

Knobe, Joshua. 2010. Person as scientist, person as moralist. *Behavioural and Brain Sciences* 33 (4). 315–365.

Koshik, Irene. 2005. *Beyond Rhetorical Questions: Assertive Questions in Everyday Interaction*. Amsterdam/Philadelphia: John Benjamins.

Kotthoff, Helga. 1996. Impoliteness and conversational joking: on relational politics. *Folia Linguistica* 30 (3–4). 299–325.

Kumatoridani, Tetsuo. 1999, Alternation and co-occurence in Japanese thanks. *Journal of Pragmatics* 31 (5). 623–642.

Kuroshima, Satomi. 2010. Another look at the service encounter: progressivity, intersubjectivity and trust in a Japanese sushi restaurant. *Journal of Pragmatics* 42 (3). 856–869.

Labov, William. 1972. Rules for ritual insults. In David Sudnow (ed.) *Studies in Social Interaction*, 120–169. New York: The Free Press.

Lakoff, George. 1972. Hedges: a study in meaning criteria and the logic of fuzzy concepts. *Chicago Linguistic Society* 8. 183–228.

Lakoff, Robin. 1973. The logic of politeness; or minding your p's and q's. *Chicago Linguistics Society* 9. 292–305.

Lee, James L & Steven Pinker. 2010. Rationales for indirect speech: the theory of the strategic speaker. *Psychological Review* 117 (3). 785–807.

Leech, Geoffrey. 1983. *Principles of Pragmatics*. London: Longman.

Leech, Geoffrey. 2007. Politeness: is there an East-West divide? *Journal of Politeness Research* 3 (2). 167–206.

Lerner, Gene. 1996. Finding "face" in the preference structures of talk-in-interaction. *Social Psychology Quarterly* 59 (4). 303–321.

Lerner, Gene. 2013. On the place of hesitating in delicate formulations: a turn-constructional infrastructure for collaborative indiscretion. In Makoto Hayashi, Geoffrey Raymond & Jack Sidnell (eds.) *Conversational Repair and Human Understanding*, 95–134. Cambridge: Cambridge University Press.

Levinson, Stephen C. 1979. Pragmatics and social dexis: reclaiming the notion of conventional implicature. *Berkley Linguistics Society* 5. 206–223.

Levinson, Stephen C. 1983. *Pragmatics*. Cambridge: Cambridge University Press.

Levinson, Stephen C. 1988. Putting linguistics on a proper footing: explorations in Goffman's concepts of participation. In Paul Drew & Anthony Wootton (eds.) *Erving Goffman. Exploring the Interaction Order*, 161–227. Boston, MA: Northeastern University Press.

Levinson, Stephen C. 1995. Three levels of meaning. In F. Palmer (ed.), *Grammar and Meaning. Essays in Honour of Sir John Lyons*, 90–115. Cambridge: Cambridge University Press.

Levinson, Stephen C. 2000. *Presumptive Meanings. The Theory of Generalised Conversational Implicature*. Cambridge, MA: MIT Press.

Levinson, Stephen C. 2006. Cognition at the heart of human interaction. *Discourse Studies* 8 (1). 85–93.

Levinson, Stephen C. 2011. Multi-action turns. Paper presented at the 12th International Pragmatics Association Conference. University of Manchester, U.K., 3–8 July.

Levinson, Stephen C. 2013. Action formation and ascription. In Tanya Stivers & Jack Sidnell (eds.) *Handbook of Conversation Analysis*, 103–130. Malden, MA: Wiley-Blackwell.

Li, Charles N. & Sandra A. Thompson. 1981. *Mandarin Chinese: A Functional Reference Grammar*. Berkeley, CA: University of California Press.

Lindström, Anna & Lorenza Mondada. 2009. Assessments in social interaction: introduction to the special issue. *Research on Language and Social Interaction* 42 (4). 299–308.

Lindström, Anna & Marja-Leena Sorjonen. 2013. Affiliation in conversation. In Jack Sidnell & Tanya Stivers (eds.) *The Handbook of Conversation Analysis*, 350–369. Malden, MA: Wiley-Blackwell.

Locher, Miriam. 2004. *Power and Politeness in Action. Disagreements in Oral Communication*. Berlin: Mouton de Gruyter.

Locher, Miriam. 2011. Situated impoliteness: the interface between relational work and identity construction. In Bethan Davies, Michael Haugh & Andrew John Merrison (eds.) *Situated Politeness*, 187–208. London: Continuum.

Locher, Miriam. 2012. Politeness research from past to future, with a special focus on the discursive approach. In Lucia Fenandez-Amaya, Maria de la O. Hernandez-Lopez, Reyes Gomez Moron, Manuel Padilla Cruz, Manuel Mejias Borrero & Marianna Relinque Barranca (eds.) *New Perspectives on (Im)Politeness and Interpersonal Communication*, 1–22. Newcastle upon Tyne: Cambridge Scholars Press.

Locher, Miriam & Richard Watts. 2005. Politeness theory and relational work. *Journal of Politeness Research* 1 (1). 9–34.

Lorenzo-Dus, Nuria. 2009. "You're barking mad, I'm out": impoliteness and broadcast talk. *Journal of Politeness Research* 5 (2). 159–187.

Lorenzo-Dus, Nuria, Pilar Garces-Conéjos Blitvich & Patricia Bou-Franch. 2011. On-line polylogues and impoliteness: the case of posting sent in response to the Obama Reggaeton YouTube video. *Journal of Pragmatics* 43 (10). 2578–2593.

Lwanga-Lumu, Joy. 1999. Politeness and indirectness revisited. *South African Journal of African Languages* 19 (2). 83–92.

Macaulay, Marcia. 2001. Tough talk: indirectness and gender in requests for information. *Journal of Pragmatics* 33 (2). 293–316.

Mandelbaum, Jenny & Anita Pomerantz. 1991. What drives social action? In Karen Tracy (ed.) *Understanding Face-to-Face Interaction. Issues Linking Goals and Discourse*, 151–166. Hillsdale, NJ: Lawrence Erlbaum.

Mao, Luming. 1994. Beyond politeness theory: 'face' revisited and renewed. *Journal of Pragmatics* 21. 451–486.

Marcoccia, Michael. 2004. On-line polylogues: conversation structure and participation framework in internet newsgroups. *Journal of Pragmatics* 36 (1). 115–145.

Marmaridou, Sophia. 2000. *Pragmatic Meaning and Cognition*. Amsterdam: John Benjamins.

Marquez-Reiter, Rosina. 2000. *Linguistic Politeness in Britain and Uruguay. A Contrastive Study of Requests and Apologies*. Amsterdam: John Benjamins.

Marti, Lelya. 2006. Indirectness and politeness in Turkish-German bilingual and Turkish monolingual requests. *Journal of Pragmatics* 38 (11). 1836–1869.

Matsumoto, Yo. 1995. The conversational condition on Horn scales. *Linguistics and Philosophy* 18 (1). 21–60.

Matsumoto, Yoshiko. 1988. Reexamination of the universality of face: politeness phenomena in Japanese. *Journal of Pragmatics* 12. 403–426.

Maynard, Douglas W. 2013. Defensive mechanisms: *I-mean*-prefaced utterances in complaint and other sequences. In Makoto Hayashi, Geoffrey Raymond & Jack Sidnell (eds.) *Conversational Repair and Human Understanding*, 198–233. Cambridge: Cambridge University Press.

Maynard, Senko. 1997. *Japanese Communication. Language and Thought in Context.* Honolulu: University of Hawai'i Press.

Mayol, Laia & Elena Castroviejo. 2013. How to cancel an implicature. *Journal of Pragmatics* 50. 84–104.

Mazzone, Marco. 2011. Schemata and associative processes in pragmatics. *Journal of Pragmatics* 43 (8). 2148–2159.

McCafferty, Andrew. 1990. Speaker plans, linguistic contexts and indirect speech acts. In Henry Kyburg, Ronald Loui & Greg Carlson (eds.) *Knowledge Representation and Defeasible Reasoning*, 191–220. Dordrecht: Kluwer Academic.

McKinlay, Andy & Chris McVittie. 2006. Using topic control to avoid the gainsaying of troublesome evaluations. *Discourse Studies* 8 (6). 797–815.

Mead, George. 1934. *Mind, Self and Society.* Chicago, IL: University of Chicago Press.

Mercier, Hugo & Dan Sperber. 2009. Intuitive and reflective inferences. In Jonathan Evans & Keith Frankish (eds.) *In two minds: Dual processes and beyond*, 149–170. Oxford: Oxford University Press.

Merrison, Andrew John. 2011. 'Doing aphasia – are you with me?': analysing face-work around issues of (non-)competence. In Linguistic Politeness Research Group (eds.) *Discursive Approaches to Politeness*, 221–244. Berlin: Mouton de Gruyter.

Mey, Jacob. 2010. Societal pragmatics. In Louise Cummings (ed.) *The Pragmatics Encyclopedia*, 444–446. London and New York: Routledge.

Mills, Sara. 2003. *Gender and Politeness.* Cambridge: Cambridge University Press.

Mills, Sara. 2009. Impoliteness in a cultural context. *Journal of Pragmatics* 41 (5). 1047–1060.

Mills, Sara. 2011. Discursive approaches to politeness and impoliteness. In Linguistic Politeness Research Group (eds.) *Discursive Approaches to Politeness*, 19–56. Berlin: Mouton de Gruyter.

Moeschler, Jacques. 2012. Conversational and conventional implicatures. In Hans-Jörg Schmid (ed.) *Cognitive Pragmatics*, 405–436. Berlin: Mouton de Gruyter.

Mooney, Annabelle. 2004. Co-operation, violations and making sense. *Journal of Pragmatics* 36 (5). 899–920.

Morency, Patrick, Steve Oswald & Louis de Saussure. 2008. Explicitness, implicitness and commitment attribution: a cognitive pragmatic perspective. *Belgian Journal of Linguistics* 22 (1). 197–219.

Morgan, Jerry. 1978. Two types of convention in indirect speech acts. In Peter Cole (ed.) *Syntax and Semantics, Volume 9. Pragmatics*, 261–280. New York: Academic Press.

Morgan, Marcyliena. 1991. Indirectness and interpretation in African American women's discourse. *Pragmatics* 1 (4). 421–451.

Morgan, Marcyliena. 1996. Conversational signifying: grammar and indirectness among African American women. In Elinor Ochs, Emanuel Schegloff & Sandra Thompson (eds.) *Interaction and Grammar*, 405–434. Cambridge: Cambridge University Press.

Morgan, Marcyliena. 2010. The presentation of indirectness and power in everyday life. *Journal of Pragmatics* 42 (2). 283–291.

Mori, Junko. 1999. *Negotiating Agreement and Disagreement in Japanese. Connective Expressions and Turn Construction.* Amsterdam: John Bejamins.

Mori, Junko & Kanae Nakamura. 2008. Negotiating agreement and disagreement in Japanese: an analysis of designedly ambiguous turn completion points. In Junko Mori & Amy Snyder Ohta (eds.) *Japanese Applied Linguistics. Discourse and Social Perspectives,* 52–79. London: Continuum.

Morita, Emi. 2005. *Negotiation of Contingent Talk: The Japanese Interactional Particles Ne and Sa.* Amsterdam: John Benjamins.

Morita, Emi. 2012a. Deriving the socio-pragmatic meanings of the Japanese interactional particle *ne. Journal of Pragmatics* 44 (3). 298–314.

Morita, Emi. 2012b. 'This talk needs to be registered': the metapragmatic meaning of the Japanese interactional particle *yo. Journal of Pragmatics* 44 (13). 1721–1742.

Neale, Stephen. 1992. Paul Grice and the philosophy of language. *Linguistics and Philosophy* 15 (5). 509–559.

Nemesi, Attila L. 2013. Implicature phenomena in classical rhetoric. *Journal of Pragmatics* 50. 129–151.

Nevile, Maurice & Johanna Rendle-Short. 2009. A conversation analysis view of communication as jointly accomplished social interaction: an unsuccessful proposal for a social visit. *Australian Journal of Linguistics* 28 (3). 75–89.

Nicolle, Steve & Billy Clark. 1999. Experimental pragmatics and what is said: a response to Gibbs and Moise. *Cognition* 69 (3). 337–354.

Norrick, Neal. 1993. *Conversational Joking: Humour in Everyday Talk.* Bloomington, IN: Indiana University Press.

Noveck, Ira. 2001. When children are more logical than adults: experimental investigations of scalar implicature. *Cognition* 78 (2). 165–188.

Noveck, Ira. 2004. Pragmatic inferences linked to logical terms. In Ira Noveck & Dan Sperber (eds.) *Experimental Pragmatics,* 301–321. Basingstoke: Palgrave Macmillan.

Noveck, Ira & Dan Sperber. 2007. The why and how of experimental pragmatics: The case of 'scalar inferences'. In Noel Burton-Roberts (ed.) *Advances in Pragmatics,* 184–212. Basingstoke: Palgrave.

Obana, Yasuko. 2012. Re-examination of *yoroshiku onegaishimasu* – the routine formula as the linguistic implementation of one's tachiba-role . *Journal of Pragmatics* 44 (1). 1535–1548.

Obeng, Samuel Gyasi. 1994. Verbal indirection in Akan informal discourse. *Journal of Pragmatics* 21 (1). 37–65.

O'Driscoll, Jim. 2007. Brown & Levinson's face: how it can – and can't – help us to understand interaction across cultures. *Intercultural Pragmatics* 4 (4). 463–492.

Okamoto, Shinichiro. 2002. Politeness and the perception of irony: honorifics in Japanese. *Metaphor and Symbol* 17 (2). 119–139.

Okamoto, Shinichiro. 2007. An analysis of the usage of Japanese *hiniku*: based on the communicative insincerity theory of irony. *Journal of Pragmatics* 39 (6). 1143–1169.

Ono, Tsuyoshi, Sandra Thompson & Yumi Sasaki. 2012. Japanese negotiation through emerging final particles in everyday talk. *Discourse Processes* 49 (3/4). 234–272.

Osvaldsson, Karin. 2004. On laughter and disagreement in multiparty assessment talk. *Text* 24 (4). 517–545.

Padilla Cruz, Manuel. 2007. Metarepresentations and phatic utterances: a pragmatic proposal about the generation of solidarity between interlocutors. In Piotr Cap & Joanna Nijakowska (eds.) *Current Trends in Pragmatics*, 110–128. Newcastle: Cambridge Scholars Publishing.

Panther, Klaus-Uwe & Linda Thornburg. 1998. A cognitive approach to inferencing in conversation. *Journal of Pragmatics* 30 (6). 755–769.

Parikh, Prashant. 2001. *The Use of Language*. Stanford, CA: CSLI Publications.

Paris, Scott G. 1973. Comprehension of language connectives and propositional logical relationship. *Journal of Experimental Child Psychology* 16. 278–291.

Parret, Herman. 1994. Indirection, manipulation and seduction in discourse. In Herman Parret (ed.) *Pretending to Communicate*, 223–238. Berlin: Mouton de Gruyter.

Perez Hernandez, Lorena & Francisco Ruiz de Mendoza. 2002. Grounding, semantic motivation, and conceptual interaction in indirect directive speech acts. *Journal of Pragmatics* 34 (3). 359–284.

Perrault, C Raymond & James F. Allen. 1980. A plan-based analysis of indirect speech acts. *American Journal of Computational Linguistics* 6 (3/4). 167–182.

Pighin, Stefania & Jean-Francois Bonnefon. 2011. Facework and uncertain reasoning in health communication. *Patient Education and Counselling* 85 (2). 169–172.

Piirainen-Marsh, Arja. 2005. Managing adversarial questioning in broadcast interviews. *Journal of Politeness Research* 1 (2). 193–217.

Pijnacker, Judith, Peter Hagoort, Jan Buitelaar, Jan-Pieter Teunisse & Bart Geurts. 2009. Pragmatic inferences in high-functioning adults with autism and asperger syndrome. *Journal of Autism and Developmental Disorders* 39 (4). 607–618.

Pillet-Shore, Danielle. 2012. The problems with praise in parent-teacher interaction. *Communication Monographs* 79 (2). 181–204.

Pinker, Steven, Martin Nowak & James Lee 2008. The logic of indirect speech. *Proceedings of the National Academy of Sciences of the United States of America* 105 (3). 833–838.

Pizziconi, Barbara. 2003. Re-examining politeness, face and the Japanese language. *Journal of Pragmatics* 35 (10/11). 1471–1506.

Pfister, Jonas. 2010. Is there a need for a maxim of politeness? *Journal of Pragmatics* 42 (5). 1266–1282.

Pomerantz, Anita. 1978a. Compliment responses: notes on the cooperation of multiple constraints. In Jim Schenkein (ed.) *Studies in the Organization of Conversational Interaction*, 79–112. New York: Academic Press.

Pomerantz, Anita. 1978b. Attributions of responsibility: blamings. *Sociology* 12 (1). 115–121.

Pomerantz, Anita. 1980. Telling my side: "limited access" as a "fishing" device. *Sociological Inquiry* 50 (3/4). 186–198.

Pomerantz, Anita. 1984a. Agreeing and disagreeing with assessments: some features of preferred/dispreferred turn shapes. In J. Maxwell Atkinson & John Heritage (eds.) *Structures of Social Action. Studies in Conversation Analysis*, 57–101. Cambridge: Cambridge University Press.

Pomerantz, Anita. 1984b. Pursuing a response. In J. Maxwell Atkinson & John Heritage (eds.) *Structures of Social Action. Studies in Conversation Analysis*, 152–163. Cambridge: Cambridge University Press.

Pomerantz, Anita. 1988. Offering a candidate answer: an information seeking strategy. *Communication Monographs* 55 (4). 360–373.

Pomerantz, Anita & John Heritage. 2013. Preference. In Jack Sidnell & Tanya Stivers (eds.) *The Handbook of Conversation Analysis*, 210–228. Malden, MA: Wiley-Blackwell.

Pomerantz, Anita & Jenny Mandelbaum. 2005. A conversation analytic approach to relationships: their relevance for interactional conduct. In Kristine L. Fitch & Robert E Sanders (eds.) *Handbook of Language and Social Interaction*, 149–171. Mahwah, NJ: Lawrence Erlbaum.

Potter, Jonathan. 1998. Discursive social psychology: from attitudes to evaluative practices. *European Review of Social Psychology* 9 (1). 233–266.

Potter, Jonathan & Alexa Hepburn. 2010. Putting aspiration into words: 'laugh particles', managing descriptive trouble and modulating action. *Journal of Pragmatics* 42 (6). 1543–1555.

Potts, Christopher. 2005. *The Logic of Conventional Implicatures*. Oxford: Oxford University Press.

Potts, Christopher. 2007. Into the conventional-implicature dimension. *Philosophy Compass* 2 (4). 665–679.

Raymond, Geoffrey. 2003. Grammar and social organization: yes/no interrogatives and the structure of responding. *American Sociological Review* 68 (6). 939–967.

Raymond, Geoffrey. 2004. Prompting action: the stand-alone 'so' in ordinary conversation. *Research on Language and Social Interaction* 37 (2). 185–218.

Raymond, Geoffrey & John Heritage. 2006. The epistemics of social relations: owning grandchildren. *Language in Society* 35 (5). 677–705.

Recanati, Francois. 1989. The pragmatics of what Is said. *Mind and Language* 4 (4). 295–329.

Recanati, Francois. 2004. *Literal Meaning*. Cambridge: Cambridge University Press.

Reynolds, Edward. 2011. Enticing a challengeable in argument: sequence, epistemics and preference organisation. *Pragmatics* 21 (3). 411–430.

Roberts, Richard & Roger Kreuz. 1994. Why do people use figurative language? *Psychological Science* 5 (3). 159–163.

Robinson, Jeffrey D. 2004. The sequential organisation of "explicit" apologies in naturally occurring English. *Research on Language and Social Interaction* 37 (3). 291–330.

Robinson, Jeffrey D. 2006. Managing trouble responsibility and relationships during conversational repair. *Communication Monographs* 73 (2). 137–161.

Robinson, Jeffrey D. & Galina B. Bolden. 2010. Preference organization of sequence-initiating actions: the case of explicit account solicitations. *Discourse Studies* 12 (4). 501–533.

Robles, Jessica. 2012. Troubles with assessments in gifting occasions. *Discourse Studies* 14 (6). 753–777.

Rouse, Joseph. 2001. Two concepts of practices. In Theodore Schatzki, Karin Knorr Cetina & Eike von Savigny (eds.) *The Practice Turn in Contemporary Theory*, 198–208. London: Routledge.

Ruhi, Şükriye. 2007. Higher-order intentions and self-politeness in evaluations of (im) politeness: the relevance of compliment responses. *Australian Journal of Linguistics* 27 (2). 107–145.

Ruhi, Şükriye. 2008. Intentionality, communicative intentions and the implication of politeness. *Intercultural Pragmatics* 5 (3). 287–314.

Ruiz de Mendoza Ibanez, Francisco. 1998. Implicatures, explicatures and conceptual mappings. In Jose Luis Cifuentes (ed.) *Estudios de Linguistica Cognitiva I*, 419–431. Alicante, Spain: University de Alicante.

Rundquist, Suellen. 1992. Indirectness: a gender study of flouting Grice's maxims. *Journal of Pragmatics* 18 (5). 431–449.

Ruytenbeek, Nicolas. 2012. Interpreting standardized indirect requests from a relevance theoretic perspective. *Cercle Belge de Linguistique* 7. 1–15.

Sacks, Harvey. 1992. *Lectures on Conversation*. Oxford: Blackwell.

Sacks, Harvey, Emanuel Schegloff & Gail Jefferson. 1974. A simplest systematics for the organisation of turn-taking for conversation. *Language* 50 (4). 696–735.

Sadock, Jerry. 1978, On testing for conversational implicature. In Peter Cole (ed.) *Syntax and Semantics Volume 9. Pragmatics*, 281–297. New York: Academic Press.

Salmon, William, 2009. Double subjects and conventional implicatures. *International Review of Pragmatics* 1 (2). 249–292.

Salmon, William. 2011. Conventional implicature, presupposition and the meaning of *must*. *Journal of Pragmatics* 43 (14). 3416–3430.

Sanders, Robert. 1987. *Cognitive Foundations of Calculated Speech*. Albany, NY: State University of New York Press.

Sanders, Robert. 2012. Creativity and strategy in dialogue. In Lorda Clara-Ubaldina & Patrick Zabalbeascoa (eds.) *Spaces of Polyphony*, 11–24. Amsterdam: John Benjamins.

Sanders, Robert. 2013. The duality of speaker meaning: what makes self-repair, insincerity and sarcasm possible. *Journal of Pragmatics* 48. 112–122.

Sanders, Robert. Forthcoming. A tale of two intentions: intending an utterance to mean something and intending utterances to achieve something. *Pragmatics and Society*.

Sanders, Robert, Yaxin Wu & Joseph Bonito. 2013. The calculability of communicative intentions through pragmatic reasoning. *Pragmatics & Cognition* 21 (1). 1–34.

Sandlund, Erica. 2004. Feeling by Doing: The Social Organisation of Everyday Emotions in Academic Talk-in-Interaction. Unpublished PhD Thesis, Karlstad University.

Sauerland, Uli. 2010. Embedded implicatures and experimental constraints: a reply to Geurts and Pouscoulous and Chemla. *Semantics and Pragmatics* 3 (article 2). 1–13.

Sauerland, Uli. 2012. The computation of scalar implicatures: pragmatic, lexical or grammatical? *Language and Linguistic Compass* 6 (1). 36–49.

Saul, Jennifer. 2002a. Speaker meaning, what is said and what is implicated. *Nous* 36 (2). 228–248.

Saul, Jennifer. 2002b. What is said and psychological reality: Grice's project and relevance theorists criticisms. *Linguistics and Philosophy* 25 (3). 347–372.

Sbisà, Marina. 1992. Speech acts, effects and responses. In John Searle, Herman Parret & Jef Verschueren (eds.) *(On) Searle on Conversation*, 101–111. Amsterdam: John Benjamins.

Sbisà, Marina. 2001. Illocutionary force and degrees of strength in language use. *Journal of Pragmatics* 33 (12). 1791–1814.

Sbisà, Marina. 2002. Speech acts in context. *Language and Communication* 22 (4). 421–436.

Sbisà, Marina & Paolo Fabbri. 1980. Models(?) for a pragmatic analysis. *Journal of Pragmatics* 4 (4). 301–319.

Schegloff, Emanuel. 1968. Sequencing in conversational openings. *American Anthropologist* 70 (6). 1075–1095.

Schegloff, Emanuel. 1984. On some questions and ambiguities in conversation. In J. Maxwell Atkinson & John Heritage (eds.) *Structures of Social Action*, 28–52. Cambridge: Cambridge University Press.

Schegloff, Emanuel. 1988a. Presequences and indirection: applying speech act theory to ordinary conversation. *Journal of Pragmatics* 12 (1). 55–62.

Schegloff, Emanuel. 1988b. Goffman and the analysis of conversation. In Paul Drew & Anthony Wootton (eds.) *Erving Goffman. Exploring the Interaction Order*, 89–135. Boston, MA: Northeastern University Press.

Schegloff, Emanuel. 1992a. Repair after next turn: the last structurally provided defense of intersubjectivity in conversation. *American Journal of Sociology* 97 (2). 1295–1345.

Schegloff, Emanuel. 1992b. To Searle on conversation: a note in return. In Herman Parret & Jef Verschueren (eds.) *(On) Searle on Conversation*, 113–128. Amsterdam: John Benjamins.

Schegloff, Emanuel. 1995. Discourse as interactional achievement III: the omnirelevance of action. *Research on Language and Social Interaction* 28 (3). 185–211.

Schegloff, Emanuel. 1996a. Confirming allusions: toward an empirical account of action. *American Journal of Sociology* 102 (1). 161–216.

Schegloff, Emanuel. 1996b. Issues of relevance for discourse analysis: contingency in action, interaction and co-participant context. In Eduard H. Hovy & Donia R. Scott (eds.) *Computational and Conversational Discourse. Burning Issues – an Interdisciplinary Account*, 3–35. Berlin: Springer-Verlag.

Schegloff, Emanuel. 2001. Getting serious: joke → serious 'no'. *Journal of Pragmatics* 33 (12). 1947–1955.

Schegloff, Emanuel. 2003. The surfacing of the suppressed. In Phillip Glenn, Curtis LeBaron & Jenny Mandelbaum (eds.) *Studies in Language and Social Interaction*, 241–262. Mahwah, NJ: Lawrence Erlbaum.

Schegloff, Emanuel. 2005. On complainability. *Social Problems* 52 (4). 449–476.

Schegloff, Emanuel. 2006. On possibles. *Discourse Studies* 8 (1). 141–157.

Schegloff, Emanuel. 2007. *Sequence Organization in Interaction*. Cambridge: Cambridge University Press.

Schegloff, Emanuel. 2010. Commentary on Stivers and Rossano: 'mobilising response'. *Research on Language in Social Interaction* 43 (1). 38–48.

Schegloff, Emanuel, Gail Jefferson & Harvey Sacks. 1977. The preference for self-correction in the organization of repair in conversation. *Language* 53 (2). 361–382.

Schegloff, Emanuel & Gene Lerner. 2009. Beginning to respond: *well*-prefaced responses to *wh*-questions. *Research on Language and Social Interaction* 42 (2). 91–115.

Schegloff, Emanuel, Elinor Ochs & Sandra Thompson. 1996. Introduction. In Elinor Ochs, Emanuel A. Schegloff & Sandra Thompson (eds.) *Interaction and Grammar*, 1–51. Cambridge: Cambridge University Press.

Schegloff, Emanuel & Harvey Sacks. 1973. Opening up closings. *Semiotica* 8 (4). 289–327.

Schenkein, James N. 1972. Towards an analysis of natural conversation and the sense of *heheh*. *Semiotica* 6 (4). 344–377.

Schneider, Stefan. 2010. Mitigation. In Miriam Locher & Sage L. Graham (eds.) *Interpersonal Pragmatics*, 253–270. Berlin: Mouton de Gruyter.

Schwenter, Scott. 1999. *Pragmatics of Conditional Marking: Implicature, Scalarity and Exclusivity*. New York: Garland.

Searle, John. 1969. *Speech Acts*. Cambridge: Cambridge University Press.

Searle, John. 1975. Indirect speech acts. In Peter Cole & Jerry Morgan (eds.) *Syntax and Semantics, Volume 3. Speech Acts*, 59–82. New York: Academic Press. Republished in Searle 1979, 30-57.

Searle, John. 1979. *Expression and Meaning. Studies in the Theory of Speech Acts*. Cambridge: Cambridge University Press.

Searle, John. 1983. *Intentionality*. Cambridge: Cambridge University Press.

Searle, John. 1992. Conversation reconsidered. In Herman Parret & Jef Verschueren (eds.) *(On) Searle on Conversation*, 137–148. Amsterdam: John Benjamins.

Searle, John. 2007. What is language: some preliminary remarks. In Istvan Kecskes & Laurence Horn (eds.) *Explorations in Pragmatics. Linguistic, Cognitive and Intercultural Aspects*, 7–37. Berlin: Mouton de Gruyter.

Searle, John. 2010. *Making the Social World*. Oxford: Oxford University Press.

Searle, John & Daniel Vanderverken. 1985. *Foundations of Illocutionary Logic*. Cambridge: Cambridge University Press.

Selting, Margaret. 1994. Emphatic speech style – with special focus on the prosodic signalling of heightened emotive involvement in conversation. *Journal of Pragmatics* 22 (3–4). 375–408.

Selting, Margaret. 1996. Prosody as an activity-type distinctive cue in conversation: the case of so-called 'astonished' questions in repair initation. In Elizabeth Couper-Kuhlen & Margaret Selting (eds.) *Prosody in Conversation*, 231–270. Cambridge: Cambridge University Press.

Sendra, Verònica Crespo, Constantijn Kaland, Marc Swerts & Pilar Prieto. 2013. Perceiving incredulity: the role of intonation and facial gestures. *Journal of Pragmatics* 47. 1–13.

Sew, Jyh Wee. 1997. Power pragmatics in Asian languages. *Language Sciences* 19 (4). 357–367.

Shaw, Chloë, Alexa Hepburn & Jonathan Potter. 2013. Having the last laugh: on post-completion laughter particles. In Phillip Glenn & Elizabeth Holt (eds.), *Studies of Laughter in Interaction*, 91–106. London: Bloomsbury.

Sidnell, Jack. 2010. *Conversation Analysis: An Introduction*. Malden, MA: Wiley.

Sidnell, Jack. 2011. 'D'you understand that honey?': gender and participation in conversation. In Susan Speer & Elizabeth Stokoe (eds.) *Conversation and Gender*, 183–209. Cambridge: Cambridge University Press.

Sidnell, Jack. 2012. "Who knows best?": evidentiality and epistemic asymmetry in conversation. *Pragmatics and Society* 3 (2). 294–320.

Sifianou, Maria. 1993. Off-record indirectness and the notion of imposition. *Multilingua* 12 (1). 69–79.

Sifianou, Maria. 1997. Politeness and off-record indirectness. *International Journal of the Sociology of Language* 126 (1). 163–179.

Sifianou, Maria. 2012. Disagreements, face and politeness. *Journal of Pragmatics* 44 (12). 1554–1564.

Silverstein, Michael. 2010. "Direct" and "indirect" communicative acts in semiotic perspective. *Journal of Pragmatics* 42 (2). 337–353.

Sinkeviciute, Valeria. 2014. "When a joke's a joke and when it's too much": *mateship* as a key to interpreting jocular FTAs in Australian English. *Journal of Pragmatics* 60. 121–139.

Soltys, Jessica, Marina Terkourafi & Napoleon Katsos. 2014. Disentangling politeness theory and the strategic speaker approach: theoretical considerations and empirical predictions. *Intercultural Pragmatics* 11 (1). 31–56.

Spencer-Oatey, Helen. 2005. (Im)politeness, face and perceptions of rapport: unpacking their bases and interrelationships. *Journal of Politeness Research* 1 (1). 95–120.

Spencer-Oatey, Helen. 2009. Face, identity and interactional goals. In Francesca Bargiela-Chiappini & Michael Haugh (eds.) *Face, Communication and Social Interaction*, 137–154. London: Equinox.

Sperber, Dan & Deirdre Wilson. 1995. *Relevance: Communication and Cognition* (2nd edn). Oxford: Blackwell.

Sperber, Dan & Deirdre Wilson. 2002. Pragmatics, modularity, and mind-reading. *Mind and Language* 17 (1/2). 3–23.

Sperber, Dan & Deirdre Wilson. 2008. A deflationary account of metaphors. In Raymond Gibbs Jr. (ed.) *The Cambridge Handbook of Metaphor and Thought*, 84–105. Cambridge: Cambridge University Press.

Sperber, Dan, Fabrice Clement, Christophe Heintz, Olivier Mascaro, Hugo Mercier, Gloria Origgi & Deirdre Wilson. 2010. Epistemic vigilence. *Mind and Language* 25 (4). 359–393.

Steensig, Jakob & Paul Drew. 2008. Introduction: questioning and affiliation/disaffiliation in interaction. *Discourse Studies* 10 (1). 5–15.

Sterelny, Kim. 1982. Against conversational implicature. *Journal of Semantics* 1 (2). 187–194.

Stevanovic, Melisa. 2011. Participants' deontic rights and action formation: the case of declarative requests for action. *InLiSt (Interaction and Linguistic Structures)* 52.

Stevanovic, Melisa. 2013. Constructing a proposal as a thought: a way to manage problems in the initiation of joint decision-making in Finnish workplace interaction. *Pragmatics* 23 (3). 519–544.

Stevanovic, Melisa & Anssi Peräkylä. 2012. Deontic authority in interaction: the right to announce, propose and decide. *Research on Language and Social Interaction* 45 (3). 297–321.

Stevanovic, Melisa & Anssi Peräkylä. 2014. Three orders in the organization of human action: on the interface between knowledge, power, and emotion in interaction and social relations. *Language in Society* 43 (2). 185–207.

Stivers, Tanya. 2010. An overview of the question-response system in American English conversation. *Journal of Pragmatics* 42 (10). 2772–2781.

Stivers, Tanya. 2011. Morality and question design: 'of course' as contesting a presupposition of askability. In Tanya Stivers, Lorenza Mondada & Jakob Steensig (eds.) *The Morality of Knowledge in Conversation*, 82–106. Cambridge: Cambridge University Press.

Stivers, Tanya & Makoto Hayashi. 2010. Tranformative answers: one way to resist a questions's constraints. *Language in Society* 39 (1). 1–25.

Stivers, Tanya, Lorenza Mondada & Jakob Steensig. 2011. Knowledge, morality and affiliation in social interaction. In Tanya Stivers, Lorenza Mondada & Jakob Steensig (eds.) *The Morality of Knowledge in Conversation*, 3–24. Cambridge: Cambridge University Press.

Stivers, Tanya & Federico Rossano. 2010. Mobilising response. *Research on Language in Social Interaction* 43 (1). 1–31.

Stivers, Tanya & Federico Rossano. 2012. Mobilising response in interaction: a compositional view. In Jan P. Ruiter (ed.) *Questions: Formal, Functional and Interactional Perspectives*, 58–80. Cambridge: Cambridge University Press.

Storto, Gianluca & Michael Tanenhaus. 2005. Are scalar implicatures computed online? In Emar Maier, Corien Bary & Janneke Huitink (eds.), *Sinn und Bedeutung 9*, 431–455. Nijmegen: Nijmegen Centre for Semantics.

Straehle, Carolyn. 1993. "Samuel?" "Yes dear?" Teasing and conversational rapport. In Deborah Tannen (ed.) *Framing in Discourse*, 210–230. Oxford: Oxford University Press.

Tanaka, Hiroko. 2000. Turn-projection in Japanese talk-in-interaction. *Research on Language and Social Interaction* 33 (1). 1–38.

Tannen, Deborah. 1981. Indirectness in discourse: ethnicity as conversational style. *Discourse Processes* 4 (3). 221–238.

Tannen, Deborah. 2010. Abduction and identity in family interaction: ventriloquizing as indirectness. *Journal of Pragmatics* 42 (2). 307–316.

Terasaki, Alene Kiku. [1976]2004. Pre-announcement sequences in conversation. In Gene Lerner (ed.) *Conversation Analysis: Studies from the First Generation*, 171–224. Amsterdam: John Benjamins.

Terkourafi, Marina. 2001. Politeness in Cypriot Greek: A Frame-Based Approach. Unpublished PhD dissertation, Cambridge University.

Terkourafi, Marina. 2002. Politeness and formulaicity: evidence from Cypriot Greek. *Journal of Greek Linguistics* 3 (1). 179–201.

Terkourafi, Marina. 2003. Generalised and particularised implicatures of linguistic politeness. In Peter Kuhnlein, Hannes Rieser & Henk Zeevat (eds.) *Perspectives on Dialogue in the New Millennium*, 149–164. Amsterdam: John Benjamins.

Terkourafi, Marina. 2005. Beyond the micro-level in politeness research. *Journal of Politeness Research* 1 (2). 237–262.

Terkourafi, Marina. 2007. Toward a universal notion of face for a universal notion of cooperation. In Istvan Kecskes & Laurence Horn (eds.), *Explorations in Pragmatics*, 313–344. Berlin: Mouton de Gruyter.

Terkourafi, Marina. 2008. Toward a unified theory of politeness, impoliteness and rudeness. In Derek Bousfield & Miriam Locher (eds.) *Impoliteness in Language*, 45–74. Berlin: Mouton de Gruyter.

Terkourafi, Marina. 2011a. The puzzle of indirect speech. *Journal of Pragmatics* 43 (11). 2861–2865.

Terkourafi, Marina. 2011b. Why direct speech is not a natural default: rejoinder to Steven Pinker's 'Indirect speech, politeness, deniability and relationship negotiation'. *Journal of Pragmatics* 43 (11). 2869–2871.

Terkourafi, Marina. 2013. Re-assessing the speech act schema: twenty-first century reflections. *International Review of Pragmatics* 5 (2). 197–216.

Thaler, Verena. 2012. Mitigation as modification of illocutionary force. *Journal of Pragmatics* 44 (6/7). 907–919.

Thomas, Jenny. 1995. *Meaning in Interaction: An Introduction to Pragmatics*. London: Longman.

Thomason, Richmond. 1990. Accommodation, meaning and implicature: interdisciplinary foundations for pragmatics. In Philip Cohen, Jerry Morgan & Martha E. Pollack (eds.) *Intentions in Communication*, 325–363. Cambridge, MA: MIT Press.

Tsohatzidis, Savas L. 1989. Two consequences of hinting. *Philosophy and Rhetoric* 22 (4). 288–293.

Tsuda, Sanae. 1993. Danwa bunseki riron to komyunikeeshon riron no tetten [Development of discourse analysis theory and communication theory]. *Tokai Gakuen Joshi Tanki Daigaku Kiyo* [Bulletin of Tokaigakuen Women's College] 28. 77–85.

Ueda, Masashi. 1995. *Otoboke Kachoo 10*. Tokyo: Hobunsha.

Ueda, Masashi. 1998. *Kobochan 45*. Tokyo: Soyosha

Vanderverken, Daniel. 2013. Towards a formal pragmatics of discourse. *International Review of Pragmatics* 5 (1). 34–69.

Verschueren, Jef. 1999. *Understanding Pragmatics*. London: Arnold.

Vicente, Begona. 1998. Against blurring the explicit/implicit distinction. *Revista Alicantina de Estudios Ingleses* 11. 241–258.

Vöge, Monika. 2008. All You Need is Laugh – Interactional Implications of Laughter in Business Meetings. Unpublished PhD dissertation, University of Southern Denmark.

Walker, Gareth. 2007. On the design and use of pivots in everyday English conversation. *Journal of Pragmatics* 39 (12). 2217–2243.

Walker, Gareth. 2012. Coordination and interpretation of vocal and visible resources: 'trail-off' conjunctions. *Language and Speech* 55 (1). 141–163.

Walker, Traci, Paul Drew & John Local. 2011. Responding indirectly. *Journal of Pragmatics* 43 (9). 2434–2451.

Watanabe, Yasuhisa. 2009. Face and Power in Intercultural Business Communication: The Case of a Japanese Company in Australia. Unpublished PhD dissertation, Griffith University.

Watts, Richard. 2003. *Politeness*. Cambridge: Cambridge University Press.

Watts, Richard. 2005. Linguistic politeness research: *quo vadis?* In Richard Watts, Sachiko Ide & Konrad Ehlich (eds.) *Politeness in Language: Studies in its History, Theory and Practice* (2nd edn), xi–xlvii. Berlin: Mouton de Gruyter.

Watts, Richard. 2008. Rudeness, conceptual blending theory and relational work. *Journal of Politeness Research* 4 (2). 289–317.

Wedgwood, Daniel. 2011. The individual in interaction: why cognitive and discourse-level pragmatics need not conflict. *Intercultural Pragmatics* 8 (4). 517–542.

Weiner, Matthew. 2006. Are all conversational implicatures cancellable? *Analysis* 66 (2). 127–130.

Weiser, Ann. 1974. Deliberate ambiguity. *Chicago Linguistics Society* 10. 723–731.

Weiser, Ann. 1975. How to not answer a question: purposive devices in conversational strategy. *Chicago Linguistics Society* 11. 649–660.

Weizman, Elda. 1985. Towards an analysis of opaque utterances: hints as a request strategy. *Theoretical Linguistics* 12 (2/3). 153–163.

Weizman, Elda, 1993. Interlanguage requestive hints. In: Gabriele Kasper & Shoshana Blum-Kulka (eds.) *Interlanguage Pragmatics*, 123–137. Oxford: Oxford University Press.

Wierzbicka, Anna. 1985. Different cultures, different languages, different speech acts. *Journal of Pragmatics* 9 (2/3). 145–178.

Wierzbicka, Anna. 1987. *English Speech Act Verbs. A Semantic Dictionary*. New York: Academic Press.

Wilkinson, Sue & Celia Kitzinger. 2006. Surprise as an interactional achievement: reaction tokens in conversation. *Social Psychology Quarterly* 69 (2). 150–182.

Wilson, Deirdre. 2012. The explicit-implicit distinction revisited. Paper presented at the 1st International Conference of the Americas (AMPRA), University of North Carolina, Charlotte, NC, 19–21 October.

Wilson, Deirdre & Robyn Carston. 2007. A unitary approach to lexical pragmatics: relevance, inference and ad hoc concepts. In Noel Burton-Roberts (ed.) *Pragmatics*, 230–259. Houndmills: Palgrave Macmillan.

Wilson, Deirdre & Dan Sperber. 1981. On Grice's theory of conversation. In Paul Werth (ed.) *Conversation and Discourse*, 155–178. London: Croom Helm.

Wilson, Deirdre & Dan Sperber. 1986. Inference and implicature. In Charles Travis (ed.) *Meaning and Interpretation*, 45–75. Oxford: Basil Blackwell.

Wilson, Deirdre & Dan Sperber. 1993. Linguistic form and relevance. *Lingua* 90 (1). 1–25.

Wilson, Deirdre & Dan Sperber. 1998. Pragmatics and time. In Robyn Carston & Seiji Uchida (eds.) *Relevance Theory. Applications and Implications*, 1–22. Amsterdam: John Benjamins.

Wilson, Deirdre & Dan Sperber. 2002. Truthfulness and relevance. *Mind* 111 (443). 583–632.

Wilson, Deirdre & Dan Sperber. 2004. Relevance theory. In Gregory Ward & Laurence Horn (eds.) *Handbook of Pragmatics*, 607–632. Oxford: Blackwell.

Wilson, Deirdre & Dan Sperber. 2012. *Meaning and Relevance*. Cambridge: Cambridge University Press.

Wilson, Thomas P. 2012. Classic ethnomethodology, the radical program and conversation analysis. In Hisashi Nasu & Frances Chaput Waksler (eds.) *Interaction and Everyday Life*, 207–238. Lanham, MA: Lexington.

Wong, Jean & Hansun Zhang Waring. 2010. *Conversation Analysis and Second Language Pedagogy*. London: Routledge.

Wrong, Dennis. 1995. *The Problem of Order*. New York: Free Press.

Wu, Regina. 2004. *Stance in Talk: A Conversation Analysis of Mandarin Final Particles*. Amsterdam: John Benjamin.

Xie, Chaoqun. 2008. (Im)politeness. Toward an evaluative and embodied approach. *Pragmatics and Cognition* 16 (1). 151–175.

Yamada, Haru. 1997. *Different Games, Different Rules*. Oxford: Oxford University Press.

Yang, Pang. 2009. Limao hanyi: limao xianxiang de jiaoji hudong guang [The notion of politeness implicature: introducing interactional perspective into politeness research]. *Foreign Language Research* 148 (3). 83–86.

Yu, Changrong. 2013. Two interactional functions of self-mockery in everyday English conversations: a multimodal analysis. *Journal of Pragmatics* 50. 1–22.

Yu, Kyong-Ae. 2011. Culture-specific concepts of politeness: indirectness and politeness in English, Hebrew and Korean requests. *Intercultural Pragmatics* 8 (3). 385–409.

Yule, George. 1996. *Pragmatics*. Oxford: Oxford University Press.

Yus, Francisco. 1999. Misunderstandings and explicit/implicit communicatioin. *Pragmatics 9* (4). 487–517.

Zhang, Yanyin. 1995. Indirectness in Chinese requesting. In Gabriele Kasper (ed.), *Pragmatics of Chinese as a Native and Target Language*, 119–164. Honolulu: Second Language Teaching and Curriculum Center, University of Hawai'i at Manoa.

Index

Made in the USA
Lexington, KY
09 January 2017